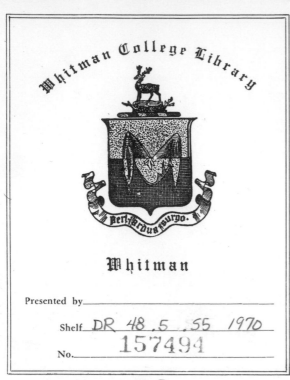

AN EMPIRE
LOSES HOPE

ANATOLE   SHUB

AN EMPIRE
LOSES HOPE

The Return of Stalin's Ghost

W · W · NORTON & COMPANY · INC · New York

DR
48
.5
.55
1970

The lines of poetry appearing in the Prologue
are from "The Heirs of Stalin" by Yevgeni Yevtushenko
from *The Poetry of Yevgeni Yevtushenko,* Revised and Enlarged Edition
Translated by George Reavey
Copyright © 1965 by George Reavey
Reprinted by permission of October House Inc.

To Joyce,

whose love and coffee were
not always fully appreciated

CONTENTS

FOREWORD

This book attempts to describe what has happened during the last decade among the diverse peoples who together constitute the lesser-known, eastern half of Europe, and among whom I was privileged to live and work for seven years.

It is neither a memoir nor a definitive history, but is intended, rather, as a kind of personal history. I have relied primarily on what I have seen myself, and secondarily, on the voices, experiences, and judgment of men and women whom I have come to know and respect personally. Most of these people still live in the region, or did so until recently; some are outside scholars whose work I have come fully to appreciate as a result of my travels.

I have adopted this personal approach because of my own experience. From the morning of August 2, 1962, when I freely crossed the Italian border into Yugoslavia, to the evening of May 23, 1969, when I was compelled to leave Moscow, hardly a day passed in which I did not learn anew that the complex, living reality in the region bore only a tenuous relationship to most preconceived ideas about it, including my own.

This contrast between Eastern reality and Western images of that reality was partly due, of course, to the secrecy and other well-known habits of the Soviet Empire which often make it virtually impossible for scholars of the greatest erudition, perception, and integrity even to guess at the answers to crucial historical questions (*e.g.*, the precise political circumstances of Stalin's death).

However, for me, the constant discovery and rediscovery of the *relevant* in Communist Europe was even more difficult than questions of precision or accuracy. Thus, on my first visit to Prague in March 1963, I realized that Franz Kafka's prophetic novels provided greater insight into the Czechoslovak atmosphere of that day than most of the political speeches or economic statistics I had been studying. (The reader will learn in Chapter 6 and subsequently how, indeed, the Kafka "question" became acute for Czechoslovakia and its neighbors.)

Intentionally, therefore, I have minimized in this book places, events, and problems of which I have little or no direct knowledge and concerning which I could contribute, at best, inspired plagiarism. I have not described Albania, for example, because I have never been there. More generally, I have excluded, to the largest extent possible, the entire world of East-West relations (diplomacy, the military competition, crises in the third world, etc.)—except insofar as such relations have directly affected the internal evolution within Communist Europe, which is the subject of this book.

On the other hand, for the benefit of the reader who is not an expert on the region, I have included, in the early chapters, historical and cultural background which I consider necessary to some understanding of what follows. Although the narrative in this book begins in 1961, obviously the history of the region does not; nor do the historic memories of its living inhabitants. I have attempted to keep such background to the indispensable minimum and am quite aware that all such summary is inevitably arbitrary, sketchy, and subjective. Readers interested in pursuing the historical background further should consult the books listed in the bibliography, which I hope will lead them to other bibliographies and still other books.

However, I also hope that historians of East European nationalism, for example, will not imagine that I am pretending to teach *them* anything new in Chapter 1; on the contrary it is to them that I owe deep gratitude. Specialists on the heritage of Lenin and Stalin will similarly understand, I am sure, that Chapter 2 is partly an attempt to distill the relevant essence of their prodigious labors for readers who have not had the opportunity to study their works.

I hope that readers generally, both expert and amateur, will pardon my reluctance to conclude this book with generalized "answers," predictions, or prescriptions. I have written this book with a sense of human fallibility heightened by my own experiences. When I first thought of writing such a book early in 1967, my tentative title was "The Fading Nightmare." This title reflected mainly my experiences in Yugoslavia, Hungary, Czechoslovakia, Rumania, and a month in Khrushchev's Russia. In retrospect, I was soon aware that I had chosen unconsciously to dismiss or disregard contrary experiences in East Germany, Poland, and Bulgaria, as well as clouds already apparent on the horizon of Brezhnev's Russia. I am now older but not necessarily wiser; I was one of the thousands who left Prague for vacation between August 4 and 20, 1968 (see Chapter 16).

I volunteer such confessions not out of any false humility but precisely because one of the major points of this book is that the experience of living history is far more complex, mysterious, specific, fragile—in short, human—than any single theory can comprehend. There are many questions raised in this book whose answers remain mysteries to me, and I shall be the most pleased if the pessimism implicit in the present title proves short-lived. I have written the book in the manner that I have in the conviction that the writing and understanding of history today is a collective effort, to which each can best contribute what he knows—or thinks he knows—best.

The faults of this book are strictly my own, but many others share responsibility for whatever merits may be found here. The generosity of the Institute of Current World Affairs, and the steady encouragement of its executive director Richard H. Nolte, first enabled me to live in Communist Europe. I would not have been so interested in doing so, nor understood half of what I saw, without the priceless political education provided by my father, David Shub, and my late brother, Boris Shub.

During my five years as their Central European and Moscow correspondent, Mrs. Katharine M. Graham, Benjamin C. Bradlee, and others at the *Washington Post* offered unstinting support with a rare grace; since then, they have been remarkably indulgent in permitting me to write my book on their time.

I owe an enormous debt to scores of political and cultural figures, diplomats, and colleagues in Communist Europe who have helped me at countless crucial points. I cannot possibly mention all their names, but Dessa Trevisan of *The Times*, a peerless companion and guide, helped me most of all.

Leopold Labedz patiently read the manuscript and offered provocative, constructive criticism on matters large and small. Patricia Blake breached my research gap, at a distance of 3,000 miles, with alacrity and discernment. Without such dedicated friends—and other friends mentioned in the text and in the bibliography—this book would have been impossible and my life would be much poorer.

Paris, June 1970

ILLUSTRATIONS

MAPS

PHOTOGRAPHS

Between pages 158 and 159

Between pages 382 and 383

AN EMPIRE
LOSES HOPE

Prologue

The deed was done in darkness, and none who were there have yet told how it was done. Among the simple folk, the legend grew that the body, which had been so artfully preserved more than eight years, dissolved into dust during the half hour it was being moved—out of the sealed crypt, through the frosty night air, behind the wall, and into the damp earth. A poet feared that the spirit still lived:

> *Mute was the marble.*
> > *Mutely glimmered the glass.*
> *Mute stood the sentries,*
> > *bronzed by the wind.*
> *The coffin smoked slightly.*
> > *Breath seeped through the chinks*
> *As they bore him out of the Mausoleum doors.*
> *The coffin floated slowly,*
> > *grazing the fixed bayonets.*
> *He too was mute—*
> > *he too!*
> > > *—but mute and dread.*
> *Grimly clenching his embalmed fists,*
> *He watched from inside, pretending to be dead. . . .*

On Monday, October 30, 1961, all had seemed normal on the cobblestones of Red Square. Tourist guides still brought provincials and foreigners to watch the change of the goose-stepping young guards outside the porphyry Mausoleum. For a fortnight, reverent delegations from eighty-four countries had been laying great wreaths of flowers before its bronze doors. Scarcely ten days earlier, the prime minister of China, Chou En-lai, had solemnly deposited two wreaths—one "to Vladimir Ilyich Lenin, the great leader and teacher of proletarian revolution," the other "to Josef Vissarionovich Stalin, the great Marxist-Leninist."

Until Sunday, October 29, visitors could still pass, hushed and in single file, through the bronze gates to view the holy of holies— the deep cave in which under glass, brilliantly lit, side by side with the wizened Lenin, the embalmed body of Stalin lay, his hands crossed against his bemedaled chest, his lips curled beneath the wispy moustache in an imperceptible smile.

On the Monday, the crypt was closed to visitors, as it had often been before. The only stirring was that of old Russian cleaning women, whisking away the strewn petals which had been scattered from the bouquets by the night's rain. The granite slab above the doorway still bore the two chiseled names, Lenin— Stalin, as military units entered the square shortly before midnight to rehearse for their traditional parade a week later.

By Tuesday morning, October 31, Stalin was no longer in the Mausoleum. He lay instead behind the Kremlin wall, buried beneath a simple black slab in a row with former colleagues. Chou En-lai's wreaths disappeared from the Mausoleum.

Stalin's reburial was ordered by the 22nd Congress of the Soviet Communist party, which had been summoned to approve the party's first new program since 1919. The congress had been meeting since October 17 in the handsome, white, new Kremlin Palace of Congresses—which, with its geometrical modern lines and spacious, air-conditioned interiors, seemed itself to augur a new beginning. Its air-conditioning and electrical wiring had come from Western Germany, its refrigerators and tiles from Britain; provincial delegates marveled at its silent automatic escalators and simultaneous translation systems.

The congress had started slowly, with marathon reports which caused many to doze. But then, with gathering force, speaker after speaker began to attack the men who had ruled Russia for thirty years. They spoke of the crimes, cruelties, and conspiracies not merely of Stalin and other confederates safely dead, but of the living. They attacked all three former prime ministers—Vyacheslav Molotov, Georgi Malenkov, and Nikolai Bulganin, who along with Stalin had headed the Soviet Government from 1930 to 1958. They attacked also the former defense minister and chief of state, Marshal Kliment Voroshilov; the former master of heavy industry and transport, Lazar Kaganovich; the former foreign minister and editor of *Pravda* ("Truth"), Dmitri Shepilov.

These were the men who had industrialized Russia, driven its peasants into collective farms, purged its Communist party and Red Army, allied their country first with Nazi Germany and then with the West, led it through the Second World War and into the "cold war." These were the men who had helped create, and ruled, a vast multinational empire extending from the Elbe to the Ussuri rivers. Now the citizens of that empire were told, officially and publicly, that nearly all these men were steeped in crime and innocent blood.

Five years before, many of Stalin's crimes had been denounced in a secret report delivered by Nikita S. Khrushchev, the new party leader. The report was read afterward at closed-door meetings of Communist party cells—and the text widely published in the outside world—but it was never published in *Pravda* or any of the other papers of the empire.

Even so, the disclosures had unloosed havoc. Most citizens of Budapest and Warsaw, Prague and Moscow, did not have to be persuaded of the monstrosity of Stalinist rule; they had borne the suffering on their persons, and few families had escaped tragedy in the terrible Stalinist years. Hungarian workers tore Stalin's statue off its pedestal in Budapest, and Soviet tanks were sent to crush the revolution.

The dread dictator's embalmed body had remained in the holy Moscow Mausoleum. Although Molotov, Malenkov, and others were removed from leadership, little more was said from high places, then or later, about the murders, tortures, and suffering that these men had visited on half of Europe. Khrushchev himself had been compelled to declare that "the term Stalinist, like Stalin himself, is inseparable from the high title of Communist." A great statue of Stalin still stood on the Letna Hill in Prague.

It was only at the 22nd Congress in October 1961 that Stalin and his chief accomplices were attacked frontally, in speeches published in the newspapers and broadcast on the radio. From the highest tribune of the Soviet Communist party, Stalinism was being denounced and exposed by Soviet leaders themselves: by Khrushchev, Nikolai Podgorny, Alexander Shelepin, and others.

They told how Malenkov conspired "to slaughter honest Communists" in Byelorussia and Armenia through "intrigues, frame-ups, lies"; how he "personally interrogated prisoners, using proscribed methods"; how he engineered the postwar purge of Leningrad, in which "totally innocent people" perished on charges "fabricated and slanderous from begining to end."

The Soviet leaders described Kaganovich as a "sadist" and "degenerate," Shepilov as a "careerist, schemer and political prostitute." They explained how Molotov, Kaganovich, and Malenkov had "sealed the fates of many people with a stroke of the pen," with "criminal thoughtlessness." They illustrated the "brutal attitude" shown in the "cynical notations" written by Stalin, Kaganovich, Molotov, Malenkov, and Voroshilov on petitions from prisoners. (Molotov: "For the traitor, scum and * * * one punishment—the death sentence.")

Khrushchev himself now hinted publicly that Stalin and his confederates had arranged the murder of Leningrad leader Sergei Kirov in 1934, as a pretext for the Great Terror which followed. He described how Stalin's old Georgian friend, Sergo Ordzhonikidze, had committed suicide after the execution of his brother; how Stalin had doomed and cursed his own brother-in-law; how the leaders of the Soviet Army had been shot as a result of charges planted on the suspicious Stalin by the Nazi Gestapo.

"You cannot bring dead men to life again," Khrushchev declared, "but this whole story must be recorded with full candour . . . so that such things shall never happen again in the future." It was a promise full of hope for the victims of Stalin's empire. To many, it seemed to portend a magic possibility—the beginning of moral reform of Communism from above, by the

Communists themselves, without the bloodshed provoked in the Hungarian uprising.

The congress reached its emotional peak in a speech on the morning of October 30 by an old woman, Dora Lazurkina. She said that she had joined Lenin's underground party in 1902, had been imprisoned and exiled many times under Tsar Nicholas II, but survived to hold Communist office in Leningrad. She was arrested in 1937 and spent the next two decades in prisons, camps, and exile.

"When they arrested me and when the prison doors closed behind me," Dora Lazurkina said, "I felt such a horror, not for myself but for the Party." She described how in 1937 "people slandered one another, they lost their faith, they even slandered themselves. Lists of innocent people who were to be arrested were drawn up. We were beaten so that we would slander others. We were given these lists and forced to sign them. They . . . threatened: 'If you don't sign, we'll torture you.'" She recalled the "cruel eyes" and brutal threats of Andrei Zhdanov, who had ruled Leningrad from 1935 until his own sudden death in 1948— a death followed by the extermination of his colleagues in the notorious "Leningrad case."

The only reason she had survived, Dora Lazurkina said, was because "Ilyich"—Lenin— "was in my heart, and I sought his advice, as it were." Now she called for the removal of Stalin's corpse from the sacred crypt with these words:

> Yesterday I asked Ilyich for advice; and it was as if he stood before me alive and said: "I do not like being next to Stalin, who inflicted so much harm on the party."

Stalin was reburied behind the Kremlin wall, still a place of Communist honor. A vase with twelve white crysanthemums stood at the foot of his new grave. The demands for the punishment of Molotov, Malenkov, and the others led to no trials or inquests—perhaps because such demands by Khrushchev's friends had not been joined by such other Soviet leaders as Leonid Brezhnev, Mikhail Suslov, and Alexei Kosygin.

Nevertheless, within the empire, the reburial of Stalin appeared a portent of impending change. For the act performed in darkness at the Mausoleum had been directed not only against Stalin's ghost in Russia but against the Communist government of 700 million Chinese.

In its conflict with Khrushchev's Russia, China had chosen to make Stalin's cause its own. It had been joined, for obscure Balkan reasons, by tiny, backward Albania. Now, even before dwelling on Stalin's crimes, Khrushchev had opened the Soviet 22nd Congress by attacking China through its ally. The Albanians, Khrushchev declared on October 17, had objected to his repudiation of Stalinism. However, the Russian leader proclaimed defiantly, "we cannot concede on this fundamental question to either the Albanian leaders *or anyone else.*"

The Chinese delegation to the congress refused to applaud Khrushchev. Two days later, Chou En-lai rose to warn that "openly exposing disputes" between Communist countries could "only pain friends and gladden enemies." But Khrushchev's supporters continued to attack "Albania" and demand conformity.

On October 21, the Chinese delegates paid a demonstrative visit to the Mausoleum and left their wreath to Stalin. On October 23, before the Moscow congress was half over, Chou En-lai flew home to Peking. He received a joyous welcome at the airport from Chairman Mao Tse-tung and all the other members of the Chinese leadership.

Khrushchev was undismayed. Four days after Chou's departure, the Soviet leader denounced the Albanians even more fiercely, accusing them of arrests and murders of "loyal Communists," including pregnant women. The final congress resolution on October 31 assailed the Albanians as "slanderous" and "divisive."

The Albanian chief, Enver Hoxha, replied a week later. He defended Stalin, denounced Khrushchev, and declared pointedly, "We are not without friends in the socialist camp. They have not left us in the lurch, and they will not leave us in the lurch in the future." The next day, Mao Tse-tung's official newspaper, the Peking *People's Daily*, announced that China's alliance with Albania would be "shaken by no force on earth."

The conflict between Moscow and Peking was complex in

origin. Several of its real causes (such as the manner in which Khrushchev first promised, then refused to deliver the Chinese a "sample" nuclear bomb) did not become known for several years. In the early 1960s, however, much of the world tended to view the struggle as a conflict between the forces of darkness and the forces of light—between Mao Tse-tung, the proponent of violent world revolution and nuclear war, and Khrushchev, the man of peace and consumer goods. Mao preached guerrilla war and said that "imperialism is a paper tiger." Khrushchev campaigned for "peaceful economic competition" with the West, "general and complete disarmament." At the congress, Khrushchev promised to end the Soviet housing shortage by 1970 and increase consumer goods output fivefold by 1980.

While the Chinese seemed to be isolating themselves from the world, Khrushchev had already made sixty-five voyages abroad, visiting twenty-seven non-Communist countries including the United States. He told the congress, "Our society is open to those people who come to us from abroad with open hearts. It is open to honest trade, to scientific, technical and cultural exchanges, to the exchange of truthful information." If there was such a thing as an "iron curtain," he said, it existed only in the West.

Skeptics noted that Khrushchev concluded the congress by boasting of the latest Soviet hydrogen bomb test (55 megatons) and that he had just called off a dangerous confrontation with the Western powers in divided Berlin. Still, despite such discordant notes, the reburial of Stalin and Chou En-lai's demonstrative departure from Moscow raised hopes of fundamental change.

The eviction of Stalin's corpse from the Mausoleum raised hopes among his former subjects that justice might at last be done and that a measure of freedom might enter an empire so long governed by fear. The conflict between Russia and China raised hopes among the smaller nations of the empire that some measure of independence might yet be their reward—and that, as the conflict grew, the Kremlin would be compelled further to review its stance toward the peoples it governed and toward the outside world.

It was a time of change and revived hope elsewhere. In the

United States, the "torch had been passed to a new generation" by John F. Kennedy. At the Holy See, Pope John XXIII renewed the ancient Church in a spirit of openness. Each spoke of new approaches to lands and people long abandoned, hermetically sealed like Stalin's crypt from "Europe" and the West.

CHAPTER 1

The Other Europe

For nearly a generation, to all but a hardy few, Europe meant the West: great jets circling over Orly and Heathrow, Volkswagens and Fiats speeding along autobahns and autostradas, huge freighters unloading at Rotterdam and Antwerp, polyglot tourists descending on the ski runs at Davos and the beaches of the Costa del Sol. It was the Europe of the Marshall Plan, the Common Market, and the North Atlantic Treaty Organization—of Charles de Gaulle, Konrad Adenauer, and Harold Macmillan. As it emerged from the ashes of the Second World War, this Europe—from Dublin to Palermo, the Atlantic to the Elbe—geographically resembled that of Charlemagne and his heirs a thousand years before. With military and economic aid from the United States, this Europe appeared in the 1960s on the way to becoming a giant Switzerland—increasingly prosperous, self-contained, self-satisfied. Its rising younger generations seemed oblivious to the broader European history of past centuries, relatively indifferent even to Europe's tragedies since 1914.

In the mid-sixties, occasional visionaries, notably General de Gaulle, began speaking of a single Europe "from the Atlantic to the Urals," "l'Europe toute entière." But most Westerners still seemed to agree unconsciously with the old Austrian chancellor, Prince Metternich, that "Asia begins at the Landgasse," the

9

street leading eastward out of Vienna. For the great millions of the West, only an occasional flash in the Eastern skies served to recall the existence of the other Europe, which, in the tragic chaos of two world wars, had been consigned to a different form of existence called Communism.

The other Europe, stretching eastward from the sandy yellow banks of the Elbe and the white karst cliffs on the Adriatic shore, had been more or less closed to the West for a generation by Adolf Hitler's Nazis, Stalin's Communists, or both. By 1960, only Yugoslavia had even begun to encourage travel in either direction across its borders.

For the shoppers along London's Oxford Street or Zurich's Bahnhofstrasse, the inhabitants of Leipzig and Riga, Bratislava and Cracow, Constanta and Debrecen, were part of another world—a remote planet more difficult to observe than the surface of the moon ultimately televised by American astronauts. The symbols of this forbidding world were the "Iron Curtain"—the barbed-wire fences, watchtowers, and plowed fields created after the war to bar its inhabitants from the West—and the concrete wall built across the center of Berlin in the early hours of August 13, 1961. At both grim barriers, machine gunners had orders to shoot.

It was, as the decade began, a sad, dark, silent world in which the atmosphere of the Great Depression appeared to have been permanently preserved. Only a handful of travelers entered, shepherded through by state tourist agencies with their prearranged visas, currency declarations, prepaid tours and meal vouchers. They arrived at deserted little airports and delapidated railroad stations, or at designated cross-points along winding, pitted, narrow macadam or dirt roads. They saw scarcely any traffic, beyond an occasional jeep or truck emitting pungent black smoke. In once-great cities, antiquated hotels and grimy restaurants reeked with soft coal, onions, and carbolic acid. Unwashed shop windows displayed unappetizing sausages, tinned foods, and fading fabrics. Queues waited for crowded old tramways and sparking trolleybuses. Neon lights were as rare as gasoline stations or citrus fruits, and after dark only principal avenues glowed with the sickly yellow of underpowered street lamps. Men wore baggy trousers and women lisle stockings as they shuffled to the dance tunes of 1935.

Some Western visitors, weary of the frantic tempos of their homelands, found in the other Europe quaintness, repose, and relief. Here time had seemingly stood still—it could be 1932, or even 1902. Few men rushed, few women bustled. There was a strange equality in submission to a common fate. Yet the air was heavy with fear as well as fatigue, and even innocent visitors soon sensed the presence of the police: from the security troops handling passports to the currency speculators poised outside "international" hotels, the all-day newspaper-readers camped in their lobbies, and the blowsy hard-currency whores who gathered in their bars after dark. (The later appearance of amateur tarts was to be a mark of "liberalization.") A notorious political prison, the scene of infamous tortures, adjoined Prague's main airfield at Ruzyne, while the Moscow Lyubyanka—headquarters of the dread KGB—was just up the block from the "Children's World" department store.

Nevertheless, the first Western visitors rediscovering Communist Europe in the sixties were surprised to find that it had remained so European. Although the authorities emphasized the new and Communist, "the stones spoke Latin." Everywhere amid the wreckage of war and revolution, there were signs of a history as rich and meaningful for all Europe as that of the old domains of Charlemagne. Indeed, in some areas the heritage was older. Ancient Illyria, the territory of present Yugoslavia, had given Rome a dozen emperors. Ovid had been exiled to the Rumanian Black Sea Coast. A Soviet Army garrison flanked the East German road leading from the Weimar of Goethe and Schiller to the Buchenwald of Hitler and Himmler. In nearby Leipzig, Johann Sebastian Bach had written his greatest music and Napoleon had suffered his first major defeat. His greatest triumph, immortalized by Tolstoy in *War and Peace*, had come at Austerlitz, now Slavkov, in southern Moravia. The palace in which Talleyrand had then dictated the Peace of Pressburg (1805) was used during the Bratislava Communist conference of 1968.

Moreover, the longer a visitor stayed in any of the nations of Communist Europe, the more he came to realize how deeply their historical traditions remained alive in the consciousness of their peoples—and how superficial, by comparison, was the apparent uniformity of the "Communism" which had been imposed on them. The *states* of Eastern Europe were governed by Communist methods; but the *nations* were *themselves*, created over the centuries by historical, cultural, and spiritual experiences that were at the same time both universal and particular.

From afar, from Glasgow, Denver, or Yokohama, the monotony of Communist rule seemed the most striking feature of the area. But, on the ground, both to its peoples and to those who came to live among them, the underlying reality was the historical consciousness of European and national experiences far older and stronger than the Iron Curtain or the men who built it.

It had clearly been, for many centuries, a single Europe. Italian architects had designed much of the Moscow Kremlin as well as the palaces of St. Petersburg. An Anjou dynasty had ruled Hungary and Bohemia. The last of the Valois, the homosexual Henri III, had been king of Poland. The Kremlin's mad Ivan the Terrible had sought the hand of England's Elizabeth. More recently, a west German princess had ruled Russia as Catharine the Great. Haydn composed quartets for Hungary's Esterhazy counts; Mozart premiered *Don Giovanni* in Prague, Verdi *Le Forze del Destino* in St. Petersburg; Liszt and Chopin stormed the keyboards of Europe from Budapest and Warsaw.

To be sure, there had long been a debate as to whether Russia was, properly speaking, part of Europe at all or some outpost like the Americas. As for the terrain between the Baltic and the Aegean, the peoples who inhabited it had often been dismissed since the nineteenth century (by Marx and others) as a group of unruly tribes who could only be the objects rather than the subjects of great History. Yet in the 1960s, few who visited it could seriously doubt the "Europeanness" of a region which had produced Copernicus and Jan Hus, Kant and Hegel, Tolstoy and Dostoyevsky, Conrad and Kafka, Stravinsky and Bartók, Nabokov and Ionesco, Teller, Szilard, and Werner von Braun. It was, moreover, the region which had sparked both world wars—the first set off by an assassin's bullet on the narrow quay at Sarajevo in deep Bosnia, the second by the lunge of panzer divisions across the Polish plains to settle the fate of the Baltic seaport of Danzig, now Gdansk. The threat of a third war had already been posed three times since 1948 at divided Berlin.

Politically, the region had been dominated before 1914 by the four empires of the Hapsburgs, Ottomans, Romanovs, and Hohenzollerns. Now, in the sixties, it was divided among nine nominally sovereign states. The most powerful of these, more populous and rich in resources than all the others combined, was the old Russian Empire which had reemerged as Stalin's Soviet Union; three-fourths of its inhabitants lived west of the Urals.

Six of the other eight states were formally bound to the Soviet system through the Warsaw Treaty military organization and the Council for Mutual Economic Assistance (usually known as Comecon). Of these, three—Poland, East Germany and Hungary —had been garrisoned by Soviet armies since the end of the war. Each had unsuccessfully sought, in great mass movements, to quit the Soviet system. But a show of Soviet tanks had halted the East German workers' revolt of June 17, 1953, the threat of similar force had contained the "Polish October" of 1956, while massive Soviet military intervention was required to quell the Hungarian Revolution of October 23–November 4, 1956.

Rumania also belonged to the Warsaw Pact and Comecon, but Soviet occupation forces had been withdrawn in 1958. Czechoslovakia and Bulgaria had not been occupied since the war's end. Their loyalty to Moscow was partly assured by native pro-Russian sentiments as well as by the control of their security police by Soviet advisers.

Albania had been a founding member of both the Warsaw Pact and Comecon, but in 1961 ceased to participate in either.

Yugoslavia had long been a special case. It had defied Stalin in 1948 and thereafter practiced a policy of "nonalignment" with either the Soviet or the Western bloc. As a result of its broadening contacts with the outside world, the atmosphere in Yugoslavia was more nearly normal by European standards in the early sixties than any of the other Communist states became at the end of the decade.

On the surface, these nine states presented outsiders with the image of apparent harmony and order. Many mapmakers, drawing in black and white, found it simple to delimit these "Communist countries" from the "free world," and mutual professions of loyalty to "Marxism-Leninism" seemed to link the nations of the region irrevocably. Within the individual Communist states, it was widely presumed, similar order prevailed. The "iron curtain" had made it difficult to detect signs of discontent, instability, conflict, or change.

Actually, the very boundary of what Westerners called the Soviet "sphere of influence" had rarely stood still. When Churchill defined the "iron curtain" in 1946, he said it extended "from Stettin to Trieste"—thus placing Yugoslavia and Albania within Stalin's empire but leaving Czechoslovakia, eastern Germany, and Soviet-occupied eastern Austria west of the line. In 1948, Czechoslovakia and East Germany came under Soviet control. But in the same year Yugoslavia proclaimed its independence, and in the distant north, Finland—which seemed about to go the way of Czechoslovakia—maintained both democracy and a considerable measure of independence.

In 1955, Austria obtained the withdrawal of the Soviet occupation forces and guaranteed neutral status by peace treaty. Hungary appeared on the way to similar status, for a few days, during the 1956 upheaval. The border of the Soviet imperial system continued subtly to shift during the 1960s as well, and by the end of the decade there were three independent Communist states in the Balkans (Yugoslavia, Rumania, and Albania) constituting a "gray zone."

Within Communist Europe, moreover, none of the states had long, continuous identities and fixed "natural" frontiers in the manner of England, France, or Spain. East Germany had only been proclaimed a state in 1949, and was not recognized as such by most of the world twenty years later. Czechoslovakia and Yugoslavia had been created in 1918, when Poland had re-emerged after more than a century's absence from the map. The Albanian state dated only from 1912, Rumania and Bulgaria from the late nineteenth century.

There had been other states in the area within living memory. Serbia and Montenegro, independent kingdoms before 1918, were now part of Yugoslavia. Estonia, Latvia, and Lithuania, independent republics between the two wars, were now part of the Soviet Union. Slovakia and Croatia, which had maintained separate governments under Nazi auspices during World War II, were once again parts of Czechoslovakia and Yugoslavia respectively.

The frontiers among the nine surviving states were neither as old nor as natural as the English Channel and the Pyrenees. The entire western border of the Soviet Union, as well as the frontier between East Germany and Poland, dated only from 1945. None of these borders were fully and formally recognized by the outside world.

To the south, along the Danube and in the Balkans, none of the frontiers had been fixed earlier than 1918; several had been revised twice or more since then. The Yugoslav border with Italy near Trieste was not settled until 1954. Several of the borders were still contested among the peoples of the area even when recognized by governments.

In the most dramatic of the frontier changes, Poland has been moved several hundred miles westward after World War II. Once-great Hungary had been drastically shrunk in 1920, expanded in 1940, and shrunk again in 1947. Rumania had had the opposite experience.

The shifting frontiers and political vicissitudes of the area were reflected in the changing names of regions, towns, and even streets. Old Pomerania and East Prussia became the Polish "northern territories," once-German Silesia the new "western territories." To the Germans, however, Polish Wroclaw and Soviet Kaliningrad remained Breslau and Koenigsberg. Cluj, Rumania, was still called Koloszvar by Hungarians and Klausenburg by Germans. The Polish-Ukrainian-Jewish town of Lemberg in once-Austrian Galicia became Lviv in the present-day Soviet Union. Many an East European town could duplicate the experience of one of Budapest's main boulevards, currently called the Avenue of the People's Republic, previously named after Stalin—but still known to taxidrivers as "Andrassy Ut" after one of the old Magyar noble families.

Beneath the surface of unity and order, long-controversial European provinces, such as Silesia, Transylvania, and Macedonia, remained sensitive. The fate of these backwaters often aroused more passion than the broad political issues which agitated world capitals. Such concern was typified by the story of the Rumanian soldier on the Russian front in World War II who, asked why he was fighting, replied, "For Transylvania." He might have replied "For Bessarabia" as well.

The political boundaries of Communist Europe still did not—despite "self-determination" votes after World War I and mass deportations after World War II—fully demark the ethnic peculiarities of the region, historically a crazy quilt of nationalities. Six million Jews had been murdered during World War II, as had perhaps a million Gypsies. Some 10 million Germans had fled west of the Elbe after the war—from Poland, Czechoslovakia, Yugoslavia, Hungary, Rumania, and the Baltic states. An additional 3.5 million had escaped from East to West Germany before the building of the Berlin Wall.

The war and postwar settlement had given the region more "ethnic" frontiers than it had ever had before. Nevertheless, more than 2 million Hungarians lived outside Hungary. More than a million Albanians lived outside Albania. There were hundreds of thousands of Macedonians in northern Greece and western Bulgaria. At least 350,000 Germans remained in Rumania, some 150,000 each in Czechoslovakia and Hungary, and many others in Poland—their very number was a major controversy.

Within the various postwar states, moreover, even the officially recognized "peoples of state" were not all homogeneous. Czechoslovakia contained, apart from lesser minorities, 9 million Czechs and 4 million Slovaks with differing histories, heroes, traditions, and temperaments. Yugoslavia was an ethnic mosaic, organized as a federal state to harmonize five languages and eight major peoples.

The Soviet Union, with its fifteen constituent republics and 120 recognized nationalities, was itself the last of the great multinational empires. It was clearly dominated by its 115 million Great Russians, to a lesser extent by the other Eastern Slavs: the 40 million Ukrainians and 8 million Byelorussians.

Most of the other Soviet nationalities were in the Asian part of the empire, or in the Caucasus mountain range from which the Georgian Stalin had arisen. However, even within the unquestion-

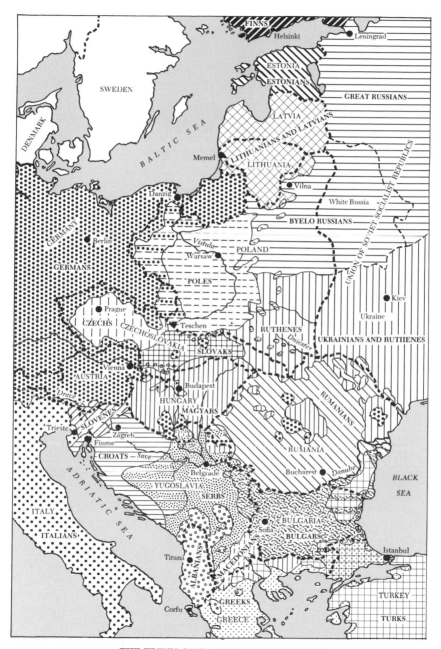

THE TRIBES OF EASTERN EUROPE (1920)

ably European part of the Soviet Union, there were more than a million Moldavians who were indistinguishable from the Rumanians across the oft-disputed Bessarabian border. Along the Baltic, there were 2.5 million Lithuanians, 2 million Latvians, and nearly a million Estonians, on whose lands Russian settlers, soldiers, and officials had replaced deported Germans, murdered Jews, and transferred Poles. Dispersed throughout Soviet territory were perhaps 3 million surviving Jews and as many Crimean Tartars.

Even the recognized "nations" of the region represented distillates of countless older tribes which had, for the most part, settled during the era of great migrations between the fourth and the tenth centuries—and which had been absorbed or "lost" by the time nationalism had begun to assert itself in the nineteenth century. Such once-dread invaders as the Huns, Avars, and Pechenegs had disappeared. But pockets of historical curiosity still survived—such as the 100,000 Lusatian Wends or Sorbs, a Slavic group in the area of Dresden, East Germany, which was officially recognized. The more numerous Ruthenians of eastern Slovakia, southern Poland, and the western Ukraine had been recognized by interwar Czechoslovakia, but they were declared to be Ukrainians, with appropriate frontier adjustments, after 1945. The Albanians were thought to have descended from the pre-Roman Illyrians, but in modern times were divided into northern Gegs and southern Tosks. Such tribal and clan differences, as well as the larger national distinctions, continued to play a role: most of the pro-German and pro-Yugoslav Albanians during and after the war were Gegs, while most of the leaders of the subsequent anti-Yugoslav regime were Tosks.

Two major alphabets, three major varieties of Christian religion, and four major linguistic groups fragmented the recognized "nations" of the region. In the Soviet Union and in the southern part of the Balkan peninsula, the Eastern Slavs and the South Slavic Serbs, Montenegrins, Bulgarians, and Macedonians all used varieties of the Cyrillic alphabet, a ninth-century blend of Greek and native Glagolithic scripts. These peoples were also Orthodox in faith, originally subject to the Greek Patriarch of

Byzantium (Constantinople), later organized into separate national churches.

The Latin alphabet reigned from the Baltic southward to the Sava River and the Eastern Danube, embracing Germanic, Romance, Slavic, and other tongues. The Western Slavs—Poles, Slovaks, and most Czechs—were Roman Catholic. So were the Southern Slavic Slovenes and Croats. However, these two groups of Slavs had been geographically separated since the tenth century by two distinctly different cultures. The Rumanians spoke a Romance language but practiced the Orthodox faith. The Magyars of Hungary, predominantly Catholic, spoke a language which was not even Indo-European but belonged to the so-called Finno-Ugric group of the Ural-Altaic family.*

Protestantism or evangelical Christianity was largely identified with the German language and people. Present-day East Germany was the cradle of Luther's Reformation and remained the only one of the nine states in the region dominantly Protestant. However, the reform movement had been prefigured by Hus and others in fifteenth-century Bohemia and Moravia.

The religious wars of the sixteenth and seventeenth centuries were won, by and large, by the Catholic Counter-Reformation, which planted its baroque churches from Vilnius in Lithuania to Dubrovnik on the Adriatic shore. Nevertheless, significant protestant traditions remained not only among Germans but also among the Czechs and Magyars. There was, in addition, the Uniate Church in Poland, Rumania, and the Ukraine, which practiced a Slavic rite but recognized papal authority. The schisms of Russian Orthodoxy meanwhile spawned the Old Believers and countless other dissident sects, of whom the most tenacious under Soviet rule were the Evangelical Baptists.

Religion was, early on, identified with nationalism, which after the Napoleonic wars became the true religion of the entire continent. The defense of the faith was the defense of the nation among Montenegrins resisting the Turk, Poles resisting Germani-

---

* Estonian and Finnish were similar. Elsewhere, the Latvian, Lithuanian, and Albanian languages, while technically Indo-European, were neither Romance, Germanic, nor Slavic. The Albanians were mostly but not entirely Moslem. The Baltic peoples were mostly but not entirely Catholic. All used the Latin alphabet.

zation. Distinctions in social class often accentuated religious and national differences: Moslem beys in the Ottoman Empire confronted Orthodox peasants; Evangelical German landowners along the Baltic faced Catholic peasants; Germans and Jews adopted commercial occupations spurned by Polish, Magyar, and Croat magnates.

Despite genocide, mass deportations, and the numerous ethnic and religious subconflicts of the Second World War, many East European towns in the 1960s still bore witness to an often uneasy coexistence among three or more cultural traditions. In Bosnian villages, Moslem minarets, Catholic church spires, and Orthodox cupolas stood on opposing hillsides. In Transylvania, Orthodox and Uniate Rumanians contended with both Lutheran Germans and Catholic, Calvinist, and Unitarian Magyars. Visitors to the Soviet Baltic states, two decades after the war's end, found German as useful a *lingua franca* as Russian.

The postwar order east of the Elbe had been largely created by the armed forces of the Soviet Union, which as late as 1955 numbered 5.7 million men—more than the adult male population of East Germany, Czechoslovakia, Hungary, or Bulgaria.

Even united—which they had never been in all of recorded history—the assorted peoples between the Baltic and the Aegean would have found it difficult to resist the compact military, economic, and cultural mass represented by the 85 million Germans, let alone the 165 million Eastern Slavs. Since the early Middle Ages, in fact, these peoples had been inviting outside sovereigns and greater powers to intervene in their quarrels—an intervention symbolized by the nineteenth-century Montenegrin boast, "We and the Russians are 100 million." In modern times, Russia intervened in the name of pan-Slavism or "socialism," Germany in the name of civilization and European unity, the Western democracies in the name of liberal principles and self-determination. For the smaller peoples, the basic principle of survival was the old Balkan proverb, "The enemy of my enemy is my friend." (Albania had leagued with distant China largely because it feared a Soviet rapprochement with its Yugoslav foes.)

Before the rise of nationalism, the Latin culture of the Middle Ages and, to some extent, the French culture of the eighteenth century had unified the elite of large areas. Latin continued as the language of the Croatian Diet until 1844, while French was the language of the St. Petersburg court. (The last Russian tsar spoke English with his family.) Often, Roman Catholicism acted as a supranational force even into the 1960s, as Stalinism sought to become one after 1945. However, nationalism permeated and transformed both of these nominally universal creeds, just as it had undermined the old order of the dynastic empires.

Literacy, urbanization, and the expansion of the new civil service or bureaucracy were the keys to the nationalist upheaval of the nineteenth century. The passion for knowledge and education had been stimulated in the seventeenth century by the British Royal Society and the Czech scholar Jan Amos Komensky, better known by his Latin name of Comenius. It received decisive impetus in the eighteenth century from the French Enlightenment.

Ironically, it was a cosmopolitan Baltic German, Johann Gottfried Herder, whose teachings inspired the dormant Slavs. In 1784, Herder proclaimed them the future leaders of Europe, collected their folklore, and urged them to develop their native languages instead of yielding to French or German. Herder taught that "a people, and especially a non-civilized one, has nothing dearer than the language of its fathers. Its whole spiritual wealth of tradition, history, religion and all the fullness of life, all its heart and soul, live in it."

Other German scholars, and before long Poles, Czechs, Croats, and others, pursued the quest for the "spiritual wealth" residing in national languages throughout the nineteenth century. It was, however, a long time before this idea was fully absorbed everywhere. Even in 1918, for example, friends of the new Czechoslovakia estimated that there were no more than 750 educated and "nationally conscious" Slovaks. A Macedonian dictionary was not compiled until after World War II—by American scholars, and to the dismay of Bulgarians who considered Macedonian merely a Bulgarian dialect.

With the defeat of Napoleon, most of what is now Communist Europe, outside the decaying Ottoman Empire, was ruled by three monarchs: one Russian and two Germanic (Hapsburg and Hohenzollern). Neither Latin nor French was adequate any longer for the conduct of their complex affairs. Outside the Russian heartland, moreover, nearly all the major towns had been built and predominantly settled by Germans, even when surrounded by Slav, Magyar, or Baltic peasants. Marx and Engels, among others, believed that "the physical and intellectual power of the German nation" was "one of the mightiest means by which the civilization of Western Europe had been spread in the East." Writing in 1852, they dismissed the Slavs of Central and Eastern Europe as "a few physical bodies of men who . . . from time almost immemorial have had, for all purposes of civilization, no language but German . . ." However, the Slovene poet Franc Preseren, among others, looked at it differently:

> In our country they generally speak German,
> The Lords and Ladies who command us;
> But Slovenian speak those who serve them.

The Hohenzollerns in Prussia and (to a lesser extent) the Romanovs in Russia succeeded in imposing the German and Russian languages respectively. However, not only in the new Balkan states but also in the Hapsburg Empire, Germans were a minority, and many of the other peoples (notably the Magyars, Poles, Czechs, and Croats) were settled on compact territories. The nineteenth-century revolution in industry, transport, and communication brought their peasant masses for the first time into the cities, old and new. These new city-dwellers were converted to nationalism less often by marching armies than by the new breed of literary intellectuals and journalists—groups which continued to play a seminal role in evolving Communist Europe.

"In Western Europe," Professor Hans Kohn sums up, "modern nationalism was the work of statesmen and political leaders; the political reality and the social-economic transformation came first and created the frame in which the young nation could develop with a sense of social reality and political responsibility. In Central and Eastern Europe it was the poet, the philologist and the historian who created the nationalities. From the Elbe to the Volga, from the Eider to the Tiber, from Flanders to the Morea, intellectuals began to cultivate their mother tongue and study the past with a new feeling of pride, and they aroused the peasants to aspirations and demands never felt or voiced before. Europe east of the Rhine and the Alps seemed . . . to slumber in the provincial drabness of small towns. . . . But underneath, the foundations were being undermined, much less by an actual change of the social structure than by the dreams of the intellectuals."

The scholars rescued languages previously relegated to illiterate peasants, codified their usage and grammar, freed them from competing dialects and "impure" alien influences—and turned them over to poets, schoolteachers, journalists, lawyers, and politicians, who enriched the national movements with new myths, realities, and demands.

It mattered little that some of the most eloquent prophets of national revival originated in the cultural peripheries of the nations they aroused. The greatest Polish poet, Adam Mickiewicz (1789–1855), who called Poland a crucified Christ among the nations, was born in Lithuania, spent much of his life abroad, and never saw either Warsaw or Cracow. None of this in any way reduced the impact, in his own time or even in Communist Poland, of his fiercely anti-Russian play *Dziady*. Similarly, the nineteenth century bard of Hungarian nationalism, Sandor Petofi, was a Slovak by origin; it was the Petofi Club of Budapest writers which sparked the 1956 Hungarian Revolution.

National self-assertion among the peoples of the region was further stimulated by a deep and universal sense of economic inferiority to the booming West. A century ago, the national income of the Hapsburg Empire was about half that of France; Russia and the Balkan states were still poorer. The Industrial Revolution took root fairly early in Bohemia and what is now East Germany, but the rest of Eastern Europe was fated to become the first of the great "underdeveloped areas." Its traditional pattern was to export food and raw materials westward in exchange for machinery and manufactured goods. But this pattern was slowly undermined by the competition of richer granaries, pastures, mines, and oilfields in the Americas, Asia, and the Middle East.

The rulers of the region oscillated between two development policies. Some looked to British, French, and German capital investments. Others tried to promote self-sufficiency, through state-subsidized industries and protective tariffs. Progress was made, but tens of millions emigrated from Eastern and Southeastern Europe to the United States; and the "East-West gap" remained.

Communist rule saw similar vacillations. Lenin before his death looked to foreign "concessions" to develop what he called "barbaric Russia." Stalin, who in 1931 promised to "overtake and surpass" the West within a decade, strove for self-sufficiency. By the 1960s, however, Communists in Belgrade, Bucharest, and elsewhere were again seeking Western capital.

Down to the very end of Hapsburg rule, many of the subject peoples recognized the political and economic advantages of the empire with its protected free trade area. "If the Austrian state had not existed for ages," the Czech leader Frantisek Palacky declared in 1848, "we would be obliged in the interests of Europe and of mankind to create it as fast as possible . . . Think of the Austrian Empire divided up into a number of republics and dwarf republics—what a delightful basis for a universal Russian monarchy!" Many of his countrymen, as well as Magyars, Slovaks, Slovenes, and Croats, continued to share this view even as the empire was collapsing seventy years later. Indeed, there were Communist officials in Prague, Budapest, and Zagreb in the late 1960s who still yearned for the old Danubian "common market," as well as for a strong state which might resist Russian and German hegemony.

However, nationalist passion could override both economic advantage and the striving for democratic government. German or Russian radicals and revolutionaries between 1848 and 1918 might well place their accent on constitutions, parliaments, and social reforms. For the smaller peoples, political freedom and social justice were often less important than "national rights." Among them, only the Czechs developed and maintained a consistent democratic tradition. "For my part," declared the Rumanian patriot Nicolae Balescu in 1848, "the question of nationality is more important than liberty."

The four old empires were only partly undone by dramatic political and military conflicts, such as the series of Russo-Turkish wars through which the Balkan peoples gained independence, or the Hungarian Revolution of 1848–49, which was crushed by "fraternal aid" from the Russian armies (with the aid of Croat troops loyal to the Hapsburg sovereign). In large measure, the complex, confusing nationalities conflict, before 1914 as afterward, involved nagging squabbles over "community control" of schools, over the ethnic composition of the civil service, and over which languages should be used on government forms and railroad platforms.

Such controversies continued to echo in the Communist Europe of the 1960s. The old pattern was visible on the bank notes of Yugoslavia, which were printed in four languages after 1965, and evident also in the federal administrative structure for Slovakia which emerged from the Prague events of 1968. Similar controversies lay just beneath the surface in Transylvania, Bessarabia, the Baltic states, and elsewhere.

Linguistic and political demands bred each other like the chicken and the egg. To resist the fatal attractions of cosmopolitan and especially German culture, the nationalist intellectuals employed history, archeology, and anthropology in order to revive (or create) traditions and myths which vindicated national pride. "This miserable generation has to be told," wrote the Czech journalist Karel Havlicek (1850), "the story of their great ancestors, who had feared neither the tyrannical worldly Popes nor the land-hungry Emperor."

Some of the new traditions were pacific, democratic, and relatively free of hatred of neighboring peoples. The Czechs, for example, venerated Hus and Comenius as forerunners of the European enlightenment, of universal humanism. The Serbs, in the national epic mourning the defeat by the Turks at Kossovo (June 28, 1389), sang of how their Tsar Lazar had renounced victory and an earthly kingdom for a heavenly kingdom.

But many of the new traditions tended to be xenophobic and aggressive, partly in defense against the rising Pan-Germanism which suffused the area from 1848 to 1945. Russian Slavophiles heaped scorn on the decadent West and praised the virtues of barbaric Muscovy, even as "Westernizers" like Turgenev preferred European values. In Transylvania, the Hungarian noble looked down on the Rumanian peasant as a "wild animal, murderous Wallachian . . . snapping at his master, sprung from a

mountain rat, suckled by a shabby wolf . . ." The Croat Bishop
Josip Juraj Strossmayer declared that religious differences with
Orthodox Serbs were "unimportant details," but a popular Serb
poem declared:

> My father is Serb, my mother is Serb.
> All my ancestors were Serb.
> The heaven is blue, Serbia's color.
> God who lives in heaven is Serb, too.

Among the Magyars and Poles, nationalism at first was aristocratic; the glory and responsibility of historic tradition were fairly
recent. Thus, in calm periods, there was among them a tradition
of realism, which securely accepted the fact that their realms had
been created by nobles and priests as much at home in Latin,
French, or German as the native tongue. However, poets like
Mickiewicz and Petofi provided a more fiery romantic tradition,
as the insurrections and revolts of the nineteenth century created
new heroes and martyrs for national legend.

For other peoples, whose languages and states had been sub-
dued much longer, tradition often had to be exaggerated or
manufactured, usually at the expense of neighboring peoples.
Professor Thomas Garrigue Masaryk, who founded the Czechoslovak Republic and became its first president (1918–35), first
made his public reputation by exposing one such Czech nationalist fraud. In the Russian Empire and among the peasant peoples
rebelling against Ottoman rule, however, the yearning for national pride frequently overwhelmed scholarly scruples and led
to absurd controversies, some of which continue to the present
day.*

Inevitably, the search for national traditions led to dreams of
reviving what had been, or was thought to have been, a "golden
age." The movement for German unity, completed by Bismarck's
Prussia in 1871, fed dreams of the medieval Holy Roman Empire.

---

* Thus, Rumanian Communist historians claim several Transylvanian heroes of
renaissance Hungary as ethnic Rumanians. Yugoslav and Bulgarian polemicists
quarrel over the dubious honor of heir to the Macedonian terrorist organization of
the early twentieth century. In emigration, Russians and Ukrainians still dispute
the ethnic identity of Gogol.

Russia since the fifteenth century had been fitfully tempted by the vision of Muscovy as a theocratic "third Rome," after the failure of Caesar's city on the Tiber and its eastern successor, Byzantium. In the same way, the historians and poets of central and eastern Europe harked back to the glories and territorial conquests of earlier empires and kingdoms.

The Poles recalled the great, united Kingdom of Poland and Lithuania under the Jagellonian kings (1386–1572), who at times ruled Hungary and Bohemia, and their successors who penetrated the Ukraine and even briefly occupied the Moscow Kremlin.

The Magyars venerated the Crown of St. Stephen (969–1038) and the glorious fourteenth and fifteenth centuries culminating in Mattias Corvinus (1458–1490), who had also been king of Bohemia and duke of Austria.

St. Stephen, the date of whose canonization, August 20, became the national holiday (Constitution Day under the Communists), was only one of several East European kings who had received sainthood. The Czechs recalled their Kingdom of Bohemia, founded by the martyred St. Wenceslas (924–29), as well as the Golden Age of Charles IV of Luxembourg (1346–1378), who annexed Silesia, Brandenburg, and Lower Bavaria and reigned in Germany as Holy Roman Emperor.

The Serbs had their princely St. Sava, son of the founder of the Nemanja Dynasty (1167–1389), which reached its zenith under Tsar Dushan, "Emperor of the Serbs and Greeks," who nearly captured Byzantium.

The Bulgarians gloried in the memories of Tsars Simeon (893–927) and Ivan Asen II (1218–1241), who conquered Albania, Epirus, Macedonia, and Thrace.

The Croats recalled the kingdom of Tomislav and his successors (910–1102), Bosnia had its King Tvrtko (1377–1391), and the Montenegrins had maintained a quasi-independence in their mountain crags even under the long Turkish occupation. The Rumanians looked back to the ancient Roman province of Dacia (106–271), and Macedonians, of course, could recall Alexander the Great.

Each of these peoples, armed with historic as well as ethnic claims to sovereignty and territory, naturally tended to empha-

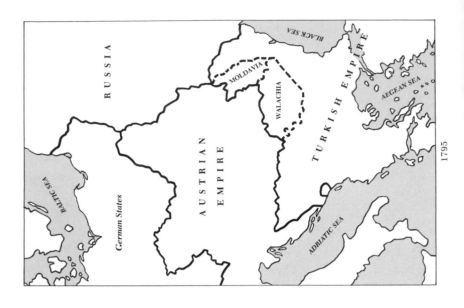

1795

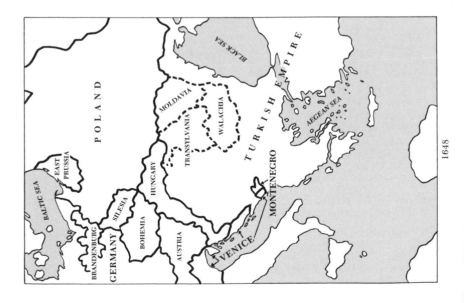

1648

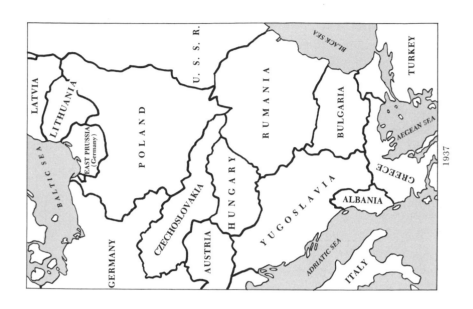

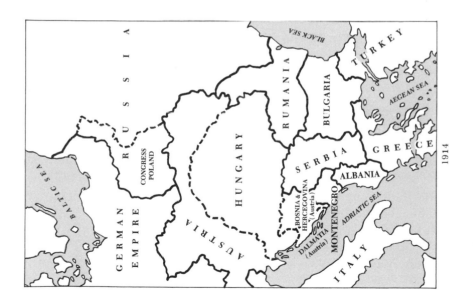

size the claim most favorable to its own aggrandizement. Most of the territorial and cultural claims conflicted with one another, breeding mutual hatred as the "national revivals" proceeded.

The nationalist claims also disturbed the political balance which had been precariously maintained by the dynastic empires since the end of the seventeenth century. The century's two leading statesmen—Metternich from 1815 to 1848 and Bismarck from 1867 to 1890—sought to maintain the unity of the three Eastern empires against the nationalist challenge. The subject nationalities in turn summoned the other two European powers, Britain and France, to redress their grievances, employing "liberal public opinion" in the West as a means of pressure on their own monarchs.

Both liberal opinion and the Western statesmen who embodied it were often sentimental or ignorant of Central and East European conditions, sometimes with fateful consequences. Thus, partly through the influence of British publicists devoted to the Czech and South Slav national causes, the Western Allies in 1917 began to promote as a war aim the complete dissolution of the Hapsburg Empire; until then, the leading Czech and Croat parties had sought only federal status within the empire. At the Paris peace conference in 1919, Dr. Eduard Beneš secured the "historic frontier of the Bohemian Crown" as Czechoslovakia's western border, with few at the conference immediately aware that 3 million Germans were to remain inside it—to be exploited by Hitler in the Munich crisis of 1938.°

The conflicting new nationalisms, the rivalries and rigidities among the four empires, and the tinkering of the Western powers were the chief ingredients of the "Eastern Question" which dominated European politics for nearly a century, spawned new nationalist legends, and further shaped the pattern of sympathies and hatred among the peoples of the region. The great powers managed to limit the Crimean War (1852–55), the Austro-Prussian War (1866), Franco-Prussian War (1870–71), the

° Neville Chamberlain described this conflict as a "quarrel in a far-away country between people of whom we know nothing." He somehow overlooked, among countless past contacts, the election as King of Bohemia of the son-in-law of James I, an election which provoked the Thirty Years War. James, like Chamberlain, permitted Prague to fall in the traumatic defeat at the White Mountain on November 8, 1620—which Czechs of the 1960s continued to cite as the ultimate argument against armed resistance to superior force.

Russo-Turkish War (1875–78), and the two Balkan Wars (1912–13). They were unable to prevent, limit, or control the great war of 1914–18, in which both sides freely employed nationalist subversion and what the Germans called *revolutionierungspolitik* (the policy of fomenting revolution) to undermine the other.

The two most fragile empires were the first to collapse. Russia, which had suffered 7 million casualties, erupted in revolution; and, when its inexperienced new democratic rulers failed to halt the war, power fell to the Bolshevik Lenin, whom the Imperial German government had helped to return and had freely subsidized. The Hapsburg Empire, unable to obtain a separate peace, was dismembered and replaced by "succession states" whose identities and boundaries had been largely forged by exiles, under Allied auspices, in Philadelphia, Paris, and Corfu.

The years between 1918 and 1939, ironically, saw far greater sufferings in Russia under Communism than under the Romanovs, while nationalist conflicts continued to bedevil the succession states. As A. J. P. Taylor explained: "The Czechs could outplay the Slovaks; they could not satisfy them. Masaryk had hoped that the Czechs and Slovaks would come together as the English and the Scotch had done; the Slovaks turned out to be the Irish. In the same way, the Serbs could master the Croats; they could not satisfy nor even, being less skillful politicians, outplay them."

In the Second World War, Western Allies, Nazi Germans, and Soviet Russians all made use of nationalist resentments and revolutionary radicalism—producing murder and carnage the like of which the world had never seen before. The Russians won the war and remade the map. In the words of Mao Tse-tung, "they appropriated a part of Rumania. Having separated a portion of East Germany, they chased away the local inhabitants to West Germany. They divided a part of Poland and annexed it to the Soviet Union and gave a part of East Germany to Poland. . . . They took everything they could."

"Marxism-Leninism-Stalinism" was supposed to unify the area. But the ethnic loyalties and resentments forged in a century of struggle were not so easily repressed. The Poles continued to hate both the Russians and the Germans, and to look down on the Czechs; their traditional friends were the Magyars. The Magyars and Rumanians, however, hated each other. So did the Bulgarians and Serbs, who had fought against each other in three wars since 1913. The Russians worried about nationalism in the Ukraine and the Baltic states, which the Germans had exploited in both world wars. Yugoslavia between 1941 and 1945 had been the scene of horrible ethnic and religious slaughter among Croatian Ustashi, Bosnian Moslems, and Serbian Chetniks—permitting the Communist Partisans to rally the victims of such racism under the slogan of "brotherhood and unity."

Even as de Gaulle and Adenauer were reconciling France and Germany, the legacy of nationalist conflict survived into the Communist Europe of the 1960s. Although young Germans no longer spoke of the 1919 Treaty of Versailles, Hungarian Communists in 1966 were still denouncing as a "shameful *diktat*" the Treaty of Trianon (1920), while Bulgarians in 1968 were celebrating the anniversary of the Treaty of San Stefano (1878), which had briefly awarded them all of Macedonia and outlets to the Aegean.

In the other Europe, moreover, in addition to the national hatreds between the various peoples, there was among each of them still another legacy of bloodshed: between Reds and Whites, collaborators and resistance fighters, and even between rival Communist factions during a half-century of total wars and total revolutions. The national experiences were primal, but the nations shared the experience of having had impressed upon them, by force, a model of government forged in Russia.

CHAPTER 2

The Model

Shortly before the fiftieth anniversary of the Soviet revolution, a European visitor fell into conversation with a Moscow official. The Russian was enthusiastically describing new plans for bringing Western capital to the Soviet Union. Fiat of Italy would build a great new automobile factory on the lower Volga. Renault of France would reequip the older auto works on the upper Volga. British, Swedish, West German, and Japanese firms would help Russia build a chemical industry, unearth the mineral riches of Siberia, mechanize agriculture, and introduce the wonders of automation and electronic computers. These advanced Western techniques, said the Soviet official with pride, would now enable the Russian economy to make a great leap forward. It was a grand and inspiring vision.

The European quietly remarked that the vision was not exactly new. Between 1865 and 1914, the United States had been largely developed by European capital. And, in the decades before the 1917 revolution, the old Russian Empire had also begun its industrialization by calling on French, British, German, Belgian, and other Western capital.

Exactly, the Soviet official agreed, the only real way to develop was to adapt and utilize the most progressive techniques in the world, wherever they came from.

Quite so, the European noted—but this conclusion had already been reached by the Tsar's ministers before the turn of the century. Now it was suddenly being embraced as a new discovery. "If it was true then, and it is true now," asked the European, "what was the point of these last fifty years—revolutions, civil war, dictatorship, isolation, so much suffering and sacrifice by so many millions?"

"Ach, yes," the Russian sighed glumly. "We made a few mistakes, didn't we?"

This sense of error and loss, of a bewildering series of wrong turnings, was felt throughout Communist Europe in the 1960s. It was felt most strongly in Russia itself, where Khrushchev had sought to cleanse Communism of Stalin's heritage and restore the morale of revolutionary days. Yet each doubt shed on some portion of the recent past raised new doubts about the more remote past, new questions about the murky present and future. In a famous ballad in 1963, the Soviet poet Alexander Tvardovsky had observed:

> Hard to admit it's all in vain,
> The years of hope and work and pain.
> If there were a God, we'd pray.
> But since there's not—what then?
> What then, in this evil hour,
> Bitter hour of reckoning?

Slowly, the history of Communism had begun to reveal itself as a study in tragic irony. Stripped of the magical power of words, of such shimmering concepts as "progress," "revolution," "the left," and "socialism," the movement had come in crucial respects to resemble the very system it had originally arisen to combat. Stalin had recognized this almost explicitly. In one of his last interviews, published only in 1956, he praised Tsar Ivan the Terrible as "a great and wise ruler who had protected the country from the infiltration of foreign influence." He singled out "the progressive role played by the Oprichnina," the dread Tsar's political police.

After Stalin's death, the Hungarian Revolution of 1956 had dramatized anew the awful irony of Communism's evolution.

There were poignant parallels with the first of the Russian revolutions, the revolution of 1905. Both in St. Petersburg in 1905 and in Budapest in 1956, the risings began when police unexpectedly fired on peaceful demonstrations. Both revolts soon became nationwide, and everywhere threw up spontaneous councils of workers' deputies. ("Soviet" is the Russian word for "council.") Both revolts were finally checked when the leaders of these workers' councils were arrested—in St. Petersburg by the police of Tsar Nicholas II on December 16, 1905, in Budapest by the Communist police on December 13, 1956. While Nicholas II had frankly proclaimed his dedication to political absolutism, however, the Communists who crushed the 1956 revolt claimed to be "progressives" building "socialism."

In retrospect, there was almost an eerie inevitability in this tragic evolution. A century ago, the Russian radical Alexander Herzen had observed that "Communism is Russian autocracy turned upside down." Lenin himself had warned (in 1905, when he still considered himself a Social Democrat) that "he who wishes to proceed to socialism by any path other than political democracy must inevitably arrive at absurd and reactionary conclusions, both in the political and economic sense." In 1959, the young Russian critic Andrei Sinyavsky looked backward on the path that his country had traversed:

> So that prisons should vanish forever, we built new prisons. So that all frontiers should fall, we surrounded ourselves with a Chinese Wall. So that work should become a rest and a pleasure, we introduced forced labor. So that not one drop of blood be shed any more, we killed and killed and killed. . . .
>
> Yes, we live in Communism. It resembles our aspirations about as much as the Middle Ages resembled Christ, modern Western man resembles the free superman, and man resembles God. . . .

As the Borgia and Medici popes had stood on the rock of St. Peter, the East European Communist rulers of the 1960s claimed apostolic succession from the "scientific socialism" of Karl Marx, a quintessential West European (born in Trier on the Rhine, died at Hampstead Heath). Almost to the end of his life Marx was virulently anti-Russian, contemptuous of the Western and Southern Slavs, and so unconsciously a German nationalist that, for example, when German armies invaded Denmark in 1848, his *Neue Rheinische Zeitung* could declare that "it is a well known fact that Hamburg is the capital of Denmark, and not Copenhagen." However, Marx also wrote that "no nation can be free so long as it oppresses other nations," and he called revolution "the conversion of all hearts and the raising of all hands in behalf of the honor of man."

Marx left the socialist movement a rich and ambiguous prophetic legacy capable of continuous reinterpretation to serve the most diverse ends. During his own lifetime, to be sure, Marx's doctrines never gained full ascendancy even in his "own" German Social Democratic party; in more developed Western countries, his influence was soon absorbed in other radical traditions. By 1898, Eduard Bernstein and other "revisionists" were challenging Marx's analysis of social conditions as outdated and his "final aims" as utopian.

Even after Lenin had proclaimed "Marxism" the established faith of the old Russian Empire, his theory and practice were condemned by Social Democratic Marxists. In a famous critique in 1918, his radical antagonist Rosa Luxemburg declared that, while democracy had its limitations, "the remedy which Trotsky and Lenin have found, the elimination of democracy as such, is worse than the disease it is supposed to cure." The most orthodox of the German Marxists, Karl Kautsky, stated even more bluntly that Lenin's dictatorship constituted "the gravest menace to the struggle of the modern working class for liberation."

Although Lenin and such colleagues as Nikolai Bukharin continued to think in Marxist terms, from the late 1920s onward Marx and Marxism exercised less and less influence on Soviet development. The Marxist heritage became largely decorative. By the 1960s, most of the practical politicians who ruled Communist Europe hardly read Marx at all, although archivists and speechwriters furnished them with tactically appropriate quotations from time to time. On the 150th anniversary of Marx's birth, in 1968, when there were parallel celebrations, discussions, and symposiums in Western and Eastern Europe, it was clear that the elaboration of Marx's ideas was largely confined to a handful of individual philosophers, politically powerless, nearly all of them in Western countries. The ranking ideologists of the Soviet empire, who all made long speeches on the occasion, seemed to know little beyond the simple liturgy of "The Communist Manifesto," written when Marx was thirty.

In fact, the complex, cosmopolitan, teachings of Marx had been subsumed for decades in the ideological trinity of "Marxism-Leninism-Stalinism." The basic texts on which most Communists had been reared were Stalin's two primitive catechisms, "Foundations of Leninism" (1924) and the "Short Course in the History of the Soviet Communist Party" (1938). Indeed, as T. H. Rigby observed, even "Leninism" as such had been invented by Stalin, who systematized, simplified, and embodied the basic Communist creed.

When Khrushchev sought to end the worship of Stalin, a new cult of Lenin was substituted. Everywhere Khrushchev traveled, he distributed little white plaster busts of Communism's founding father. *"Lenin is forever alive," "Lenin is always with us,"* proclaimed red streamers hung from apartment windows and solemn posters on factory walls. On the nights of great Soviet holidays, when previously Stalin's floodlit portrait, towed by dirigibles, had looked down from the heavens over Red Square on the multitudes below, now Lenin's illuminated portrait smiled benignly down from the celestial heights. ("My God!" exclaimed an American seeing this for the first time. "Precisely," a French cynic replied.)

Nevertheless, few who were not compelled to do so actually read Lenin's turgid pamphlets, polemics, and tactical instructions. Those who did read Lenin, even in a spirit of piety, found contradiction and embarrassment. In the conflict between Mao and Khrushchev, both sides could freely stuff their bitter jeremiads with equally authentic Lenin quotations, proving diametrically opposite points. Western radicals meanwhile cringed on encountering some of Lenin's more naïve statements on economics—the idea, for example, that money could so easily be abolished that gold would be used to plate workers' bathtubs. (The latter thought was especially painful when, half a century after Lenin's revolution, tens of millions of Soviet citizens still lacked running water.)

By 1970, even the professional ideologists of the Soviet Communist party Central Committee could no longer get their Lenin straight. In the official party "theses" for the hundredth anniversary of his birth, they presented as Lenin's own view a statement by an Austrian Socialist which Lenin had explicitly condemned as the height of "banality."

Nevertheless, the system that Stalin created in Russia, which was imposed on its East European neighbors after 1945, had been constructed on foundations laid by Lenin. Communism had triumphed in Russia less as a result of Marxist philosophy than of Lenin's unique personality, powerful will, and strategic revolutionary instincts. In a series of fateful decisions between 1903 and 1921, Lenin created first a party, then a state, then an international movement in his own image: purposeful, militant, unscrupulous, intolerant. By the time Lenin began to have second thoughts, he was a dying man. He had impressed on Russia not only the institutions which made Stalin's rule possible, but a legacy of bloodshed and hatred from which, for his followers, there was no easy turning back.

Like Marx but unlike any of his own successors, Lenin was a cosmopolitan intellectual of impeccably *bourgeois* origins. The second son of a well-to-do government official, he spoke German, French, and English, was admitted to the Imperial bar, and was able (thanks to the income from his parents' estates) to postpone earning a living until the age of twenty-seven. When he was only seventeen, his older brother was executed for a conspiracy to assassinate Tsar Alexander III. He himself was drawn into radical student disorders, and revolution soon became his life and career. By the age of twenty-five, he was in prison; by thirty, in exile, one of the recognized leaders of the small Russian Marxist refugee group. He spent fifteen of the years between 1900 and 1917 wandering in Western and Central Europe—directing his network of followers inside Russia, quarreling incessantly with his socialist comrades.

In 1903, Lenin split the fledgling Russian Social Democratic Labor party to form his own "new type of party," the Bolsheviks.

He shaped it as a tightly organized elite corps of disciplined professional revolutionists, directed from the top. He insisted that no revolutionary movement could succeed without "an organization of leaders that is strong and maintains its primacy." The party, he stressed, "must be a hierarchy," and he artfully labeled this principle "democratic centralism." It remains the basic principle of Communist organization.

Trotsky, a critic of Lenin's at the time, forecast that under this principle "the organization will replace the party; the Central Committee will replace the party organization; and, finally, the dictator will replace the Central Committee." But this did not prevent Trotsky from joining Lenin's party in August, 1917, or urging still more dictatorial measures later. By that time, Lenin himself professed to see no contradiction between what he called "Soviet democracy" and "the application of dictatorial power by individual persons." He defined dictatorship as "government unlimited by any laws, absolutely unhampered by any rules, relying directly on force."

Lenin's historic achievement was to establish this kind of government in Russia eight months after tsarism had been overthrown —that is, in a Russia which he himself called "the freest country in the world." The strategems and methods employed by Lenin between 1917 and 1921 remain, as Stalin called them, the foundations of Leninism. These methods, emulated by Stalin's followers in Eastern Europe between 1944 and 1948, also constituted a formidable moral obstacle to those Communists who sought, after 1956, to replace the Stalinist heritage with a "return to Leninism."

When the tsarist regime collapsed in war-weary Russia, power fell to a Provisional Government of liberals and democratic socialists. Lenin returned from exile determined to overthrow them. In his first speech on arrival, he predicted imminent "civil war throughout Europe" and called for a new "socialist" revolution which, he argued, would surely ignite a world revolution. "Any day now," he said, "the whole of European capitalism may crash." (He continued to expect the crash, momentarily, for five years.)

In June and again in July 1917, Bolshevik attempts to seize power failed. But when the German Army captured Riga, Russian soldiers began to desert en masse, and their generals turned against the Provisional Government. In September, the Bolsheviks gained a majority in the Petrograd Soviet and promptly began organizing a Military-Revolutionary Committee, headed by Trotsky, to seize power. From his underground hideaway, Lenin pressed his followers for an immediate coup. His reasoning was less philosophical than tactical. If the tsars could rule Russia with 130,000 nobles and landed gentry, he argued, 240,000 Bolsheviks could do just as well. It would be "naïve", Lenin said, to wait for a "formal majority" in the long-awaited Constituent Assembly (constitutional convention) which was to be elected by universal suffrage on November 25.

On November 7, Trotsky's military units overthrew the Provisional Government and proclaimed Lenin head of a new Council of People's Commissars.* Russia's labor unions, however, demanded a broader coalition government including all of the democratic socialist parties. Eleven of the fifteen members of Lenin's cabinet supported their demand; the alternative, they argued, "was the constitution of a purely Bolshevik government by means of political terror."

Lenin, backed by Trotsky and Stalin, rejected the demand. Two days after seizing power, the Bolsheviks began suppressing opposition newspapers.** Marauding Red Guards killed prominent liberals and drove socialist leaders into hiding. On December 22, 1917, Lenin named the Polish Bolshevik Felix Dzerzhinsky to head a new political police, the Cheka—later renamed the OGPU, GPU, NKVD, MVD, and KGB. According to its own reports, its agents executed 6,300 alleged "counter-revolutionaries" in the first year of its existence (more than the total number of executions under tsarism between 1821 and 1913).

---

* Most of its members were later executed by Stalin, so that when the revolution's fiftieth anniversary was celebrated in Moscow, official posters reproducing the historic proclamation of the first Soviet Government were cropped to omit their names.

** "As soon as the new order is consolidated," Lenin promised in his decree suppressing opposition papers (November 9, 1917), "all administrative measures against the press will be suspended. Full liberty will be given it within the limits of responsibility before the law, in accordance with the broadest and most progressive regulations in this respect." The promise was quoted widely in Prague in 1968—and brought fierce Soviet attacks on every Czech who quoted it.

Although the Bolsheviks already held power, they received less than 25 percent of the vote in the elections to the Constituent Assembly. A clear majority of votes and seats went to the democratic Socialist Revolutionaries. Even in Petrograd, where Lenin's hold was firmest, the Bolsheviks received only 424,000 of 950,000 votes.

When the Constituent Assembly met on January 18, 1918, Lenin dispersed it with the aid of Lettish sharpshooters, machine guns, and artillery. Publicly Lenin acknowledged that "civil war is inevitable," swearing that "nothing in the world will induce us to surrender the Soviet power." To Trotsky privately, he called dissolution of the Assembly "a complete and frank liquidation of the idea of democracy by the idea of dictatorship." This remained the Communist view of elections and parliaments.

In three years of civil war, the Red Army under Trotsky's command ultimately prevailed over several armies of "Whites" and local nationalists, as well as fitful intervention by foreign powers. Incalculable suffering was produced by Lenin's economic policy of "war Communism," which through "class war in the villages" and hasty nationalization decrees attempted to establish instant socialism. More than 2 million Russians, including most of the prerevolutionary elite, fled the country into permanent emigration. Famine and epidemics ravaged wide areas. An official Soviet report later disclosed:

> The living standards of the Russian worker in 1919–1920 were at least three times lower than before the war. . . . Famine and cold, disease and infant mortality are hidden behind these figures. There were over 5 million typhus cases during these two years. . . . The number of prematurely dead is calculated as above 7 million for the period January 1, 1918 to July 1, 1920, in those territories in which registration of the dead was carried out.

Among the total population under Soviet rule, the loss of life between 1918 and 1922, when the Civil War ended, was estimated at more than 9 million, not including the war's military casualties. Industrial production had fallen by more than 80 percent. The 1920 grain harvest was barely 18 million tons—as compared with

74 million tons in 1916 and 92 million before the war.*

In March 1921, Lenin faced peasant revolts against government grain seizures, growing anti-Bolshevik feeling among the workers, and dissident groups within Communist ranks demanding broader internal freedoms. Strikes in Petrograd led to full-scale rebellion by the radical sailors of the Kronstadt naval base, who had helped carry Lenin to power. They now denounced the Communists as "usurpers" who, "instead of giving the people liberty, have instilled in them only the constant fear of the Cheka, which by its horrors surpasses even the gendarme regime of Tsarism . . ."

Red Army and Cheka detachments led by Trotsky crushed the Kronstadt revolt, but the upheaval finally persuaded Lenin that change was necessary. Rather than yield a monopoly of political power, Lenin made economic concessions. He abondoned "war Communism" and proclaimed a New Economic Policy (NEP), which restored the free market in agriculture, legalized trade, encouraged artisans and small private enterprise, and invited foreign investment. The NEP came too late to avert the horrible famine of 1921–22, in which some 5 million Russians died, but thereafter the Soviet economy swiftly reattained pre-revolutionary levels.

The 10th Communist Party Congress, at which the NEP was proclaimed, was a decisive turning point in Communist history. For Lenin, even as he was abandoning his costly economic theories, resolved to strengthen the political dictatorship. "Terror cannot be dispensed with," he wrote, "notwithstanding the hypocrites and the phrasemongers." A few days after the 10th Congress, the Cheka was authorized to deport anyone "recognized as dangerous to the Soviet structure" to a forced labor camp. Dzerzhinsky had opened the first such camps for Civil War prisoners in 1919, and by 1921 there were already several notorious "death camps."

Lenin also ordered the end of organized opposition groups within the Communist party itself. A resolution of the 10th Congress "On Party Unity," drafted by Lenin, forebade party mem-

* By way of comparison, the grain harvest in 1952, Stalin's last year, was 80 million tons—less than in 1913 or in 1928.

bers from organizing groups or circulating political protests against decisions of the Central Committee. Moreover, even Central Committee members who challenged the party line could now be excluded.

For a few years after Lenin's death in 1924, the party's Central Committee continued to witness live political struggles among his principal heirs. However, even during his lifetime, power had already begun gravitating from the Central Committee to two smaller groups. One was the compact, policy-making directorate called the Political Bureau or Politburo. The other was the permanent Secretariat of the Central Committee. The Secretariat coordinated the work and assigned the personnel of the party organizations throughout the country, which in turn enforced "the leading role of the party" over the government, army, police, trade unions, and social organizations. Under Stalin, who became the party's general secretary on April 4, 1922, the Secretariat came to rule the party, and thus the nation.

In contrast to the Westernized intellectuals who had originally surrounded Lenin, Stalin was an authentic proletarian from the Caucasus mountain village of Gori. He had drifted from the Tiflis theological seminary into the revolutionary movement, where he helped organize bank holdups and other "expropriations" to aid the Bolshevik cause. (Several historians believe that he also collaborated with the tsarist police.) From April 1917 on, Stalin was one of the "hards" who supported Lenin unflinchingly in the numerous internal crises of the Boshevik party, but, once in control of the party machine, his crudeness offended even Lenin, who urged—too late—that he be removed.

Within five years after Lenin's death, Stalin had triumphed first over Trotsky and other "leftists," then over Bukharin and other "rightists" who considered the NEP a sound basis for long-term Soviet economic development. In 1929, Stalin launched a "second revolution" more terrible than the first. The essentials of the party's new "general line" were the forcible collectivization of the peasants, and an extensive, breakneck industrialization concentrated on heavy industry and war production. These concepts continue to form what *Pravda* likes to call "the general laws of socialist construction."

It took the OGPU, Red Army, and armed Communist youth from the cities to drive the peasants into collective farms, often amid pitched battles and mass executions. Stalin later told Churchill that collectivization had cost Russia 10 million lives. The process was chaotic as well as brutal. It was only after a terrible famine in 1932–33 * that Stalin conceded the collective farmers the right to small private garden plots and a few cattle of their own.

Even veteran Communists were dismayed. Sergei Syrtsov, an alternate Politburo member, observed in 1930 that the Stalinists —far from being "scientific socialists"—were "acting according to the rule: Let us see what comes out of it, and if life should punch us on the head, then we shall become convinced that we should have acted otherwise."

Bukharin noted privately that "the mass annihilation of completely defenseless men, together with their wives and children," had brought about "deep changes in the psychological outlook of those Communists who participated in this campaign and, instead of going mad, became professional bureaucrats for whom terror was henceforth a normal method of administration. . . ."

Industrialization was accelerated largely by driving peasants into the cities, depressing the workers' real wages, and forcing women into the factories. (Between 1928 and 1937, the number of women industrial workers increased fivefold.) Piecework became the basis of the wage system, with workers constantly spurred on to ever higher output by speedup movements and production races ("socialist competition").

Food, housing, clothing, and other consumer goods were held to bare subsistence levels. Stalin's "second revolution" wiped out private trade, wrecking the country's distribution network in the process.** Between 1928 and 1937, the average housing space per person in Moscow was reduced by half.

* To hide this famine from the outside world, Stalin sharply restricted travel by foreigners to and inside Russia—restrictions which remained in force many years after his death. To bring in the harvest from the demoralized countryside, urban "volunteers" as well as Army conscripts were sent out to the farms each fall—another practice which has proved permanent.

** In 1912, Russia had 1,166,000 department stores, wholesale units, and retail outlets. By 1937, this had been reduced to 228,000 stores and 98,000 warehouses. Stores lost their names and received numbers instead; thus, Eliseyev's famous grocery in Moscow became "Gastronom No. 1."

Russia was virtually cut off from the world market, and prices were fixed arbitrarily from Moscow. Turnover taxes on basic necessities (which the consumer paid in the form of higher prices) channeled funds from agriculture and light industry to capital goods and war production. The forced priority of heavy industry continued for decades after World War II. By 1952, the disparity in real wages between the average Russian and the average American worker was twice as great as it had been in 1913.

While ravaging the countryside and depressing urban living standards, Stalin created a new ruling class of privileged party, government, police, military, and economic officials. In the factories, the ratio between the wages of a director and those of an unskilled worker rose to 30:1. Members of the new class also received priority rights to better housing, vacation resorts, and scarce imported consumer goods.

The permanent party apparatus expanded vastly. In 1922, only 15,000 of the party's half-million members were full-time officials. By 1939, there were twelve times that many professional party functionaries—one for every nine party members. No figures were ever provided on the expansion of the secret police, but both its size and influence grew rapidly throughout the 1930s. As Bernard Shaw observed (admiringly!) in 1932:

> A considerable share of the success of Russian Communism consists in the fact that every Russian knows that, if he will not make his life a paying enterprise for his country, then he will most likely lose it. An agent of the GPU will take him by the shoulder and will conduct him to the cellar of this famous department and he will simply stop living.

Until 1934, the "proletarian sword" of the GPU spared the members of the Communist party itself. For this reason, Khrushchev and his followers continued to insist, at the "de-Stalinization" congresses of 1956 and 1961, that the upheaval of 1929–1934 still represented the "good" Stalin, and that his crimes only began with the mysterious murder of Sergei Kirov, the Leningrad party leader, on December 1, 1934. It was this murder that set the stage for the Great Terror of 1935–40—the time of ultimate horror when, in the words of the poet Anna Akhmatova, "only the dead smiled," "the stars of death stood over us, and innocent Russia writhed under bloody boots and the tires of Black Marias."

At the height of the great purge in 1937 and 1938, at least 7 million Soviet citizens were arrested, including more than 1.2 million Communist party members. Only 50,000 of the Communists ever regained freedom; 600,000 were executed. New victims joined their ranks down through World War II and afterward—including whole peoples, such as the Crimean Tartars and Volga Germans, whom Stalin suspected of disloyalty. In 1968, the Soviet nuclear physicist, Andrei Sakharov, asserted:

> At least 10 to 15 million people perished in the torture chambers of the NKVD from torture and execution, in camps for exiled kulaks (well-to-do peasants) and so-called semi-kulaks and members of their families . . . People perished in the mines of Norilsk and Vorkuta from freezing, starvation and exhausting labor, at countless construction projects, in timber-cutting, building of canals, or simply during transportation in prison trains, in the over-crowded "death ships" in the Sea of Okhotsk, and during the resettlement of entire peoples. . . .

Stalin's terror claimed the lives of nearly all Lenin's closest associates, more than half the delegates to the 1934 party congress, virtually the entire Red Army high command, and almost half the Soviet officer corps. Of 139 Central Committee members, no fewer than 98 were shot; others committed suicide or died mysteriously.

The annihilation of the old Bolsheviks cleared the way for ambitious young men who had proved themselves during collectivization and the purge. In 1939, Stalin reported that some 500,000 young men had been promoted to executive positions since 1934. Many of these men came to rule Russia in the 1960s. Suslov and Kosygin were among those who filled the vacant places at the Moscow summit. Brezhnev, Frol Kozlov, Andrei Kirilenko, and Gennadi Voronov earned party office in the provinces at a time when denunciation of old revolutionaries was the party's main activity.

Stalin's purge also ravaged the ranks of the Communist International (Comintern) which Lenin had created. In 1928, as part of his new "general line," Stalin proclaimed the Social Democrats of Europe the main enemies of the working class. German Communists following his line helped clear the way for Hitler, whom they regarded as the "icebreaker" of their own revolution. In 1935, alarmed by the growing power of the Third Reich (and Nazi cancellation of the secret agreements between the Red Army and the German General Staff), Stalin publicly proclaimed a "Popular Front" campaign against fascism. Secretly, however, he sought a pact with Hitler.

By the mid-1930s, fascist or other dictatorial regimes held power throughout Central and Eastern Europe, with the single exception of Czechoslovakia. Thousands of foreign Communists had sought refuge in Moscow, where most of them fell victim to Stalin's terror. Virtually all the party leaders of Poland and the Baltic states were shot. Casualties were nearly as heavy among Hungarian, Finnish, and Yugoslav party leaders. Several hundred German and Italian Communists also perished—many of the Germans at the hands of Hitler's Gestapo, to which the NKVD delivered them after the Nazi-Soviet Pact of August 23, 1939.

Stalin described his alliance with Hitler as "cemented by blood" and hoped to the last that Hitler would keep the bargain. Even after the war, according to his daughter Svetlana, he often said, "Ech, together with the Germans we would have been invincible!"

When the Nazis invaded Russia on June 22, 1941, Stalin initially panicked: "All that Lenin created, we have lost forever," he told intimates. Although Soviet forces were equal to the Germans in manpower, artillery, planes, and tanks, in less than five months the Nazi Wehrmacht swiftly occupied a vast territory which included 40 percent of the Soviet population. In many areas, particularly the Baltic states and the Ukraine, the Germans were welcomed as liberators. By the end of 1941, the Wehrmacht had taken 3.6 million prisoners.

Nazi barbarism in the occupied territories, along with the deliberate starvation of Russian war prisoners, stiffened Soviet morale as the German offensive was halted before Moscow on December 5, 1941. And Allied military and economic aid, continuous bombing of German industry, and the opening of new fronts in North Africa and Italy helped enable the Red Army to begin rolling back the Wehrmacht in 1943. But Russian losses by the end of the Second World War were estimated at 20 million dead.

Once Soviet territory had been cleared of the Nazi invaders, Stalin moved to expand the Communist realm. He acted on the principle that "this war is not as in the past. Whoever occupies a territory also imposes on it his own social system. Everyone imposes his own system as far as his army can reach. It cannot be otherwise." Stalin's Western allies, with greater or lesser reluctance, conceded the point.*

Communism was imposed west of the Russian frontiers by the Soviet Army, the MVD and—to an extent which varied greatly—local Communists. The strength of native Communist movements ranged from miniscule (as in Rumania, where the party numbered 884 members before the Red Army's arrival) to mass, as in Yugoslavia and Czechoslovakia. Before the war, Communism had been largely an ethnic phenomenon in Eastern Europe—weak in non-Slavic areas, strongest among disturbed Slavic minorities such as the Ruthenians and Macedonians.

Wartime experience had also varied widely. In East Germany and in Hungary, Rumania, and Bulgaria, which had been allied with Hitler, there had been little or no resistance to the Nazis until the arrival of the Soviet armies. In Czechoslovakia, the wartime experience was mixed. Some Czechs collaborated with the Germans; most practiced passive resistance; many who had escaped abroad fought in the Allied Armies. In briefly independent Slovakia, there was little resistance until Communists led a national uprising in the Tatra mountains in August 1944.

* At the Moscow Conference in October 1944, Churchill and Stalin agreed on the following division of influence between Russia and the West in southeastern Europe:
  Rumania—Russia 90 percent, the others 10 percent
  Greece—Britain and the U.S. 90 percent, Russian 10 percent
  Yugoslavia—50–50 percent
  Hungary—50–50 percent
  Bulgaria—Russia 75 percent, the others 25 percent
  Poland, already occupied by the Red Army, was in effect ceded to Communist domination at the Yalta Conference of February 1945. The respective occupation zones in Germany were fixed at the Potsdam meeting in June 1945. There was never any formal agreement among the Allies concerning Czechoslovakia.

In Poland, there was a strong resistance to the Nazis, but it was non-Communist and suffered a tragic fate. On July 29, 1944, Soviet armies under Marshal Konstantin Rokossovsky reached the industrial suburbs of Warsaw. Moscow's Polish-language radio proclaimed the hour of liberation at hand and called on Poles for "direct, active struggle in the streets of Warsaw, in its houses, factories and stores . . ." On August 1, the underground forces of the Polish Home Army rose, and for sixty-three days battled eight German divisions. The Soviet Army did not move to help them. More than 200,000 men and women were killed or wounded before Warsaw surrendered on October 2. On Hitler's orders, the Wehrmacht razed the city. A few weeks later, Stalin recognized a Communist committee formed in Moscow as the Provisional Government of Poland.

The Yugoslav experience was unique. The initially small Partisan bands in the mountains of Bosnia, western Serbia, and Montenegro managed to weather numerous German assaults, to outmaneuver and defeat Serb and Croat nationalists, to organize Communist-led resistance in Macedonia and Albania. From 1943 on, they received millions of dollars of Western equipment, as well as nearly all the arms surrendered when Italy left the war. They liberated large areas before the Soviet Army advanced on Belgrade, and came out of the war with 141,000 seasoned Communist party members.

More than three years were required to impose Communist rule throughout Eastern Europe. The climax of the struggle came in February 1948, when Communist-controlled police and the so-called "People's Militia," the party's private army, seized full power in Prague.

The years 1945–48 were later enshrined in East European Communist mythology as a "heroic" period of dedication and idealism—in contrast to the Stalinist terror of 1949–52 which followed. Yet, even in the early years, for every tale of Communist idealism, there were agonizing sagas of violence, cruelty, skullduggery, and slander applied to so-called "class enemies." As in Russia between 1918 and 1921, a wave of refugees flooded west before the frontiers were sealed. As in Russia between 1929 and 1933, an even greater number of non-Communists were imprisoned or sent to forced-labor camps before the terror struck Communist ranks.

The Communist leaders who assumed power between 1945 and 1948 were by no means a uniform group. The most striking division was between the "Muscovites" and the "natives"—the Communists who had spent the war years in Russia and those who had remained in their home countries, either in the underground or in fascist prisons. There were contrasts, too, in social origins—middle-class intellectuals alongside former manual workers, passionate nationalists alongside Jewish "cosmopolitans." Several key East European leaders had also worked directly for the MVD or other Soviet agencies.

In the first few years, the differences among these Communists seemed small in the face of the larger task of imposing minority rule on hostile populations. Before long, however, each of them faced what was to be the permanent dilemma of how to stay in power—by winning support within his own party and nation or by pleasing the Kremlin. The two alternatives were largely incompatible, and those who attempted to accomplish both objectives usually achieved neither. The capriciousness of the aging Stalin —swinging suddenly from one favorite to another, from "rightist" to "leftist" policies—made the dilemma even more cruel. In successive purges between 1949 and 1954, a host of high East European Communists were executed or imprisoned, only to be "rehabilitated" (most of them posthumously) in later years.

Two of the original East European leaders remained continuously in power, surviving Stalin and all his pallbearers, by making an early and unequivocal choice. In East Germany, Walter Ulbricht staked all on pleasing the Kremlin and the proconsuls of the Soviet occupation army—and outlasted a succession of Russian leaders who each in turn toyed with the thought of liquidating his East German regime. In Yugoslavia, on the other hand, Josip Broz-Tito struck out for popularity and independence—ultimately presiding over the emergence of a different kind of Communism.

The clash between Stalin and Tito erupted into the open on June 28, 1948 (the anniversary of the Serbian defeat at Kossovo and of the assassination at Sarajevo). However, as in the later

Soviet conflict with China, the trouble went back a long time—to Stalin's high-handedness and bad advice to Yugoslav Communists before and during the war. Above and beyond all the real and spurious issues between Belgrade and Moscow, however, there loomed Stalin's suspicion of Tito as a restless, ambitious, and independent personality.*

"I will shake my little finger and there will be no more Tito," Stalin told Khrushchev. Instead, Tito called on the West for aid, arrested Stalin's sympathizers, and proclaimed that Yugoslavia would now seek and find its own, specific "path to socialism." He denounced Stalin's Russia as "an enormous terror state" ruled by the MVD, and declared that never before in history and "nowhere are men so inhumanly treated as in the Soviet Union. . . ."

Stalin hastened to purge suspected "Titoists" elsewhere and to impress on Eastern Europe the tested Soviet model of Communism, with its barbed wire, police terror, forced labor, war economy, and cult of his own personality. East European leaders pledged their unconditional allegiance. In Czechoslovakia, Deputy Premier Vilem Siroky asserted that "for a Communist there is a rule which must be observed at all times and expecially in difficult circumstances—unreserved confidence in the Soviet Union and the great Stalin." Soviet ideologists, led by Suslov, described such limitless loyalty as "proletarian internationalism." (The independent Yugoslav Communists, on the other hand, were denounced as "a gang of hired Anglo-American spies and murderers.")

After Stalin's death on March 5, 1953, his heirs ended the terror among Communist party leaders, shut down most of the forced labor camps, permitted the beginnings of a cultural "thaw," and slowly renewed contact with the outside world. There was much talk of a "return to Lenin," and two of Stalin's former victims—Wladyslaw Gomulka in Poland, Janos Kadar in Hungary —returned to power in the convulsions of 1956. However, throughout the empire in the early 1960s, much of the old Stalinist "general line" remained in place, as did many old Stalinists in high office: Ulbricht in East Germany, Antonin Novotny in Czecho-

* Tito's career and personality will be discussed in Chapter 4.

slovakia, Kozlov, Suslov, and Kosygin at Khrushchev's right hand in the Kremlin. Together with Khrushchev, they alternately embraced and condemned the pragmatic Titoist system in Yugoslavia. Yet in every wave of change in Communist Europe, the peculiar Yugoslav example inevitably came to the fore in one form or another. It had done so in Poland and Hungary during the fifties and seemed likely to do so elsewhere in the new decade.

CHAPTER 3

The Halfway House

Yugoslavia in the early 1960s was often described as a "halfway house"—halfway between East and West, halfway between Balkan sloth and European industry, halfway between Stalinism and democracy. Indisputably, as contact between the two Europes resumed, Yugoslavia was the halfway house at which curious travelers from both sides stopped first. For Westerners long frightened by reports of the grimness of Stalinist rule, Yugoslavia was usually the first Communist country to which they dared venture. For citizens of the Soviet empire long sealed off from the decadent, imperialist West, Yugoslavia was often the first non-Stalinist country to which they were permitted to venture.

Under Khrushchev, Communists seeking alternatives to the Stalinist model were naturally drawn to Yugoslavia, which was the only other model in existence in Europe. The Yugoslav leaders still proclaimed their loyalty to "Marxism-Leninism," but had in fact departed from its Soviet version in many respects.

In 1950, Tito had proclaimed a system of "workers' self-management," in which elected workers' councils (in theory at least) chose their directors and decided enterprise policies. In 1952, the Yugoslavs had heralded the ultimate "withering away of the state," by according broad powers to the (theoretically) self-governing communes, or municipalities. Both of these innovations

53

were drawn directly from prophecies of Marx which Lenin and Stalin had in practice repudiated. Moreover, in 1954, the Yugoslavs had abandoned the forced collectivization of agriculture, and thereafter 85 percent of the land was worked by private peasants. They had accepted Western loans and, in 1961, embarked on an economic reform stressing the profitability of enterprises and a "socialist market economy." In these respects, they seemed to be applying the logic of Lenin's New Economic Policy which Stalin had so ruinously abandoned.

In the West, on the other hand, there was a feeling that Yugoslavia might perhaps represent the wave of the Soviet future. In 1955 and 1956, Tito had persuaded Khrushchev to endorse the pluralist slogan of "different paths to socialism." Khrushchev retreated from this concept when Hungary went too far down its own path, but he had often given the impression that he wished to emulate Titoist innovations, and Yugoslav officials themselves said privately, "Our policy is what Soviet policy ought to be." When the Chinese began to attack Khrushchev through the Yugoslav "revisionists," Western interest in the Yugoslav experience grew more intense.

For, apart from the Titoist theoretical innovations that had been drawn from Marx and Lenin, the Yugoslavs had made a number of changes which in Western, non-Communist eyes seemed hopeful and reasonable. They had begun to open the borders to Western tourists, imported Western films, translated Western books, and welcomed Western trade. Their economic reform had been coordinated with international lending agencies, and its ultimate aim was a convertible currency—when the other Communists were still operating basically war economies with money no better than scrip.

In foreign policy, the Yugoslavs had long been preaching the gospel of "nonalignment" between the two main military blocs. Their missionary efforts among African, Asian, and Arab nationalists and neutralists reached an impressive climax in the Belgrade conference of 1961, assembling dozens of heads of states of all hues and colors. Yugoslav leaders vigorously pursued "peaceful coexistence" with everybody, and urged negotiations between the Great Powers in place of cold wars.

For those Western diplomats and scholars who had known Stalin's empire, moreover, Yugoslavia in the early 1960s represented great progress. There was none of the wild police terror and violence which had distinguished Stalin's empire—and had been prominent in Yugoslavia itself after World War II. The Yugoslav Communists themselves, too, possessed a vitality and curiosity that had not been seen in Russia since the 1920s.

Therefore, Western statesmen hoping for a "mellowing" or "erosion from despotism" in Russia and its empire based at least some of their hope on Yugoslav influence and example. If Khrushchev's Russia were to emulate Yugoslavia, and Yugoslavia continued to be susceptible to influence from the West, then perhaps the Kremlin and the West could yet be reconciled and the cold war could give way to a more relaxed peace.

It was often said in those days that the Yugoslavs were "ahead" of the Russians and their satellites—five years "ahead," ten years "ahead," twenty years, depending on the relative optimism of the observer. Now that Khrushchev and his friends seemed committed to working their way out of the dead end of Stalinism, it appeared that they might well adopt at least some of the "revisionist" theories of the Yugoslavs. Such was the reasoning among the Yugoslav theorists themselves, among many in the West, and apparently among many in the Soviet empire as well.

Both Eastern and Western visitors found Yugoslavia a disconcerting experience. It was certainly *different* and full of life, but what was fascinating about it seemed to have little to do with either Eastern or Western notions of what Communism was about.

For the traveler arriving from Moscow or Sofia, Belgrade seemed like Paris in comparison. Indeed, diplomats stationed in Bulgaria, which had once been the "garden of Europe," frequently drove the 90 miles from Sofia to the Yugoslav frontier to shop for meat and vegetables. Diplomats stationed in Tirana, Albania, came out to Yugoslavia's most backward southern towns and sighed with relief as if they had reached Venice.

When the European Athletic Championships were held in Belgrade in September 1962, Soviet athletes rushed into the shops, drawn (as Tito later put it) "like bees to honey" by the relative abundance. Soviet women discus-throwers and hurdlers, enthralled by nylon stockings but accustomed to rationing, amused their Yugoslav interpreters by asking how many pair they were entitled to.

A delegation of officials from the Soviet Writers Union was shocked by the bohemian airs of their Yugoslav hosts, their absorption and familiarity with Western literature, their enthusiasm for such forbidden Russian classics as Boris Pasternak's *Doctor Zhivago*. Soviet security officials, conferring with their Yugoslav counterparts, asked how the Yugoslavs could really afford to plan for a million or two million foreign tourists, since they would surely need an equal number of police agents to control such dangerous foreigners.

The traveler coming from the West in the early 1960s also felt that he had reached another world. If he came, as many tourists did, by car from Italy, he might notice that the shops and open-air markets of Trieste were jammed with Yugoslavs frantically buying clothing and other necessities.* There was no longer any "iron curtain" on the frontiers with Italy and Austria, across which hundreds of thousands of Western tourists had begun to pour in the late 1950s, and tens of thousands of Yugoslavs had begun to move in the early 1960s.

Yugoslav border guards and customs officials were hardly tougher than those encountered at West European frontiers. They simply seemed more disorganized, and tourists complained of confusion rather than high-handedness. The first change one noticed was not so much the red star in the cap of the border guard, but the faded gray of his uniform, which looked as though it had been laundered too often, or perhaps had never been a very clear gray. It was a signal of things to come, for once inside the country the familiar consumer world of Western Europe, with its Shell and Agip gas stations, Coca-Cola signs, and bright boutiques, had been left behind.

The same bright Adriatic sun shone on both the Italian and Yugoslav sides of the frontier. Yet nearly all the man-made colors

---

* In those days, even Belgrade housemaids who had never left Serbia knew—through friends and relatives—just what was selling, in what colors, sizes, and styles, 400 miles away in Trieste. The situation changed after 1965, for reasons to be described in Chapter 12.

in Yugoslavia somehow seemed vaguer, paler, faded. Many houses appeared not to have been painted or plastered in years. New buildings were cleaner, but not much brighter, for the local paint was water-based. Clothing seemed to have been tinted with weak dyes, posters printed with watered-down inks. Even the grass in the fields seemed paler, seared by the sun, with few sprinklers to water it.

There was much that was new to greet tourists who moved slowly down the Adriatic coast, explored the mountains of Bosnia or Montenegro, and finally arrived in the fertile plain where the Sava and Danube rivers met at Belgrade. Scattered along the coast, there were new hotels and motels in the cheesebox international modern style, contrasting with twelfth- and fourteenth-century churches and their slim bell towers. New apartment houses, built of poured concrete or brick faced with stucco, were dressed up in the Italian manner with brightly colored balconies, window frames, or curtains. New roads were promptly marked with international safety symbols.

Yet these new elements stood out against a background that felt prewar or older. In Rijeka, the country's largest port, black coal smoked from ship funnels, and horse-drawn carts helped unload the ships. In Sarajevo, the famous Moslem artisans' market, the *bas carsija,* was a scene from the *Thousand and One Nights.* In Belgrade, scruffily dressed Albanians cut wood, washed the streets at night, or begged for alms, while their women sometimes nursed their babies in the street. In the moon-crater mountains of Montenegro, peasants drove sheep and goats across the main highway as a woodburning locomotive went by, flashing cinders into the air.

The contrast between pretensions and realities was equally striking. The popular magazines were full of familiar "international" themes: Hollywood and Cinecitta films, Paris fashions, Scandinavian home design, Fiats and Volkswagens. Yet economic journals casually noted in passing that most women worked 14 to 16 hours a day and that half the children born in 1961 had entered the world without benefit of doctor or nurse. The country was dispensing foreign aid and sending specialists to Africa, Asia, and Latin America, yet coping with a large hidden unemployment by such primitive means as all-day parking attendants in the smallest village squares, waiting to collect the equivalent of ten cents per car per hour.

The crews building the Adriatic highway (ultimately completed in 1965) worked without bulldozers or pneumatic drills. As far as the road went, it was good enough. But where it ended, or the traveler was compelled to risk roads officially marked as "macadamized," the experience could be tragicomic. In the rainy seasons, such roads were often impassable mud. In summer, the motorist churned up huge clouds of pink-white dust, so fine it penetrated closed suitcases in locked baggage trunks. Every twenty miles or so, little old men with brooms stood by the roadside, waiting to sweep gravel into the more egregious potholes. Tourists in those days vied with one another with tales of incredible breakdowns in the middle of nowhere, desperate searches for repairmen, local smiths who forged new parts in deserted barns.

The country had begun to introduce supermarkets (after Tito had admired an American one displayed at the Zagreb international fair), but the best fruits and vegetables, eggs and meat, were still to be found at the traditional open-air markets—to which peasants traveled by night from miles around to hawk their wares in the morning. A fashion show for tourists might display chic summer dresses as well as handsome imitation fur coats; but such stylish wares were rarely to be found in most shops, as exports took priority. Yugoslavia had developed Western tastes and appetites—yet a visit to almost any factory or office disclosed that it was far from Western productivity: the Yugoslavs had discovered the coffee break before the time clock.

Universities, old and new, were jammed with the children of workers and peasants, but professors complained that there were few real students of prewar quality among them. Most just "sat" year after year, with even the meager government stipend enabling them to enjoy life in the big city. Bonuses were offered to young graduates willing to go teach in the illiterate boondocks —but the few who did so stayed only long enough to save money for an apartment in Belgrade, Zagreb, or Rijeka. Peasant girls came to universities and teachers' colleges hoping to marry doctors or engineers, and were occasionally seduced by taxidrivers posing as medical students. In the country's backward south, there were modern, glass-fronted university buildings at Skoplje and Pristina; scarcely a week went by in which the glass was not shattered by youthful rock-throwers.*

The foreign tourist on the Dalmatian Coast might well be pleased by the absence (or discretion) of the police control. But once a foreigner settled a while in Belgrade, the picture changed. He might pick up his phone and overhear the conversation of three or four of his Western colleagues—or, on occasion, police headquarters. His mail, wherever it came from, was inevitably sealed with the thick, familiar Belgrade glue. In numerous government offices, he discovered, many a high official was a former officer of the UDBA, the secret police. Among the Yugoslav citizens who seemed freest to mingle with foreigners, several were rumored to be UDBA collaborators—a few were reputed to be working for the even more secret and rival KOS, the military intelligence.

At the same time, after years of Khrushchevite denunciations of Stalin's "cult of personality," it was disconcerting to find the main street of nearly every Yugoslav town named after Marshal Tito, his portrait on restaurant and hotel walls, his most routine appointments reported on every front page. Whole towns were still named after him: Titograd, Titov Veles, Titovo Uzice, Titovo Korenice. When he entered a public place, sound and light effects enhanced his every word and gesture with royal authority. Crowds chanted "We are Tito's, Tito is ours," or sang the song beginning, "Comrade Tito, we pledge to you we will never swerve from your path."

The Marshal moved around the country, from one elegant villa to another, from his private island of Brioni to Belgrade, in stately pomp: on the royal yacht *Galeb*, in the special blue train the *Sutjeska*, or in a long motorcade of American limousines.** These monarchical trappings inspired lesser members of the "new class"

* An exchange professor once gave an entire course in American literature at Skoplje without a single question being asked. When he finally forced the students to participate, the first question was, "Do you know Elizabeth Taylor?"

** A Slovenian mechanic who occasionally serviced the Marshal's car, and who had done the same for King Alexander before the war, was once asked the difference. "The King," he replied, "used to come up here with three cars, only one of them new. The Marshal comes with sixteen, all of them new."

to seek their own villas, foreign cars, and Western clothes. At one point, in a mood of reform, the regime granted long-term credits to several thousand officials to help them buy their own automobiles, so that they would stop using government cars for private errands. The car imported was the Peugeot 404, and the officials were soon known as the "peugeoisie." These upper-class airs contrasted sharply with the poverty of much of the population, and with the proletarian origins and Marxist rhetoric of the leaders themselves.

For the foreigner, however, the most vivid discovery in actually seeing Yugoslavia was its variety—the striking contrasts between the different regions of the country. Even a tourist who did not venture far inland could see that the Dalmatian coastal towns bore the marks of Venetian empire, while a score of miles up the mountain—in the Montenegrin hills, in wild Hercegovina—one felt the presence of the Turk. Austrian influence was clear in the northwest, the traces of the Magyars in the northeast—a wild mixture of Turkish, Bulgarian, Byzantine, and Greek legacies in the deep south.

Bosnia, in the mountainous heart of the country, was not only naturally beautiful but culturally incredible: crossing mountain after mountain, from one valley to another, one moved from the thirteenth century to the nineteenth, from the twentieth to the fifteenth and back again. In a few hours, a motorist could pass hydroelectric stations built by the Communists, railroads built by the Hapsburgs, mosques and bridges built by the Turks, khaki-clad Army units in American jeeps, blonde Slavic girls in Moslem culottes, swarthy peasants roasting lamb on outdoor spits.

No other country in Europe offered such variety in such a kaleidoscopic mixture. Geography, history, economics, and culture cut Yugoslavia up along axes that were by no means identical. It is at the same time an Alpine, Danubian, Balkan, and Adriatic country. From northwest to southeast, roughly parallel to the coast, mountain ranges and highlands divided the country geographically into three broad strips—among sea, mountain, and plains people. The coastal area was the narrowest, least populated, and most beautiful—with hundreds of ravishing islands just off its winding bays and gulfs.

Most Yugoslavs lived in the plains, in the fertile valleys of the Sava, Danube, Morava, and Vardar rivers—the historic route from Vienna and Budapest to Athens and Byzantium. Here stood the main cities, some of them settled two thousand years: Ljubljana, Zagreb, Novi Sad, Belgrade, Nis, Skoplje. The civilization of the Yugoslav peoples had developed in these cities, and along the coast.

But the mountain people had played a decisive role in the country's history. For while foreign occupation armies, from Suleiman the Magnificent and Eugene of Savoy to the Nazi Wehrmacht, camped in the cities of the plain, the mountaineers shouldered arms in the guerrilla uprisings that constituted the national epic. In the first two decades of Communist rule, most of the new masters of the country were mountaineers—and resented as such by city folk.

The geographic divisions were only the beginning of Yugoslav complexities. History had drawn another, more significant line from the coast right across the mountains and plains (roughly north-south along the Drina, Sava, and Drava rivers). The Emperors Diocletian and Theodosius were the first to draw the line, to partition their realm into Western and Eastern empires— Roman and Byzantine, Latin and Greek. Virtually the same line soon came to divide Catholic and Orthodox Christianity—and, still later, to divide the Hapsburg and Ottoman Empires.

Nine-tenths of the citizens of Yugoslavia were considered ethnically *Yugo* (South)-Slavs. However, the South Slavs were divided into six major "nations" with different histories and traditions, two alphabets, three different languages, and three religions.

In the extreme northwest, along the Italian and Austrian frontiers, there lived the *Slovenes*, who were Catholic, wrote the Latin alphabet, had their own distinct language, and had been ruled for centuries by Austria. Most of them lived in the Julian Alps, although others had reached the coast near Trieste.

To the south and east of the Slovenes, there lived the *Croats*, who were dispersed rather in the form of a horseshoe: along the Adriatic Coast and up around to the plains adjoining Hungary. The Croats, too, were Catholic and wrote the Latin alphabet. But,

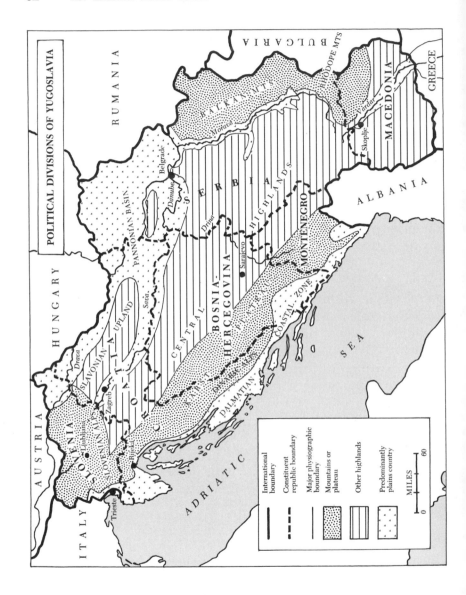

unlike the Slovenes, the Croats spoke the dominant language of Yugoslavia, which they called Croato-Serbian. (Most others called it Serbo-Croatian or simply "Yugoslav.") The coastal Croats had been ruled by Venice, briefly by Napoleon, then by Austria. The plains Croats had been under Magyar domination.

The Catholic Slovenes and Croats were considered the two "Northern" peoples economically, "Western" culturally.

In the mountainous middle of the country, right along the old Imperial divide, there were the provinces of Bosnia and Hercegovina. Here there were Croats, Serbs, and a million *Slavic Moslems*. These Slavic Moslems were not Turks, but Slavs who had accepted Islam during the Ottoman occupation. They too spoke "Yugoslav" (Serbo-Croatian), and most of them used the Latin alphabet.

The *Serbs* were the most numerous of all the Yugoslavs. Indeed, they constituted two-fifths of the entire population. They lived in the east of the country, from the Hungarian border down through the Danube and Morava valleys, adjoining Rumania and Bulgaria. They spoke the same language as the Croats and the Slavic Moslems—Serbo-Croatian—but they used the Cyrillic alphabet and they were Orthodox. They had had a great kingdom in the Middle Ages, and were the first to win independence from the Turks in the nineteenth century.

Closely akin to the Serbs were the *Montenegrins,* who lived in the Crna Gora (Black Mountains) in the southwest corner of Yugoslavia, just north of Albania. They often considered themselves "pure Serbs"—they were Orthodox, spoke Serbo-Croatian, and used the Cyrillic alphabet—but had had an independent kingdom of their own before World War I.

In the very south, adjoining Bulgaria and Greece, there were the *Macedonians*. They, too, were Orthodox and used the Cyrillic alphabet. But they had a language of their own, philologically halfway between Serbo-Croatian and Bulgarian.

Thus, apart from the Slovenes and Macedonians, all the ethnic "Yugoslavs" spoke Serbo-Croatian. But the differences in dialect, idiom, and alphabet had been causing controversies between Serbs and Croats for more than a century; and every new dictionary was a political event.

To complete the picture, in addition to the ethnic "Yugoslavs," there were hundreds of thousands of Magyars in the northeast, nearly a million Albanians in the southwest. The country was an absolute delight to the ethnographer, especially since its people enjoyed migrating, intermarrying, and asserting their individuality in bizarre ways.*

The old Imperial dividing line between Catholic West and Orthodox East coincided only roughly with the economic division of the country into developed north, semideveloped center, and backward south. By and large, the territories which the Hapsburgs had held the longest (inhabited by Slovenes, Croats, Magyars, and the Serbs north of the Danube) were the most developed. The territories which the Ottomans had occupied longest (including Macedonians, Albanians, Bosnian Moslems, and southern Serbs) were the most backward.

The interwar Kingdom of Yugoslavia, dominated by the Serbs from Serbia, had attempted to redress the balance in their favor. Their hegemony was so thorough that even the Serbs living in Croatia were offended. The Communist regime, multinational in principle but leaning heavily on backward mountaineers, sought for years through heavy investments to build up the country's underdeveloped areas. Nevertheless, in the early 1960s it was surprising how little these twentieth-century efforts had altered the old patterns. The Slovenes were 98 percent literate; in Bosnia-Hercegovina, on the other hand, 36.5 percent of the population (including half the women) were illiterate. The Slovenes and Croats had children at about the same rate as West Europeans; the Albanians in the Kossovo region had a birthrate four times as high. The backward areas made progress, to be sure, but the "north-south" gap remained because—even with less of an investment—the more skilled peoples progressed faster. Winter motorists on the *autoput*, Yugoslavia's main north-south highway, could always tell where they were: in Slovenia, the snow was

---

* Thus, there were not only a million Serbs living in Croatia. There were important families in Dubrovnik (Ragusa) who insisted on calling themselves "Catholic Serbs" rather than Croats. Moreover, among the Serbs in Serbia, "pure" Serbs, who were supposedly Slavic and blond, were distinguished from Tsintsars and Vlachs who had been absorbed into Serbdom but were, it was believed, mostly Rumanian in origin.

neatly cleaned; in Croatia, it was half-cleaned; in Serbia, not at all.

The essence of the Yugoslav nationalities problem—which was and remains its most sensitive political issue—was that the various nationalities were neither evenly balanced nor dominated by a single people. The 8 million Serbs were the pivot around which the state revolved—indeed, fertile, mineral-rich Serbia was the key to the entire Balkans. Yet, even together with the half-million Montenegrins, the Serbs remained a numerical minority in a population of more than 18 million. The prices of their raw materials kept falling on world markets, and their own native bent was for politics and horse-trading rather than industry. They had great traditions both of radical democrats and of cunning police chiefs—as well as of inspired maneuvering between Paris, Vienna, and St. Petersburg during their century of independence before Yugoslavia's creation. They felt they had earned the right to rule by their long struggles against the Turks and their heroic campaigns in World War I—the retreat to Albania, the march from Salonika—which had made Yugoslavia possible.

The 4.5 million Croats and 1.6 million Slovenes had the skilled workers, technicians, and businessmen, along with diligence and various other "German" virtues. They considered themselves best qualified to lead the country—yet constituted less than a third of the population. Nor did the two peoples follow the same course in practice, however they might agree in theory. The Croats had a long tradition of obstinate resistance to their rulers—in Budapest before 1914, in Belgrade afterward. The Slovenes, on the other hand, somehow managed to draw economic and cultural advantage out of limited accommodations with the central power. (Tito, whose father was Croat and mother Slovene, combined both traditions on a world scale.)

To casual outsiders, the various Yugoslavs resembled one another more than any of them did such neighbors as the Germans, Magyars, Rumanians, or Greeks. Yet, in the country itself, Tito sometimes seemed to be the only "Yugoslav"; others were indelibly typed as Serbs, Croats, Slovenes—and sometimes even according to their districts and villages. Serbs regarded Croats as lawyers and Germans; Croats considered Serbs policemen and

Turks. Both looked down on Slovenes the way Prussians viewed the Swiss—as pedantic, efficient businessmen who lacked "heart." Montenegrins considered heroism their national industry, and valor, loyalty, and honesty the great virtues lacking in the lowland peoples—but the others told tales of Montenegrin laziness, aversion to the modern age, and patriarchal attitudes toward women. All looked down on Macedonians as somewhat comical, on Bosnian Moslems as infidels or savages. The latter two peoples, for their part, regarded the Croats as haughty, the Serbs as overbearing, the Slovenes incomprehensible.

The "national question" had destroyed the interwar Yugoslav state, and led to horrible fratricidal conflict. Of the 1.9 million Yugoslavs who died in World War II, at least 600,000 perished at the hands of their own countrymen.

Tito's government had created a federal state with six constituent republics, plus autonomous regions for the Albanian and Hungarian minorities, but the old suspicions died hard. A housekeeper in Belgrade refused to touch fish for twenty years because in 1942 she had cut open a fish and found a ringed finger inside, belonging to one of the Serb victims of the Ustaše massacres, whose bodies were tossed into the Sava in Croatia to float down the river to Serbia. The Croats had their own tales of Serb repression before the war.

While foreign experts could cooly note the "leadership qualities" of the handsome Montenegrins and the business acumen of the Slovenes, a Serb artisan remarked: "The Montenegrins? You can keep them here a hundred years, dress them up any way you wish—all they know is the fist. They are the police, and would be under King Alexander, Franz-Josef or God-knows-whom." As for the Slovenes, "they decide everything that has to do with money. The Slovenes aren't Communists or socialists. They aren't even nationalists. They are simply egotists."

A Serb writer took an equally emotional view: "Belgrade is no longer our capital, it's become a Federal city. Tito is a Croat, the Croats run the Army, the Slovenes run the economy—and most of us Serbs were Chetniks anyhow." On the other hand, a Croat economist declared: "There is no real federalism. The republics have no powers. Everything is run from Belgrade; Zagreb is ignored. The Serbs control the police and that is what counts. Tito may be a Croat but his closest cronies are Serbs."

There was usually some, but not much, truth in such statements. What was striking, however, was that they dominated most conversation among Yugoslavs who were not Communist officials dealing with foreigners. For years, the Communist regime had ignored or throttled these man-in-the-street prejudices, pretending that they had disappeared, or would disappear so long as the party kept saying that its slogan of "brotherhood and unity" had "solved" the nationalities problem. In fact, the problem had merely been repressed—partly by the lingering trauma of the war, partly by the centralized party dictatorship after the war, and then by the necessity for national unity in the resistance to Stalin.

By the early 1960s, however, the nationalities conflict had already come to divide the Communist regime itself. Often, the essentially nationalist thrust of various arguments was masked by high theory and objective argument which impressed foreigners—but failed to fool other nationalities.* Nevertheless, the national tensions which had been so destructive in World War II proved to be creative in Yugoslavia during the 1960s. With the stable figure of Tito presiding and balancing as a "Yugoslav" monarch, the quarrels among Serb, Croat, Slovene, and other Communist leaders gradually brought diversity into both the economic and political system.

The long, in-and-out struggle over economic reform, which dominated Yugoslav political life throughout the 1960s, was largely a continuation of nationalist politics by other means. Slovenes and Croats favored decentralization—greater power for the republics, more money for local banks, lower taxation for the economic enterprises themselves. In this way, more efficient Slo-

---

* There was, for example, the contest within the regime over where to locate an aluminum plant. Bauxite and power were available in both Hercegovina and Montenegro. Economists proved that, over a fifty-year period, a plant in Hercegovina would be roughly 5 percent more economical. The Montenegrins, however, showed that a plant in their republic would be 3 percent more economical over a hundred-year span. The Montenegrins won. A Croat economist called the decision a farce—first, because a hundred-year life for such a plant was ridiculous in the modern age; second, because the key decision-maker was himself a Montenegrin. (Later, aluminum plants were authorized for all three regions—sacrificing economy of scale for ethnic harmony.)

vene and Croat industries would have more money and more freedom to spend it.

Serbs, on the other hand, favored continued centralization. They argued that the underdeveloped south could never be rescued from backwardness without heavy, planned investment by the federal authorities. The Slovenes and Croats did not win the argument until after many years they persuaded the Macedonians that the Belgrade bureaucracy was siphoning off too much of the money.

These pork-barrel controversies acquired a larger significance, going beyond both economics and nationalism. For centralism in the economy also implied tight political control from Belgrade. Such control was personified by the Serb Alexander Rankovic, long-time master of the UDBA, party secretary for personnel and organization, and from early 1963 vice-president of the Republic. The "strong-hand" approach naturally commended Rankovic and his followers to the Soviet Union—which in Yugoslav politics counted mainly on pan-Slavic sentiment among Serbs and Montenegrins, distrusting the Catholic Slovenes and Croats.

On the other hand, the economic decentralization and market economy urged by the Slovenes and Croats implied a higher degree of political pluralism. This liberal approach in turn was personified by Edvard Kardelj, the former Slovene schoolmaster, former foreign minister and National Assembly president. Kardelj was the main architect of the new constitution adopted in 1963 which promised both economic and political "liberalization."

Furthermore, Slovenes and Croats naturally looked westward, both culturally and for capital investments and export markets. In seeking close economic and cultural relations with the West, the Slovene and Croat reformers were aware that they would need a foreign policy to match. Since the late fifties, Tito had been balancing between Rankovic and Kardelj, as between East and West.

The struggle between the two factions in the leadership was touch-and-go from 1960 to 1966, with frequent compromises which satisfied neither side. The new constitution, promised for 1961, was delayed two years and then amended at the last moment to create the office of vice-president for Rankovic. The first economic reform, undertaken in early 1961, was broken off in mid-1962 and new controls reimposed; a second reform was not risked until 1965.

The issues dividing the leadership were rarely clear to the population at large, however—partly because there were so many compromises, partly because the Communists used such abstruse language, partly because of ingrained popular suspicion, partly because the deeds of Rankovic's party cadres and police diverged so often from the words of Kardelj and other earnest theorists.

It was the liberal theory, in the early 1960s, which won the world publicity—leading to hopeful claims of a "new communism" among sympathizers in the West, and grim suspicion of "revisionism" among Stalinists to the East. However, in practice advocates of the old "strong-hand" approach were well entrenched, especially in the smaller towns and villages. In addition to the schisms among the party leaders and its regional complexities, Yugoslavia as a whole was still a fairly primitive country, with a charming but disarming disposition to individualism, anarchism, and clannish wheeling and dealing.

The result was that, while *Pravda* and the *New York Times* might earnestly analyze Yugoslav theoretical texts, Russians and Americans living in the country often privately agreed that there was no coherent system at all, mainly Balkan confusion. Moreover, educated non-Communist Yugoslavs, who had been excluded from responsibility by the Partisan mountaineers, seemed in full agreement that confusion had been the chief result of hasty innovations and compromises among often semiliterate politicians—some of whom made speeches about "self-management," others of whom made sure the UDBA collected the taxes.

Examples of such politically created confusion were readily at hand. Thus, for quite a few summers, tourists found it impossible to eat fish on the Yugoslav coast, even though the restaurants of Venice, Trieste, and other Italian towns were stocked largely with fish from Yugoslav waters. The reason was that Yugoslav hotels and restaurants could only pay the fishermen through bank transfers—which meant that the police knew exactly what the fishermen were earning. Most fishermen therefore preferred to fish for their own families and friends. The tourist restaurants were not well supplied until the regulation was changed.

In contrast to Communist leaders to the east, the Yugoslav authorities showed a frequent readiness to admit mistakes and change course when policies failed. However, the population had heard too many such confessions of error from the same politicians. As a Belgrade physician ruefully remarked, "They make the mistakes, but it is *we* who pay for them."

Thus, in the fall of 1962, many abroad reading the new draft constitution found it a serious and hopeful document. Yet in Belgrade its abstract Marxist formulations contrasted bizarrely with the pungent smell of the city itself—sweet, sharp, and sickly sour in a uniquely Balkan mixture. The sweet smell was lignite or soft coal used for heating. The sharp smell came from onions, scallions, garlic, peppers, cabbage, and cauliflower—all staples of the local diet. The sickly sour aroma was bad plumbing. Turkish coffee and plum brandy further spiced the blend.

In this atmosphere, anyone trying to deal with day-to-day Belgrade realities inevitably read the abstruse Communist theoretical discussions with a smile.

My family and I were then engaged, for example, in trying to find a place to live in Belgrade. We found the housing market incredibly tight and anxious, mainly for political reasons. Owners of older houses and flats suspected that the new constitution would be the prelude to new expropriations. And a tough speech by Tito against "speculators" had brought a new regulation forbidding people who had taken bank loans to build houses from renting space to help pay the mortgage. Any mortgaged house which was even partly rented out would "revert to the community." House after house, flat after flat, were taken off the market. However, the inflation of the preceding year had made some homebuilders rather desperate. An agronomist we met had borrowed to build a house, but it had cost more than he had planned. He could not now manage the mortgage, taxes, and final improvements without help. Although by renting the house he risked a jail sentence, he saw little alternative to doing so. "It would only be eight months," he said.

An electrician we encountered had an even stickier problem. He was driven to desperate adventure by the campaign against "speculation," which in Belgrade as elsewhere had turned into a general drive against private artisans. In his case, the police seemed bent on taxing him out of business. A well-to-do appliance merchant before the war, he had been thoroughly expropriated, but had managed to retain a prewar summer cottage on the fashionable Dedinje hill overlooking Belgrade—mainly, he said, because "it was the only house bombed by both the Germans and the Americans." He had slowly repaired it as best he could, but now feared that the house as well as his shop might be lost. The "protection" provided by a foreign tenant might save the house, and also guarantee some income in case he had to give up the shop.

There were only four very small rooms, none of them a kitchen or a bath, and virtually no furniture. He proposed that we "invest" the equivalent of six months' rent in all the necessary improvements—bathtub, stove, sinks, furniture, the lot. Thus we would have a "modern" flat and he, after six months, would have an income.

We accepted this proposition and in the course of the adventure learned a bit about Yugoslav life as Yugoslavs lived it. For example, Belgrade has no municipal gas network, and anyone with a gas stove must use bottled butane. However, the bottles often leaked, no matter how firmly closed, and getting a repairman or a new bottle might take days. At one point the entire city was out of butane for a fortnight. This artificial shortage was a common maneuver, on the part of the butane and other enterprises, to compel the political authorities to sanction a rise in prices.

Other experiences similarly demonstrated the living realities beneath the formal pretense to system. The Yugoslavs' best refrigerator, for example, was the Obodin, made in Montenegro with a Kelvinator motor on U.S. license. However, the production was sold out two years in advance. The electrician explained how to get one: "Don't go to the store. Go to the Obodin sales office and tell them you're a friend of that Montenegrin correspondent in New York." The refrigerator was delivered by bicycle-truck two hours later.

A sink was bought in a big department store on Marx-Engels Square, which promised to deliver "next day." Five such days went by with no delivery, until the store finally confessed it had no truck. We had to fetch the sink at a deserted warehouse by the Danube, lift it onto our auto luggage rack, and drive it home.

Furniture stores featured five- and six-piece dining and living room ensembles, but we already had a few pieces. "Sorry," said one salesman after another, "we cannot sell individual tables or chairs, you must buy the *komplet*." We finally located an export manager willing to sell us floor samples, but wondered how Yugoslav wage earners could ever afford the *komplet*, and how profitable furniture stores could possibly be.

Ultimately, we left the electrician to his own troubles because the lignite-burning stove was too weak to heat the house and the electric current was insufficient to install electric heaters. However, we thought of our former landlord some eight months later, when the controlled press suddenly "discovered" that private artisans were being unjustly driven out of business, and there was no one to replace them. Of 116,000 artisans in the country, more than 13,000 had given up in 1962. There were practically none left in such major towns as Split and Subotica, where the campaign had been especially virulent. In the Osijek district, there was one locksmith per 33,500 inhabitants; one plumber per 18,700 inhabitants; one mechanic per 100,000 inhabitants. Of 538 villages in the district, 158 did not possess a single craftsman of any kind. The result of the shortage was thoroughly predictable: in Zagreb, Sisak, and elsewhere, workers in "socialist" enterprises, most of whom regarded themselves as underpaid, began doing private crafts on enterprise time.

Time and again in Yugoslavia, liberal intentions proclaimed by Tito, Kardelj, and others at the summit of the regime were ignored or vitiated at the level of local party bosses and policemen. The slightest hint of toughness from above, on the other hand, often led to overzealous and ruinous campaigns by local authorities.

One Belgrade artisan summed up the situation with a fable about a fox and a wolf, who were on the best of terms until hunger struck in the forest. "Forgive me," the wolf said to the fox, "I am very hungry and must eat you."

"Don't," replied the fox, "It would do no good—I'm as skinny as you are. But look—there are fat sheep in the pen at the edge of the forest. You should eat them."

"But what about the dogs and shepherds?"

"Don't worry: an order has been received that you can freely eat sheep."

The wolf started moving toward the pen, but the dogs sensed the danger and alarmed the shepherds, who chased the wolf back into the forest. Beaten and tired, he came to the fox's lair and asked, "Why did you lie to me?"

"I wasn't lying," the fox replied. "The order has been received, but the shepherds do not observe it."

Some of the troubles experienced in the early 1960s stemmed from the top leaders' continuing addiction to orthodox Communist doctrines. For example, late in 1962 the leadership proclaimed a new drive to "increase the socialist sector" in agriculture by buying up private farms. A year later, it was discovered that 25 percent of the "socialist" farm enterprises were operating at a loss, and an additional 30 percent had no funds whatever.

Often, however, such economic failures, as well as the regime's recurrent troubles with intellectuals, stemmed from the contrast between its rationalist, scientific pretensions and the backroom political atmosphere in which decisions were actually taken.

"Our society," Professor Mihajlo Markovic of Belgrade University pointed out, "pretends that it is developing in accord with scientific principles" and "is making experiments with millions of people." Yet "we do not even possess sufficiently comprehensive and trustworthy knowledge about the following:

—How individual classes in our society live, what their political views are, what their moral formations are like;

—What the effective role of the working class is in our society;

—What changes are taking place in the countryside;

—What the present relations are between the various nationalities in our country. . . .

—What are the effects of various great changes taking place in our society—technical progress, social self-management, decentralization . . . etc.

About all these problems we have, it is true, various partial, hastily prepared and insufficiently reliable reports, papers, analyses, inquiries, statistics and so forth. The great question is . . . how many facts are to be found in all this and how much idealization, apologetics, the desire to please those who have requested the documents and have preconceived notions on these matters?

"In a nutshell, there is a great question as to how much *scientific truth* is to be found in these texts. . . ." Yet, without such knowledge—the Belgrade professor argued—"politics are more or less a matter of brilliant and inspired improvisations, more or less a process of painful and expensive learning from mistakes."

The regime's difficulties with such restive intellectuals had begun before Marshal Tito suddenly launched a surprising campaign against abstract art and Western influences early in 1963. There was little doubt that the campaign went deeply against the grain. Yugoslavia already had a plethora of talented abstract artists, who had attracted attention even in Paris, and several years later the government was to build a striking modern art museum in New Belgrade to house their works. At the same time, theaters, movie houses, and bookshops in Belgrade, Zagreb, Ljubljana had been thoroughly oriented to the West since the break with Stalin, as they had been before the war. Even some Communist officials had been identified with *avant garde* culture: Koca Popovic, then foreign minister, had once been a surrealist poet.

Yet by and large the intellectual level in the party was low, indeed, and young intellectuals in the cities of the plain barely concealed their resentment of the mountaineers who frequently presumed to judge their works.

In an interview with Yugoslav editors in February 1963, Tito acknowledged the bitterness of the intellectuals but defended his sudden cultural campaign.

Some people have shouted loudly against me over what I said about culture. . . . They say: Tito knows how to conduct politics well enough, but he is not competent to deal with cultural affairs.

But, comrades, those who say such things do not grasp what a Communist party is, what socialism is, or what communism is. I am not only responsible for industrialization and agriculture, but I am also responsible for culture itself, because I am not only the President of the Republic but I am also the Secretary General of the League of Communists. And, as the Secretary General of the party, I am responsible both before history and the people for a correct course in our country's development. . . . Moreover, as an average man who looks at art, I can know what is good and what is not. I cannot grant that something is good if it is not.

In fact, the cultural campaign had arisen less out of the Marshal's sudden interest in art than out of the exigencies of his ambitious foreign policy. For, just as economic discussions in Yugoslavia were often really nationalist conflicts, and discussion of the constitution veiled a struggle over the power of the police, so Tito's cultural campaign was a curious way of extending a helping hand to his beleaguered Soviet comrade, N. S. Khrushchev.

CHAPTER 4

Two for the Seesaw

For nearly a decade, Nikita Khrushchev and Josip Broz-Tito conducted a remarkable political affair. They faced suspicion or opposition within the Soviet Politburo and Yugoslav Communist party, among the East European satellite chiefs, from the Western powers, and from Communist China. Their relationship was frequently stormy, several times broken off, and often seemed a kind of seesaw in which neither man could gain satisfaction without compromising the other. Nevertheless, Khrushchev and Tito were drawn together time and again by mutual need, a common vision, and the mysterious cords of personality.

Both were cocky, crafty, curious, restless, gregarious self-made men—peasant sons who had been drawn as youths into the industrial proletariat, who had been fired by the romance of the Russian Revolution and Civil War, who had discovered in Communist agitation and organization a life and a career. Both had witnessed and weathered the terrible tyranny of Stalin, the drama and heroic sacrifices of World War II, the insane suspiciousness of Stalin's last years.

Tito, born in 1892, was two years older than Khrushchev and far more experienced, both in the ways of the world and in revolution. He had been a rover from the age of fifteen, and qualified almost as an Old Bolshevik. Before the First World War, as a locksmith, metalworker, and auto mechanic, he had roamed the Hapsburg Empire and beyond—from Zagreb and Ljubljana to Trieste, Mannheim, Pilsen, Munich, and Vienna. As a sergeant-major in the Austro-Hungarian army, taken prisoner on the Russian front, he had worked in the Volga region and Siberia, marched in Lenin's unsuccessful July 1917 uprising in Petrograd, been imprisoned briefly in the historic Fortress of St. Peter and St. Paul, joined the Red Guards in Siberia, fought in the Civil War, lived among the Moslem horsemen of wild Kirghizia.

In Yugoslavia in the 1920s, he became a Communist organizer among the metalworkers, was arrested, tried, and imprisoned. In the 1930s, he moved back and forth between Yugoslavia, Western Europe, and Moscow—as "Comrade Walter," agent of the Comintern, then after 1937 as general secretary of the Yugoslav Communist party. In Prague, Vienna, and Paris, he organized the recruitment of Communist volunteers for the Spanish Civil War. In Moscow, he somehow escaped the purge of the Yugoslav leadership and was permitted to move the party's headquarters back into Yugoslavia.

In the Second World War, Tito had written a new epic in the pages of his country's history—pinning down twelve German divisions, outmaneuvering nationalist rivals, ignoring Stalin's counsels of caution, profiting from British and American aid, winning the day by boldness. Without asking Moscow, he had himself proclaimed marshal of Yugoslavia and head of a provisional government. He conferred confidently with Churchill before his first interview with Stalin. He had imbued his colleagues with the kind of pride which Stalin called "boundless ambition, arrogance and conceit."

Stalin had pronounced anathema on him in 1948, but within five years Tito was being received by the Queen of England and his armies were being equipped by the Pentagon. Once the danger was past, he resumed his restless roving—traveling endlessly to Asia, Africa, Latin America. In the course of his colorful career, he picked up German, Russian, English, Czech, and some French; he liked women, dogs, fishing, cameras, resplendent uniforms, diamond rings, good food and drink.

Although Soviet power far exceeded that of Yugoslavia, Khrushchev was a provincial in comparison with the worldly Tito, and he often showed it by his personal deference to the Yugoslav marshal. Khrushchev was fifty before he ever ventured outside Russia; he was already in his thirties when he first saw Moscow and Kiev. As a boy, he had tended cattle in the village of Kalinovka, on the border steppes between Russia and the Ukraine. His family moved when he was fourteen to the industrial Donets basin—to Yuzovka, named after a Welshman, John Hughes, who had developed the local mines. At fifteen, he began working as an apprentice fitter in a German-owned engineering works. At eighteen he was a mechanic in mines owned by a French company.

Khrushchev became a Communist in 1918, well after Lenin's seizure of power, but emerged from the Civil War as a political commissar. Afterward, he served the party as a junior official, and the party schooled him—first at a technical college in Yuzovka (renamed Stalino), then at an industrial academy in Moscow. Under the patronage of Stalin's henchman Lazar Kaganovich, Khrushchev began quickly rising as the Stalinists drove Trotsky, Bukharin, and other Old Bolsheviks first out of office, then to traitors' deaths. By 1935, Khrushchev was party chief in Moscow, directing the construction of its famous subway. Three years later, at the height of the Stalinist blood purges, he took over the shattered party in the Ukraine. During the Second World War, as a political commissar on the southern fronts, he participated in the defense of Stalingrad. As party chief in the Ukraine and again in Moscow after the war, he managed to survive a new round of Stalinist intrigues and purges—and then moved swiftly to outmaneuver his rivals within two years after Stalin's death.

In September 1953, Khrushchev demanded a better deal for agriculture. In October 1954, he journeyed to Peking and, through a number of concessions, won the confidence of the Chinese Communists. By a series of travels outside the Soviet bloc (starting with a visit to Belgrade in May 1955), he sought to break out of the isolation to which Stalin's policies had condemned Russia. He seized the issue of "de-Stalinization" in February 1956 and made it his own. In May 1957, he promised that within a few years Russia would be producing more meat, milk, and butter than the United States.

Like Tito, Khrushchev showed little concern for ideology, little understanding of the higher economics, little patience with the preoccupations of intellectuals. Both men were "practicists"—concerned with results rather than theories, confident of their personal ability to fathom the real needs of the workers, determined that their countries should cut a figure in the world, convinced that the discipline of dedicated Communists could overcome economic handicaps, political obstacles, and social contradictions.

Khrushchev, however, was the more emotional, impulsive, and irrepressible of the two men. He threw himself vigorously into all-out campaigns and offensives, first in one direction, then in another—often failing to leave himself a dignified line of retreat. His Soviet colleagues first admired his combative spirit, but later came to regard him as a bull in the china shop.

Tito, on the other hand, possessed an almost animal instinct for sensing possible dangers, present or future, from all sides. He exercised constant self-control, rarely went too far, cautiously neutralized competing pressures, was a master at blurring issues. In moments of great crisis, Tito could be a lion; but at all times he was a fox, endowed with the patience which Khrushchev often lacked.

Khrushchev and Tito shared the dream of restoring the dynamism, vitality, and flexibility of the Communist movement in its halcyon days; of sweeping away the rigidity, narrow-mindedness, and fear which had been Stalin's legacy; of a revolutionary "opening" which would make Communism appeal to the new forces stirring in the dark continents, and render it more palatable to their own peoples.

Yet each man inevitably embodied native traditions. Khrushchev was the master of a sprawling continental power, and of a people whom long isolation and unique suffering had endowed with a deep apathy and sense of inferiority to the West. He thought in great power terms and was especially consumed by the desire to "overtake and surpass" the West, which Stalin had first vowed to do in 1931. He was proud that Russia had been first to explode a hydrogen bomb, first to launch a sputnik into outer space. Yet, the more he saw of the outside world, the more he realized that far greater efforts would be required to overcome the West. The United States was never far from the center of his thinking—whether he was challenging it in direct confrontations, attempting to turn its flanks, promoting summit conferences, or goading the Soviet economy.

His intense concentration on the United States led him to careless disregard of the other great power, China—until Peking turned on him with devastating effect in 1960 and impeded his freedom of action even within the Communist camp, just as the United States had already barred Soviet pretensions to world authority. Once the conflict with China had begun, however, it influenced Khrushchev's every act. In such imperial struggles, as in Khrushchev's efforts to maintain personal supremacy, lesser nations, causes, and individuals became expendable pawns. Significantly, Khrushchev cared least about Yugoslavia when his own position in the Kremlin was strongest and when he was most confident of success at home and abroad—namely, in the period between the launching of the first sputnik in October 1957 and the U-2 incident in May 1960.

When Khrushchev was in trouble, however, he looked to Tito for support. As a symbol of successful anti-Stalinism, Tito was useful in mobilizing Communist opinion against the "Stalinists" who were Khrushchev's chief rivals and critics—Malenkov and Molotov in the mid-fifties, Kozlov and Suslov in the early 1960s. At the same time, Tito provided Khrushchev with a useful bridge both to Western opinion and to the nationalists and neutralists of the "third world."

Tito's ambitions were as great as Khrushchev's—he would never be content to see Yugoslavia become just another middle-sized European country like Sweden. Yet he could never hope to realize his ambitions by raw power—only by political skill, by enlisting others to reinforce his cause.

As Tito skillfully balanced the competing nationalities and party factions inside Yugoslavia, so on the world scale he maneuvered between the West, the Soviet bloc, and the "nonaligned" Asians, Africans, and Arabs. He was determined to maintain his independence at all costs. Yet there was little doubt, at least between 1953 and 1965, that of the three relationships—with the

West, with the Soviet bloc, and with the nonaligned—Tito personally cared most about his relations with Russia. The West was indispensable, if only for the military security it offered and the more than $3 billion in aid it provided between 1945 and 1961; the nonaligned countries enhanced Tito's bargaining power with both West and East. Yet, like the rulers of medieval Serbia who fought yet also sought honors from Byzantium, Tito never lost sight of the Kremlin. He consistently denied that there was any such thing as "Titoism" or "national Communism." He sought Soviet legitimation of his regime to prove that he, rather than Stalin, was the true Communist, as well as to justify retrospectively the decades he had devoted to Moscow's service.

Moreover, only the misgoverned states of Communist Europe offered any possibility for the extension of Ttio's power and influence. The non-Communist neighbors—Italy, Austria, and even Greece—increasingly exercised more of an attraction for Yugoslavia than Titoism exercised on them. So long as the Soviet bloc treated Tito as a pariah, Yugoslavia was perforce permeated by Western economic, cultural, and ideological influences which, unchallenged, tended to undermine Communist theory and practice.

Among some Yugoslav Communists, Western influence produced mainly a desire for the sweet life—a tendency symbolized by Rankovic's sleek Jaguar and smartly cut Italian suits. But among others, particularly among the Slovenes and Croats closest to the frontiers, contact with the West promoted all sorts of unorthodox ideas which made for conflict not only with the Serb centralizers and the suspicious masters of the UDBA, but also with the larger party mass of primitive "mountain boys" who had shed blood to establish their dictatorship, to become "little Stalins" in their villages, factories, and committee rooms, and who feared any change that might affect their own place.

Each time Moscow pronounced anathema on Tito, each time the "capitalist" West proved friendlier than the "socialist" East, the Yugoslav Communists were confronted anew with the dilemma of where they were going—a dilemma which Milovan Djilas had been first to articulate in 1953. Djilas argued that, having made their revolution and having rejected the Soviet system (which he considered identical with Stalinism), the Yugoslav Communists could only advance by moving toward a democratic socialism, even if that meant sharing power with others or yielding it altogether.

Tito refused to make such a choice, believing that Soviet Communism might yet reform. He sought to sidestep the "Yugoslav dilemma" by limiting his country's uniqueness. In harmony with Moscow, the Yugoslav party could more easily avoid ideological disintegration and justify its own dictatorship. Among all the Soviet leaders, Tito saw in Khrushchev the best hope for influencing Russia's evolution, as well as for extending Yugoslav influence.

The Khrushchev-Tito affair moved through many phases but one important contradiction was built in from the start. Within the Soviet empire, Tito symbolized "de-Stalinization," economic "liberalization," greater scope for nationalism—all of which evoked popular hopes but also mobilized vested interests against him. In Yugoslavia, on the other hand, collaboration with Khrushchev promoted centralism, party discipline, police control, and doctrinaire economics—and thus encountered increasing resistance not only from the Slovenes and Croats but from the rising younger generation which did not share Tito's romantic memories of revolutionary Russia. The result of this contradiction was that each attempt at collaboration between Khrushchev and Tito proved more difficult than the last.

The very first attempt, in 1955–56, was the most dramatic and far-reaching. It brought the restoration of diplomatic relations and trade, Khrushchev's denunciation of Stalin, and Tito's triumphant Russian tour in May 1956. "There are no longer any serious and difficult problems between us," said Tito. Yugoslavia and Russia were "part of the same family, marching shoulder to shoulder." Tito's worst enemies in Hungary and Bulgaria were dismissed, "national Communists" were rehabilitated, and the way seemed clear for the reconstruction of Eastern Europe on Titoist lines.

The stormy autumn of 1956—the "Polish October" and the Hungarian Revolution—destroyed this dream. The fast-moving events forced both Tito and Khrushchev into embarrassing compromises and reversals. In the Kremlin, Khrushchev lost ground to

Molotov, Malenkov, and others who largely blamed Tito for the upheaval. Tito imprisoned Djilas for having condemned Yugoslav ambivalence toward the Hungarian revolt. Nevertheless, Tito himself criticized the Russians for having failed to reform quickly and thoroughly enough. He still counted on Khrushchev to do so.

"Can we ever trust them again?" asked Tito in April 1957. "It would be a mistake to say no, because one day, we hope in the not too distant future, this improper, insincere and uncomradely behavior toward us will subside." When Khrushchev triumphed over Malenkov and Molotov in July, Tito thought the day had come. In August, he met Khrushchev secretly in Bucharest. In September, Gomulka came to Belgrade, and Tito for the first time since 1948 acknowledged "the leading role of the Soviet Union . . . the first country of socialism." On October 15, Yugoslavia demonstrated its "solidarity" by recognizing East Germany (thereby inducing the West Germans to sever diplomatic relations for a decade).

Yet, within a month, this second Khrushchev-Tito entente had begun to turn sour. In November, the heads of the twelve ruling Communist parties assembled in Moscow, with both Khrushchev and Mao Tse-tung in confident mood. In August, the Russians had successfully tested their first intercontinental ballistic missile. In October, they had launched the first sputnik. They had also promised to provide China "new technology for national defense"—a "sample" atomic bomb and the technical detail for its manufacture.

As the world's senior Communist leader, Mao dominated the Moscow conference. He argued that the United States, despite its nuclear strength, was politically a "paper tiger"; that "the East Wind was prevailing over the West Wind"; that in fifteen years (i.e., by 1972) Russia would economically outstrip America, China would outstrip Britain, and the Communist camp would then be invincible. He publicly urged consolidation of the camp under Soviet leadership for a more adventurous policy. Mao's insistence on tightening Communist unity was strongly supported by Suslov, the perennial Soviet champion of doctrinal uniformity and an old foe of the Yugoslavs. Suspicion of Tito was widespread. The memory of his "divisive" influence in Hungary was still fresh, and the Communists of Albania and Bulgaria could well recall his earlier plans to absorb them or dominate them through a Balkan federation.

Tito had been invited to the Moscow conference, but when he saw the draft of the joint declaration which Suslov and the others had prepared, he pleaded lumbago and sent Rankovic and Kardelj in his stead. Khrushchev reportedly told them that Yugoslavia could not continue to sit "in two chairs." They signed a vague appeal for "peace," but they could hardly sign the main conference declaration, which asserted that among Communists "the main danger at present is revisionism," a code word for Tito's freewheeling pragmatism. The Russians scoffed at Yugoslav doctrinal scruples. Khrushchev's colleague, Anastas Mikoyan, remarked contemptuously that the Soviet Union could easily buy Yugoslav collaboration, and make all ideological differences disappear, for $100 million a year.

There was no overt break for nearly six months. In March 1958, Tito sent Moscow the draft of the new Yugoslav party program, and partly altered it to meet Soviet objections. Nevertheless, the Soviet bloc boycotted the April Yugoslav party congress, and on May 5 the Chinese launched an attack on "Judas Tito," declaring that his excommunication in 1948 had been "basically correct." *Pravda* reprinted the Chinese onslaught the next day. Within a month Russia and its satellites had canceled the credits they had promised Tito, and Khrushchev himself was assailing Yugoslavia as a "Trojan horse" staked by American "alms."

This time, the Yugoslavs turned their back on Moscow for more than two years—and, even after Khrushchev and Tito had sought contact once again, an additional year was required before a new collaboration could even begin to be acknowledged openly. Between 1958 and 1961, the Yugoslavs obtained new loans from the West and introduced notable domestic reforms, with Kardelj, the Croatian leader Vladimir Bakaric, and other decentralizers setting the pace.

Meanwhile, the unity which Russia and China had precariously maintained since 1950, and reaffirmed in 1957, was slowly unraveled in the course of 1958 and 1959—by crises in the Middle East, the Formosa Straits, and on the Chinese-Indian border; by Khrushchev's courtship of the United States; and by his definitive refusal in October 1959 to deliver the nuclear aid promised to Peking.

Then, in the spring of 1960, Khrushchev's position was radically altered. His plan to reduce the Soviet armed forces met resistance from the Red Army marshals and the heavy-industry directors who supplied them. The Chinese launched a militant series of attacks entitled "Long Live Leninism!" The U-2 incident in May was a turning point. It doomed the Big Four summit conference toward which Khrushchev had been pointing, strengthened the hand of the Soviet "military-industrial complex," appeared to justify Chinese criticism of Khrushchev's naïveté toward the Americans, and brought immediate and significant changes within the Kremlin itself.

While several Khrushchev loyalists were demoted or dismissed, Brezhnev, a consistent spokesman for the marshals and heavy industry, became Soviet chief of state; Kosygin reentered the Politburo, from which he had been absent since 1952, and became first deputy premier; and Kozlov, the tough, handsome Leningrader, became the party's second secretary and Khrushchev's heir presumptive.*

From May 1960 onward, Khrushchev was in trouble—and his personal competition with Kozlov, Suslov, and the "military-industrial" leaders became entangled with the broader conflict between Moscow and Peking. Hoping to outmaneuver his rivals, Khrushchev at times sought to force the breach with China, at other times to outbid Peking in militancy by daring anti-Western moves at Berlin, Cuba, and elsewhere.

Immediately after the U-2 incident, the new Soviet collective leadership sought reconciliation with the Chinese and arranged a conference of some fifty Communist parties in Bucharest in June. The Chinese expected it to be a quiet private meeting aimed at compromise. Khrushchev, however, took the offensive and attacked Mao by name. Although the meeting was held behind

---

* Like his ally Suslov, Kozlov had been closely identified with the virulent anti-Western, anti-Yugoslav, and anti-Semitic campaign of Stalin's last years. Kozlov and Kosygin had also been the principal survivors of the notorious "Leningrad case" in 1949, when Stalin had purged all the city's other Communist leaders, partly for alleged sympathies with Titoism.

closed doors, Khrushchev's spokesmen let it be known that the Soviet leader was fighting the Chinese, with "peaceful coexistence" and the prevention of war as his platform.

But Khrushchev failed to score a clear-cut victory either at Bucharest or at home in the Kremlin. The Soviet party Central Committee took the fateful step of recalling Soviet technicians from China, yet also moved to prepare a world conference of Communist parties by means of a smaller meeting in September—a meeting at which Kozlov and Suslov represented Russia.

Khrushchev's troubles tempted Tito, once again, to take a hand in the politics of the Soviet bloc. In August, the Yugoslavs began publishing Kardelj's polemic, "Socialism and War," which attacked the Chinese directly, quoted Khrushchev respectfully, presented the conflict with Peking as an "issue of principle," and rejected the compromise formulas devised within the Soviet Politburo. In October, Tito resumed personal contact with Khrushchev at the United Nations General Assembly in New York, and reportedly agreed to begin "normalizing" relations with an exchange of foreign ministers' visits.

Yet, once again, as in 1957, the Soviet leadership cared more about China than about Yugoslavia. Despite the personal animosity between Khrushchev and Mao, the stormy Moscow conference of eighty-one Communist parties in November managed to produce a joint declaration (drafted mainly by Suslov and Liu Shao-chi) which papered over Sino-Soviet differences. There was little agreement on larger issues, but the declaration condemned Yugoslavia for carrying on "subversive work against the socialist camp."

Tito branded the declaration "a rotten compromise" and waited for Khrushchev to improve his situation. An ambitious Yugoslav economic reform, secured by new Western credits, proceeded on schedule. Djilas was released on parole in January 1961. A summit conference of "nonaligned" heads of state was scheduled for Belgrade in September. On June 7, Tito prodded the Soviet leaders in a speech at the Bor copper mines:

> On the one hand they say, "We want good state relations, we want to trade with you, we want this, we want that, we want ex-

changes!". . . . On the other hand, they smear us and believe we will forget everything and trade normally with them. No, this is impossible. In Yugoslavia there is no difference between ideology and state policy. They are one, and everybody should be aware of it.

Three weeks later, the Yugoslav Foreign Minister was welcomed to Moscow after numerous previous postponements of his visit. When the Belgrade "nonaligned" conference took place, Tito refused to condemn Khrushchev for having resumed nuclear tests and endorsed the Soviet view of the German problem in the midst of a new crisis over Berlin. However, the internal atmosphere within Yugoslavia continued to be easygoing, while the Soviet bloc gave Tito little credit for his support.

At the Soviet 22nd party congress in October, backstage efforts to appease the Chinese failed. Khrushchev and his friends insisted on condemning the Albanians; Chou En-lai's wreath to Stalin provoked the ejection of the dictator's body from the Mausoleum; de-Stalinization was once again a weapon in Khrushchev's hands against his rivals.

Now, Tito moved more quickly to accommodate the Russian leader. In November 1961, he initiated a retreat in Yugoslav domestic policy, from liberal decentralization and pragmatic experimentation to tighter party control. Rankovic and the Serbian centralizers slowly gained ascendancy over the Slovene and Croat reformers. On April 7, 1962, on the eve of a visit to Belgrade by the Soviet foreign minister, Andrei Gromyko, Djilas was arrested anew for having published the book *Conversations With Stalin,* which allegedly disclosed state secrets. Apart from personal impressions, the book contained no facts that had not previously been disclosed in official Yugoslav documents. But Djilas poignantly recalled the causes of the original Soviet-Yugoslav split, and concluded with a somber warning: "Those who wish to live and to survive in a world different from the one Stalin created, and which in essence and in full force still exists, must fight." Tito, in contrast, believed that de-Stalinization in Russia was irreversible and could best be encouraged by joining forces with Khrushchev.

Soon after Gromyko's Belgrade visit, Khrushchev publicly welcomed Tito back into the fold. In a speech at Varna, Bulgaria, on May 16, Khrushchev pledged that Russia "will do everything to bring about good cooperation with Yugoslavia and thus help its peoples to fortify themselves in positions of socialism." Meanwhile, the Orthodox Patriarch of Moscow visited Serbia, and lesser Soviet delegations followed throughout the summer.

Within Russia, the second wave of de-Stalinization was in full flow. In September, Khrushchev personally approved the publication of the novel *One Day in the Life of Ivan Denisovich*, by Alexander Solzhenitsyn. It was not merely a powerful literary work which reminded many Russians of the young Dostoyevsky, but the first Soviet book to describe, even in fictional terms, life in a Stalinist forced-labor camp. Introducing the novel to the readers of his magazine *Novy Mir* (New World), the editor and poet Alexander Tvardovsky wrote that the effect of Solzhenitsyn's book, "which is so unusual for its honesty and harrowing truth, is to unburden our minds of things thus far unspoken, but which had to be said. It thereby strengthens and ennobles us."

At about the same time that he authorized the publication of Solzhenitsyn's masterpiece, Khrushchev quietly informed the widow of Nikolai Bukharin that her late husband's memory would be cleared of the treason charges for which he had been executed in 1938.

In September, Brezhnev arrived in Yugoslavia on a state visit. It was hardly a personal triumph. The Yugoslav population was almost demonstratively apathetic, while officials were repelled by Brezhnev's crudeness, boasting, and transparent attempts to compromise his hosts. At the final Belgrade reception for the Soviet visitors, foreign guests observed Kardelj in protracted argument with Brezhnev while Rankovic smirked and Tito, silent, regarded the Russian leader with glowering contempt. Nevertheless, Brezhnev's delegation also included Khrushchev's son-in-law, Alexei Adzhubei, and, despite Brezhnev's performance, contacts between the two parties were quietly intensified.

The Cuban missile crisis of October 1962, accompanied by a Chinese attack on India, hastened the new Khrushchev-Tito entente. Khrushchev was now very much on the defensive. The Chinese publicly (and others privately) attacked him for "adventurism" in putting missiles into Cuba and "capitulationism" in taking them out. Although Khrushchev claimed that his object had been to defend Cuba against American attack, Fidel Castro disclosed that the Russians had urged installation of the missiles in the interest of "strengthening the socialist camp as a whole." Throughout Eastern Europe, credulous Communists who had been impressed by Khrushchev's sputniks and 55-megaton bomb tests were demoralized by Kennedy's bold demonstration of American power. In Moscow, Khrushchev could no longer conduct political talks with important visitors alone: Kozlov and Brezhnev were at his side in every meeting, and often Kosygin or Suslov as well. The discussion of the economic reforms proposed by Kharkov professor Yevsei Liberman was halted. Old reactionaries pressed for an end to de-Stalinization and a crackdown in the arts. Soviet party secretary Boris Ponomarev declared in *Pravda* once again that "revisionism" was the main danger and that it found its "fullest expression" in Yugoslavia.

Tito's concern for Khrushchev's position had been evident during the Chinese-Indian border conflict. Despite Belgrade's oft-proclaimed friendship with India in the "non-aligned" movement, Yugoslavia hesitated to give New Delhi prompt or unequivocal support. Tito was obviously waiting to see what Moscow would do—an open question. For Khrushchev had demonstratively embraced the Chinese ambassador shortly before the two crises, and in the very midst of them the Soviet press suddenly applauded the Chinese—even though Khrushchev had refused to back them in 1959 (and would criticize them anew a few weeks later).

Tito waited, characteristically, until an agreement had been signed to provide Yugoslavia with American wheat for the coming year, until Kozlov and Brezhnev had left Moscow to attend party congresses in Rome and Prague respectively, and until Kardelj had left on a long tour of the Far East. Then, on December 5, 1962, accompanied by Rankovic, Tito arrived in the Soviet Union for the first time since 1956—ostensibly for a "vacation."

For two days, Tito and his group conferred privately with Khrushchev and Mikoyan, who had just returned from Cuba. Then they briefly toured the country. In Kiev, Rankovic spoke as if the break with Stalin had never occurred. He talked of the "working class of the entire world, together with all progressive forces, led by the Soviet Union," thus going farther than Tito was ever to do.

Nevertheless, Tito's very presence in Russia intensified the attacks from the Chinese and Albanians, as Khrushchev had probably foreseen. At a series of Communist party congresses in Sofia, Budapest, Rome, and Prague, Chinese "fraternal delegates" had pressed the attack in the presence of Soviet representatives, and the Russians—including Kozlov and Brezhnev—had been compelled to answer.

On December 12, Khrushchev brought the Yugoslav leaders with him to the semiannual session of the Supreme Soviet. He used the opportunity to widen the breach with the Chinese and cement his new ties with Tito.

"Why is it precisely the Albanian leaders who are now more vociferous than anyone?" Khrushchev asked—and answered his own question with a homey parable.

> I remember that in the miners' towns foulmouths used to do this: they would find a little boy who had barely learned to repeat words and did not understand their meaning; they would teach him the dirtiest oaths and would tell him, "Go under the windows of people's homes and say these words to the people." Or, worse, they would say to such a child, "Go to your mother and repeat these words to her. Here is three kopeks for this, and afterwards we shall give you five more."
>
> Now the Albanian leaders are acting like those silly boys. Someone taught them to pronounce foul words, and they walk under windows and shout hooligan curses at the Communist Party of the Soviet Union. . . . For their swearing they get promised three kopeks. And when they begin to swear more violently and colorfully, they get another five kopeks and are praised.

Western "imperialism" might be a "paper tiger," Khrushchev declared, echoing Mao's pet phrase,—but "those who say this know that this 'paper' tiger has atomic teeth." He deplored the conflict on the Chinese-Indian frontier, and made his own sympathies clear:

Would it not have been better if the sides had not resorted to hostilities at all? Yes, of course, this would have been better. . . . Here is the Chinese People's Republic, now withdrawing its troops actually to the line on which the conflict began; wouldn't it have been better not to have moved from the positions where they formerly stood? Such arguments are understandable. . . .

Khrushchev returned again and again to the inadmissability of a major war in the nuclear age, to the necessity for "reasonable compromises by negotiation." He appealed strongly to the Western powers to agree on banning nuclear tests. Behind the scenes, Soviet diplomats and scientists had already agreed to international controls to guard against secret underground testing. Khrushchev formally offered the concession in a letter to President Kennedy the following week—but such was the uneasy situation in the Soviet Politburo that he was later compelled to withdraw it. For the same reasons, Khrushchev was obliged to shade his praise of the Yugoslavs, and to speak of "some dogmatists" and "the Albanian leaders" when he clearly meant the Chinese.

Serious differences with the Yugoslavs remained, Khrushchev declared, but in the Cuban crisis, the Yugoslavs had taken a "correct" position, while the Chinese ("ultra revolutionary loudmouths") had "wanted to bring on a clash between the Soviet Union and the United States . . . a world thermonuclear war." Therefore, whatever may have been true about "Yugoslav revisionism" in 1960, whatever "some people" (including Ponomarev in *Pravda* three weeks earlier) were still saying about it, was largely "irrelevant." Khrushchev now proclaimed that "the dogmatists"—the Chinese—were clearly the "main danger."

The next day, Tito himself addressed the Supreme Soviet, an unprecedented honor which led some Western observers to conclude that Yugoslavia had rejoined the Soviet bloc. Tito, however, continued to be prudent. He spoke briefly, said little about Soviet-Yugoslav difficulties past or present, placed the emphasis on "peaceful coexistence," and declared that Soviet and Yugoslav views on "all major" international issues were "identical or close to each other." He, too, called for an agreement to halt nuclear testing.

Perhaps most important, Tito defended Khrushchev against the charges of "capitulation" in Cuba. It was already an open secret that Khrushchev had personally contacted Kennedy through unofficial channels at the height of the crisis, offering a settlement on terms softer than the Politburo majority were ready to consider. Kennedy had accepted Khrushchev's "unauthorized" terms, while ignoring the official Politburo policy paper. Now Tito paid a public tribute "to the Soviet Government and to Comrade Nikita Khrushchev personally, who acted so boldly at the most critical moment, taking into account the interests of all mankind and displaying the farsightedness of statesmanship."

In view of Yugoslav opinion, Tito could not go much farther. Photographs of him and Khrushchev kissing each other, which appeared in the Western press, were not published in Yugoslavia. When Tito's blue train finally returned to Belgrade on the morning of December 22, he felt compelled to denounce as "ridiculous" the speculation that Yugoslav policy had changed. He did so, however, in a manner that in fact indicated considerable change.

"We do not need to change our policy," Tito said, "but only to abide by our principles of cooperation and friendship with all peoples of the world . . . but also by the principle of closest cooperation with the socialist countries, which is self-evident, because ours is a socialist country. Why would we have worse relations with them than we have with some Western countries?"

Every Belgrade taxidriver knew the answer to Tito's question: since 1948 the Western countries had given Yugoslavia steady aid and support, while the "socialist" countries, when not actively hostile, had supplied mainly broken promises. By coincidence, heavy snow began falling on Belgrade the morning of Tito's return; it was the first result, several citizens remarked, of the Marshal's mission to Moscow.

The first half of 1963 was difficult for both Khrushchev and Tito. Each faced opposition or resistance within his own party to the new course—for in both parties, Soviet-Yugoslav cooperation was only part of a larger complex of issues.

Both Khrushchev and Tito succeeded in compelling their respective parties to accept a new orientation—but not without compromises and difficulties. Khrushchev endorsed a campaign against liberal writers and artists, a retreat from de-Stalinization, new powers and authority for the "military-industrial" leaders, and a serious new effort to appease the Chinese. Only when Kozlov suddenly suffered a heart attack on the night of April 10-11 was Khrushchev able to begin regaining lost ground; and not until June could Khrushchev move decisively toward resumption of the conflict with China and a nuclear test-ban agreement with the West (signed August 5).

Tito echoed Khrushchev's campaign against abstract art and Western influences in the early months of the year. In March, he put through the last-minute changes in the new Yugoslav constitution mentioned earlier: the very name of the country was changed to the "Socialist" (instead of "People's") Federative Republic, and the post of vice-president, with important powers, was suddenly created for Rankovic. (The red-white-and-blue national flag was also nearly replaced by the red party flag, but resistance proved too strong.) Kardelj was in virtual eclipse for many months, and Tito rode to and from the May Day parade with Rankovic alone. A few weeks later, Tito told the party central committee that "we make up a part of" the international Communist movement and "we do not stand outside of it." *

In prevailing over domestic resistance, Khrushchev and Tito dramatically illustrated the difference between them as political operators. Both had studied politics under Stalin, the master of "dosage," the art of how far and how fast to go, of how to measure out political change in proper proportions. But Tito proved the more discerning student. His vague attacks on the arts in the spring of 1963 mentioned no names. The vice-presidency created for Rankovic was constitutionally limited to a single four-year term. While moving prudently toward a more pro-Soviet position, Tito kept other options open: receiving the American secretary of state and the presidents of Mexico, Finland, and Liberia; obtaining new loans from the World Bank.

Khrushchev, on the other hand, attempting to appease Soviet reactionaries in the early months of 1963, praised Stalin's "mer-

---

* Nevertheless, it was noted that none of the Slovene or Croat leaders spoke in favor of the new pro-Soviet line—just as it was observed in August that most of the Soviet Politburo absented itself when Khrushchev formally signed the nuclear test-ban treaty.

its," brandished 100-megaton bombs, spoke again of "burying" capitalism, and humiliated publicly the very intellectuals he had encouraged to speak out. These and other excesses alienated many of his natural supporters, and then no sooner did he feel himself in the clear than he prematurely embarked on a new initiative—making overtures to West Germany in July—which could only arouse his conservative critics anew.

When Khrushchev arrived in Belgrade for a fifteen-day "vacation" on August 20, 1963, he looked ten years older than the jaunty Tito. His gait and movements were slow, the flashes of ebullient energy rare. He seemed for the most part tired, self-conscious, depressed. The "rest" he had ostensibly sought turned out to be a strenuous tour of the major Yugoslav regions and towns, designed mainly—it seemed—to demonstrate to the Soviet leader how nicely the Yugoslavs had been doing without him.

Tito had Khrushchev's plane met at the border by U.S. Sabrejets, flew him down to Skoplje in a Douglas DC-6, drove him around the country in an endless column of Cadillacs, Chevrolets, and Mercedes (with a few large Fiats and a Rolls-Royce for good measure). The first factory Khrushchev visited outside Belgrade was a tractor plant working under licenses from Massey-Ferguson and Leyland; the last, near Zagreb, was an automated chemical plant, financed by the U.S. Government and Imperial Chemical Industries. On every Yugoslav street, Khrushchev could see the Serbian-produced version of the Fiat 600. While Khrushchev was resting at Tito's private island of Brioni, the president of the Italian Senate casually dropped in—and word leaked out that Tito would conclude his fall tour of Latin America by meeting with President Kennedy in Washington.

The Khrushchev tour turned into a kind of political *pas de deux*, in which the Soviet leader was clearly the wooer, Tito the wooed. Khrushchev attempted to bind the Yugoslavs to him by verbal concessions, pan-Slavic oratory, and statements which might compromise Belgrade in the West. Tito, while fending off these attempts, sought to commit Khrushchev to Yugoslav-type reforms in Russia itself, to all-out struggle against China, to more active support of Asian and African neutralists, and (last but not least) to Soviet aid without strings to Yugoslavia.

"I like the form of workers' councils and find it a progressive phenomenon," Khrushchev told factory workers at Rakovica, explaining that the Soviet party was studying the question of how to democratize management in industry. His remarks, though amply reported in the world at large, were never published in the Soviet press. Later, Khrushchev felt compelled to retreat gently; without mentioning workers' councils, he spoke of different Communist countries adapting to local conditions. Tito soon replied that the Yugoslav system was not a response to local conditions, but represented "the basic ideas of Marx, Engels and Lenin."

Throughout the tour, Khrushchev stressed the issue of peace, the necessity of averting thermonuclear war, his own program for besting the West in economic competition. He predicted that Russia would outstrip the United States in absolute production "in six-seven years" (i.e., by 1970), and in per capita output by 1980. Yet, unexpectedly, he shied away from attacking China, Albania, or the dead Stalin by name, although when he did speak of "dogmatists" and "pseudo revolutionaries," his face showed genuine fury. His prepared speeches predicting Soviet economic superiority to the United States contrasted sharply with his obvious personal sense of inferiority in viewing the more developed towns and factories of Yugoslavia.

The high (or low) point of the tour came when a British journalist asked Khrushchev to compare Yugoslav and Soviet living standards. Livid, Khrushchev replied, "You are looking for the nasty smell of the backside, and that is not the most beautiful part of the body." Tito looked demurely aside, but the Albanian party newspaper promptly commented, "The history of the civilized world has never known a case in which the principal head of a state used such hooligan language."

When Tito finally bade Khrushchev farewell, the props were the same as on the day he had greeted him. There was a bear hug for the photographers, flowers from the children of the Russian colony, a blue-coated honor guard, and all the rest. Yet the atmosphere was not quite as warm as it had been a fortnight earlier. Although the Yugoslavs had hoped for a restoration of the credits promised in 1956, Khrushchev had brought few gifts. Although Khrushchev expected to address the Yugoslav National Assembly, in return for Tito's speech to the Supreme Soviet, Belgrade blandly scheduled the Assembly for a week after the Russian leader's departure. By the end of the tour, both Khrushchev and Tito were referring to their discussions as an "exchange of views" —the diplomatic phrase indicating disagreements.

In the most spontaneous utterance of the entire tour, at a mass meeting in the model Slovenian miners' town of Velenje, Khrushchev hinted at some of the difficulties besetting him. He asked rhetorically whether there could be different approaches among Communists in settling practical problems as well as on matters of principle. "Yes, there can," Khrushchev said. "Various conceptions of the same problem sometimes appear in a party among its leaders."

What should be done in such cases? Khrushchev said that "one must fight to achieve unanimity in that which is essential, decisive, in that which unites us. At the same time, one must have patience when differences arise and not start accusations. . . ." The Yugoslav leaders and he had common views on essential problems, "and that is a good thing," Khrushchev said. "Even if there are certain little matters between us, let time do its work, so that they may all disappear or, as the metalworkers say, be ironed and polished up." All would be well, Khrushchev remarked, "if we . . . conduct affairs without looking for dead cats and without planting them on each other. . . ."

What seemed clearest after Khrushchev's visit was that, with all the "good will" on the part of both leaders, with all the nominal attachment of both sides to "Marxism-Leninism," the Yugoslav experience since the break with Stalin in 1948 had been psychologically decisive. For that experience set the Yugoslav leaders free to mold their society in practical fashion and to play an easy-going, freewheeling role in the world. That inner freedom had, over fifteen years, brought not only Tito but Yugoslavia great rewards. It was a freedom which Khrushchev, presiding over the Stalinist heritage, had yet to attain.

The last meeting between Tito and Khrushchev took place in Leningrad in June 1964. It was brief, secret, and without results. It was already too late for either man to deflect the movement of their two countries and parties away from each other.

CHAPTER 5

October Afterglow

For several years after October 1956, Poland was considered "a case history of hope." After fifteen years of agony under Nazi and Soviet occupation, Poland in 1956 had been stirred to self-assertion. First, there had been the shock of Khrushchev's revelations of Stalin's crimes, including the murder of the entire prewar Polish Communist leadership. Then, Poznan workers had erupted in violent demonstrations, shouting "No Bread Without Freedom, No Freedom Without Bread!" Writers and journalists had taken up the cry and in October 1956—a month of exaltation and mass meetings—there had been great changes *without* the bloodshed and tragedy that had ensued in Hungary. The Soviet Marshal Konstantin Rokossovsky, whose presence as Poland's defense minister was the symbol of the national humiliation, returned to Russia. The Soviet agents who directed the Polish secret police were also sent packing. The Polish Communist leaders who had most servilely executed Stalin's bidding were dismissed, and many policies of the Stalinist period were reversed.

Thus, in the early 1960s, Poland was still often paired with Yugoslavia as an example of successful, hopeful "national Communism" which might yet inspire other countries, perhaps even Russia. Wladyslaw Gomulka, the austere Polish party chief who had emerged from Stalinist confinement to power in October 1956, was sometimes compared with Tito, even though the two men instinctively disliked each other from their first meeting.

Like Yugoslavia, Poland permitted private peasants to work 85 percent of its land. Uniquely in Eastern Europe, Poland's Communist regime had achieved a modus vivendi with the Roman Catholic Church, which was virtually a state within the state. Catholic newspapers provided intelligent if loyal criticism of the regime, and a talented group of Catholic deputies sat in the Polish Sejm (parliament). The Polish regime not merely tolerated artistic experimentation but appeared to welcome independent intellectual distinction. There was world respect for such figures as the philosopher Leszek Kolakowski, the economists Oskar Lange and Wlodimerz Brus, the sociologist Stefan Ossowski, the writers Antoni Slonimski and Maria Dombrowska. There was growing recognition, too, for such younger talents as Slawomir Mrozek, the playwright, Krzsztof Penderecki, the composer, and Andrzej Wajda, the film director.

In contrast to the restrictions which Stalin and Khrushchev had placed on Jewish culture in Russia, the Polish state maintained, among other institutions, a famous Yiddish Theater in Warsaw—whose most distinguished actress, Ida Kaminska, won international renown in the Czechoslovak film *The Shop on Main Street.* Poland had long ceased to jam Western radio broadcasts, permitted a significant import of Western books and periodicals, and in the early Gomulka years allowed hundreds of thousands of citizens—including distinguished intellectuals—to travel abroad. The theaters, movie houses, and concert halls of Warsaw and Cracow featured the latest products of Western culture, and the Polish press appeared the liveliest and most literate of all the Communist countries.

Furthermore, the regime's own grip on the country seemed light, its approach modest and aloof. There was little of the oppressive party sloganeering common in most Russian dependencies, no "personality cult" for Gomulka in the manner of Stalin or Tito. The Communist Party itself was numerically small—proportionally a third smaller than those of Russia, East Germany, or Yugoslavia. Nearly half its members in 1964 had been enrolled less than five years. The Polish security police—the UB—had disintegrated in 1956, and not until 1959 had it been sufficiently rebuilt to resume its normal surveillance duties. Even in 1963, it seemed less in evidence than Rankovic's UDBA in Yugoslavia, let alone the KGB and other ubiquitous police agencies of the Soviet empire.

Freedom of religion, toleration of private farming, cultural diversity, and the mildness of police control—these were the major elements of the "Polish way" which had won widespread recognition from friend and foe in the late 1950s. Poland's distinctiveness was recognized by many anti-Communist Polish emigrants abroad, who urged aid and support to Gomulka. It was recognized by the United States, which between 1957 and 1963 provided more than $500 million in surplus wheat, as well as other aid, and extended to Poland (alone among the Soviet-bloc countries) most-favored-nation treatment in trade. It was, finally, recognized by Khrushchev himself in 1958, who assured the Polish leaders that they could pursue autonomous policies at home so long as they supported his foreign policy. While Moscow attacked Yugoslav "revisionism" and Chinese "dogmatism," the "Polish way" escaped Soviet criticism.

The traveler arriving in Poland in the early 1960s was inevitably impressed not merely by an atmosphere of relaxation, but by the Western and non-Communist character of so much that he saw and heard. Most often, he was impressed first by the rebuilding of Warsaw, which had been 87 percent destroyed in World War II. Virtually all the capital's historic places were rebuilt just as they had been before the war, from plans found in the cellars of the architectural school and from old paintings by a nephew of Canaletto which were held by Polish collectors. The Old Town Square, the New Town Square, and the charming quarter just below, sloping down to the Vistula, called the Mariensztadt, were recreated in their original gothic, renaissance, and baroque styles. The restored monuments included not only baroque squares and former royal and noble palaces, but cathedrals, churches, and religious statues. At first look, historic Warsaw hardly seemed to be a Communist city at all.

To be sure, the architecture of Stalinism had left some mark—notably in his 30-story gift, the "Palace of Culture and Science in the Name of J. V. Stalin," which dominated the Warsaw skyline and which John Gunther has described as a "gangster's wed-

ding cake." Stalinist grandiosity was also apparent in the four-
and six-lane boulevards by which one entered and traversed the
city, broad enough for May Day military parades but capable of
sustaining ten times the daily traffic of the early 1960s.

However, Polish architects had moved swiftly after Stalin's
death to abandon such pretentiousness. They built first in the
Khrushchevian style of prefabricated, poured-concrete boxes, then
in the more contemporary international style with its neat lines
and light-metal trim, colored terraces and balconies, blending
such structures into what was left of the prewar city and around
the restored monuments of their proud history.

In Cracow, Poland's "second capital," which had not been significantly damaged by the war, the Catholic religion, Latin alphabet, and Franco-Italian architecture impressed the visitor with
a similar sense of Poland's "Westernness." In both cities, and particularly in and around their great universities, the vitality and
excitement of Polish youth were strongest. Because 6 million citizens of Poland (including 3.5 million Jews) perished in the war,
at least half the population in the early 1960s was under twenty-
seven years of age. The normal street scene included a few elderly
folk, hardly any middle-aged, and throngs of youths—pale, slim
blonde girls with blue eyes and blue jeans; boys with berets,
beards, guitars, leather jackets, motorscooters—all in search of gay
adventure. At sidewalk cafés and in wine cellars, at abstract art
exhibitions and jazz concerts, Polish writers, artists, musicians,
and film-makers—many of whom had recently traveled to Paris,
Rome, and Hollywood—dazzled visitors with their nonconformist
wit and sparkling intelligence.

Talkative and volatile, the young Polish intellectuals who set
the tone for fashionable Warsaw and Cracow often reminded
British visitors of the Irish. They much enjoyed the freedom in
those days to talk, grouse, and grumble without looking over
their shoulders for a police spy. (It took some years for them to
realize that freedom of conversation was somewhat less than freedom of speech.) There was a touch of old-fashioned gallantry in
the manner in which all Poles, including Communist officials,
bowed to kiss ladies' hands. But there was none of the heavy
earnestness of Germans or Russians. Instead, there was irony and

insouciance, a light and casual approach to life's tragedies and follies, a gay contempt for the Communist system and its primitive spokesmen.

Looking back at the horrors of the Nazi and Stalinist past, looking east and west at the rigors of the Soviet Union and East Germany, the young Polish intellectuals rejoiced in the limited freedoms achieved in 1956 and made light of the new difficulties which had begun in the early 1960s. For them, Warsaw was still the "Paris of the East"—even though their own conversation and private lives seemed more to resemble the forced gaiety, the bittersweet desperation of Berlin in the Weimar Republic.

A poetess (whose father had died of tortures in a Stalinist prison) could gaily recount why she had become "the most erudite Marxist-Leninist in People's Poland" in her teens. With universities virtually barred to youths of "bourgeois origin," and party officials sitting on admission boards, she could only obtain entrance by committing whole volumes of Marx, Engels, and Lenin to memory and thus overwhelming her ideological examiners.

A writer could describe the hours, weeks, and months spent in struggling with the censorship, in running from one publishing house and party commission to another, gaining the support of an influential friend of a friend of a friend. Yet he could happily conclude, "They can tell us what *not* to say, but they can no longer tell us what to say or how to say it. And that is a big difference."

A Communist journalist, linked to the rising "Partisan" faction of the party, could scoff not only at the mediocrity of Gomulka and the boorishness of Khrushchev but at Marx's sacred doctrine itself. The working class, he observed airily, was "just a meteor which streaked across the sky of History before sinking in the sea of automation."

Such Poles were "cool" long before the word became fashionable, cool in their personal detachment and in their disdain for the primitive functionaries who ruled them, the alcoholic masses who surrounded them, and the bigoted priests who judged their morals. This was the old tradition of Polish aristocracy.

Yet the urbane intellectual elite of Warsaw and Cracow had far less influence than the former aristocracy—less, too, than their own counterparts in Paris, London, or even Prague. In those cities, the intellectuals were part of a larger, historic middle class with civic traditions and international horizons. In old, partitioned Poland, cleft between the landed aristocracy and the peasant masses, the role of a middle class had been assumed largely by Jews and Germans. These had nearly all been murdered or driven out of the country between 1939 and 1948. The purely Polish interwar urban classes, from army officers to Socialist industrial workers, had also been thoroughly decimated. Hundreds of thousands perished in the anti-Nazi resistance. Other hundreds of thousands, who had fought in the Western Allied armies, preferred to remain abroad. Still others had been morally if not physically crushed under Stalinism. Poland's human loss during the war—22 percent of the population killed—was proportionally greater than that of any other country. The losses were highest among the very age and social groups that might have provided effective leadership in the 1960s.

More than ever, and despite statistics showing industrial growth, Poland was a nation of peasants or former peasants. Urban industry expanded in the first post-war decades largely by absorbing the former peasant handicrafts and cottage industries (as well as through the acquisition of the former German coal-steel basins in Silesia). Peasant youths and women swelled the urban work force.

For culturally sensitive Poles, there were few more poignant contrasts than that between historic Cracow, lovely, gentle, and eminently civilized, and the raw steel town of Nowa Huta which the Communists built alongside it—in which teen-age hillbillies were thrust to create an atmosphere compounded of brutality, alcoholism, and fanatic Catholicism. If in Cracow and Warsaw, Polish faces often recalled Chopin and Marie Walewska, in Nowa Huta, Katowice, and other industrial boom towns, the image of Stanley Kowalski predominated. Lodz, Poznan, and other centers of the older textile and consumer industries were relatively neglected in the new emphasis on coal, steel, and heavy machinery. But in these cities, too, peasants from the neighboring countryside, as well as from the "eastern territories" ceded to Russia in 1945, had filled the places of the former townspeople.

The Polish countryside—a defenseless plain from Cracow north to the Baltic, from Berlin eastward to the Pripet Marshes—had a timeless, deserted quality. Only occasional clusters of youthful motorcyclists at a road junction served to recall that it was not still 1908. Elsewhere, slow-moving horsecarts far outnumbered motor vehicles or tractors.* Stefan Cardinal Wyszynski, the Catholic Primate, was criticized for saying that Poland could support a population of 80 million; yet the fact was that much of the country was sparsely inhabited.

The Polish villages seemed primitive and disorderly compared with those of neighboring Germany or Slovakia. Along the roadside, there were, here and there, some new one- and two-room houses of brick and stone. But weathered wooden shacks and log cabins were more common, and there were numerous thatched huts as well. The peasants and their families seemed to work longer hours, particularly in summer, than the collective farmers of other Communist countries. But even in the early 1960s, nearly two-thirds of the farms lacked electricity, and the long, misty northern nights in fall and winter kept both vodka consumption and the birth rate high. The peasants seemed as suspicious of the agronomists bringing chemical fertilizers as they had been of the Germans, Russians, and Jews who in the past had appeared to threaten the old rural economy and pure Catholic faith.

The Communist party barely existed in the country-side, which was the domain of the Catholic Church—as powerful a church as any in Europe, often compared in its ardor with that of Spain. Perhaps 90 percent of Poles considered themselves practicing Catholics. The Church regarded itself as "the emanation of the nation," and fostered the national virtues of patriotism, courage, and loyalty. At the same time, it preached "struggle against the national vices of drunkenness, laziness, frivolity, extravagance and excess."

In the cities, among laymen and part of the hierarchy alike,

* In 1960, there were 2.8 million horses, barely 230,000 automobiles and trucks, and only 62,000 tractors. Most of the tractors belonged to state farms, rather than private peasants.

there was an enlightened liberal current, in sympathy with the advanced Catholic opinion of Western Europe and the spirit of Pope John XXIII. Yet in Poland as a whole, and especially in the villages, the clergy was often narrow, traditional, obscurantist. From 1957 to 1965, the Church proclaimed a "Great Novena" consecrating the nation to "Mary, Queen of Poland." At the Vatican Council, the Polish hierarchy proposed the "universal motherhood of Mary" and supported the conservative resistance to the reforms of John XXIII.

The symbol of Polish Catholicism was the shrine of the miraculous "Black Madonna" of Czestochowa—an icon at the Jasna Gora monastery which, according to the national legend, had saved Poland by repelling an army of Swedish "heretics" in 1655. Each year Czestochowa was the site of an annual pilgrimage by tens of thousands of Poles, mostly peasants, artisans, and women. Before the war, pilgrims often engaged in pogroms en route to the shrine. In 1960, the Church launched from Jasna Gora a "Women's Crusade" against birth control and abortions. "If the sins of the mothers, who murder their unborn children, do not cease," a Church leaflet declared, "the whole nation may be ruined."

By the 1960s, there were more churches in Poland than before the war, and their number kept growing. The Communist regime attempted to limit Catholic prerogatives in education and elsewhere, but refrained from direct confrontations. It hoped that time and apathy would gradually erode the Church's influence. Yet, as the party failed to provide the mass of Poles with either spiritual inspiration or material affluence, even nonbelievers often took to attending Church as a demonstration of their anti-Communism.

Although it refrained from questioning the Soviet occupation, the Church was strongly nationalist. It energetically catholicized the former German territories and identified itself with a thousand years of Polish history, including the wartime resistance movement. "When the hate of the aggressors attacked us," said Cardinal Wyszynski in 1960, "the love and faith of the Warsaw insurgents defended the sacred altars. . . . Is not this hallowed blood the truest expression of the strange unity of human and divine things in our fatherland?"

While the Communist party ostensibly ruled the country, the Church in large measure did represent the real Poland. Although Gomulka had come to power in 1956 on a wave of national feeling, the Communist regime had been installed in 1944 by the Russian Army and could not survive without it. "The Soviet Union," said Gomulka in 1963, "is the decisive main strength of the socialist camp, without which no socialist state could hold out. . . ." Thus, while Gomulka rehabilitated the victims of Stalinism between 1944 and 1952, including the anti-Communist wartime resistance, he remained convinced that only the Soviet Union could maintain Communist rule in Poland. Close relations with the dominant Kremlin faction were especially necessary to forestall the temptation of yet another Russian-German collaboration (as in 1939) at the expense of Polish sovereignty.

In Poland's situation between Russia and Germany, only a few basic combinations were possible. The interwar dictator, Josef Pilsudski, had staked all on an alliance with France, and had urged Allied intervention against Hitler in 1933. When the West failed to budge, Pilsudski attempted to appease Nazi Germany, and the colonels who succeeded him rejected any possibility of alliance with Russia down to the eve of the war. After Gomulka took power, Poland made tentative overtures toward a normalization of relations with West Germany and proposed various measures to reduce tensions, such as the plan by Foreign Minister Adam Rapacki for a nuclear-free zone in Central Europe. But Bonn's initial response in 1957 and early 1958 was suspicious and negative. When Khrushchev moved to strengthen East Germany and launched a Berlin crisis in the fall of 1958, Gomulka seemed to have little choice but to join him.

To some extent, therefore, Poland's geography and recent history set limits on the extent to which Gomulka could emulate Tito on the path of "national Communism." Yet Gomulka's own character also doubtless played a role. In the view of a sympathetic observer, Hansjakob Stehle:

> The real Gomulka has little in common with the people's tribune that the legendary "October" made of him. He posseses the wide but not especially profound wisdom of the self-taught; he has much

common sense but is without imagination, without the versatility and shrewdness of a Khrushchev. His tactics are practical, but he has no ideological finesse. In questions of principle, he is inelastic, stubborn, persistent and incorruptible. In the home-baked Communism of Gomulka, there is a firm instinct for power; like Pilsudski, he regards gradual doses of authoritarian methods as a sort of medicine against Polish anarchy.

In contrast to Tito, an inordinately curious, restless "original," Gomulka all his life followed a fairly straight and narrow path. He was born in Austrian Galicia in 1905, the son of a socialist activist among the oil-refinery workers. He himself moved into trade-union organizational work as a teen-ager, and was a Communist labor official by the age of twenty-two. It seems doubtful that he ever left Poland before World War II. Even during his years in power—when Poland's image was brightest in the world, and when Khrushchev was barnstorming the continents—Gomulka rarely traveled outside the Soviet bloc. Dour, puritanical, ascetic in his own habits, he preferred a simple, quiet, gray order to the tumultuous and often pretentious experiments in which Tito and Khrushchev indulged. While Tito viewed Yugoslavia itself from the perspective of world strategy on his private island of Brioni, Gomulka viewed the world from the standpoint of the Polish problem in his modest three-room apartment in downtown Warsaw.

In Catholic, peasant, anti-Communist Poland, Gomulka's search for a popular base inevitably led him to rebuild the party and police apparatus which had crumbled in 1956. In his need to maintain the truce with the Church and the peasantry, he soon came to rely on the Soviet leaders to discourage those in his own party urging more radical measures. He tried for a time to maneuver—between Belgrade and Peking, and among the different Kremlin factions—but his room for maneuver was narrow, especially after the Polish economy had begun to stagnate and Polish intellectuals became restive.

Unlike Yugoslavia, Rumania, and the Soviet Union itself—all potentially rich countries—Poland was essentially poor in natural resources. Its land was not especially fertile, and the peasants were mostly inefficient small holders. Once released from the collective farms in 1956, they produced a marked upsurge in production for several years—climaxing in the record harvest of 1961. But peasant productivity was lower than on the collective farms of East Germany, and even in the good years Poland was importing grain, for consumption and for fodder, in order to produce the hams and other farm exports needed to finance imports of machinery. The nation's major mineral resource was the coal of Silesia, but by the 1960s there was a glut of coal on the world market, and export prices continued to fall. Despite aid from the United States, trade deficits grew.

Shortly after taking power, Gomulka had had the opportunity to pioneer a new path for the Polish economy. Polish economists led by Professor Lange prepared the essentials of a "new economic model" to replace the centrally planned, command economy inherited from Stalinism. Lange's proposals in 1957 comprised two inseparable elements: First, autonomy for enterprises, which were to be financially self-supporting, and directed by skilled managers along with elected workers' councils. Second, reform of prices and wages, so that prices reflected actual costs, as well as the supply and demand on a relatively free market. Lange's proposals in fact anticipated and went beyond the reforms suggested five years later by Professor Liberman in Russia. However, Lange emphasized that without realistic prices, mere structural tinkering would not provide Poland with the flexibility and efficiency required by a modern economy.

During 1957 and 1958, several of Lange's recommendations were carried out, but not the essential price and wage reform. Between 1958 and 1960, there was some adjustment of wholesale prices, without much effect on the consumer market. The half-reforms failed to stimulate either economic growth or productivity. In the autumn of 1959, meat shortages, inflationary tendencies, and popular discontent frightened Gomulka, who turned back to the methods and men associated with the old centralized planning.

The squeeze on the Polish economy intensified in the early 1960s, with the loss of the China market and the new pressure for heavy-industry investments and defense production at the time of the Berlin and Cuban crises. In response to the record harvest

of 1961, Gomulka raised land taxes on the peasantry by 20 percent—thereby contributing to the economic troubles which began
for the regime with the bad harvest of 1962.

In 1963, with both Poland and its Communist neighbors
plunged into new economic troubles, the Liberman discussions in
Russia reawakened hopes for a new round of economic reform in
Poland. But when the Liberman debate was halted in Moscow,
Gomulka in December 1963 dissolved Professor Lange's Economic
Council. Real wages from 1962 onward either stagnated or tended
to decline, and the numerous compromises, official and unofficial,
produced a hybrid, inefficient economy which lacked even the
discipline and uniformity of Soviet planning, let alone the freedom
and flexibility urged by the reformers.

A symbol of the confusion was the Polish currency, the zloty,
which operated at half-a-dozen rates of exchange. Western tourists received 24 to the dollar, Soviet-bloc tourists twice as much,
Polish recipients of cash from abroad three times as much—while
black-marketeers in the streets offered 100 zlotys to the dollar.

The Polish state itself participated in this confusion. It operated
commission stores and trading firms which sold Western and
higher-quality Polish goods to its own population for hard currency at triple the tourist rate of exchange. Private currency speculation, along with corruption among economic officials and the
widespread theft of state property, occupied the principal concern of the police. Gomulka and his colleagues, however, refused
to consider a radical currency reform which might limit such
speculation. (A realistic exchange rate might have disclosed that
Polish living standards were lower than those of undeveloped
Bulgaria; even a Polish minister of state earned only about $50 a
week in real purchasing power.) Instead, in 1965, a new scrip was
created as a bonus for foreign tourists, in the form of coupons
issued by the state tourist agency; the coupons merely added to
the confusion.

Corruption was so widespread that it was widely believed in
Warsaw that the authorities really operated not so much on the
basis of the officially published five-year plans but on the basis of
secret plans which wrote off as much as 20 percent of national
income for uncontrollable bribery, speculation, and pilfering.

"The greatest mistake you Westerners make about us," a Polish acquaintance told the British literary critic V. S. Pritchett, "is that you think we are enslaved by a rigidly organized system from which one cannot escape. But the truth is that there is no real system. There is a state of continual disorder. Planners make small miscalculations which lead to enormous mistakes, and the ordinary man spends a lot of his time picking his way through chaos."

Professor Lange himself disclosed that there had been no ladies' hairpins in Poland for a time simply because the planners had forgotten to include them in the plan. A journalist, Karol Malcuzynski, returning from several years abroad in 1962, described days "when I was unable to get toothpaste in Warsaw, when I was searching high and low for simple, unadorned drinking glasses, and when I finally had to comb the streets of this capital, not for one day but for weeks, looking for toilet paper. . . ."

A Western automobile engineer of Polish origin who toured the Zeran plant just outside Warsaw wondered how any cars were ever produced there at all. There were, he said, four times as many workers on the crowded factory floor as were needed.

A survey of women in a Warsaw factory showed that the average working woman rose at 4:45 A.M., prepared breakfast for her family without eating any herself, spent an hour and twelve minutes getting to and from work, some 53 minutes a day waiting on line for groceries, about nine hours at the factory, and had less than six-and-a-half-hours' sleep. Another inquiry disclosed that some 30 million paper forms—one for every statistical Pole—had to be filled out daily.

The quality of Polish daily life was described by Slawomir Mrozek just before Christmas 1963:

> We wanted to get carp for the holidays. To keep it alive until cooking time, it has to be kept in the bathtub. But to put the carp in, you have to take the coal out. The coal could be dumped in the vestibule, but where would we put the potatoes? We thought and thought, and finally my mother-in-law suggested: put the potatoes in the kitchen, the coal in the vestibule, and the carp in the bathtub. But what about the rabbits? . . . We thought and thought and finally somebody said, put them in the cellar. But grandpa is in the cellar. What do we do with grandpa? We could put him where the TV

set is, but what about the set? It could go where the tenant's folding cot now stands. But what do we do with the tenant? He could sleep in the bathtub, but that's where the carp is supposed to be. . . .

The dilemma was solved by coincidence:

Returning home from work a little earlier one day, I found the tenant sleeping with my wife in my place. So we took the coal out of the tub and put it into the vestibule, the potatoes out of the vestibule and into the kitchen, the rabbits out of the kitchen and into the cellar, grandpa out of the cellar and in place of the TV set, and the TV set in place of the tenant's folding cot. But what about me, you ask? No problem there. I have to stand in line for the carp.

The economic stagnation that set in after 1962 was partly caused by the failure to reform the system, partly by the fact that farm exports outstripped farm output, partly by the high investment rate to which Gomulka committed the regime. The big investments were to some extent motivated by the demands of the Soviet bloc, to an equal extent by the party penchant for huge new projects for their own sake.*

The economic stagnation led to little conscious pressure for change among the mass of peasants and workers. Polish living standards in the early 1960s were certainly higher than those in the great eastern neighbor, the Soviet Union. They were also not that much worse, and for the poorest classes actually better, than in the depression years before the war; in any case, there were fewer and fewer Poles alive to argue the contrary from personal experience. The United States continued to supply wheat, and American relatives to send dollars and food packages. Inchoate resentments could always be directed, and were, at familiar targets—the Germans and the Jews. Having fought and lost millions of people between 1939 and 1947, most Poles seemed in no mood for heroics and quite prepared to regard the stagnation as a "small stabilization."

* Thus, the regime committed itself to a long-term project for developing the copper deposits near Legnica in Silesia, including a large refinery estimated to cost 30 billion zlotys ($300 million at the black-market rate)—partially because copper was short elsewhere in the Soviet bloc, with Russia's most extensive reserves located beneath the ice near the Arctic Circle. The project could only pay for itself if world copper prices remained high in the 1970s.

Discontent appeared, instead, within the party and among the intellectuals. In the party, the "Partisans"—a group consisting mainly of younger officials, several of whose leaders had fought in the wartime underground—sought to turn nationalist resentment against the "Muscovites" or former "Stalinists," many of them Jewish, who had been prominent before 1956. Ironically, the former "Stalinists" had later become most insistent on the need for political and economic reform. Gomulka balanced between the two groups, but as time passed, adherents of a "strong hand" gained ground while more open-minded officials gradually dropped out of public life. The rising figure was the Partisan leader and minister of the interior, General Mieczyslaw Moczar.

The discontent among the intellectuals became apparent during the winter of 1961-62. It had been encouraged by Khrushchev's new wave of de-Stalinization. There were stormy meetings of the Writers' Union, and of the so-called Crooked Circle Club, a discussion group in which intellectuals attempted to restoke the fires of October 1956. But the club was closed down, and the censorship became more difficult for journalism, literature, theater, and cinema alike.

Gomulka, echoing Khrushchev's March 1963 attacks on "decadent" and Western influences, at the same time throttled criticism of the country's economic failures. In June 1963, Warsaw's two most distinguished intellectual journals were shut down. A new publication, *Kultura,* was founded in their place—dedicated to "the struggle against reactionary ideology."

Polish intellectuals were disturbed and boycotted the new publication. A Western traveler a few weeks later remarked that the change need not, necessarily, be for the worse. The same sort of merger had recently taken place in Czechoslovakia and there the new magazine had proved more liberal than its predecessors.

"What is liberal in Czechoslovakia," a Polish novelist snapped angrily, "is nothing here."

There was, indeed, little doubt that the atmosphere in Warsaw in the summer of 1963 was still far more cheerful than in Prague, not to mention East Berlin or Moscow. But Poland and Czechoslovakia were moving in opposite directions—Poland backward from 1956, Czechoslovakia forward to 1968.

CHAPTER 6

The Haunted Castle

Czechoslovakia was different from all the other states of Communist Europe. It was, from the beginning, the special case—the great exception to most theories as to why Communism takes hold and what it accomplishes.

Elsewhere, it could be argued that pre-Communist regimes had been brutal tyrannies or corrupt dictatorships, dominated by great landowners, foreign capitalists, or military and police cliques. It could be argued that the other nations of Communist Europe had been socially backward, economically underdeveloped—masses of illiterate, priest-ridden peasants and slum-herded proletarians, exploited by a privileged few. It could be argued that, despite the human cost, Communist rule had smashed old class barriers; broken the primitive peasant mentality; built industries, cities, and universities; established, despite "excesses," the bases of modernization and future prosperity. In short, it could be argued that elsewhere in Communist Europe a mass of once very poor people were somewhat better off, at least in some respects, after decades of Communist rule than they had been under the old tsars, kings, regents and colonels.

Such arguments, even for the other countries of Communist Europe, were accepted more readily by outsiders than by the living inhabitants of the region. Yet no such argument could even be made about Czechoslovakia, to which Stalinist rule brought no "progress" by any sort of definition, but economic, national, and moral degradation. In Czechoslovakia, Stalin had seized a garden and turned it into a wasteland.

The perfect society has never existed, but by mortal standards the Czechoslovak Republic of Thomas G. Masaryk and Eduard Beneš was an eminently civilized and happy country. It was the only nation east of Switzerland and south of Scandinavia which successfully practiced democracy throughout the years between 1918 and 1938. The republic was progressive, egalitarian, prosperous, and efficient. It had strong unions and cooperatives, disciplined and socially conscious workers, expert craftsmen, distinguished scientists and intellectuals, hardy independent farmers. (The great landowners of Hapsburg days had disappeared in 1918.)

Czechoslovakia inherited 70 percent of the industrial capacity of the empire; Bohemia and Moravia alone had accounted for more than half the empire's industrial production. The Republic's economy was remarkably diverse. There were great heavy industries like the Skoda metal and munitions works, and world-famous consumer-goods plants like the Bata shoe factory (Europe's largest). Smaller concerns and cooperatives employed the century-old skills in glassware, jewelry, ceramics, printing, and precision instruments. Czech industrial products competed successfully on world markets. Lacking great natural resources, Czechoslovakia, like Britain, specialized and traded, refining and reshaping imported raw materials and semifinished products and exporting them on the basis of superior quality. Czechoslovak agriculture was intensive, and productivity on the farms was well above the European average. Living standards of workers and farmers compared favorably with those in France and Germany. Prague's shops were as elegant as those of Paris.

In many respects—with the notorious exception of its fatal geographic position, gripped in the German vise—Czechoslovakia resembled Holland, Denmark, and Switzerland. The country would never be a great military power or a flaming inspiration to rebellious youth across the continents. Its peoples exuded little of the glamour of the Latins, none of the pride of the Poles, warmth of the Russians, or boldness of the Serbs. They were cautious, prudent, solid—inward in their wry humor, subtle in their fantasy, rational, earnest, methodical. Romantics found the Czechs, particularly, easy to despise (the Slovaks less so—they had, over the centuries, imbibed some of the romanticism of their Magyar masters). The people and their leaders valued peace above all, and had little taste for adventures. The Czechoslovak Republic provided its citizens with a sober, decent, dignified life in which industriousness, learning, and civic responsibility were fostered and respected. The liberty of the human conscience was prized above all—for Bohemia was the land of Master Jan Hus, and the motto of Masaryk's Republic was the Hussite slogan *"Veritas Vincit,"* Truth Prevails.

The Great Depression and the rise of Nazism provoked increasing difficulties for the Republic. There were troubles not only with the German minority (which constituted 24 percent of the population), but also with clerical-led nationalists in Slovakia, who had roused depressed peasants and mountaineers against Prague rule. Nevertheless, democracy in Czechoslovakia held firm until the Western powers betrayed the country to Hitler in 1938. In 1936, a year before his death, Professor Masaryk could write with modesty and justice to his friend Karel Capek (the author of *R.U.R.* and *War of the Newts*): "Perhaps in fifty years our times will appear to people living then in such a haze of splendour that they will almost envy us."

Masaryk's appreciation of his handiwork was shared, much less than fifty years later, by the overwhelming majority of his countrymen, who considered the interwar republic by far the happiest time in their peoples' history. They were able to say so openly, in countless public-opinion polls, during the spring of 1968, but their feelings were equally strong, though ruthlessly suppressed, in the long night through which Czechoslovakia passed between 1948 and 1963.

The harshness of those years was dictated by no objective threat or challenge. Czechoslovakia might instead have become Communism's showplace. It faced few radical social problems or domestic political contradictions. The Nazi occupation of Bohemia and Moravia, while brutal, had been nowhere near as murderous as elsewhere and had actually expanded Czech industrial capacity. Slovakia, independent under a clerical regime, had been relatively prosperous during the war. The country as a whole had suffered little damage from bombing or land battles. Many big industrialists who had collaborated with the Nazis fled abroad in 1945 and their factories were promptly nationalized.

Furthermore, the Czechoslovak Communist party was one of the few anywhere which had enjoyed significant popular support before the war. It had regularly polled between 10 and 13 percent of the vote, even though the rival Social Democrats as well as Beneš's liberal National Socialists were usually stronger. Between 1936 and 1946, the Communists had won additional prestige. They had been vociferous in the opposition to Nazism before and during the Munich crisis. Some of them (including the Slovak intellectual Vlado Clementis, the future foreign minister) had even criticized the Stalin-Hitler Pact. Many of their abler young leaders became martyrs in the resistance or in Nazi concentration camps. The Slovak Communists had led a national uprising in 1944, at Banska Bystrica in the Tatra mountains. The peoples of Czechoslovakia, betrayed by Britain and France in 1938, had been liberated by the Soviet Army, and (unlike the Poles, Hungarians, or Rumanians) they had never been anti-Russian. The Communist party took the lead in the expulsion of the 3 million Germans from Bohemia and Moravia, and won new supporters as it supervised the seizure and distribution of the Germans' lands and properties.

In May 1946, the Communists won 38 percent of the vote in a free election—the highest proportion ever won by a Communist party anywhere. Under President Beneš, Communist Premier Klement Gottwald headed a multiparty coalition pledged to make Czechoslovakia a democratic, socialist society and a bridge between East and West. During 1946 and early 1947, Gottwald and other Communist leaders often stressed that they would follow their own "path to socialism," a moderate and independent course suited to Czechoslovak traditions. There was no need, they implied, to follow the brutal example of backward Russia. Even years later, several anti-Communist émigrés who had known Gottwald in those days believed that he, and at least a few of his colleagues, may have been sincere in such democratic professions.

Czechoslovakia's very advantages, and the obvious temptations these offered to at least some of its Communist leaders, may well have impelled Stalin to inflict a cruel and humiliating fate on the party and the country. The mystery, in retrospect, is why Gottwald and his colleagues (who sometimes referred privately to Soviet officials as "those idiots") accepted and abetted this degradation, step by step, going farther in some respects even than the more dependent Communists of Poland and eastern Germany. Perhaps it was precisely because Czechoslovakia had been different: men who became professional Communist leaders in a socially progressive democracy tended to be of a different moral caliber than those who became Communists in order to fight fascist dictatorships. They were more committed emotionally to the Soviet ideology than to the best traditions of their own country—and they were weaker characters. Gottwald and his colleagues between the wars had enjoyed the protection of liberal Czechoslovak republican institutions, and during the war the solicitous hospitality of the Kremlin. They were not, like the Yugoslav Communists, proud, ambitious fighters steeled in the fires of underground conspiracy, guerrilla war, and violent revolution.

While Tito resented the activities of the Soviet secret police on Yugoslav soil, the Czechoslovak Communist leaders accepted the aid of Beria's "gorillas" in Communizing the police and army, in infiltrating the Social Democrats and other parties with paid or blackmailed Soviet agents. While Tito's Partisans had survived the Wehrmacht's onslaughts virtually alone at first, then aided mainly by the West, neither Communists nor non-Communists in Czechoslovakia could think of going it alone, or turning to the West, after the shame of Munich. While Tito's authority in his own party was undisputed, in Czechoslovakia Stalin was able to play one leader or faction off against another—the moderate, weak Gottwald against the hard-bitten fanatic Rudolf Slansky; rational centralist Czechs against such passionately nationalistic Slovaks as Gustav Husak and Laco Novomesky.

Thus it was that, between 1947 and 1962, Stalin, his envoys, his agents, and his heirs imposed their will and their needs on the Communists of Czechoslovakia. Major decisions were, time and again, dictated in the halls of the Kremlin, in Stalin's *dacha* at Kuntsevo outside Moscow, or at the Soviet leaders' villas in the Crimea. From 1949 onward, Soviet secret police officers stationed in Czechoslovakia acted as a separate power within the state, responsible not so much to Gottwald or his colleagues as to Stalin and his heirs.

The great turning point came in the summer of 1947. On July 4, Gottwald's coalition cabinet voted unanimously to participate in discussions of the U.S. Marshall Plan for European economic recovery. Stalin immediately summoned Gottwald to the Kremlin and ordered him to reverse the decision. "I have never seen Stalin so furious," Gottwald told colleagues afterward, and reversed the decision without a second thought.

Two months later, at the secret Silesian conference which created the Cominform, Russia's Andrei Zhdanov proclaimed an end to the policy of "coexistence" and coalition with the West and with democratic parties in Eastern Europe. Zhdanov enunciated a hard, new "general line" of preparation for a new world war.* The new line not only divided Europe into hostile military and economic blocs, but divided humanity, inside as well as outside the Soviet empire, between Stalinists and "class enemies" with whom no honest cooperation was possible.

The new policy spelled an end to the Czechoslovak Communists' coexistence with democracy and prompted the Party to seize sole power in February 1948. Four months later, despite reservations among its leaders, the Czech party joined the Cominform campaign against Yugoslavia; in fact it was the Czech Communist *Rude Pravo* which announced Tito's excommunication. In the fall of 1948, Gottwald preserved his own position only after a long visit to Stalin in the Crimea.

The hard Soviet line dictated a thorough reorientation of the Czechoslovak economy—away from specialization, consumer goods, and a balanced world trade, to the role of steelmaker and munitions producer for the Soviet bloc. The Russians directly controlled the rich uranium mines at Jachymov, to which tens of thousands of forced laborers were sent after 1949. They pressed

* In accordance with Stalin's classic teaching that aggressive action should always be presented as legitimate self-defense, Zhdanov accused the West—virtually disarmed at the time of launching preparations for war.

the development of new mines and heavy industries, as well as the herding of farmers into collectives and state farms on the Soviet pattern. By 1951, the economic plan which the Czech Communists had themselves devised for the years 1948–53 had been radically distorted in the interest of Stalin's military buildup.

Stalin personally directed a wave of terror among Czech and Slovak Communists between 1949 and 1953. Soviet secret-police "advisers" installed in Prague controlled the interrogations. They often reported directly to Moscow, encountering less and less resistance from Gottwald, who turned to drink. The Soviet "specialists" introduced all-night interrogations and rigged group trials, whether of non-Communists or Communists, in the "amalgam" style of Stalin's Moscow Trials—linking together as co- "conspirators" people who had been opponents for years. Stalin's spirit was evident in the general atmosphere of paranoia (even the Boy Scouts were condemned in 1952 as a "Fifth Column pledged to support capitalism") and in the unusual severity of the punishments (as, for example, the hanging in June 1950 of a popular Socialist woman deputy, Dr. Milada Horakova).

The scenario of what became the major trial of Czechoslovak Communist party leaders was devised and revised over a three-year period to meet Stalin's personal obsessions. The persecution of prominent Communists began in the fall of 1949 as a campaign against suspected "Titoists," with Slansky leading the witch-hunt. In the first phase of "investigation," Vlado Clementis, the foreign minister, was the most prominent of those arrested. However, after countless other arrests, tortures, interrogations, and consultations with Stalin, Slansky himself was in the dock alongside Clementis in a grisly mass show-trial of alleged "Zionist agents"—an accompaniment to Stalin's anti-Semitic campaign in Russia. The commission which supervised the trial in November 1952 included Antonin Novotny, Vilem Siroky, and Karol Bacilek —who a decade later respectively held the posts of president, prime minister, and party leader in Slovakia.

Seven other major trials, and numerous individual trials, followed—despite the deaths of both Stalin and Gottwald in March 1953. Among those sentenced in the later trials were Husak and Novomesky, the Slovak leaders; Josef Smrkovsky, leader of the

Prague uprising in May 1945; Eduard Goldstuecker, the scholar and diplomat; and Josef Pavel, the security specialist. The trials continued until the end of 1954. A few prisoners were quietly released starting in 1955, but the trials remained a trauma in the party for a dozen years afterward.

Novotny, who became party leader in September 1953, had risen to the summit as a direct result of the terror. Born in 1904, a mechanic by trade, a Communist since 1921, he had been an obscure regional party secretary before the war, which he spent in the Mathausen concentration camp. He had entered the key party policy bodies in the autumn of 1951—just before the greatest single wave of arrests—and had been chosen directly by the Soviet Politburo in preference to his senior rival, Antonin Zapotocky. He earned the lasting respect of Kremlin conservatives by holding Czechoslovakia in line during the 1956 upheavals in neighboring Poland and Hungary.

A gray, hard, dull, lonely man, Novotny possessed none of the popularity once enjoyed by Gottwald or Zapotocky. His semi-literate, confused speeches evoked contempt among the educated citizens of Prague. He was resented in Slovakia for curtailing its autonomy. His chief talents were those of the back-room machine politician, a manipulator of appointments, promotions, demotions, transfers of loyal supporters or suspected rivals. His concern was for who was watching whom, and he had few, if any ideas on policy beyond bolstering his own position and proving his indispensability to the masters of the Soviet party, police, and military apparatus.

With the caution of the trained Stalinist, Novotny was slow to emulate sudden bursts of Soviet liberalism, such as Khrushchev's de-Stalinization in the spring of 1956. He was quick, however, to follow Moscow when tough policies were proclaimed, and quicker still to volunteer Czechoslovak support and resources for the Kremlin's military and subversive ventures abroad, even at great cost to the domestic economy. The symbol of his rule was the giant statue of Stalin on Prague's Letna Hill, a monstrous monument that was only completed in 1955 and was not finally dismantled until October 1962. The huge base of the monument continued to remain in place years afterward. (Czechs wondered whether a statue of Khrushchev or of Mao would replace it.)

Long after Khrushchev had begun preaching the need for contact with the outside world, Novotny's Czechoslovakia remained under lock and key. In 1955, only 2,749 Western visitors were permitted to enter the country, nearly all on official business; even in 1958 there were fewer than 25,000. Until mid-1963, Western tourists had to wait weeks for visas and to designate in advance the specific checkpoints at which they would enter and leave the country. Most of the prewar frontier stations had been closed.

The citizens of Czechoslovakia themselves were far more restricted. Before the war, more than a million Czechs and Slovaks used to travel abroad each year. Vienna was considered next door, and entire villages of Czechs thrived each summer on the Dalmatian coast of Yugoslavia. From 1949 onward, however, Czechoslovakia was a maximum-security prison. Access to Western books and periodicals was barred even to most Communist editors and publishers. As late as 1959, only 4,431 Czechoslovak citizens were permitted to travel to non-Communist countries.

Yet, Czechoslovakia could not indefinitely live in isolation from the outside world, in the manner of Russia or China. It possessed neither the great area nor the rich natural resources nor the kind of people traditionally disposed to consider their country a world in itself. For years, Novotny was able to live on borrowed time, as the Czechoslovak economy drew on the physical and human capital of pre-Communist days. Thus, growth statistics continued impressive in the late fifties.

In fact, however, the economy was already seriously overstrained. Agriculture, consumer industry, and housing had been systematically neglected for a dozen years. Incentive had been destroyed by the extreme leveling of wages. On the farms, the output of most products was either barely equal to, or lower than, the level of the depressed mid-1930s. Despite the forced emphasis on heavy industry, electric power, machinery, and engineering, Czechoslovak progress even in these fields lagged behind such comparable countries as Belgium and neighboring Austria.

In 1959 and 1960, Novotny extended Czechoslovakia's already heavy commitments to the Soviet Union and its various clients (such as the Arabs) to new Kremlin clients—to newly independent states in Africa and to Communist Cuba. These commitments, and the sudden Soviet break with China, undermined the already tenuous balance of the Czechoslovak economy.* Even according to the dubious official statistics of the time, the Czechoslovak economy barely expanded in 1961.

Khrushchev's second de-Stalinization in October 1961 provoked the first attempt to rid the party of Novotny's gray rule. As early as 1956, the ambitious Czech interior minister, Rudolf Barak, had evidenced disagreement with Novotny over de-Stalinization, urging the rehabilitation of the victims of the purge trials. Now, in January 1962, Barak wrote a letter to Khrushchev asking support in a bid to overthrow Novotny. Barak gave his letter to the Soviet Embassy in Prague for transmission to Moscow. Instead, the Embassy turned the letter over to Novotny, who had Barak arrested.

Although details of the case remain obscure, there seem grounds to suspect that Barak's betrayal was the work of elements in the Soviet party and police apparatus who were at that very time restraining Khrushchev from further de-Stalinization. (Significantly, the Albanians charged that Barak's conspiracy had been inspired by the Khrushchevites and gleefully hailed his arrest as a triumph for sound Stalinism.)

At the Czechoslovak party congress in December 1962, Novotny, in the presence of Brezhnev, dismissed de-Stalinization as a problem by declaring that "more than thirty" innocent victims had been rehabilitated. But the number of Communist victims had run into the thousands, and the non-Communist victims numbered scores of thousands. Even those Communists who had been legally rehabilitated were excluded from political power, and assigned to trivial jobs in the provinces or academic positions. Meanwhile, Novotny, Siroky, and Bacilek held the highest offices in the party and state.

In August 1962, Novotny was forced to scrap the five-year economic plan for 1961–65. There was drought in the country-side and the cities were gripped by shortages of meat and vegetables. Morale in the factories was abysmal. Absenteeism,

* China had been a large captive market for low-quality Czechoslovak products which could not be sold in the West. Between 1960 and 1962, Prague's exports to Peking were slashed by 90 percent.

pilfering, and defective products were losing the economy millions of dollars.

The winter of 1962–63 was one of the harshest Europe had experienced in decades. In Czechoslovakia, snow and ice blocked the roads and stopped the trains. Fuel and electric power were rationed. Consumer goods remained in short supply. Novotny's stage-managed party congress had produced no hint of change. Even stalwart Communists were demoralized by the grimness of the cold, darkened winter, the persistence in office of the old Stalinists, and the shock of Soviet humiliation in the Cuban missile crisis.

To the handful of Western visitors that winter, Prague presented tragic contrasts. At night, the city was unbelievably dark. Even downtown on Wenceslas Square, most of the light stancheons were turned off because of the power shortage. By day, one saw only too clearly the dirty streets, uncleaned windows, peeling plaster, and undressed stone; the rusting water pipes, overburdened old trolleys, patient queues in butcher shops and cafeterias; women's legs in unbecoming cotton and lisle, men too often in drab, ill-hanging coats of prewar style. There were few children: the Czech birthrate, which had been falling steadily for a decade, was now among the lowest in Europe. The adults were grim, depressed, silent. Compared with raw, youthful Warsaw or masculine, extroverted Belgrade, Prague gave the impression of an inward, fading dowager, living less on hope than on habit.

The dirt and depression were all the more poignant because, beneath it, Prague was perhaps the most enchanting European city north of the Alps. It lay at Europe's very center (750 miles from London, 850 from Rome, 1,600 from Moscow). Through the city flowed the Vltava—Smetana's famous Moldau—on which ducks played beneath the bridges, as the river rippled gently northward to the Elbe. Along both sides of the river, gothic towers and steeples, Renaissance cathedrals and arcades, baroque villas and palaces blended in diverse combinations, reflecting seven centuries of living traditions. The city had been relatively unscarred since the eighteenth century.

On the level bank of the river, there were the medieval Jewish cemetery, where Rabbi Loew had conjured up the Golem; the Bethlehem Chapel, where Hus had preached; the Tyl Theatre, where Mozart and Da Ponte had first presented *Don Giovanni*. Narrow cobbled streets and arcades led to the Old Town Square, with the monument to Hus and the Reformation martyrs at its center. Just off the square was the undistinguished gray apartment house where Franz Kafka had been born.

From Kafka's house, the traveler could look across the mists of the Vltava to the famous castle—Hradcany—high on the hill of the opposite bank: from afar a mysterious symbol of remote authority, approachable only by devious side roads, narrow alleys, or steep steps. There, on the grounds of the old Bohemian royal palace, through courtyards and alleys, one wonder succeeded another, evoking the glories of the past. The great St. Vitus Cathedral, begun in the fourteenth century, housed the tomb of the Bohemian kings, the Coronation Jewels, the gothic chapel of St. Wenceslas. In one of the inner courtyards of the castle, there stood, untopped, the small stone base on which Masaryk had planned to erect a modest statue of Liberty.

Yet, early in 1963, even many of the most famous old palaces and shrines were closed, boarded up, or in desultory disrepair. The Wallenstein Palace was neglected because the German soldier-adventurer who built it had fought the Czechs in the Thirty Years War. The portraits of Maria Theresa and her Hapsburg heirs had been removed from the old throne room of the castle. Of Thomas Masaryk, there was no trace. Kafka's house was unmarked—his works had been banned for years; they prefigured far too realistically the anonymous terror and helplessness which had gripped Czechoslovakia since 1949.

Symbolically, the revival of Czech liberalism began with two events. The first was the campaign to rehabilitate Kafka waged by Eduard Goldstuecker, who after his release from prison had become a professor at Charles University. The second was a bold attack by a young Prague economist, Radoslav Selucky, on "the cult of the plan"—the system of centralized command which had so plainly ruined the national economy.

Nevertheless, the impulse to change was weaker at first in the Czech lands than in Slovakia, where the cry was less for political liberalism than for national vindication. Although Novotny had made major economic investments in Slovakia, he had treated it as a dependent and somewhat suspect province. The autonomy promised after the war had long been supressed. Novotny had yet to restore the honor of Clementis, Husak, and other Slovak Communist victims of the trials, or even the honor of the 1944 Slovak uprising. The Slovak capital of Bratislava was, if anything, more neglected than Prague. But it lay on the Danube hardly an hour from Vienna, and by early 1963 there had been enough traffic back and forth so that its citizens knew how much better their Austrian neighbors were living.

Thus, Czech liberalism, Slovak nationalism, and the trauma of the purges combined with the economic collapse in the first months of 1963 to place Novotny on the defensive and force the beginnings of change. On April 3 and 4, the party central committee met in the Hradcany Castle and removed Bacilek as party leader in Slovakia. In Bacilek's place, a slim, young man named Alexander Dubcek became first secretary in Slovakia and a member of the party Presidium in Prague.*

Dubcek did not become widely known, even among his own people, for nearly five years. At first glance, his official biography seemed that of a typical party functionary, a professional *"apparatchik"* like tens of thousands of others in Eastern Europe: born in 1921, a Communist since 1939, a party official since 1949, a graduate in 1958 of the Soviet Higher Party School in Moscow. But later, when official biographies gave way to living biographies, it became clear that Dubcek had been shaped in a rather unusual mold.

To begin with, he was a second-generation Communist, who had literally been conceived in the United States. His father, Stefan Dubcek, had crossed the Atlantic in 1911, worked as a cabinetmaker, and joined the Socialist party of Illinois. Alexander's older brother, Julius, was born in Chicago in 1920. When Mrs. Dubcek became pregnant again, the family decided to re-

---

* Strangely, the changes approved in the first days of April were not publicly disclosed until six weeks later—on May 14. In 1968, it was revealed that Novotny had attempted to save Bacilek to the end. Perhaps he had reason to hope that his conservative friends in the Kremlin would veto the decisions. Kozlov's fateful heart attack (April 10–11) and the subsequent return of Khrushchev to Moscow (April 20) after a curiously long "vacation" may have swung the balance.

turn to Slovakia—to the town of Uhrovec, where Alexander was born three months after their arrival.

Stefan Dubcek joined the Czechoslovak Communist party, and in 1925 took his family to the Soviet Union to help found a kind of Utopian community, the "Inter-helpo" cooperative farm at Frunze in Central Asia. When Stalin's collectivization drive began, such cooperatives disappeared. The Dubcek family moved to Gorki (Nizhni-Novgorod), where Ford engineers were then helping to construct Russia's largest automobile factory. Alexander attended Russian schools from the age of five to seventeen, at a time when most teachers, particularly in the provinces, were still imbued with the ideals of the pre-Stalinist Russian intelligentsia.

Early in 1938, despite the Nazi menace, the Dubceks returned to Slovakia (perhaps in order to escape the Stalinist terror). Under the Slovak quisling state, Alexander worked as a machinist while maintaining contact with the Communist underground. In 1943, Stefan Dubcek was arrested and interned until the end of the war. In 1944, his sons Julius and Alexander joined the Slovak national uprising in the Tatra mountains, led by Husak and Novomesky. Julius died in battle in January 1945. Alexander was wounded twice. After the war, he married a local girl in Trencin; they were wed in a Catholic church. The years which Dubcek spent in the Moscow Higher Party School—1955 to 1958—were the years of the "thaw," of Khrushchev's secret speech denouncing Stalin, of the first sputnik.

Thus young Alexander Dubcek had (like Tito) personally experienced some of the most dramatic periods of Soviet life. He had also fought in a broad national uprising of his own people, led by Communists, only to see that uprising denounced by the Stalinists and its leaders tried and imprisoned as "bourgeois nationalists."

Three weeks after Dubcek became party leader in Slovakia, Communist victims of Stalinist repression began speaking out openly in Bratislava. On April 22, at a congress of Slovak writers, Laco Novomesky rose to denounce the trials and purges of the fifties. His own case, he said, was "only an infinitesimal part of something much bigger, much more monstrous and much more horrible." A month later, at a congress of Slovak journalists, another victim of repression—Miro Hysko, who had once been the editor of the Bratislava *Pravda*—publicly denounced Premier Siroky by name and called for an investigation not only of the "infamous political trials" of Stalin's day, but also of the period after 1956. Hysko's speech was published in the Slovak newspapers—a direct blow at Novotny as well as Siroky.

On August 22, a report on the persecutions of the fifties, which had been long delayed, finally appeared in Prague. The report announced that 481 cases had been reviewed and all but 70 of the victims cleared. The tide of liberalization was now running high—partly because Khrushchev in Moscow was basking in the glow of the nuclear test-ban treaty, but partly also because the advent of Dubcek to the Slovak leadership had given the reformers, Czech as well as Slovak, a base and a sanctuary in Bratislava.

In the summer and early fall of 1963, the most exciting periodical in the country was the Slovak literary weekly, *Kulturny Zivot*. Its pages were opened not only to Husak, Novomesky, and other Slovak nationalists, but also to free-thinking Czech economists such as Selucky and Eugen Loebl, a victim of the Slansky-Clementis trial who had become director of a Bratislava bank. At the same time that Novotny was counting on support from Kremlin conservatives, the Bratislava rebels summoned Soviet liberals to their aid. On September 14, *Kulturny Zivot* published a eulogy to the memory of Clementis by Ilya Ehrenburg.

Novotny attempted to appease the mounting opposition with small concessions. Western jazz was permitted, and youths danced the twist and listened to beatnik poetry readings. Several obstacles to tourism were removed. But there was no change in the economy. Farm production in 1963 was barely higher than in the drought year 1962. Industrial production actually declined.

Novotny was compelled to give further ground. On September 22, Prague announced the removal of Siroky and a large-scale reorganization in which several lesser Stalinists were also dismissed. The leading anti-Novotny rebels and victims of Stalinism, however, were not themselves admitted to positions of power. Instead, a generation of younger Communists, many of them technocrats, was promoted. Josef Lenart, a forty-year-old Slovak, became the new premier and promised economic reforms. Novotny ceased his attacks on the cultural publications and met "cordially" with leading writers and journalists on September 26— promising a new era of live-and-let-live. Shortly afterward, the Roman Catholic Primate, Archbishop Josef Beran, and four other Czechoslovak bishops were released from confinement.

The most important result of the changes in 1963 was cultural: Czechoslovakia was finally allowed to "catch up" with Poland, Hungary, and the Soviet Union, which had all experienced a "thaw" while Novotny had kept Prague frozen in arch-Stalinist patterns throughout the fifties and beyond. (When *High Noon* was shown in Prague in January 1963, it was the first American cowboy film exhibited there in fifteen years.)

From 1963 onward, publishing houses, theaters, and especially film producers enjoyed greater scope for experimentation, self-expression, and contact with the West. (The Czechs were, per capita, the greatest readers of translated books in the world.) Economists began discussing the causes of the 1961–63 depression, studying international economic developments more freely, and searching for means of reform. Historians moved cautiously to restore the names of Masaryk, Beneš, and other pre-Communist figures to the scholarly journals.

However, there was no further political change after the reorganization of September 1963. Barely three months later, Novotny was again inveighing against "revisionists" and other foes real and imagined. His foes had won a stalemate, not a victory. After the rapid movement in the first nine months of 1963, the deadlock lasted nearly four years. Novotny continued to reign in Hradcany Castle, and even rumors of his ouster ceased.

Was it pure coincidence that the liberal wave which had been surging forward in Czechoslovakia came to a halt just when there was yet another sharp turn in Moscow? For in the autumn of 1963, Khrushchev's authority was irreparably undermined by a disastrous harvest, and his tentative attempts at reaching some accommodation with the West were thrust in doubt by the assassination of John F. Kennedy.

CHAPTER 7

Journey into Khrushchev's Russia

A professor at Columbia University's Russian Institute once remarked that he never felt farther from knowing "what was going on in Russia" than when standing in Moscow's Red Square. It is certainly true that the foreign visitor, suddenly compelled to rely on the Soviet press and radio, soon feels cut off not only from the outside world but from the high politics of the Soviet Union itself. He misses the vast and comforting fund of news reports, analyses, press translations, and radio monitoring services culled and distilled by thousands of Western specialists for the student of Soviet affairs abroad.

On the other hand, no matter how assiduously a traveler has studied the mountains of material assembled by outside experts, the real Russia is invariably a surprise. This is not because such material is false in its detail; the standard of foreign scholarship so incomparably higher than before the war. It is, rather, a matter of proportions, of strikingly different accents and emphases which distinguish Russia-as-it-is from the image of "Russia" abroad. The disproportions are mainly the result of the country's long isolation and the continued secrecy and restrictions—which compel even the most disinterested outsiders naturally to focus on themes and

128

issues raised by the Kremlin authorities, thus often neglecting other aspects of Soviet life. Whether favorable or unfavorable, the picture formed abroad is inevitably two-dimensional—and each generation of travelers to Russia is compelled to experience it anew, rarely without an emotional jolt.

Rationalists are shocked by the disorder of Russian daily life, romantics by the prosaic immobility of the masses, revolutionists by the conservatism of Soviet institutions, conservatives by the virulence of official propaganda. Pessimists are startled to discover that real life goes on at all, while optimists are disillusioned by the quality of that life. Communists blame their disillusion on the primitiveness of Russia; admirers of historic Russian culture ascribe their disappointment to Communism.

My own first visit to Russia—a twenty-three day journey in the autumn of 1963—was full of surprises, even though I had been raised among Russian emigrants and had already spent more than a year traveling in other Communist countries. I spent a week each in Moscow and Leningrad, with briefer stops at Rostov-on-Don, Volgograd, Vilnius in Lithuania, and Kiev and Poltava in the Ukraine.

In some ways, the journey merely confirmed obvious truisms, usually taken for granted. The country is incredibly vast ("one-sixth of the earth's surface"), its landscape rarely relieved by mountains, the horizon infinite in all directions, towns isolated amid the great underpopulated open steppes and forests. Its natural resources are fantastic—the black earth of the Don fertile beyond belief, the Ukraine hardly less so. Russians as people are unusually warm, generous, familial, their women earthier and more durable than the men. The Russian language is terse, rich, melodious, emotionally subtle. Communism has deeply affected, but by no means obliterated, the Russian civilization described in the great literature from Pushkin to Pasternak, as well as in the observations of perceptive foreign visitors from the Marquis de Custine (1839) to Laurens van der Post (1963).

The problem of generations, of "fathers and sons," of which Khrushchev had spoken earlier that year, was all too real. The survivors of the very oldest generation, the grandfathers in their sixties, seemed not too different from Russians of their age in emigration. The middle generation, the adults shaped by Stalin, were very different. Those whom I talked with seemed sullen, beaten, or, at the very least, reserved. They exuded an unmistakable air of great spiritual as well as physical fatigue. (Van der Post was reminded of Shcherbatov's lines written just after Peter the Great: "How could there remain any manliness and firmness in those who in their youth trembled before the rod of their superiors and who could not win any honors except by servility? ")

But Soviet youth in 1963 resembled their "grandfathers" more than their "fathers." They seemed remarkably vivid, alert, curious, open-minded, friendly, and relatively uncontaminated by cynicism. Well educated and surprisingly aware of what was going on abroad, they sensed the backwardness of the system under which they lived, applied the word *"sovremenni"* (contemporary, modern) as the supreme compliment, and confidently expected better days. These were the youngsters who had thronged by the thousands to listen to the new poets—Yevgeni Yevtushenko, Andrei Voznesensky, Bulat Okudzhava, and Bella Akhmadulina. Their yearnings had been expressed in prose by Vassily Aksyonov, Yuri Kazakov, Vladimir Tendryakov. These young people were Russia's future, and they seemed to recall the youth of classic Russian literature far more than they did the Communists of Stalin's "iron age."

However, the spiritual chasm between these Soviet "sons" and their "fathers" had been a major theme of the new Russian writing since 1956, and had produced sharp, open clashes between Khrushchev and the young writers in the winter of 1962–63. Thus, my own conversations with Russian youngsters, while stimulating, largely confirmed impressions I had already gained by reading. The surprises were of a different character.

It took me nearly three days in Moscow to feel that I was really in Russia at all. I was eating Russian food, drinking Russian vodka, immersing myself in the language. I had already seen most of the postcard sights: Red Square, the Kremlin grounds, various theaters, rail stations, stores and markets. I still had a sense of unreality. Then one morning I was taken to visit Moscow University, on the Lenin Hills, and from its gardens exposed to a good view of the city below. Leaning on the rail, I spied, almost lost in the trees to our left, an unpretentious little church, notable mainly for the vividness of its blue and gold cupolas. On being told that General Kutuzov had prayed there in 1812, I walked over, to be rewarded as we approached by the sound of music. The church was in use; and only then—standing within its humble whitewashed walls, looking at the subtle splendor of its vivid icons, hearing the massed voices of simple men and women raised in the sublime tones of the Orthodox liturgy— at last I felt I was in Russia.

In my later travels as well, in visits to theaters and museums as well as to churches, it was impossible to escape the overpowering role played by Orthodox Christianity in Russian culture. Whether viewing the wondrous icons of Andrei Rublyov, listening to *Boris Godunov,* watching Tolstoy's *Power of Darkness* in the theater, I was constantly reminded that the Christian heritage was the matrix of nearly all that we call Russian culture.

Nearly all—because there was another notable tradition, the Westward-looking (specifically Francophile) "St. Petersburg" tradition epitomized in Pushkin and Turgenev. But this was at first a rather fragile plant, appealing more to the cultivated than to the mass. At the turn of the twentieth century, Russian intellectuals who could not root themselves consciously in Orthodoxy chose to throw over the old ways completely and to experiment, improvise, rethink. The music of Stravinsky, Prokofiev, and Shostakovich, the painting of Malevich, Kandinsky, and Chagall were among the first fruits of the new experimental modernism—the novels of Vladimir Nabokov, in the United States, among the most recent.

During the 1920s, the *avant-garde* seemed enthroned, while the age-old religious impulses were transmuted for a time in the mystique of revolution, as organized religion itself was savagely persecuted. But, starting in the early 1930s, Stalin chose to dam up both of these cultural streams, and they remained largely underground long after his death. The result was a profound discontinuity, in which the officially favored culture of "socialist realism" lacked both roots in the past and branches to the present of the outside world.

The interesting question was which of the two underground streams—the Orthodox or the experimental—would break through first and with greater force. Among such older poets as Pasternak and Akhmatova, as well as the young Voznesensky, one found both: modern forms infused with religious content. Yet, as the critic Andrei Sinyavsky pointed out, there were inherent difficulties in "attempts to unite the ununitable—to wed Andrei Rublyov to radar."

Both Stalin and Khrushchev, peasant sons, tended to repress modernism (with its Westernizing associations) more harshly than Orthodoxy. The icons were preserved, the churches restored—at first as antireligious museums, later as tourist attractions—and the tendency toward restoration grew stronger as the years passed. Many Soviet youngsters tended to rationalize their collecting of icons and their visits to churches as purely "cultural" curiosity, but their nostalgia seemed nonetheless religious in essence. One of Okudzhava's most popular ballads, entitled "François Villon," was a simple prayer:

As long as the earth keeps turning, as long as the light is strong,
Lord, give to each and every man, whatever he doesn't have. . . .
I know Thou canst do everything, I believe in Thy wisdom
As a fallen soldier believes in Paradise,
As each ear believes Thy soft words,
As we ourselves believe, not knowing what we do. . . .

What was the point, the poet Boris Slutsky asked, of pretending that the archangels in the icons of Andrei Rublyov represented mere peasants:

Rublyov, when he took the vows,
Was scarcely an unbeliever.
He fell on his knees
before the Word—the one that was in the Beginning. . . .
He was saved not by a swineherd
(symbolizing Labor)
but quite simply
            by the Savior . . .

Among educated Russians, there could be little devotion (as there was among Polish Catholics) to the institutions of the established Church, for the Orthodox hierarchy was largely viewed as a tool of the state in tsarist as well as in Communist times. The spiritual hunger nonetheless seemed far greater in Russia than in Central Europe or the Balkans—and the spiritual confusion uniquely poignant: "They have thrown down Stalin, they have thrown down God, what can we believe?" an anguished engineer in Leningrad asked me. Despite the "logic of history," my own strong feeling was that religion had a future in Russia.

One reason for this belief was that, in Russia as elsewhere, Orthodoxy was inextricably linked with nationalism. And Russian nationalism had been one of the main props of the regime, especially since 1941—both in its positive (win the war, reach the moon) and its negative (beat the Jews, jam the broadcasts) aspects. In Khrushchev's Russia, I was continually struck by the nationalist terms used to glorify a party which had originally stemmed from the extreme antipatriotic wing of European Socialism. "I spit on Russia," Lenin is once said to have remarked; for him, the world revolution was supreme. In contrast, the adjective with which the Communist party of the 1960s preferred to describe itself was *rodnaya*, literally "own" or "native," actually much more emotional in tone (derived from the verb "to give birth," as is the noun *rodina*, motherland). Of all the adjectives that Lenin might conceivably have applied to his party, this one was probably the least congenial to his entire cast of thought.

One wondered also how Lenin might have reacted to the various statues and memorials to the tsars, or to feudal princes, that abounded in Russia's major cities. Some were quite justifiable as works of art—notably Falconet's "Bronze Horseman" depicting Peter the Great and the witty monument to Catharine the Great, both in Leningrad. Yet it seemed paradoxical that, nearly a half century after Lenin's revolution and in the city now bearing his name, one of the principal squares was dominated by an equestrian statue of the very paragon of absolutism, Nicholas I, while there was not a single visible sign of any of Lenin's closest revolutionary associates, Trotsky, Bukharin, Zinoviev, or, for that matter, Stalin.

In Moscow, it was Khrushchev, after nearly four decades of Soviet rule, who sponsored the first public monument to Marx. Stalin had preferred to erect such nationalist memorials as the statue of the feudal warrior Yuri Dolgoruky, opposite the Moscow City Hall. Similarly, when he called on the Russian people to resist the German invaders in November 1941, it was in the name of old nationalist heroes: "May the manly images of our great ancestors—Alexander Nevsky, Dmitri Donskoy, Kuzma Minin, Dmitri Pozharsky, Alexander Suvorov and Mikhail Kutuzov—inspire you!" Later in the war, he replaced the *Internationale* as the national anthem with a pompous new hymn, *The Great Soviet People*, with verses praising himself by Sergei Mikhalkov (who survived both Stalin and de-Stalinization as a powerful official of the Writers Union). After the war, Stalin toasted the Great Russians as the leading people of the Soviet Union and declared war on all forms of "cosmopolitanism," foreign influence, and national individuality.

A decade after Stalin's death, Russian nationalism remained a powerful force, even as Khrushchev's attempt to revive Communist "internationalism" had withered in the Hungarian Revolution and the conflict with China. The best of the intellectuals resisted the official nationalism, or protested openly when it turned militaristic, anti-Western, or anti-Semitic. Solzhenitsyn's stories, Okudzhava's ballads, the films of Gregori Chukrai (*Ballad of a Soldier, Clear Skies*) strove for a universal humanity, eschewing patriotic bombast. Yevtushenko's "Babi Yar" * was the most famous protest against bigotry, concluding:

> Let the Internationale ring out
> When the last anti-Semite on earth is buried.
> There is no Jewish blood in mine,
> But I am hated by every anti-Semite as a Jew,
> And for this reason,
> I am a true Russian.

Nevertheless, in conversations with less educated Russians, I

---

* Deleted from the official collection of his works published in 1970, as was "The Heirs of Stalin," quoted in the Prologue of this book.

had the impression that the new nationalism was something more than an artificial creation of the regime. Rather, it seemed a deep-seated popular sentiment which the authorities were both stimulating and attempting to capture for their own purposes.

The most powerful element in the new nationalism was the memory of World War II, which in Soviet terminology was "The Great Patriotic War." During my visit, I could hardly talk to any Russian for five minutes without hearing about the devastation of the war. This was to be expected from Intourist guides, for the official line then blamed the war (along with Stalin's "errors") for nearly all Russia's troubles. But even Russians encountered casually seemed to have the impression that practically no one else did any serious fighting in the war, and that no other people had suffered half so much.

Moreover, Russians of all kinds in 1963 still talked about the war with the same sort of immediacy as Western Europeans had a decade earlier. Part of this lag could be attributed to economic conditions. However, there was also in the Russian mind a kind of blurring between the end of the war and Stalin's death eight years later. "The war swept many bad things away," a girl in Volgograd remarked—thus conveniently forgetting the persecution of war prisoners, the famine of 1946, the witch-hunts, purges, and plots of Stalin's last years. The confusion was obviously between what Russians *wanted* to happen in 1945 and what actually happened only after 1953 or 1956.

The war, the cold war, and the space race had also stimulated the great-power psychology. Most Russians I talked to considered the Soviet Union and the United States the only countries worth talking about, in any context. (The few exceptions were older men whose education had steeped them in French or German culture.) Any suggestion that both the United States and Russia might learn some useful things from the Italians, the Dutch, or the Swedes, was politely but incredulously brushed aside. If there was general indifference to most of Europe (Germany was partly an exception), I also found no great concern about China, mostly amusement at what was assumed to be Chinese poverty and primitivism. The feeling, despite bizarre frontier incidents that year, was that the Chinese simply did not matter. (This feeling began to change radically when China developed nuclear weapons.)

Russian attitudes toward the Germans were especially complex. Ordinary people commonly divided them between "our" Germans (in East Germany), for whom there was little respect or affection, and "the others" in West Germany, of whom there was considerable fear. It was admitted that Germany as a whole had, at the end, suffered considerably from the war; but the postwar West German economic recovery, so much more rapid and thorough than Russia's own, was brushed off as the product of "billions" in American aid. The fear of the Germans struck me as a fear not so much of Nazi sadism as of historic German efficiency and power. It was a fear tinged with respect: Russians did not look down on the Germans as they did on their allies in Eastern Europe, or on the no-longer-great powers of Western Europe. In discussions of Germany, more than in any conversation about the United States, one sensed a defensiveness which seemed to mask deep national anxieties. It was as though American prosperity and power were to be expected, and could easily be tolerated, while German competence somehow posed a threat to the essence of Russian national existence.

Of course, the Russians' perceptions of all foreign peoples, as of their own place in the world, continued to be deformed by their own isolation.* Official suspicion of any contact with the outside world was evident even in the most routine job applications. The questionnaires asked the applicant to specify whether and exactly when he had ever been abroad, whether he had been a war prisoner, whether he had any relatives in the outside world. Communist newspapers were still the only foreign periodicals generally available. Western theater troupes, concert artists, and films had only begun reappearing after 1956. The jamming of foreign radio broadcasts had ceased only on June 19, 1963. (It was resumed on August 21, 1968.)

The results of such isolation were twofold. On the one hand,

* In 1960, according to official statistics, some 120,000 Soviet citizens altogether (in a population of more than 200 million) traveled to all the non-Communist countries combined. More than four-fifths of this number were members of official delegations. Only 14,000 were group or individual tourists. By contrast, more than 10,000 Finns alone came to Russia in the same year.

there was, particularly among the young and the educated, a burning curiosity about the outside world, a hunger to absorb wonders which Russia had been so long denied. This was as evident in conversations with ordinary Russians as in the queues forming to see Western films and in the poems by Voznesensky, Yevtushenko, and others describing Florence, Paris, New York.

On the other hand, however, the Stalin era had deeply ingrained among Russians the habit of viewing their country as a world apart, and their own loves, sufferings, and problems as unique—not to be compared with, or significantly influenced by, the experiences of other, more fortunate peoples. Therefore, curiosity about the Russian past was at least as great as that about the outside world.

Khrushchev's de-Stalinization had directly stimulated such curiosity about the early Soviet years. It was not only a matter of exposing Stalin's crimes (although these remained the country's deepest trauma), but also of rediscovering the Russian culture which Stalin had suppressed and nearly destroyed. The curiosity of youth was particularly directed to the ebullient variety of the 1920s, which both Ilya Ehrenburg and Konstantin Paustovsky now evoked in their memoirs. In art and music as well as literature, the new generation sought to pick up the threads severed by Stalin. These were the days when Shostakovich's brilliant opera, *Ekaterina Ismailova,* banned in 1936, was revived; and when Dostoyevsky, similarly attacked, was at last reprinted and rediscovered by a new generation.

The hunger for a usable past, for a national heritage worthy of pride, was immense, and a considerable nostalgia was already discernible not only for the Communist twenties but for the "bad old days" before the Revolution. The nostalgia was not for tsarism as such (although collecting portraits of the last Tsar did become fashionable in later years), but rather for the color and variety of the old times. I was particularly struck by this in watching two Soviet portrayals of prerevolutionary Russia, within a few days in Leningrad. The first was a performance of the Stravinsky-Fokine ballet *Petrushka,* which was wildly cheered in what nearly seemed a political demonstration. (Most of Stravinsky's music had been banned for decades.) The second was a new, wide-screen film called *The Volga Flows*. In the ballet as well as the film, the pre-revolutionary scene was vivid, colorful, exciting. In the film, moreover the brief, pungent prerevolutionary scene made a longer sequence on the Khrushchevian Utopia (everyone living in concrete-block prefabs) seem pallid and dull by contrast. This nostalgia for the tsarist past became even more evident later in the loving, long new film versions of *War and Peace* and other nineteenth-century classics.

The full intensity of this hunger for the past, as well as the curiosity about the forbidden West, were difficult to imagine outside the Soviet Union. Certainly there was little to resemble it in Poland or even Czechslovakia, where Communism was relatively recent. One had to live in Russia for a while to realize just how stale, soporific, tedious was the official culture, including everything from newspapers to shop-window decorations. Only then could one fully appreciate why so many young Russians felt stifled and anxiously quaffed every fresh breeze, no matter where it originated, for spiritual oxygen.

Soviet newspapers largely peddled slogans, polemics, and "campaigns," and it was impossible to rely on them for even the most basic news of world affairs.* What the reader would learn from the press was that chemical workers and managers from all corners of the Soviet Union, led by heroic farseeing Communists, were rallying around their Leninist party to produce enough fertilizer to reach the stars. This was Khrushchev's big new campaign of the day. It was accompanied in the press by the perennial lesser campaigns—for efficiency, against bureaucracy, for ideological education, against neglect of the workers, for peace, and against the warmongers. The persevering reader would also learn that Russia was buying grain abroad—if he resisted the impulse to skip past or through the full text of Khrushchev's long speech in Krasnodar launching the fertilizer campaign.

Soviet reading-between-the-lines of an opaque press was an old story, but in 1963 there were several interesting new wrinkles on the tale of how Russians managed to get some idea of the world.

* During my journey, for example, *Pravda* briefly reported Harold Macmillan's resignation as Britain's prime minister, but for many days afterward a Soviet reader could only guess at the climate in the Tory party which led to his resignation and, ultimately, produced Sir Alec Douglas-Home as his successor.

Izvestia had become the best-selling daily, largely because its foreign news had become more substantial under the editorship of Khrushchev's son-in-law Adzhubei. The large numbers of ordinary Russians were attracted by two new periodicals: *Za Rubezhom,* which reprinted important speeches and statements by Kennedy, Nehru, and other foreign leaders and political commentators; and *Inostranaya Literatura,* which reprinted an impressive number of Western contemporary writers (including Kafka) in those days. Most surprising to me were the hundreds, if not thousands, in Moscow and Leningrad who queued up daily to buy the Yugoslav and Western Communist papers. The London *Daily Worker* was scarcely more informative than *Izvestia,* but after a week or two in the Soviet Union even the mediocre, primitive *L'Humanité* seemed like a great newspaper—not only for its news but for its advertisements (automobiles! refrigerators! department stores!).

The news, commentary, and political discussion on Radio Moscow were tendentious, uninformative, and monotonous, although resident foreigners insisted that it had become much more professional than in the Stalin years. The musical programs were dominated by snatches of nineteenth-century classics (the baroque revival had barely begun) and by folksong recitals from the national republics, also rather nineteenth-century in tone. Whole hours could be consumed with the reading of a *Pravda* editorial on "contemporary dogmatists and sectarians" (that is, the Chinese), or by reports from Byelorussian party officials on plan fulfillment as viewed from Minsk.

It was hardly surprising that millions of Russians turned their dials to the Voice of America, the BBC, even Radio Monte Carlo and Vatican Radio—not merely for news but for music as well. Two of the most animated questions I was asked about the West concerned pop musicians: in Leningrad, two young Russians demanded reassurance that Ray Anthony's popularity in the United States had not declined, and in Moscow, a larger group asked anxiously about a rumor that Paul Anka had been killed in a sports-car crash.

It was difficult to imagine the enormous impact on Russians of even the slightest Western culture fact. One consequence of the Cuban-Soviet alliance, for example, was the legitimation of Latin-

American dance rhythms in Russia. One could not hear them on Radio Moscow or in the smaller cities, but in one Leningrad hotel I saw a shouting crowd of dancers compel the band to repeat a samba three times. Outside Moscow's new Molodyozh youth club, a group of students told me all about Fellini's movie *Eight and a Half* although none of them had seen it. What they had done was to pool their money for a single black-market ticket to the restricted International Film Festival showing, and assigned the ticket to their friend with the best memory. Immediately after the showing, they had questioned him about the film, minute for minute, and now they all felt they had seen it.

Similarly, in Moscow's Pushkin Museum and Leningrad's superb Hermitage, the young people drifted to the collections of French Impressionists, only recently brought up from the cellars to which Stalin had consigned them. Even in far-off Alma Ata, an American graphic-arts exhibition (already attacked in the party press as "ideological subversion") was playing to turnaway crowds.

Similar patterns of selection were evident in almost every cultural field. My first theatrical evening, for example, was spent at the Moscow Art Theatre—a terrible disappointment in view of that theatre's great history. The play was Schiller's *Mary Stuart.* Not only was the heroine (forty-four years old at her death) played by an actress who, complaining neighbors informed me, was "at least sixty-nine"; the entire production was stylized, stuffy, wooden, declamatory. Within a few days, however, young Muscovites had explained to me that the old art theater was "hopeless, run by the same old fogeys for years." The only theater worth looking at in Moscow, they said, was the *Sovremennik* (Contemporary); while in Leningrad, "one goes" to the Comedy Theatre or, on occasion, the Gorky Drama Theatre. I found the two Leningrad theaters stimulating, indeed, but never managed to get to the Moscow *Sovremennik.* Just before the end of my journey, a rather stuffy article in one of the papers disclosed that it was almost impossible to obtain tickets for the *Sovremennik,* while the Moscow Art and a half-dozen other "leading" theaters in the capital were usually a third empty. The article chose to pretend that it was simply a matter of inadequate "distribution arrangements." It was rather, I thought, a matter of taste.

Despite Khrushchev's attacks on the liberal writers in March, the cultural climate had definitely improved that summer. In May, Alexander Tvardovsky, the editor of the liberal monthly *Novy Mir* and since 1961 an alternate member of the party Central Committee, disclosed publicly that Khrushchev had introduced Solzhenitsyn with pride to members of the government at a meeting with writers that winter. It became known, too, that Khrushchev had personally insisted on the publication of Solzhenitsyn's *One Day in the Life of Ivan Denisovich,* which the party ideologists had previously blocked. "Matryona's Home," perhaps Solzhenitsyn's finest story, was published in the January issue of *Novy Mir.* In July, the same magazine printed his novella "For the Good of the Cause," which dealt with the arbitrary "little Stalins" who continued to operate in the provinces, thwarting youthful idealism.

On August 18, just before Khrushchev's departure for Yugoslavia, *Izvestia* published Tvardovsky's long ballad "Tyorkin in the Other World," filled with satirical thrusts at virtually every aspect of Soviet life. Uncompromisingly anti-Stalinist, Tvardovsky pointedly called the roll of the forced-labor camps:

> There, row on row, according to years,
> Kolyma, Magadan,
> Vorkuta and Narym
> Marched in invisible columns. . . .
> ˙ Notch it, though it bitter be,
> Forever in the memory!

In an introductory note accompanying the ballad, Adzhubei recounted how Tvardovsky had read it to an appreciative Khrushchev on the Black Sea coast. By September, both Voznesensky and Yevtushenko, despite the attacks on them in March, were back in print, to the relief and delight of youngsters I met in my travels. As a result, my general impression of the state of the Russian spirit was optimistic. Russia struck me as a convalescent, a patient long ravaged by a deep and serious illness, still in delicate condition and just beginning to recover. But the will to recover seemed to be shared at almost every level of Soviet society. There seemed to be a direct line from the anonymous young students and engineers whom I encountered to the young poets they admired, through such older intellectual leaders as Tvardovsky, Solzhenitsyn, Ehrenburg, and Paustovsky, to Khrushchev himself.

Yet in fact the autumn of 1963 proved to be the sunset of Khrushchevian liberalism. For that autumn brought Khrushchev disaster in the very field he had personally dominated for a decade: agriculture. Despite continuing triumphs in outer space and the glittering Soviet industrial growth statistics of the late fifties, the ruinous harvest of 1963 demonstrated that the entire Soviet economy was in deep trouble. The extent of the trouble surprised many in the outside world, but it was all too clear, even to a casual tourist, inside Russia itself.

In coming to Russia, I had been prepared by reading and by photographs for the drab clothing worn by the great majority of people. But it was a shock nonetheless, not only for the lack of color and style, but because so much of it had obviously been worn too often and out of season. Nor was I quite prepared to find, in the land of the sputnik, the ever-present abacus as virtually the sole means of mass computation and bookkeeping. (I believe I saw no more than a dozen cash registers or adding machines in seven Soviet cities.) I spent an entire day in Kiev (population 1.4 million) futilely seeking a jar with a closeable top—and ended up, nine hours later, using adhesive tape to seal a plastic candy dish.

Signs of economic backwardness turned up even at presumed showplaces. At Moscow University, for example, I was shown a gymnasium and swimming pool that would have seemed quite ordinary in my Brooklyn junior-high-school days (1940); grade-school children were using the university facilities at the moment. On the handsome modern hydrofoil boat plying the Don between Rostov and Azov, half the passengers were old peasant women dragging sacks of potatoes or vegetables to take advantage of a price differential twenty miles down-river.

In one of the better districts of Moscow, I was shown the "new architecture" of what was probably the most modern farmers' market in Russia. The architecture (poured concrete square, covered by a glass center dome) was similar to that of Western bus stations and armories in the 1930s. The market itself was organized on principles far older. Each of the dozens of participating collective farms had its own set of counters. In the single market, one could thus buy, say, carrots at perhaps fifty scattered locations. At each carrot counter, there was a woman with an abacus and a counterweight scale who, inevitably, spent most of her time doing nothing. Furthermore, many of the fruits, vegetables, and meats were of a quality unsellable in most European countries. Yet the new market was surely far better—covered, heated, spacious—than most of the outdoor markets or street stalls I saw elsewhere, with their long queues at almost every hour of the day. Indeed, that new Moscow collective-farm market was doubly an earnest of Khrushchevian liberalism: not only for the new architecture, but because the very building of a new outlet for the *kolkhoz* farmers signified an end to the Stalinist pretense that food was available in state stores.

It was not necessary to wander far off the tourist trails to be aware of how difficult the food problem had become. I found it impossible, for example, to locate any orange juice whatever during this journey. Soviet menus were the first I had ever seen to carry such a notation as "tea 5 kopeks, tea with sugar 6 kopeks, tea with lemon 10 kopeks"—and, once out of Moscow and Leningrad, the lemon was fictitious. Even in Intourist hotels for privileged foreigners, many of the meat dishes were croquettes or other forms of chopped meat reinforced by copious breadcrumbs; small portions of beef or chicken were artfully concealed by french fries, succotash, parsley, etc. Yet it was depressing to discover a normal Russian, nontourist menu in a smaller town, such as Rostov or Poltava (both located in the midst of prime farm districts), and realize that the ordinary Russian most of the time could only choose among various forms of croquettes, meat substitutes, thick soups, and cabbage. It was small wonder that black bread and vodka comprised so large a part of the diet.

The troubles of Soviet agriculture had long been concealed by official statistics, which were freely falsified—first under Stalin, but then also under the same Khrushchev who had first exposed

Stalin's farm frauds. Stalinist harvest figures had been inflated at least 50 percent, according to the new figures released early in the Khrushchev period. Yet, in the fall of 1963, when Khrushchev was compelled to buy $800 million worth of grain from the West, scholars abroad reexamined Khrushchev's statistics for 1956–62. For, had those statistics been accurate, there should have been ample grain reserves to meet the crisis caused by the ruinous 1963 harvest. American specialists conservatively estimated the statistical "discrepancy" for 1956–62 at 135.7 million metric tons. The 1963 harvest was estimated at 92 million tons—or about the same as in 1913.

Defending himself in a speech late in 1963, Khrushchev argued that on the whole his costly program for developing the semiarid "virgin lands" of Kazakhstan had been profitable since 1954. His own statistics, however, disclosed that the virgin lands had been operating at a loss since 1960 (without even including the 1963 drought). In another speech, he observed that the 1959 party congress had vowed to increase spending on agriculture and the chemical industry, but that these plans had somehow fallen by the wayside. (In fact, they had been shelved by the military buildup accompanying the Berlin and Cuban crises of 1961 and 1962.) Moreover, despite party campaigns after 1959 against the peasants' private garden plots and cattle, the private plots—representing less than 4 percent of the country's cultivated land—produced nearly half its milk, meat, and vegetables, and three-fourths of its eggs in 1963.

The official line in the fall of 1963 was that "we're still paying for Stalin's mistakes in agriculture," as my Intourist guide in Volgograd put it. This was doubtless true, especially as the basic mistakes had not been rectified. But it was also true that, as a Leningrad engineer told me, "our people are indignant and disgusted." In June 1962, when meat prices were raised 30 percent and butter 25 percent, there had been bloody riots in Novocherkassk on the Don. In the fall of 1963, there was general disgust in the cities as students, workers, office employees, and even the Radio Moscow staff were rushed out to collective and state farms to help bring in the harvest.

The difficulties of Soviet agriculture were well advertised by

Khrushchev himself at various times, and again by his successors in March 1965. However, even when one looked at one of the major post-Stalin achievements, housing construction, one realized that "progress" in the Soviet Union was a very relative notion. Almost everywhere, I was taken to new housing districts and projects, either completed in the past four or five years or under construction. The volume of such construction was impressive, reminiscent of the growth of public housing projects in American cities just after World War II.

Yet, what surprised me about Soviet cities was not the new, but the old—how much of the physical plant, even in Moscow and Leningrad, clearly dated back to prerevolutionary times. It was quite easy, walking through many a Russian street, to imagine oneself back in the times of Dostoyevsky. Venturing into some of the older apartment houses, I was appalled by the utter lack of maintenance over those many years: hallways dingy, dirty, unpainted, scarcely lit. I did not enter any of the new apartments, but was told that complaints had already begun in them over faulty construction and lack of maintenance. Still, the new one- and two-room apartments were doubtless an improvement over the "communal apartments" in which Stalin had forced the great majority of Soviet city-dwellers to live—six or seven families, with one room each, sharing a common kitchen and bathroom.

The symbol of Soviet construction was the giant crane poised over half-finished apartment houses or factory buildings. There were probably more such cranes on view than in the United States (where elevators do much of the same work). Yet many if not most of these cranes were standing idle—and many of the partly built projects were completely empty of workmen. At the 1961 party congress, Khrushchev called for a halt to new construction projects, so that the old ones could be finished. Yet not merely the Soviet press but the naked eye in 1963 disclosed countless building sites on which little or no work was being done. Khrushchev himself complained that major industrial projects were taking twelve years to finish, when they should have been completed in three or four.

If the landscape of the Soviet city was disappointing, the countryside aroused mixed emotions. On the one hand, nature had given Russia so much: majestic river valleys, broad horizons, forests and woods suffused with an enchanting hush, birches and firs romantic in all seasons. The hand of man was rarely to be seen; the scale was human, preindustrial. There was a stillness, an immemorial peace, in the unspoiled countryside which engulfed and protected smaller towns, villages, and farm settlements from the harshness of Soviet modernity. One understood immediately why so many Russians had always loved to walk in the woods, search for mushrooms, or hunt.

Yet the villages themselves were desultory and sad, for a nation whose scientists had already mastered the secrets of atomic energy and space flight. On a four-hour drive from Moscow to the Tolstoy estate at Yasnaya Polyana (via Tula on the main road to Kharkov), I was disheartened by the old, unpainted one- or two-room wooden peasant shacks, the rickety fences closing in the private plots, the collective fields empty and untended, the occasional tractor abandoned to the rain, the old women and children leading a cow or a goat through the mud in search of some grass as if they had been doing so since time immemorial. An occasional new stone building was, almost always, the administrative headquarters of a state farm.

On the boat ride down the Don from Rostov to Azov, the atmosphere was, if anything, even more timeless and somnolent: the fertile fields broad and empty, jerry-built fishing shacks and landings on the shore, the wooden peasant houses liberally interspersed with thatched-roof huts. One felt in the opening pages of a Sholokhov novel—except that this was 1963, Sholokhov's novel had been written thirty years earlier, and its opening pages described the Don before the First World War. There was no sign, however, of the proud, prosperous Cossack horsemen who once considered themselves the freest people in the Russian Empire.

Other travelers who managed to penetrate farther into rural areas during this period were even more saddened. Ota Richter, a young Czech photographer who visited a model collective farm in the black-earth country 30 miles north of Odessa, was shocked by diseased cattle, the lack of machinery and transport, the utter poverty of the farmers. "Not even with the liveliest imagination," a Slovak colleague of his remarked, "could I have visualized that life in a Soviet collective could be so bad."

Anthony Sylvester, who toured southern Russia the following summer, took a bus from Kiev 70 miles into the countryside, to Belaya Tserkov: "What I saw reminded me sharply of wartime German propaganda pictures of Russia. Thick clouds of dust enveloped the roads, which were pitted in places with holes a foot deep and more. Barefooted girls were carrying buckets of water. In a stagnant pool, some middle-aged women were splashing about in the summer heat, naked save for their black cotton pants. A man who sat down next to me for a sunbath told me that he had not been paid any wages for the past two months. 'This happens quite frequently,' he added."

To the Western eye, the sadness of the Russian countryside lay in its material poverty. But to sensitive Russians, indifferent to Western materialism, there was a deeper sadness—expressed in a sketch by Solzhenitsyn:

When you travel the byroads of Central Russia, you begin to understand the secret of the pacifying Russian countryside.

It is in the churches. They trip up the slopes, ascend the high hills, come down to the broad rivers like princesses in white and red; they lift their bell-towers—graceful, shapely, all different—high over mundane timber and thatch; they nod to each other from afar; from villages that are cut off and invisible to each other, they soar to the same heaven. And wherever you wander in the fields or meadows, however far from habitation, you are never alone; from over the hayricks, the wall of trees, and even the curve of the earth's surface, the head of some bell-tower will beckon to you from Gorki Lovetskie, or from Lyubichi, or from Gavrilovskoye.

But when you get into the village, you find that not the living but the dead greeted you from afar. The crosses were knocked off the roof or twisted out of place long ago. The dome has been stripped, and there are gaping holes between its rusty ribs. Weeds grow on the roofs and in the cracks in the walls. Usually the graveyard has not been kept up, the crosses have been flattened and the graves churned. The murals over the altar have been washed by the rains of decades and obscene inscriptions scrawled over them.

On the porch there are barrels of lubricating oil and a tractor is turning towards them. Or else a lorry has backed into the church doorway to pick up some sacks. In one church there is the shudder of lathes. Another is locked up and silent. In another there are groups and clubs. *"Let Us Aim at High Milk Yields!" "A Poem About Peace." "A Heroic Deed."*

People were always selfish and often unkind. But the evening chimes used to ring out, floating over villages, fields and woods. Reminding men that they must abandon the trivial concerns of this world, and give time and thought to eternity. These chimes, which only one old tune keeps alive for us, raised people up and prevented them from sinking on all fours. . . .

In Russia in 1963, I saw enough that had been built "last year," "two years ago," or "five years ago" to accept the general view that life had improved considerably since Stalin's death. But the largest question on my mind was, Precisely what had been accomplished *before* 1953? Few would dispute any longer the somber human price paid for Lenin's and Stalin's harsh experiments and provocative foreign policies; 40 million Russians, at the very least, had perished unnaturally since 1917.

Many Westerners felt compelled to agree that this heavy price was paid for *something,* although it was never quite clear just what. There was a blurry image compromising neatly plotted "growth" curves, the Dnepropetrovsk hydropower station, the Moscow Subway, and Colonel Yuri Gagarin hurtling in space. Yet my own impression after seeing a good slice of Russia (including the new Volgograd hydroelectric station and the Volga-Don canal) was that the Russian people paid this price for less than nothing—nothing, that is, that could not have been accomplished with much less strain in half the time by any normal nontotalitarian government with a minimal respect for human dignity and economic realities.

The myth of Soviet "progress" was dependent, of course, on the legend of pre-Communist backwardness in Russia—a backwardness deliberately exaggerated by the Russian reformers of the time, as well as by the Communists later, to prove that the tsarist autocracy and the Russian "bourgeoisie" were *completely* incompetent. To be sure, the last tsar, Nicholas II, was probably the most dull-witted sovereign Russia had seen in more than a century, and his regime in its last years, dominated by the dissolute monk Rasputin, was (as, former Premier, Sergei Witte, put it) a "tangle of cowardice, blindness, craftiness and stupidity."

Nevertheless, after 1890 and particularly between 1908 and 1914, Russia made enormous economic strides. In 1914, Russia was already the world's fifth leading industrial power. It led the world in oil production, was second only to the U.S. in railroad mileage, was fourth in production of pig iron and cotton textiles. Coal, iron, and steel output had quadrupled since 1890. Lumber exports had increased twelvefold in a decade. Three-fourths of the army recruits in 1914 were literate, and universal primary education seemed attainable by 1922. The real purchasing power of the Russian worker in 1914 was only half that of the German worker, only a fourth that of the American worker—but the gap had been narrowing.

Russia had been nearly three decades behind the United States in launching industrialization, but the United States itself had been sixty years behind Britain and caught up in half a century. By this standard, Russia with its great natural resources (and the technical advantages of late starters) should have caught up. Instead, Russia had become an awesome military power, but its people remained poor by almost any other standard.

Despite the ambitious promises of the 1961 Communist party program, I met no ordinary Russian during my journey who professed to believe that the Soviet Union, under its current system, could aspire to Western levels of output or income in the foreseeable future. The Russians I met did not seem at all impressed by the official Soviet growth statistics which Western analysts felt compelled to take seriously. The Russians, after all, could make the proper allowances from life experience for wretched quality, lack of maintenance, unused capacity, distribution bottlenecks, a ridiculous price system, padded employment rolls, and the millions of man-hours of human effort wasted in the travail of eking out a daily existence.

There was little cheer in high Soviet output of coal and steel, when the rest of the world was moving into light metals and plastics; little comfort in industrial growth statistics, when the developed world was expanding its services (and paying farmers to restrict surpluses).

One of the principal bases of Khrushchev's support had been

the general conviction that life for the average Soviet citizen was gradually improving. Largely, this conviction stemmed from the end of the Stalin terror, the relaxation in the arts, the attempts at "coexistence" with the West. But there had also been a sense of steadily rising living standards for nearly a decade after Stalin's death. The difficulties which remained could still, in large measure, be blamed on Stalin or on the war.

However, the sense of steady economic improvement had already been shaken by the price increases of June 1962. The harvest of 1963 was an even greater shock, and "patriotic" voices were soon raised to declare that even Stalin had never stooped so low as to buy grain in the West. I heard such opinions from several middle-aged men during my journey. More significantly, an experienced French colleague who revisited Moscow later that winter heard similar grumbling from Communist party insiders who, only two years earlier, had been singing Khrushchev's praises. Indeed, by November 1963, Khrushchev's fertilizer plan was being criticized in the party press, and by the end of the year Soviet Army leaders were openly resisting the cuts in the military budget through which he hoped to finance agricultural improvement.

The economic hopes that Khrushchev had aroused were being cruelly disappointed. The spiritual vacuum, engendered by the combination of Stalinism and partial de-Stalinization, remained. A philosophy professor whom I met in Vilnius, Lithuania, seemed to be expressing a more general anguish. "One must have a world view," he insisted. "If Marxism-Leninism is false, must we believe in God again?"

To secular Westerners like myself, it seemed that the only way out of this void lay in more thorough reform, broader opening to the diversity of the modern world. Among veteran Communists, however, there were complaints about the "disorder" and "confusion" which Khrushchev's innovations had already introduced, about the doubts which he had permitted to be sown among the Party faithful.

On November 29, 1963, one week after the assassination of President Kennedy in Dallas, Texas, Khrushchev dispatched a letter to Peking, seeking a truce with the Chinese Communists.

C H A P T E R   8

Balkan Mystery

On Christmas Eve 1963, the Orient Express was six hours late. Heavy snows were falling throughout Central Europe and the Balkans. The train had left its dining car somewhere in southern Austria, and by the time it reached Belgrade, on route to Sofia and Istanbul, the lights and heat were out in half the sleeping cars. Angry porters cursed the Belgrade stationmaster for having let the electrician go home before the train's arrival. They showed us to our berths with candles, and asked why on such an awful night four Westerners with typewriters would want to go to Sofia.

We were going on a tip, or perhaps it was an invitation. Three days before, a Western press agency in Belgrade had received a call from its man in Sofia, a quiet little Bulgarian who rarely did anything more politically adventurous than report the football scores. "You have heard about the spy trial?" he asked. No, not yet. "Well, it will be on the wire in a few hours. It will be worth your while to come here. It should be interesting."

A few hours later, the wire reported that a high Bulgarian diplomat would be tried for espionage and treason on December 26. The man's name was Ivan-Asen Khristov Georgiev. He was fifty-six years old, and for five years had served as counselor of the Bulgarian permanent mission to the United Nations. According to the wire report from Sofia, he had entered the service of the U.S. Central Intelligence Agency in November 1956, had received more than $200,000 for the support of his "ten mistresses," and

151

had been recruited for the C.I.A. by a distinguished American scholar—Professor Cyril E. Black, chairman of the Slavics Department at Princeton University.

Professor Black's name aroused attention because only three months earlier, another noted American scholar, Professor Frederick C. Barghoorn of Yale University, had been detained by the KGB in Russia. President Kennedy had intervened publicly to compel his release. Attacks on such scholars, widely respected for their activities in cultural exchange, hardly seemed a logical way of advancing the East-West dialogue to which Khrushchev appeared to have committed himself.

Yet, it seemed to be developing into quite a year for spy trials. In May 1963, a Soviet military intelligence officer, Colonel Oleg Penkovsky, had been tried in Moscow as a C.I.A. agent and shot. Various Soviet officers and officials had been disgraced as a result. Then there had been lesser trials of alleged Western agents in Poland and East Germany.

The Penkovsky trial, moreover, appeared to have marked a new phase in the long, tortured history of Communist trials. For few observers doubted, after the trial was over, that Penkovsky had been actually guilty of the acts of which he was accused— and that was a great difference.

In Stalin's Moscow Trials of the 1930s, Old Bolsheviks had been condemned as Nazi and Japanese agents, saboteurs, poisoners, and the like, when, plainly, their only real crime had been to disagree with Stalin. In Eastern Europe after the war, the Communists had staged great show trials of non-Communist political leaders, once again concocting hysterical accusations as a means of discrediting political opponents. Then, in Stalin's last years, Hungarian, Czech, Slovak, Bulgarian, and other East European Communists had suffered the same fate as the Old Bolsheviks in Moscow in the 1930s. They had been framed as "imperialist," "Titoist," or "Zionist" agents, forced by torture to "confess" to incredible plots, simply because the paranoid Stalin suspected them of having independent ideas.

The major defendants, however, had gone to their deaths devout Communists; and many of those who had escaped the death sentence emerged from prison to prove anew their devotion to the party and the Kremlin, notably Gomulka and Kadar. Since 1956, Khrushchev had been "rehabilitating" the Communist honor of the victims of the postwar trials, and of many of the prewar victims as well. The old type of Stalinist trial—in which, for example, a Jewish Communist would be labeled a Gestapo agent—seemed a thing of the past.

Colonel Penkovsky, on the other hand, represented a new phenomenon. Here was, in fact, a high Soviet Communist official who had not merely doubted, or criticized, the wisdom of Kremlin policies but had deliberately risked his life to collaborate with Western intelligence in active efforts to undermine, defeat, and if possible destroy the Soviet system. Serving in one of the most secret and security-conscious Soviet agencies, he had for years consciously betrayed his masters to the "imperialist" foe—and, worse yet, done so out of a sense of patriotic duty.

The questions raised by the Penkovsky trial were, indeed, disturbing. Was the turncoat colonel an isolated case, or were there perhaps other apparently loyal Communist officials driven by the same desperation to betray the cause? Furthermore, would East-West contact and parting of the Iron Curtain lead, as Khrushchev believed, to greater loyalty to Communism—or would it tend to create new Penkovskys?

Once the Penkovsky affair had set off a wave of prosecutions in Eastern Europe, it seemed only natural that the Bulgarians would get into the act sooner or later, for at least two reasons.

First, the Bulgarians were the most devoted of all the Communist-ruled nations to the Russians. Their language was closest to Russian. Tsarist armies had freed them from the Turks. They had fought in both world wars, to be sure, on the side of the Germans—but, because of the special circumstances of their involvement, that had little to do with Russia. The Bulgarians' presence on the losing side of both world wars could be traced to their defeat in the second Balkan war (1913), in which the Serbs and Greeks had won most of Macedonia. Because the Serbs and Greeks were on the Allied side, the Bulgarians joined the Germans in the hope of winning Macedonia. Despite that, in World War II they had never declared war on the Soviet Union.

The Macedonian question had poisoned Bulgarian politics ever since 1913. Immediately after World War I, their popular Agrarian leader Alexander Stambulisky had sought reconciliation with Belgrade. But Stambulisky had been assassinated in 1922, and from then on reactionary officers and the so-called IMRO, a Macedonian terrorist organization, had dominated Bulgarian life down through World War II.

Immediately after the war, the Bulgarian Communist leader, Georgi Dimitrov, had, like Stambulisky, sought reconciliation with Yugoslavia, now ruled by Marshal Tito. But Dimitrov died mysteriously soon after Stalin's conflict with Tito and his successors again began claiming Macedonia and instantly echoed every Soviet initiative in the hope of winning Russian backing for their claim. The Kremlin encouraged the claim whenever it sought to put pressure on Tito.

In addition to their devotion to the Russians, the Bulgarian Communists had long been addicted to show trials, first of non-Communists, then of their fellow Communists. (One of the early trials inspired Eric Ambler's 1951 thriller *Judgment on Delchev.*)

The most dramatic of the trials was that of Traicho Kostov, who had been leader of the underground Communist resistance during the war. In 1949, he appeared in the dock in the first of the East European trials of alleged "Titoist" agents. The brave Kostov, although he had made a "full confession" under torture, repudiated it in open court. One of Kostov's closest associates, Anton Yugov, who had been interior minister during the Communist seizure of power, somehow had survived and even became prime minister. But Yugov had suddenly been removed in a mysterious coup in November 1962, just after Khrushchev's defeat in the Cuban missile crisis.

Thus, thirteen months afterward, the trial of Ivan-Asen Georgiev appeared to promise all sorts of potential clues not only toward the future of Bulgaria's politicians but toward the state of mind of the Russian leaders on whom they were so dependent.

The Sofia morning papers provided the following portrait of Asen Georgiev: he was born in Sofia in 1907, joined the underground Communist movement before he was twenty-one, studied law at the Sorbonne from 1928 to 1931, completed his law studies in Sofia and practiced law there until September 9, 1944. On that day, the day the Soviet armies entered Bulgaria, Georgiev became secretary general of the Interior Ministry—that is, chief of staff of the political police—under none less than Anton Yugov. In other words, Georgiev was obviously a rather high Communist trusted by the Soviet MVD, and not a career diplomat.

In 1946, Georgiev was posted as counselor to the Bulgarian Legation in Paris. The indictment spoke of various contacts with the French Socialist Léon Blum. Late in 1950, however, Georgiev and a Legation colleague, Rosa Aronova, were recalled from Paris. For five years, Georgiev taught the history of the state at the Sofia University Law School, with the rank of docent.

Georgiev was nominated counselor at the U.N. in October 1956, and arrived in New York on November 3. From September 1960, he also represented Bulgaria in financial claims negotiations with the United States. After his recall from New York in December 1961, he took part in United Nations meetings in Europe and at an international conference of astronautical organizations held at Varna, on the Bulgarian Black Sea Coast. The Varna meeting established an International Institute of Space Law, and Georgiev was chosen president of this East-West organization. He traveled widely in this capacity before his arrest on September 8, 1963.

The newspaper summary of the indictment charged Georgiev on four counts: He had divulged classified information concerning the Bulgarian U.N. mission, the Foreign Ministry, and "other state institutions;" as counselor to the U.N. Mission, he used his position to the detriment of Bulgaria "and other socialist states;" he betrayed the Bulgarian position in the financial talks with the U.S.; and he divulged information on internal political and economic conditions in Bulgaria. The prisoner had made a full confession and the state would ask the death penalty.

Wandering around Sofia that day, we found several of the trial exhibits in a propaganda window which the Bulgarian authorities maintain next door to the American Legation. A short-wave radio, tape recorder, microphone, and documents were displayed to prove Georgiev "an enemy of the people." Elsewhere, on Russky Boulevard, we found other propaganda windows filled with anti-American posters and cartoons from the more virulent Soviet, East German, and North Vietnamese papers. In the National Museum, we saw great placards and maps recalling the "historic" frontiers of medieval Bulgaria, including all of Yugoslav Macedonia and substantial portions of Albania and Greece. On the main square, there was a monument to Russia's Tsar Alexander II, the "Tsar-Liberator." ("Not because he emancipated the Russian serfs," it was explained, "but because the Russian Army liberated Bulgaria from the Turks in 1877.") Nearby, there was the famous Alexander Nevsky Cathedral—built to honor the Russian prince who defeated the Teutonic knights.

The Palace of Justice was the largest building in Sofia, with 640 rooms and 25 courtrooms. The largest courtroom had been taken to try Asen Georgiev, and it was crowded with movie and television cameras, spotlights, and four large klieg lights. Before long, we realized that the cameramen were working from a scenario; their lights invariably went on a minute or so before the appearance of a new witness or the introduction into evidence of some new tape recorder, invisible ink, or some other "spy" paraphernalia.*

Most of the questions at the trial were posed by the chief judge, Angel Velev, or the prosecutor, Ivan Vachkov. The two other judges and three lay jurors were silent. The four defense attorneys, who conceded Georgiev's guilt from the outset, asked perhaps a dozen questions in all.

Judge Velev began by reading the detailed indictment, which traced Georgiev's contacts with American intelligence to Paris in the winter of 1949–50, where he met a Bulgarian-born French banker, Angel Kuyumdzhisky. In October 1956, when Georgiev was on route to the United Nations, he met Kuyumdzhisky again in Paris and asked to be placed in contact with the C.I.A.

On November 3, 1956, Georgiev arrived at Idlewild Airport in New York. In the glass-enclosed immigration booth, he was greeted by a man who said "I'm a friend of Angel's," introduced himself as "George Anderson," and arranged to meet Georgiev next day in Central Park. At the meeting in the park, according

---

* The local correspondent of Tass, the Soviet news agency, was even better briefed. She phoned in a story one morning describing testimony which was not even foreshadowed until much later that afternoon. We had to rely mainly on official translators, who were quick with denunciations of "American imperialism" but frequently censored or garbled factual details.

to the indictment, "Anderson revealed to Georgiev that his real name is Cyril Black, and that he is the son of the former director of the American College in Sofia, Floyd Black." (From Princeton, Professor Black categorically denied any connection with the Georgiev case.)

According to the indictment, Georgiev and "Anderson" met frequently between November 1956 and September 1957 at a series of New York hotels. Georgiev received the cover name "Georges Duval" and the C.I.A. phone number (National 8–0972) with instructions to "ask for Salance." From September 1957 to October 1958, Georgiev and Anderson continued their meetings in an apartment at 44 East End Avenue. In the course of this year, the microbiologist Tonka Karabashova, who was allegedly Georgiev's mistress, was brought to the United States three times to visit him. In August 1958, Rosa Aronova was also brought to the United States for the first of three visits.

In October 1958, Georgiev broke off his connections with the C.I.A. after a quarrel with Anderson. However, in May 1959, Georgiev wrote a personal letter to Allen Dulles, the director of the C.I.A. The letter was signed "Georges Duval," reviewed the quarrel with Anderson, and offered Georgiev's services anew to the intelligence agency.

Between March 1960 and December 1961, Georgiev met continuously with Bonnard, identified as a higher C.I.A. official— first at the Sheraton Hotel, then at an apartment at "338" East 77th Street.* At the last meeting in the 77th Street apartment, Bonnard allegedly gave Georgiev two sheets of white, chemically treated paper suitable for secret messages, as well as a bottle of developing fluid.

During 1962 and 1963, Georgiev's space-law activities allegedly enabled him to meet Anderson, Jackson, Salance, and other C.I.A. agents abroad. He met with Anderson in Geneva in May 1962, and in March and again in April 1963. (Professor Black said that his Princeton colleagues could easily confirm his presence on the university campus at those times.)

At the March 1963 meeting, in an apartment near the Swiss

---

* After the *New York Times* disclosed that there was no such address, because numbers 336 and 340 were adjacent, Bulgarian television presented a film clip of Georgiev saying that he may have mistaken the number.

Legation in Paris, Anderson and an American cryptographic expert allegedly gave Georgiev a decoding block and a conversion table, as well as earphones for his Hamarlund SF-600 radio receiver. On the radio, Georgiev was to receive secret coded radiograms from the "U.S. spy center in Greece" (apparently, the powerful Sixth Fleet transmitter on Mount Imetos near Athens).

The secret writing paper, code blocks, and clandestine radiograms were heady, exciting details; but it was noteworthy, even before the actual testimony began, that all of this equipment only entered Georgiev's life after December 1961 (that is, more than five years after Georgiev was said to have begun working with American intelligence).

Concluding the indictment, Judge Velev read the four counts which had been published and then added a significant charge which had not appeared in the press: namely, that Georgiev had revealed secret information "on the differences between the Communist party of the Soviet Union and the Communist party of China."

Immediately afterward, Georgiev himself took the stand to read his confession. Even with the pallor of a hundred days of prison on him, he radiated a definite magnetism. Of medium height and stocky build, he had the strut of a proud rooster, rugged shoulders, close-cropped gray hair, a firm jaw and arresting blue-gray eyes.

Georgiev was quick to disclose that he was no mere common spy. He was, for example, the translator into Bulgarian of Hegel's *Philosophy of Law* and had himself written seven books, including studies of ancient Sparta and wartime France. He seemed a fascinating representative of a certain type of Balkan Communist: the Westernized intellectual of comfortable middle-class background who, under the prewar dictatorship, had chosen the life of Communist conspiracy and revolution and emerged from World War II high in the new elite.*

* There were many famous Communists of this type, among them Enver Hoxha in Albania, Lucretiu Patrascanu and Ion Gheorghe Maurer in Rumania, Vladimir Bakaric and Koca Popovic in Yugoslavia. Patrascanu, Maurer, and Bakaric had been lawyers, like Georgiev. Patrascanu, the most brilliant, was arrested in 1948 as a potential Rumanian Tito and executed in 1954. Maurer and Bakaric, both subtle as well as witty men, discreetly influenced their countries' evolution from within, largely from behind the scenes.

Yugoslav Partisan leaders, 1943 (l. to r.): Rankovic (deposed, 1966),
Djilas (turned democrat, 1954), Tito, Zujovic (supported Stalin, 1948),
Hebrang (died mysteriously, 1948), Pijade (died naturally, 1957),
Kardclj (survives)

Soviet leaders, 1958: Khrushchev, Suslov, Brezhnev

Andrei Voznesensky   Alexander Solzhenitsyn

Tito welcomes Khrushchev to Belgrade, August 20, 1963

"Uncle Asen" Georgiev

Walter Ulbricht (above) and the traditional welcome extended visitors to his "DDR" at Berlin

Rumania's strong man, Nicolae
Ceausescu (above) and diplomatic charmers, Ion Gheorghe
Maurer and Corneliu Manescu
(right)

Janos Kadar

Wladyslaw Gomulka

Pleading guilty, Georgiev at once declared that he had made a full confession at the moment of his arrest "*in the Hotel Metropol in Moscow.*" This was the first indication that he had not been arrested in Bulgaria. He then described his meetings with Angel Kuyumdzhisky, who early in 1950 had warned him against returning to Bulgaria in the atmosphere of terror surrounding the fall of Traicho Kostov. "I was afraid because I was sure Kostov was not guilty," Georgiev said. "I was worried because I had very many people against me. I lived in fear. My hair turned gray in that period."

When Georgiev turned to his fateful meeting on a Central Park bench with "George Anderson," he stressed the date—Sunday, November 4, 1956—reminding us that it was the day the Soviet Army had intervened to crush the Hungarian Revolution. Anderson's face "seemed familiar," Georgiev said, "from my days as a Communist party secretary and my work in the Interior Ministry." This was the first suggestion that Georgiev had been a Communist party functionary as well as a security official.

The defendant said that he maintained contact with Anderson until the fall of 1958. "*Later I learned* that he was Cyril Black. . . ." This contradicted the indictment, which claimed he learned it on the Central Park bench. It was also an incredibly weak identification of Professor Black as a spy.*

Georgiev said he was disappointed because the agents were less interested in political intelligence than in such trivial details as his opinion of "some petty Bulgarians who had crossed the border." What he had really wanted from the Americans was aid in financing an international institute of Hegel studies, open to both Eastern and Western scholars. Anderson was favorable to Georgiev's proposal, but "the others" vetoed the idea.

Georgiev also disclosed that his letter to Allen Dulles began as a condolence message on the death of the latter's brother, John Foster Dulles. He then described how he had reestablished contact in March 1960 with Bonnard, who was "intelligent, well-educated" and "understood my ideas."

The next morning, the court pressed Georgiev for an identifi-

* The Black family had been well known in prewar Sofia. Black himself had been in Bulgaria in 1945 investigating Communist police pressures at the very time that Georgiev was secretary general of the Interior Ministry.

cation of Professor Black. Asked to describe "George Anderson," he replied that Anderson spoke Bulgarian well, was about fifty years old, was restrained and talked very little. Anderson struck Georgiev as "narrow-minded" in comparison with Bonnard. "No matter how they are educated," Georgiev said, "when it comes to really understanding, these people are formalistic idiots. . . ."

For the third time now, Georgiev was asked how he knew that Anderson was really Black. This time his reply was, "I remember that *Black told me* that his father was the director of a college." From a trained attorney and professor of law, this statement was also most unsatisfactory. (Georgiev might have met the real Professor Black, as Black, in the course of his U.N. activities.)

The court turned back to Georgiev's women and finances. Why had the C.I.A. paid for Mrs. Karabashova's three trips from Paris to New York; why had she come? "She had gone to Paris at my personal expense. I decided to ask American intelligence to bring her to the United States *in order that she could see it. . . .*" This seemed rather implausible. Why did the C.I.A. satisfy such requests? "They knew I was an important political figure. I could get whatever I wanted because I had joined them at the time of the Hungarian events."

As for Rosa Aronova, she had been "wrongly accused of spying." He felt a definite "moral obligation" to her. Georgiev said that he had given 4,000 Bulgarian leva to Mrs. Evgenia Delcheva, who "was also my mistress," to arrange for the care of his sick mother. But he insisted that he had not collaborated with the C.I.A. for financial gain: "I didn't go for money. . . . I had money and I have money. The Americans never supported *me.*"

Georgiev vigorously denied that his work in space law was connected with the C.I.A., and disclosed that he had been nominated to the presidency of the space-law institute "by *Soviet* scientists."

This was a provocative disclosure, indeed. The late Colonel Penkovsky had worked with a Soviet scientific-research committee which was largely a front for Russian military intelligence. Might Georgiev have been a double agent, who had first contacted the C.I.A. as part of some Bulgarian or (more likely) Soviet intelligence operation? He had been secretary general of the Interior

Ministry when the Soviet Army was still occupying the country. His posts as counselor in Paris and at the U.N. were traditional intelligence slots. He had been arrested in Moscow just a few blocks from the main headquarters of the KGB. These were intriguing leads, but the court failed to follow them.

Prosecutor Vachkov asked Georgiev about his confession: how had the security police treated him, had he confessed voluntarily? Georgiev's response was one of the high points of the tiral:

> Before, I had the idea that the methods of security would be the same as in 1950. I thought that after my arrest I would be thrown into a dungeon and tortured, that I would have to sign reports denouncing my relatives and friends, etc. . . . I still had this idea when I was arrested in 1963.
>
> However, when I was taken to prison, I was given a room five by six meters (roughly 16 x 19 feet) with two big windows, a very sunny room. I had very friendly relations with the other prisoner in the room; we discussed Marxist problems and played chess. . . . The living conditions were better than those I had at home.
>
> Not only the material conditions were excellent, but I was treated by the investigators with such humanism! We had many really interesting conversations. The chief investigator had a very intelligent mind and really humane attitude. . . .
>
> Because of the high intellectual standards of the state security service—probably the highest of any in the entire world—I decided to confess everything. Everything!

This statement could only be interpreted as deliberate irony, a *reductio ad absurdum* intended to discredit the entire proceeding. Bulgarian prisons were notorious, and the Bulgarian police was hardly known, even by Balkan standards, for its intellectual level.

After Georgiev's paean to police "humanism," the court adjourned, to reconvene in closed session later that afternoon, in open session the next morning. The closed session, we were told, was devoted to Georgiev's account of the various "secrets" he had divulged.

The morning session on December 28 was not far advanced when Georgiev was asked the reasons for his conduct. "Political instability and ideological confusion played a great role," he said.

After the trial of Kostov, he had developed certain ideas about social classes in Communist countries:

> I came to believe that there was a definite type of class struggle in the socialist countries. . . . On the one hand, there were the masses of manual workers in the factories and fields, who . . . could not reflect on or participate in social life. On the other hand there was the class of intellectual, political workers who guide, direct and manage political life. . . . Their living conditions cannot even be compared with those of the workers. . . . Thus, despite common ownership of the means of production, I thought that society had been divided into two such antagonistic classes. . . .

Judge Velev asked whether Georgiev had been influenced by Milovan Djilas's book, *The New Class* (1957). "Yes, I read the book later and was impressed by his theories . . . [but] I had these ideas before his book was published, probably before it was even written. . . ."

In 1962 and 1963, when he had returned to Bulgaria, Georgiev said, he had continued to work for the C.I.A. "But the investigators know very well that I hesitated about my collaboration with the Americans as far back as 1961. . . . I was afraid, however, of being denounced, so I continued to collaborate."

In Vienna a few months earlier, Georgiev had remarked that he was sure he would be arrested upon his return to Bulgaria. He had come back "because I couldn't stay away from my country, my people and my culture." A few minutes later, Georgiev left the stand.

The first and most important witness was Mrs. Tonka Ivanova Karabashova, a short, stooped, bespectacled woman of fifty-six with the air of a longtime spinster. She had known Georgiev since 1928; her husband had been a fellow student of Georgiev's. The two families had become neighbors after Georgiev's return from Paris in 1950.

When, the judge asked, did you and Georgiev begin having sexual relations? In 1955, Mrs. Karabashova replied. All those who saw her found it difficult to believe that the handsome, worldly, confident Georgiev—after knowing this dry, plain woman for twenty-seven years—would make her his mistress at the age of forty-eight. Yet Mrs. Karabashova's testimony to Georgiev's relations with the C.I.A. proved to be the only direct testimony to such relations apart from his own ambiguous confession.

Mrs. Karabashova was asked how she had come to visit New York as a guest of the C.I.A. She had come to Paris in 1957 to attend a medical course—first staying at a hotel, later sharing an apartment with a young lady named Julia Ivanova. A French microbiologist urged her to seek a grant from the World Health Organization.

Georgiev, who was begging her to come to New York, told her to contact Dr. Lora Bakalova, another Buglarian professor then in Paris. Mrs. Bakalova asked her for six photographs and said everything would be arranged. Ultimately, "a big, gray-haired fellow about forty" met Mrs. Karabashova, took her Bulgarian passport, and gave her a West German passport with an American immigration visa in the name of Margaret Anna Sadler, nurse.

In New York on her first visit, Mrs. Karabashova was escorted by a "charming" lady named Mary Graine. In Washington, Mary introduced her charge to George Anderson. Mrs. Karabashova identified Anderson in 1957 as a "man of about fifty with a moustache." (Professor Black was then forty-two and clean-shaven.) Anderson, who referred to Georgiev as "Uncle Asen," accompanied Mrs. Karabashova back to Paris, returned her original passport, and took the false one. Her two other visits took place under similar conditions.

Mrs. Karabashova was granted a World Health Organization fellowship in the fall of 1958. She received 100,000 old francs monthly for eight months from a WHO official named Matery— who, she said, was also a C.I.A. agent. Mrs. Karabashova finally returned to Bulgaria after her relationship with Georgiev had deteriorated.

"Am I free?" asked Mrs. Karabashova when there were no more questions. The audience snickered. Judge Velev, smiling ironically, nodded. She walked briskly out of the courtroom, looking very much like a woman who had swallowed a bushel of locusts. But in describing her encounters with Anderson, she had not identified him as Professor Black.

Julia Ivanova, a tall, slim young blonde with a beehive hairdo, then testified that Georgiev had paid Mrs. Karabashova's medical bills in Paris. When Mrs. Karabashova had been away from Paris, Miss Ivanova had thought she was in a rest home. Miss Ivanova, who was now working in the Bulgarian Legation in Algiers, provided the only corroboration of the Karabashova story.

Evgeny Kamenov, the next witness, had known Georgiev since law-school days. As minister to Paris and deputy foreign minister, Kamenov had also known Georgiev as a diplomat.

What was Kamenov's estimate of Georgiev? "In the Interior Ministry, he was very active. But the opinion of his colleagues was not so high because he was unfocused, disorganized in his work. . . . Otherwise, we considered him a good Communist." In the United Nations, Georgiev was "one of the good, qualified members of the delegation . . . but was not as well-organized as he had been before. He wrote very long speeches, which then had to be cut down." As an academic, according to Kamenov, Georgiev displayed "erudition and a great knowledge of Marxist-Leninist science. Nevertheless, he did not produce results. Not even a single article of his was published in the newspapers."

The Kamenov testimony was not merely confused but surprising, for his principal complaint against Georgiev was that he was disorganized. Hardly a capital crime. And Kamenov was a witness for the prosecution.

Kiril Shterev, a rather aggressive young diplomat, testified that when Georgiev arrived at the U.N. in 1956, he had been "impressed by his culture, good manners and command of French." However, Georgiev "ignored the work of the mission" although "he fulfilled his own tasks." As for Georgiev's speeches at the U.N., Shterev said they were "very long and 'more Catholic than the Pope,' . . . very sectarian."

Evgenia Alexandrova Delcheva, who had been named in Georgiev's confession as one of his "mistresses," was a slight, birdlike creature of forty-three who trembled visibly at several points in her testimony. She had known Georgiev since 1950, when her husband had worked in the Paris Legation. But, asked whether she had ever had sexual relations with Georgiev, she replied, "We had no personal relations whatever." The question was restated.

Again Mrs. Delcheva nodded her head negatively and in a near-whisper repeated "No . . . no . . . no."

Tinka Stoicheva Velkova, a plump plain woman in her fifties, had worked as a housekeeper for Georgiev's father and known the defendant since 1938.

"Did you have any personal relations?" she was asked.

"No, not really. Though I did like him as a man."

Had they had sexual relations?

"Some, around 1946."

Mrs. Velkova's testimony, while amusing, seemed irrelevant to the accusations against Georgiev. The later prosecution witnesses seemed even less relevant, although they included many prominent figures in Bulgarian life.

Ljuben Vasiliev, who had also known Georgiev since university days and was now director of the law faculty, described how the two men had quarreled over a book written by a Bulgarian lawyer. Georgiev had privately criticized the book, but had praised it in the press. Vasiliev asked, "How is it possible for you to say one thing and write another?" Georgiev replied: "You're pretty stupid if you don't understand a basic political principle: the unity of opposites."

The only important witness, called by the defense, was Dr. Lora Bakalova, a heavy-set gray-haired woman of fifty-four. She should have been a key witness. It was she who was alleged to have taken the six passport photos from Mrs. Karabashova and arranged the latter's first visit to the United States. She was not, however, asked about any of this—nor even whether she had ever met Julia Ivanova, as that young lady had testified. Instead, Dr. Bakalova testified that Georgiev had been a prominent Communist since student days, a capable man, and "a good party member."

After Dr. Bakalova's testimony, Judge Velev announced that open sessions of the court would resume on Monday, December 30. However, after a recess, the court would resume in closed session to hear witnesses to the grave secrets disclosed by Georgiev. The secret testimony was never published although the prosecutor referred to it later.

Of the remaining witnesses whom the defense had announced

it would call in open session, five proved to be absent; the others were innocuous. Then came the turn of various groups of "experts," who testified about the spy paraphernalia allegedly found in Georgiev's apartment. They were not particularly impressive.*

Judge Velev then read depositions from witnesses who could not attend the trial. The only significant one was from Jordan Chubanov, who had succeeded Vutov as chief of the U.N. mission in 1959 and had worked with Georgiev until January 1962. Chubanov described Georgiev as a man "widely informed on world events," but who often neglected his duties. However, Georgiev's only contacts with Americans of which he, Chubanov, was aware were official contacts.

Thus, as prosecutor Vachkov prepared to sum up, there had been much testimony, some of it contradictory, on Georgiev's financial and sexual activities; considerable evidence that he had had access to codes and secret information; much talk about the spy equipment he had received in the past year, and about letters he had asked friends to mail in the West. However, on the crucial theme of Georgiev's relations with the C.I.A. and "George Anderson," there was only Georgiev's confession and the tale told by Mrs. Karabashova.

Prosecutor Vachkov attempted to fill in the gaps, as well as to define the political purposes of the trial. A tall, handsome, sunburned man of about fifty with thick, marcelled-gray hair, the careful, well-groomed prosecutor somewhat resembled Alexander Rankovic, the master of the Yugoslav UDBA. His speech was *suaviter in modo, fortiter in re.*

The trial, he said, was an event of "great political importance." The reactionary, aggressive imperialist circles headed by the United States were employing espionage and diversion as state policy. American imperialism was "the most dangerous enemy of

---

* One group of experts described a broadcast from the "spy center" on September 20, 1963 (twelve days after Georgiev's arrest) and played an alleged tape of this broadcast. The tape began with rather indistinct bars from the last movement of Schubert's *Unfinished Symphony.* (According to the indictment, which the experts seemed to have forgotten, this was the signal that the message was to be disregarded.) The music cut off in midpassage and a voice repeated monosyllables and numbers. The tone of the tape differed considerably between the music and the alleged "message." It sounded very much as though they had been crudely spliced together, a most unconvincing performance.

the peoples of the world." Even fascism was "no worse."

Bulgaria and the other Communist countries, "headed by the Soviet Union," were working for peace and doing their best to enlarge economic and cultural relations with "other" countries. But the Penkovsky trial in the Soviet Union, the exposure of "spies masquerading as tourists" in Moscow and Kiev, the recent spy trials in Poland and East Germany all showed—as did this trial—that the imperialists were using increased cultural and scientific exchange to send agents into the Communist world. A brochure distributed in West Germany advised tourists "to spread decadence among our people." In another brochure, tourists were advised to make contact with youth and even give presents to pretty girls. Great sums were being devoted to radio propaganda (which was still being jammed in Bulgaria, although jamming had ceased in Russia and Rumania that summer).

The Bulgarian people's wrath against the traitor Georgiev was great. "True to his hypocritical nature, he made a comic farce of his confession." He tried to prove that, while serving the C.I.A., he also upheld Bulgarian interests. Yet the facts showed that "spying is a typical feature of his character." Georgiev "did not understand the attitude of the investigators or the attitude of the court towards him . . . but proved his own hypocrisy and two-facedness." Georgiev's letter to Allen Dulles (which was never produced) showed that he had not stopped spying in the summer of 1959. "Allen Dulles later used the arguments furnished by Georgiev's letter, which expressed his political ideas, in a speech to businessmen."

Now, at last, the prosecutor came to what seemed the heart of the case. In 1960, he said, Georgiev had informed Bonnard about various proposals to be made by the Communist countries. During the 15th session of the General Assembly, Georgiev told the Americans in advance of the proposals, opinions and decisions taken by the *Soviet* delegation. . . ." This was the session at which Khrushchev had appeared in person to attack Dag Hammarskjold, preaching "general and complete disarmament," and banging his shoe.

In the summer of 1960, Georgiev also "gave information about the secret discussions at a meeting of very important socialist leaders . . ." This was clearly the Bucharest conference of June 1960, at which Khrushchev attacked the Chinese but was compelled to retreat.

"In 1960, he gave information concerning the naval base of a friendly socialist country. . . ." This was the departure of Soviet submarines from the Albanian base at Valona in the wake of Enver Hoxha's break with Khrushchev.

In 1961, Foreign Minister Karlo Lukanov told Georgiev "to become acquainted with the discussions going on" between Moscow and Peking. "He read very confidential materials, taking notes even though the material was secret. He transmitted these notes to the Americans . . ."

Before briefly discussing the Karabashova episode, the prosecutor made a curious statement which he did not amplify. "Pressed by Lukanov, Chubanov and Vutov," said the prosecutor, "Georgiev admitted committing treason and espionage. . . ." He did not say when this admission took place, but the impression given was that it had been sometime in 1961.

Georgiev "gave information which was directed against *all* the socialist countries. . . . Even during the crisis in the Caribbean, he did everything to help American intelligence." This was the first and only allegation that Georgiev had helped the C.I.A. in the Cuban missile crisis.

Georgiev's "debauchery and careerism have no equal," Vachkov concluded. The trial had shown that "the people must be more and more vigilant. . . . There is no place on earth for this spy and traitor!" With this call for Georgiev's death, the invited audience burst into frantic applause. Women smiled and laughed, television cameras whirred, klieg lights blinked on and off. The defendant sat impassive between two young armed militiamen.

Of the four defense lawyers, only the last made a serious argument. He noted, in a gingerly manner, that many of the secrets which Georgiev was supposed to have disclosed were not real secrets. The documents he had disclosed "concerning the Bucharest and Moscow conferences" of 1960 were "internal propaganda materials," and propaganda was not all that serious. In any case, the harm done by such disclosures was slight compared to his achievements; even the prosecutor had admitted that the financial talks with the United States had ended in Bulgaria's favor. Georgiev had rendered many signal services over the years; "I ask you to find within yourselves the strength not to condemn him to death." With this plea, the court was recessed to hear Georgiev's final statement in closed session. None of it was ever published.

Sentence was passed on the morning of December 31. Georgiev was condemned to death on two counts: (1) "between November 1956 and December 1961 . . . in the interests of the United States, he collected and delivered to United States intelligence organs . . . state secrets which he had learned in the course of his work"; and (2) "from November 1956 to December 1961 . . . as Counselor of the Bulgarian Mission to the United Nations, he intentionally carried out his duties in a manner detrimental to Bulgaria and other states. . . ."

The dates given in the verdict were surprising. Both the prosecutor and Georgiev's own confession claimed that he had actively worked for the C.I.A. until his arrest in September 1963. However, the verdict limited his treason to the period ending December 1961. The court thus ruled out Georgiev's work in space law, his alleged efforts during the Cuban crisis, the entire collection of espionage paraphernalia, coded messages from the "spy center in Greece," and all the "expert" testimony based on this hocus-pocus.

What, then, were Georgiev's real crimes? It was difficult to disentangle the reality from the confusing show in the courtroom.

For the "workers and peasants" in Bulgaria, the trial was clearly a warning to maintain "vigilance" toward every possible contact with the West. As a political morality play, the trial demonstrated how an intellectual started off by studying in the West, became exposed to "revisionist" ideas, and ended up in the most sordid espionage.*

For the Bulgarian authorities, the trial was surely a useful manifestation of solidarity with Soviet spy-hunters after the Pen-

---

* To heighten the effect of this lesson, a "spontaneous demonstration" was dispatched to the American Legation on the second day of the trial to break windows and overturn diplomats' cars. The police arrived on the scene a half hour late (although the main police station was two blocks away), but Bulgarian cameramen were there on time.

kovsky affair. Conceivably, Georgiev had been apprehended in the wake of KGB investigations following the Penkovsky scandal. Yet, if that were the case, it was difficult to understand why Georgiev's work in the space-law field (and thus, all the rigamarole of secret codes and radios, invisible ink and chemical paper) had been omitted from the final sentence. Had Georgiev been a conventional spy trafficking in military or scientific secrets, there would indeed have been little reason to discuss his "revisionist" ideas, his mistresses, and similar distractions. Moreover, had there been solid evidence of conventional espionage, it seemed improbable that so many witnesses would have appeared who either supported Georgiev's good character or, at the most, criticized him for being disorganized, arrogant, or verbose.

It was noteworthy that no further charges were ever pressed against Dr. Bakalova or the numerous other witnesses relatively friendly to Georgiev, including those in high positions who had ostensibly been responsible for his conduct. Nor did the trial prove to be (as some had expected it might be) the prelude to more dramatic action against the fallen Yugov and his followers.

Much in Georgiev's career, as well as his familiarity with codes and the equipment found in his home, suggested that his real status in Bulgarian diplomacy might have been that of a political intelligence agent—in which case he may have been contacting C.I.A. men in the manner traditional among rival intelligence services. Georgiev's links with the Russians, as disclosed at the trial, seemed suggestive. Soviet intelligence operations were traditionally "international." Moreover, the most important disclosures with which Georgiev was charged concerned the Russians and particularly the Sino-Soviet dispute: the background of the Bucharest and Moscow conferences of 1960, the withdrawal of Soviet submarines from Albania, Khrushchev's tactics at the United Nations that fall.

Georgiev may well have communicated such political intelligence to the C.I.A., directly or indirectly. However, might he not have been acting officially or semiofficially, on behalf of superiors interested in using the West to further their own aims? Nearly all the specific disclosures fell within the period between March 1960 and December 1961—a period of considerable instability marked by Khrushchev's increasing difficulties with the Chinese and with Kremlin critics as well.

There was ample precedent in Communist Europe for strategic "leaks" aimed at using the West to influence developments within the Soviet camp. Polish Communists in the spring of 1956 had given the C.I.A. the text of Khrushchev's famous "secret speech" denouncing Stalin. Later that year, Polish Central Committee members used Western journalists to spread such dramatic stories as the Soviet troop maneuvers allegedly aimed at intimidating Gomulka—accounts which were difficult to confirm from independent sources but which (repeated on Western radio broadcasts) helped create the image of Gomulka as a national hero.

In the Sino-Soviet dispute, Khrushchev supporters had often disclosed behind-the-scences "secrets" to the West in order to influence the struggle. Mikoyan communicated Soviet concern over China to trusted Western contacts early in 1959. At the Bucharest meeting in June 1960, the Khrushchev side of the dispute was leaked to Western journalists. In a struggle in which both Khrushchev and Mao since 1959 had been seeking to overthrow each other, the Khrushchev forces knew that, the more the issues in the dispute were publicized, the more difficult it would become for other Soviet leaders to compromise the dispute at Khrushchev's personal expense.

Asen Georgiev's principal disclosures seemed to be of just the kind that Khrushchev and his agents had been making—publicly and through neutral diplomats, through the Yugoslavs, through Western Communist parties. Furthermore, "when pressed by Lukanov, Chubanov and Vutov," Georgiev had "admitted his activities"; and, in Georgiev's own words, "the investigators knew that I hesitated about my collaboration with the Americans in December 1961." His subsequent conduct for more than a year and a half was not held treasonable.

Why, then, had Georgiev suddenly been arrested and placed on trial in the autumn of 1963? Conceivably, he had betrayed his sponsors to the Americans by going farther than his superiors had intended. However, it seemed equally likely that the entire line of activity in which Georgiev had been engaged—activity that had been approved at high levels before September

1963—had now suddenly been repudiated at those high levels.

During his visit to the United States in 1959, Khrushchev had jokingly suggested to Allen Dulles that both Washington and Moscow could save a lot of money by freely exchanging information and pooling their intelligence operations. "We are both paying the same spies anyhow," the Soviet leader scornfully remarked, indicating his own low opinion of the net political value of the huge, expensive, competing intelligence agencies. For several years before the fateful incident of May 1, 1960, Khrushchev had deliberately chosen to ignore American U-2 reconnaissance flights over the Soviet Union, in the interests of his larger efforts to alter the world political climate.

Khrushchev's casual attitude toward espionage operations seemed to have been justified by the C.I.A.'s misadventures at the Bay of Pigs and elsewhere, as well as by the general Western unreadiness to comprehend the reality of his sharpening struggle with China. Indeed, Soviet officials (as well as, perhaps, such intelligence operators as Georgiev) had been compelled to exert extreme indiscretion to persuade the skeptical West that Khrushchev and Mao had, indeed, quarreled seriously.

However, in the Cuban missile crisis of 1962, Khrushchev paid dearly for his casual attitude; he incurred this major political humiliation largely as a result of superior American intelligence. The U.S. superiority derived partly from the efforts of Colonel Oleg Penkovsky and perhaps (*who could be sure?*) other Soviet and East European officials whose loyalty to the Kremlin had never before been doubted. Certainly, after the Penkovsky affair, there was reason enough for the Kremlin to review all the contacts its agents had been having with the "enemy."

Penkovsky's chief contact had been a British traveler moving in and out of Eastern Europe, with thoroughly legitimate credentials as a businessman. What of the thousands of other contacts Communist agents and officials were having, all over the world, with Western diplomats, journalists, scholars, scientists, engineers, cultural figures? These, too, were now suspect—and, with them, Khrushchev's entire policy of expanding contact, symbolized by his own copious travels and loose talk.

To edgy Kremlin colleagues, raised in the Stalin tradition,

Khrushchev's policy had made few new Communists in the outside world, but had merely opened the door for the West to find
such allies as Penkovsky and Asen Georgiev. If such veteran
Communists, cleared for secret operations, were already vulnerable, what might a few more years of "de-Stalinization" and
"peaceful coexistence" bring?

Asen Georgiev had been a Communist since 1928, high in the
party, a privileged member of the "new class." Yet, despite Bulgaria's isolation from the West and traditional loyalty to Moscow,
despite all the purges and counterpurges in the Bulgarian party,
he had apparently chosen to play a most dangerous game which
he doubtless realized he could not survive. And, even after his
arrest, he had managed to discredit numerous details of his own
confession, to expound his heretical views, to inform the world of
his seizure in Moscow and his ties with "Soviet scientists."

On the other hand, however, if Georgiev had indeed been a
C.I.A. collaborator, why were there so many friendly witnesses,
including people in high authority? Why was the evidence presented at the trial so flimsy? Why were there no repercussions—
dismissals, purges, reorganizations—as there had been in the Penkovsky affair? Why, in short, with all the resources of the Bulgarian
state (including Soviet "advisers") at its disposal, had not the
prosecution been able to do better?

It had been a curious and perplexing trial indeed, and long
after Georgiev's execution was announced on January 5, 1964,
those of us who had attended it were still pondering over the
riddles the trial had posed. It was a strange performance no matter
how one guessed at the reality beneath it. Whether Georgiev
had actually been guilty as charged, whether his real "crimes"
had been different from those mentioned in court, whether he was
made a scapegoat for operations ordered by others—whichever
theory one chose, the case appeared to demonstrate a degree of
disarray and disaffection in high Communist circles which it
would have been difficult to imagine in sleepy, "loyal" Bulgaria.
The disaffection was to be dramatized in an abortive coup on
April 7, 1965, involving the commander of the Sofia military garrison, two other Bulgarian generals, and other high-ranking officers and security specialists. The plot was said to have been un-

covered by Soviet military intelligence, and Suslov himself came to Sofia to purge the Bulgarian security police afterward.

Yet, as both the Penkovsky and Georgiev trials showed, the disaffection was hardly confined to Bulgaria. To take but one example, what sort of men were the "Soviet scientists" who had nominated Georgiev to the presidency of the International Institute of Space Law in 1962? Were they actually scientists, or intelligence agents like Penkovsky? What were their real thoughts, and how far might they go in pursuing them? Such questions doubtless troubled Khrushchev and his colleagues more deeply than they disturbed the motley group of spectators who had watched the trial in Sofia. The answers to such larger questions may never be known.

However, many months later, at a social gathering, an American formerly connected with the C.I.A. took me aside to discuss the Georgiev case. "I just wanted to let you know," he said, "that I was with The Agency for ten years—and that he was one of our most interesting boys for a long, long time."

Why, then, had the Bulgarians been unable to prove it?

"They couldn't," was the reply, "but we could. Uncle Asen fooled them to the last."

CHAPTER 9

Goulash

When Khrushchev arrived in Budapest for a state visit on March 31, 1964, Hungarians were calling their country "the gayest barrack in the Communist camp." In deference to Khrushchev, who had stormed with rage when exposed to a Hollywood cancan in 1959, Budapest chorus girls remained partly clothed during the visit, while striptease artists took a holiday. Stolid Soviet visitors seemed nonetheless disconcerted by the Hungarians' taste for wine, women, and song, their mature sensuality, and mordant humor. There was no controlling the endless flow of political jokes:

What was the difference between capitalism and Communism, Hungarians asked. "Capitalism is the exploitation of man by his fellow man. Communism is exactly the opposite."

What were the terms of Karl Marx's will? "He left *The Communist Manifesto* to us, and *Das Kapital* to the West."

What would Hungary have, if not for its trade with the Comecon countries? "Everything."

How would encyclopedias of the year 2000 identify N. S. Khrushchev? "A minor literary critic in the Age of Mao Tse-tung."

Such bitter jests were as much in the national tradition as the throbbing songs of disappointed love played endlessly by violinists in candlelit cafés and rococo restaurants. This distinctive tradition had survived despite all Hungary's vicissitudes since 1918 and despite the virtual disappearance of social groups who had largely shaped the national character.

Among the peoples of Central Europe, the Magyars were perhaps the most mysterious and certainly had been the proudest, proud even of the multiple tragedies of their history. Surrounded by Slavs and Germans, they had stood firm a thousand years on the fertile black earth of the Danube valley, preserving their strange, sad language with its sibilants and pursed-lip vowels, its suffixed articles, and internal assonance. Attacked by the Mongols, later occupied for nearly two centuries (1526–1696) by the Ottoman Turks, Hungary was the great "outpost of Christendom" for Renaissance Europe. "Being martial," Machiavelli noted, "her people serve almost as ramparts."

As numerous during the Middle Ages as Englishmen, the Magyars were virtually extinguished in the wars with the Ottomans—but nevertheless rose to dominate Slovaks, Croats, Rumanians, and other minorities in their midst. From 1867 to 1917, the Hapsburg monarchy was the Austro-Hungarian Empire, and the proud Magyars ruled a realm stretching from the Adriatic to the Tatras and the Transylvanian Alps.

Although Magyar leaders were less eager than the Austrians to begin the First World War, at its end liberal Europe was determined to punish Hungary for its sins against the Slavs. The Magyars proclaimed a democratic republic in the hope of winning the sympathy of the Western democracies. When this failed, they created a Soviet Republic in the hope of prompting Russian intervention. But Lenin's hands were tied by civil war and Rumanian armies arrived in Budapest first. The brief Red Terror gave way to a White Terror, anti-Semitic as well as anti-Communist. The Allies deprived Hungary of 71 percent of its prewar territory, 60 percent of its population, 61 percent of its arable land, 83 percent of its pig iron production, 88 percent of its timber. Between the wars, Hungary rang with a cry of irredentist defiance, "Nem, nem, soha"—"No, no, never!"

The Hungary of 1964 was in many ways a new and different Hungary. The millennial persistence of the Magyars was usually ascribed to their warrior origins and to the consequent tenacity of their historic upper class. This landed aristocracy, with its great families like the Esterhazys and Andrassys, had managed to preserve until 1945 powers which its Western counterparts had ceded a century or more earlier. Ironically, some of their great estates survived as Communist collective farms, often under the same taskmasters and stewards. But the aristocracy itself was no more—as finished politically as the Junkers of old Prussia.

Finished, too, as an important influence were the Jews, who numbered nearly a million in pre-1918 Hungary, some 400,000 between the wars, barely 100,000 after 1945. Before the First World War, the Jews had assumed the role of the middle, industrial, and commercial class which Magyar nobles disdained. In journalism, literature, and the theater, they had tinged Magyar pride with their own brand of ironic, self-deprecating humor.

But even the group of deracinated Jews who provided the postwar Communist movement with so many leaders (Matyas Rakosi, Erno Gero, Mihaly Farkas) had been overthrown in the 1956 revolution. This had been accomplished partly through the libertarian eloquence of other Jewish intellectuals (Gyula Hay, Tibor Dery, Zoltan Zelk) who had been imprisoned after the Soviet intervention and, even after their release, remained apart from the new regime of Janos Kadar.

The German industrialists, engineers, and professors who, together with the Jews, had helped make Budapest a great industrial city—second only to Berlin in Central Europe—had also departed, some after 1918, most after 1945. Yet they left behind a tradition of scientific and intellectual rigor. Two decades after the Germans' departure, German remained the *lingua franca* of travelers in Hungary; Budapest professors and waitresses alike dreamed of weekends in Vienna; and Hungarian writers who had once venerated Thomas Mann pored over the works of Günter Grass and Heinrich Böll.

The Gypsies, too, who had been to Hungarian music what the Negroes are to American, were mostly gone, also victims of Nazi genocide. Their music lived on in Liszt and Bartók as well as café melodists, although the musicians were now mostly Magyars. In the same way, Magyars who were neither Jews nor anti-

Semites invented new, space-age tales about the traditional comic pair Cohen and Green.*

Despite material shortages, Budapest women remained, like the departed countesses of old, the most elegant in Eastern Europe. Budapest's shop windows managed somehow to look stylish even when their contents were not. Unlike Warsaw or Belgrade, Budapest made the most of colors, light, ribbons, tags, placards, type, space itself. Windows with only a few items looked dramatic rather than bare; windows with a wide variety appeared sumptuous rather than clogged. Food and wine shops, delicatessens, cosmetics shops and beauty parlors were smart, neat, warm, busy, and inviting. Hungary was the first Communist nation to manufacture *espresso* machines. Old-fashioned head-waiters reigned supreme in Budapest's restaurants, by far the best in Communist Europe. The Magyars' cuisine was the most pungent east of the Rhine. Their wines—particularly the red *Egge Bikaver* ("Bull's Blood")—were equally heady. Both were made for love, just as the most haunting Magyar melodies expressed (as V. S. Pritchett observed) "the music of the sexual act." Interwar Hungary had given the world the amorous comedies of Ferenc Molnar, and (although Communists hated to admit it) the most famous postwar Hungarians remained Magda, Eva, and Zsa Zsa Gabor.

Indeed, as several critics noted, Hungarian literature had a rather unique tradition of blending sexual passion with political comment. A poem by young Mihaly Ladanyi showed that the tradition was still alive in the spring of Khrushchev's visit:

> You spread your smile on my heart, and when your thighs entwine
>   my waist,
> do you even think
> that when you will be no more, I shall long remember
> your thighs with affection
> just as I did tonight
> plodding home, spiritless,

---

* After Russia's Alexei Leonov became the first man to walk in space, Cohen and Green went hurtling out into orbit. Cohen left the capsule to duplicate Leonov's feat, but as he did so, the capsule door slammed shut behind him. He knocked and knocked again on the capsule door to gain reentry. Finally Green asked, "Who's there?"

because I saw again the bitterness of broken-winded lives?
At such times, roving homeward,
what else can give me strength to start again tomorrow morning,
but your smiles and thighs? . . .

I think of you when I peer at the prices
and finger my lean pockets.
I think of you between the jaws of time-payment dates
and in the maze of hopeless apartment ads.
I think of you before the pompous office boss
I think of you in the ranks of scraping and bowing lackeys. . . .

For you, too, are fed up with the quays of the Danube and of
   Margaret Island,
since all you have is one pair of shoes and one pair of nylons,
and what is the use of youth
before you have cashed it in for a co-op apartment?

Hungary's recovery from the trauma of 1956 had not been easy, and in a deeper sense was far from complete despite the surface gaiety. The suicide rate was the highest in the world. The birthrate was the lowest in Europe. Abortions exceeded live births. (In Budapest in 1961, the ratio was three to one—and Budapest contained a fifth of the country's population.) Although there were periodic rumors that the electrified barbed wire on the frontiers would be dismantled, and other rumors that the "temporary" Soviet occupation force of 60,000 might be withdrawn, both remained in place—suggesting that the economic improvement and low-keyed political atmosphere introduced under Kadar could not alone beguile Magyar spirits.

The economic improvement was, to a large extent, the work of Khrushchev. Perhaps he felt a high degree of personal responsibility for the upheaval of 1956. He seemed determined to use Hungary to demonstrate more generally that a middle way between Stalinism and "counterrevolution" was possible and viable. In 1957, Khrushchev had canceled a number of Hungarian debts, extended new large-scale loans, and permitted Kadar's planners to concentrate on consumer goods and housing while delaying costly heavy-industry investments. At the same time, the price structure of Soviet trade with Hungary and other East European states was revised to diminish resentment of Russian "colonialism." Such aid involved some belt-tightening in the Soviet economy itself, which since 1945 had become accustomed to favorable exploitation of East European resources. (Khrushchev's Soviet critics were later to reproach him for such generosity toward Hungary and other satellites after 1956; in 1968, when Czechoslovakia sought similar generosity, it was not granted.)

The economic improvement in Hungary had been substantial. In 1960, real per capita income was one-third higher than in 1956. From 1957 onward, some 50,000 new housing units were built annually, double the previous rate. After 1961, when Hungary began repaying its debt to Russia and raised its military budget, living standards rose more slowly. Nevertheless, while most other states of Communist Europe were raising consumer prices during the economic crisis of 1962–63, Hungary actually lowered prices in the spring of 1963. Furthermore, in contrast to the former suspicion and harassment of the urban "bourgeoisie," the new middle classes of Budapest—ranging from doctors and lawyers to private cosmeticians and seamstresses—were permitted to hustle and thrive in an atmosphere of "live and let live."

The more relaxed political atmosphere was summed up in Kadar's famous slogan, "Whoever is not against us, is with us." An end was put to the former discrimination against "bourgeois elements" in education and employment. The government welcomed non-Communist specialists into the administration and economic management. The party itself strove to attract engineers, technicians, economists, and other experts into its ranks. Here, too, Khrushchev's hand was evident. For Kadar had coined his famous slogan on December 9, 1961, a few weeks after returning from the 22nd Soviet Communist party congress. By the end of 1962, some 95 percent of the political prisoners had been released and there was a broad new amnesty in March 1963.

Tibor Dery and other revolutionary writers of 1956 were published again in Hungary. Lesser revolutionaries regained posts in the government, economy, and cultural life. By 1964, many of them felt that a large part of the revolution's original objectives were quietly being realized. However, they were also sufficiently chastened to recognize that the revolution's greatest dreams—

democracy and national independence—could only be fulfilled if there was basic change in Russia itself. Hopes for such change rose in Hungary with the burial of Stalin and Khrushchev's "second de-Stalinization."

During 1962 and 1963, the cautious Hungarians permitted the Soviet liberals to make the first moves, but were quick to follow. Magyar journals speedily translated the verse of Voznesensky, Yevtushenko, and Akhmadulina, the prose of Ilya Ehrenburg and Victor Nekrasov. Early in 1963, some three months after the publication of Solzhenitsyn's *Ivan Denisovich* in Moscow, Budapest began publishing the concentration-camp memoirs of Joszef Lengyel, a Hungarian Communist victim of Stalin's 1937 purges.

Although the Hungarian "liberalization" had been stimulated in Moscow, Kadar's personal touch was also apparent. For the Communist party as well as for himself, modesty, discretion, caution, and inobtrusiveness were the watchwords. During the November 1962 party congress, there were no red banners in the streets of Budapest, no pictures of the leaders, hardly any trace in fact that such a gathering was being held. On the congress's first day, Kadar was photographed chatting with the venerable composer Zoltán Kodály, who had been specially invited for the occasion. But portraits of Kadar were rare in the country and remained so even after he had gained, as he had by 1964, a measure of genuine respect almost bordering on popularity.

Kadar was more typically Hungarian than most of his predecessors. Rakosi and his closest companions were Jewish intellectuals who had spent years in Moscow. Most other famous leaders of twentieth-century Hungary came from its Calvinist minority (the Counts Tisza before 1914, Admiral Horthy between the wars, the ill-fated Imre Nagy). Kadar had been born in Rijeka (then Fiume) in 1912, but his origins were working-class, he had lived in Budapest since boyhood, and he had been a Communist from the age of seventeen. By trade, Kadar was originally a metalworker (like Tito, Novotny, and Brezhnev).

During World War II, Kadar took part in the underground anti-Nazi resistance led by Laszlo Rajk. After the war, he followed in Rajk's footsteps three times: first as chief of the Budapest party organization, then as minister of the Interior, ultimately into a Stalinist prison. He did not, however, follow Rajk to martyrdom in 1949; indeed, according to several accounts, he helped persuade Rajk to "confess" to treason and Titoism. Kadar himself was arrested in 1951 and brutally tortured. He was released in October 1954 and soon resumed his career in the party.

During the revolution of 1956, he supported Imre Nagy almost to the end, but then lent his name to the Soviet intervention. He gave Nagy a personal safe-conduct, but was powerless to prevent his arrest by the Soviet KGB. He pledged also that Nagy would not be brought to trial, but could not prevent his execution in 1958 (after a secret trial which, according to legal experts, followed Soviet, rather than traditional Hungarian, juridical forms). This clouded, anguished past was etched in the lines of Kadar's rugged face, and, together with his unpretentious pragmatism, even began to win him a certain sympathy as a fellow victim of the national tragedy.

Everyone knew that, so long as Soviet troops and security agencies remained in the country,* Kadar's real powers were limited. Kadar, it was believed, was attempting to make the best of a difficult situation and by 1964 seemed, with Khrushchev's help, to be on the way toward succeeding.

Hungarians as well as foreigners in those days were often tempted to draw a parallel with the nineteenth century. After the Hungarian Revolution of 1848–49 had been crushed, most of its radical leaders were either hanged or forced to flee abroad (as some 100,000 Hungarians had fled in 1956). But a more moderate group of Magyar nobles, led by Ferenc Deak, rode out the storm and bided their time until Emperor Franz Josef, defeated by France at Solferino (1859) and by Prussia at Sadowa (1866), was ready to compromise with Hungarian national demands. To some observers, Kadar now seemed a second Deak, preparing the ground for the day when the Soviet empire was sufficiently weakened to permit the Magyars to go the way of independent Yugoslavia or, better still, neutral Austria.

---

* In November 1962, for example, when the British businessman Greville Wynne was abducted in Budapest by the KGB as part of the Penkovsky affair, Hungarian officials were at first visibly surprised, then plainly embarrassed by the incident.

Politically minded Hungarians carefully watched the development of the Soviet conflict with China, which had already brought them considerable amelioration since 1961, and hoped that future stages of that struggle might bring further rewards. Deep in the national consciousness was the memory of how the Magyars had miraculously been spared total annihilation by the Mongols in 1242, when the Great Khan Ogotai suddenly died in far-off Karakorum and the Mongol occupation army under Batu Khan withdrew from the Danube valley back to the Russian steppes.

There was news from the distant Orient again as Kadar greeted Khrushchev and his party at Budapest's Eastern railroad station on March 31. This time, the news was from Peking, in the form of a leading article published jointly by the *People's Daily* and *Red Flag*. For the first time since February 4, the Chinese Communists had launched a fierce new attack on Khrushchev as a "traitor," "Trotskyist," and "revisionist." In a brief speech at the railroad station, the Soviet leader gave no indication of any reaction to the new assault.

The next morning, however, Khrushchev addressed 8,000 electrical workers gathered in the square of the Tungsram light-bulb factory (built by Phillips in 1896). He had a prepared text to be read by a Magyar interpreter, a routine sermon on the blessings of electrification in Russia. However, as was his habit, he interrupted the prepared text midway in order to speak extemporaneously.

"There are some people," Khrushchev declared, "who call themselves Communists and Marxist-Leninists, and claim they are working for a better world. But they still do not consider it important to strive for higher living standards. They only call for revolution, revolution.

"But revolutionary passion alone is not enough," Khrushchev emphasized. "We also need a good plate of goulash—better clothes—good housing—schools for the children—culture. . . . That is something worth fighting for!"

The "capitalist" countries, Khrushchev observed, "manufacture goods of high quality"—"why then must we in the socialist countries make inferior products? . . . If the socialist countries have a lower productivity of labor than the capitalist countries, we can't win."

Similar themes resounded throughout his tour. It was not until the night of April 2–3, however, that Khrushchev was free to attack the Chinese by name, not for several weeks that the world learned of the behind-the-scenes drama which had been rending international Communism since early February. It was a drama which involved not only intensified conflict between Moscow and Peking, but troubled stirrings within the Soviet leadership and the emergence in a strange new role of the Rumanian Communists.

The Soviet party had refrained from public criticism of the Chinese since October 1963, but Peking had ignored Moscow's direct appeal to improve relations after President Kennedy's death. Nevertheless, when the Soviet Central Committee met in December, there were no attacks on China even from Khrushchev, who spoke twice during the session. The December meeting scaled down Khrushchev's plans for expanding the chemical industry and trimming the military budget. It also appointed as an alternate Politburo member a tough Ukrainian, Pyotr Shelest, who was now accompanying Khrushchev in Hungary.

Soviet appeasement failed to sway the Chinese. On February 4, Peking issued a thunderous attack declaring that only through "struggle" and "splits" could a new unity be achieved among Communists. It classed Khrushchev and his colleagues with previous traitors whom Lenin and Stalin had routed. The attack was entitled "The Leaders of the Soviet Communist Party Are the Worst Schismatics of Our Time." *

This was too much for the Russians. Their Central Committee had previously been summoned to convene on February 10 to

* The Chinese article was obviously drafted for maximum emotional effect on Russian audiences. I heard the text at the time on Radio Peking in both English and Russian. In English, the constant references to "splitters," "splittism," and "schismatics" sounded quaint, almost comical. In Russian, however, the word for "splitter" or "schismatic"—*raskolnik*—has deep emotional and historical resonance, conjuring up the traumatic schisms of the Russian Orthodox Church in the seventeenth century. The word *raskolnik* has as much force in Russia as "heretic" in Spain or "infidel" among the Arabs. It was no accident that Dostoyevsky named the doomed protagonist of his *Crime and Punishment* Raskolnikov. It was perhaps, equally fitting that the chief guardian of Soviet doctrinal orthodoxy, Suslov, came from a family of religious sectarians.

discuss agriculture. By February 12, the Soviet leaders had sent out a private letter to other Communist parties around the world, informing them of imminent action against the Chinese. The Soviet letter announced that the Central Committee meeting would adopt reports and resolutions condemning the Chinese, which would be published. It urged other Communist parties to join in a "collective rebuff" to Peking at an international Communist conference.

On February 14, the Central Committee heard Suslov read a long report which denounced the Chinese and formally proposed a world Communist conference. Even before Suslov had finished, however, it was decided that the report he had just read would be kept secret. For that same day, the Rumanian Communist leaders had addressed an "urgent appeal" to the Russians to delay their counterattack, and had offered to mediate between Moscow and Peking. The Soviet Central Committee accepted the offer immediately.

The next day, the Central Committee adopted a curious resolution (which, in accordance with the agreement with the Rumanians, was also kept secret). The resolution made no call for an international Communist council, but instead urged "normalizing relations" with China. There were other signs indicating discord within the Soviet leadership.

A Rumanian delegation led by Ion Georghe Maurer and Nicolae Ceausescu conferred with Mao and his colleagues in Peking, then with Khrushchev and Mikoyan in the Crimea, as both sides held their fire publicly. On March 25, the Rumanians proposed that both Moscow and Peking join them in a new appeal for Communist unity. Three days later, the Soviet leaders agreed to do so. Peking's response, however, was the sharp new attack which greeted Khrushchev on his arrival in Hungary.

On the afternoon of April 2, Hungarian officials advised foreign journalists that "important materials" would be published in their party newspapers the next morning. These turned out to be Hungarian documents condemning the Chinese. They were timed to coincide with the release in Moscow that night of the Suslov report and Soviet Central Committee resolution of February 15. There seemed no doubt that Khrushchev had seized the opportunity of the new Chinese attack to force the publication of these documents after six weeks' delay.

The incident remained perplexing even after the Rumanians, on April 28, had disclosed the details of their role in the affair. The six-week delay to permit Rumanian mediation was not particularly puzzling, but it did demonstrate an unsuspectedly deep desire within the Soviet Central Committee (despite numerous border incidents as well as bitter Chinese press attacks since July 1963) to seek compromise with Mao at almost any cost. And there were significant discordances between the official Soviet documents, which stressed Chinese "splitting" activities, and Khrushchev's much broader personal campaign for "goulash"—for raising Soviet living standards, reducing military expenditures, and relaxing tensions with the West. For Khrushchev, such a program was the other side of the anti-Chinese coin. Other Soviet leaders apparently did not view matters in the same way, as became evident in the manner that the Soviet press censored Khrushchev's remarks during his Hungarian tour.

In his first speech after the release of the February documents, a formal address at the Budapest opera house, Khrushchev mainly stuck to the common party line. He declared that the "subversive activity" of the Chinese posed a "serious threat," and suggested a search for new "organizational forms" to bind Communist Europe more closely together. However, he also emphasized the horror of war ("the destruction of cities and villages, the tears of widows and orphans") and the necessity "to proceed steadfastly along the path leading to peace, step by step, from agreement to agreement," with the West.

Khrushchev asserted, furthermore, that "the only solution" to the German problem lay in "peaceful negotiations *toward German unity.*" This was a heretical assertion, for since 1960 the official Kremlin line had stressed the permanent division of Germany. Even Khrushchev's first overture in June 1963 to the new Erhard government in West Germany had been couched only in terms of increased trade, with no hint that the Soviet leader was ready to talk about German reunification. Khrushchev had not been permitted to follow up even that first modest overture. His remarks at the Budapest opera house indicated a realization, nonetheless, that the German problem would have to be faced in order to relax the East-West military confrontation in Europe. The Soviet press censored Khrushchev's reference to German unity.

On April 6, Khrushchev journeyed to eastern Hungary and made it even more clear, in two off-the-cuff speeches, that for him the issue was not merely the Chinese heresy, but higher living standards and conciliation with the West. At the Borsod Chemical Combine, he noted that Hungary had increased industrial output fivefold since the war, and then asked the workers:

> But would you say that this is enough, that you already have everything you want? Of course not. After all, when the housewife goes to the store, she wants to buy as much as possible. If she has one dress, let us say, she wants to buy one more, or even two more, particularly if she likes to stay in fashion. And this is correct. . . .
> Some people criticize us, saying "You are always thinking about living better. These are anti-Marxists, bourgeois slogans." . . . [But] we did not make the revolution to live worse. . . . If the socialist system gives a person fewer economic and spiritual goods than the capitalist system, people are going to ask: "Why the devil did we substitute one for the other?" . . . One pair of trousers may be enough in the tropics, but not in our country—because something may freeze. . . .

There were "people" who were saying, according to Khrushchev, that he was prepared to sacrifice the interests of the world revolution. He loyally denied such a charge, but then immediately attacked those Communists who were allegedly demanding "war on the capitalists in order to wipe out exploitation in the capitalist countries."

"What exactly does this mean?" Khrushchev asked. "It means we must fight France, fight West Germany, fight the United States of America, Italy, Britain, Japan and other capitalist countries. But to fight means to kill people. Whom should we kill in these countries? . . . The overwhelming majority of the population of the capitalist countries consists of our class brothers—workers, peasants and intelligentsia. What right have we to interfere in their internal affairs? After all, they are not asking us for this. . . ."

To those who accused him of fearing war, Khrushchev replied, "only a child or an idiot does not fear war. . . . Is the man who jumps head first off a bridge the bravest? No, he is either stupid or has lost all faith in life . . ."

Khrushchev disclosed that "certain people" were "babbling" that Russia under his leadership was "begging the imperialists for peace." He rejected this as slander; there was no question of begging, but of a balance of nuclear power which compelled realism on both sides. President Kennedy's speech at American University (June 10, 1963) had shown, Khrushchev declared, that even the leaders of the United States "have not been deprived of good sense."

"I have been criticized for praising this speech by Kennedy," Khrushchev revealed, without specifying who the critics were. "But I still consider it a reasonable presentation." He noted more recent remarks by the American secretary of state, Dean Rusk, and the chairman of the Senate Foreign Relations Committee, J. William Fulbright, which were also "very reasonable." By recognizing that both the United States and Russia possessed the power to annihilate each other, such Americans were showing a "sense of reality."

"Comrades," Khrushchev concluded, "we want the question of who wins out on the world scale not to be decided by a war between states. The system that gives people more freedom, that gives people more material and cultural goods, is the system that will ultimately triumph."

Here was a definition of peaceful competition which not only the West but many people in Communist Europe would gladly accept. Such a definition could only be viewed as naïve, demagogic, or dangerous, however, by Communists devoted to the tradition of Lenin and Stalin. For such Communists knew that the entire system (including their own powers and privileges) was based on giving people less freedom and fewer material goods, in preparation for the "final conflict" which both Lenin and Stalin regarded as inevitable. A genuine competition in prosperity or freedom would compel profound changes in the Communist system. Such changes might not only open the way for "revisionists" like Milovan Djilas and Imre Nagy, or "traitors" like

Oleg Penkovsky and Asen Georgiev, but would threaten tens of thousands of careers which had been built on repression, suspicion, and hostility at home and abroad.

Khrushchev at times seemed inclined to risk the gamble, as he had opened the Pandora's box of Stalin's crimes in 1956. Tito had been enabled to play the card of nationalism. But other Communist leaders were unwilling to abandon the Bolshevik doctrines of permanent dictatorship and irreconcilable conflict. The "historic" conflict, the "international class struggle," the threat from the West, were needed to justify continuing repression and sacrifice—even though the "frightful collision" between the two systems which Lenin forecast had become unthinkable in the nuclear age. It was this dilemma, above all, which had spawned such disarray in Communist ranks since 1956.

Addressing students at an industrial institute in Miskolc later that day, Khrushchev compared the situation in the Communist world with a storm in the forest. During the storm, people "huddle together," but afterward "they scatter." In the days of John Foster Dulles, he said, "we united and drew closer together. But now, *when there is no threat,* everybody says 'Well, we can manage by ourselves.' To that, the imperialists add a piece of bacon or goulash. To some, they promise in advance; to some, they give credits; and to some they promise without giving and say, 'Just behave and you will get it.'"

This was a clear expression of Khrushchev's annoyance with the temptation in several East European countries, and especially Rumania, to seek greater independence through Western economic aid. But Khrushchev was quick to add that as Soviet premier, "I am ready to take credits from the devil himself if the rate of interest is advantageous to my country."

If "capitalism" could be conquered "merely with fists," Khrushchev said, "matters would be simpler." But this was impossible in the nuclear age; "victory over capitalism can only be won by surpassing its productivity."

Many of Khrushchev's clearest statements were either censored completely by Soviet news media or significantly reworded. For example, Khrushchev's spoken "now, when there is no threat" (from the West) was muddied by Kremlin censors to read "now that we have warded off the immediate threat of war." Such censorship of Khrushchev had become more and more frequent since 1960—and it was nearly always in the direction of hardening his line toward the West, blunting the edge of his appeals for consumer goods.

At Miskolc and later, Khrushchev was free to attack the Chinese leaders by name, and did so. Nevertheless, he also continued to refer to "certain people" who were criticizing his line. It was clear to many observers that Khrushchev could only be talking about his opponents inside the Kremlin. To some who heard him, it seemed as though Khrushchev were appealing to the West for help in the difficult struggle against these foes.

For those who had watched him closely over the years, the physical impression produced by Khrushchev at this time spoke more poignantly even than his words. The change was appreciable even since his tour of Yugoslavia seven months earlier. In his walk and his bearing, in the intonation and accents of his voice, in his facial and bodily reactions to the people and things that he saw, Khrushchev gave the impression that the power in which he had once gloried had now become a wearying burden. He had lost the illusions of Communist "victory" on which he had been raised, illusions with which he had rallied the movement until 1962. He was older and wiser for his traveling in the outside world and for his failures at home. He knew that his promise of raising Russian living standards could only be attained by emulation of the West and at least a truce in the cold war. But he also sadly realized that, with the death of President Kennedy, there was less hope that the West would help him vindicate his policies.*

---

* It will remain one of the fascinating "ifs" of history whether Khrushchev might have survived if Kennedy had lived. Perhaps nothing could have saved Khrushchev after the 1963 harvest. Indisputably, however, the prospects for his "coexistence" program were dimmed by various changes in U.S. policy between November 1963 and October 1964. Kennedy, for example, was believed ready to follow the nuclear test-ban agreement by a formal nonaggression pact between NATO and the Warsaw Treaty states. His successors permitted this project to be vetoed by Bonn Foreign Minister Gerhard Schroeder. At the same time, Washington activated the plan to give West Germany "co-possession" of atomic weapons by creating a so-called multilateral nuclear force, a project which Kennedy had viewed skeptically and Moscow regarded with horror. The U.S. also became more deeply committed in Vietnam. In any case, by the late 1960s,

Although Khrushchev continued to read the conventional Soviet propaganda texts prepared for him, it was also clear that he hardly believed the propaganda any longer. His disillusion emerged with particular force in a visit April 7 to the Martonvasar agricultural research institute twenty miles south of Budapest. At this converted aristocratic manor (where Beethoven had once made music and love with the daughters of the noble house), Hungarian agronomists described at length their achievements in developing new plant strains and hybrids to raise agricultural output. Khrushchev listened silently until one of the scientists claimed that, with a new type of hybrid corn, Hungary was obtaining yields of 27 centners per hectare—higher, the guide said, than yields in the United States.

"No, no, no, don't kid yourself," Khrushchev suddenly interrupted. "Excuse me, I don't want to praise the imperialists, but their yield is higher. I have the statistics, and so do you . . ." Khrushchev referred to his friend Roswell Garst, the Iowa corngrower, whose views on Soviet agriculture Khrushchev had most recently commended to the February Central Committee meeting.

"Your figures are more pleasant," Khrushchev told the Hungarians, "but facts are facts. Besides, that's no standard for us because the Americans don't try for very high corn yields. Their yields per hectare are much lower than those in Western Europe."

A yield of 27 centners per hectare, Khrushchev said, was much too low. "You know," he said sadly, "for us in the Soviet Union that is possible—but for Hungary it is too little. . . . You have a lot of scientific explanations but Garst, without scientific explanations, gets 87 centners per hectare."

Despite the billions of words in *Pravda* presenting the Soviet Union as the most progressive country in the world, Khrushchev did not hesitate to recognize Russia's backwardness compared even with the nations of Eastern Europe—not to mention the United States, which he obviously admired for its mobility and dynamism. When the Hungarians began discussing seed pro-

---

when Khrushchev's departure came to be generally regretted, liberal Communists in Hungary, Poland, and Czechoslovakia often reproached Westerners privately for having failed to help Khrushchev in his last, troubled year.

duction, Khrushchev again interrupted to note that the United States had placed such production on an industrial basis.

"The Americans say they do this because it's profitable," Khrushchev remarked. "You know what that means under capitalism— if you fail, either you go broke or you're dead. Whereas with us, those who fail are lectured, reprimanded, shamed, but go right on living."

Khrushchev told the Hungarians that he would soon propose another sweeping reorganization of Soviet agriculture, a large-scale shift from all-purpose farms to specialized farms. He was drafting a letter to the party Central Committee on the subject. Few of Khrushchev's remarks that day ever appeared in the Soviet press.

The next morning, the Russian leader made plain his irritation with Soviet industrial practices and with his own colleagues. He was taken to visit the Budapest Optical Combine and talk with the plant's managers. One of them informed him that the plant was behind schedule because the Soviet Union had failed to deliver motors on time. Emerging into the factory courtyard, where workers had been assembled to hear him speak, Khrushchev could not conceal his anger. After a few introductory pleasantries, he recounted the incident, and disclosed that the Soviet factory which had failed to deliver the motors was located in the Ukraine.

"Here's the culprit, here's Comrade Shelest," Khrushchev bellowed—pointing to the Ukrainian party leader alongside him. "He's eating your goulash, but not delivering the motors. . . . Look how glum he is—as if a hedgehog had been rammed down his throat!"

This public humiliation of Shelest (who revenged himself six months later) showed, once again, how deep was Khrushchev's frustration with the Sisyphean labor of reforming the Soviet system, of influencing the colleagues that system provided him.

Khrushchev's last major public appearance in Hungary was at an outdoor rally in the Budapest Sports Palace on April 9. Here, 3,000 Hungarians heard the strongest anti-Chinese speech ever delivered in Khrushchev's name. But Khrushchev did not deliver it personally. He stood grim-faced at the tribune as a Magyar interpreter read a long prepared text, and he did not interrupt the reading to speak his own mind.

The speech was full of sharp phrases, but on closer examination added nothing to the Suslov report. It expressed neither the burning anger with Peking that Khrushchev had manifested behind closed doors four years earlier, at the Bucharest and Moscow conferences of 1960, nor his current preoccupation with "goulash" and conciliation with the West. A television report on his Hungarian journey, which Khrushchev delivered after returning to Moscow, was equally stiff and formal.

Khrushchev's seventieth birthday, which was celebrated in the Kremlin Hall of Catharine the Great on April 17, was a rather sad occasion. The birthday party was boycotted not only by Mao, Ho Chi Minh, and Tito, but by the Italian Communist leader Palmiro Togliatti and the Rumanian party chief Gheorghe Gheorgiu-dej. Brezhnev pinned new medals on Khrushchev's chest and Mikoyan declared that each of the party leaders harbored "equally warm fraternal feelings toward Comrade Nikita Sergeyevich Khrushchev."

Khrushchev himself, however, at least unconsciously, recognized the dubious value of such assurances. He had "little need of doctors' services," he maintained, but "for some statesmen, political death may come before physical death. This is why, if a statesman wishes to live long, he must work with the collective. . . ." De-Stalinization had been pursued "without surgery and by therapeutic means only," he noted, "despite an enormous force of inertia." He doubtless knew how much of the inertia came from the men in the hall paying him tribute.

Soon after the birthday party, Khrushchev resumed his restless traveling. In May, he made a three-week tour of Egypt; in June, a three-week cruise to Scandinavia; in July, he was in Poland; in August, he made a lengthy tour of Soviet farm areas, followed by nine days in Czechoslovakia. Frequently during these tours, he expressed his frustration, as he had in Hungary, with the Soviet vested interests restraining him. In Egypt, for example, he complained indirectly about the Soviet marshals and their insatiable appetite for armaments. "I don't know how it is in your country," Khrushchev said, "but my esteemed friend President

Nasser could tell me whether a military person ever says to him: 'Don't give us any more weapons, there are enough of them!' " Altogether, Khrushchev was away from Moscow 135 days, not counting weekends, during the first eight months of 1964. His absence was a major reason for his fall.

There were other reasons, however. From July 18 to August 2, Khrushchev's son-in-law Adzhubei toured West Germany, conferred with high government officials, and arranged for Khrushchev himself to visit the Bonn Republic the following spring. Adzhubei made little secret of his father-in-law's willingness to go far toward accommodating the West Germans, even perhaps so far as to alter the regime in East Germany. "We are not married to Ulbricht," he told Bonn officials.

Two days after Adzhubei's return from West Germany, Khrushchev announced that a Central Committee meeting on agriculture would be held in November. The meeting would discuss vast new reorganization plans, involving high party leaders. A reliable Moscow source told Michel Tatu of *Le Monde*, "You will see, the November plenary session is going to be very interesting. There will be many changes at the top. Almost all the leaders *except Khrushchev* will be affected."

The new agricultural plans appear to have been at least partly designed as a pretext for "surgery" in the leadership. The rapprochement with West Germany, in turn, was essential to progress in agriculture, for development of chemical fertilizers and intense mechanization would require massive purchases of Western equipment on favorable credit terms. There was little enthusiasm in most Western countries for supplying such credits, but the Bonn Government, according to Chancellor Erhard, had a reserve fund of 60 billion marks ($15 billion) to smooth the way for German reunification.

On September 8, the Chinese publicly charged that Khrushchev was preparing to "barter" away East Germany; nearly a fortnight passed before the East Germans denied the accusation. But once Khrushchev left Moscow for the Crimea on September 30, other Soviet leaders forcefully denounced such plans. On October 5, Suslov declared at a Moscow rally organized for East Germany that Soviet solidarity with Ulbricht's government was "not to be bought and sold, even for all the gold in the world." Russia's relations with Bonn could not be normalized through "underhand deals."

The next day, Brezhnev, speaking in East Berlin, asserted that "only short-sighted politicians who have completely lost any sense of realities" could think of "decisions and deals of some kind to be concluded behind the back" of the East German Communists. "No, my friends," he said, "this will not happen!"

On October 11, with Khrushchev still in the Crimea, Brezhnev returned from East Berlin to Moscow. Suslov met him at Vnukovo Airport. In addition to all the other issues which had been feeding their resentment of Khrushchev, the conspirators may also have known that China was on the verge of exploding its first atomic bomb (October 16). Khrushchev had provoked the great schism in 1959 by denying China the nuclear aid he had promised earlier; now a hostile China was becoming an atomic power by its own efforts.

On the night of October 15, it was announced that Khrushchev had resigned because of "advanced age and deteriorating health." He had been overthrown by his colleagues in less than three days. Suslov, who had been Stalin's final ideologist, delivered the principal indictment of Khrushchev. Brezhnev, the former Army political commissar who had been decorated in 1961 for stimulating missile production, became the new party leader. Kosygin, who had been Stalin's consumer-goods supervisor, was named prime minister.

In Hungary, the news of Khrushchev's fall was received with near panic. For days, there were rumors that Kadar, too, would be obliged to step down. The rumors proved to be unfounded, and Kadar—along with Ulbricht, Novotny, Gomulka, and the others who had embraced Khrushchev on his birthday six months earlier—remained in place.

In the course of the following year, Kadar permitted Professor Imre Vajda and other experts to elaborate an economic reform, rational in its assumptions and projections, which helped raise both the efficiency and quality of Hungarian production. But, with the cautious Kadar obliged to keep one eye on the new masters of the Kremlin, Hungary could not afford to go too far. The

rising hopes of 1962–64 leveled off, and during the tenth anniversary of the 1956 revolution, the Government refused entry
visas even to friendly foreign newsmen.

Nevertheless, most Magyars continued to enjoy their *gulyas*
(goulash), and to consider their country "the gayest barrack in
the camp." It took a while for them to realize that, during the
long twilight of Khrushchev's decline, their Rumanian neighbors
had stealthily begun to move out of the camp altogether.

CHAPTER 10

Totul Pentru Tara

The Rumanians were often described as the only people in the world who could follow you into a revolving door and come out ahead. Quick, gay, roguish, they achieved by charm, shrewdness, and timing what others sought by heroic confrontations. Some thought they did it with mirrors; others called it a high-wire act without a wire. The upright Magyars swore that, while anybody in Eastern Europe would sell his grandmother, only a Rumanian would deliver. The Russians, outplayed, fell back to quoting Tsar Nicholas II: "Rumania is not a nation or a state; it is a profession." (The Tsar in turn was paraphrasing Bismarck.) Even the Yugoslavs, their most friendly neighbors, sneered that "the Rumanians betrayed the Russians when they were weakest—we defied them when they were strongest."

Nonetheless, the Rumanians' achievement during the 1960s was extraordinary. Their Communist party was, to begin with, the smallest and least representative in the Balkans; 884 members in 1944, most of them not even ethnic Rumanians. Their country was occupied by 55,000 Soviet troops until July 1958. They had no common borders with the non-Communist world, and controversial frontiers with several of their Communist neighbors. They started out the decade as "super-Stalinists."

Yet, by the end of the 1960s, the Rumanians were receiving

political support from China, economic aid from West Germany, and a visit from the President of the United States. Their foreign minister, Corneliu Manescu, had been unanimously elected as the first Communist president of the United Nations General Assembly. And their Communist party, 1.5 million strong, had turned its back on its origins and many of its original leaders.

Few would have predicted it, even as late as 1959; but then, few outsiders ever pretended to understand Rumania, a land of strange legends and exotic habits. A beautiful country and potentially rich, it was the land of Gypsy bear-tamers and love potions, the evil eye, and the Dracula myth. Even the Saxons who farmed the valleys of Transylvania were said to have been lured there by the Pied Piper of Hamelin. Under Hohenzollern kings and Communist commissars alike, Rumanian scientists explored the secrets of eternal life or, at the least, prolonged potency—Dr. Voronov and his "monkey glands" before the war, Dr. Aslan and her Geriatrics Institute afterward. In the 1920s, Europe gossiped about Queen Marie's lovers; in the 1930s, about King Carol and Magda Lupescu, or about the Rumanian Army officers who wore girdles, powder, and pomade. In 1966, the Communist authorities suddenly forebade abortions; and in 1967, as the squalls of newborn Rumanians echoed throughout the nation's overcrowded maternity wards, Europe gossiped again.

Who were the Rumanians anyhow? Hostile historians said that they had only discovered, or invented, themselves in the eighteenth century, when a group of Transylvanian Uniate theological students came to Rome and saw the Column of Trajan, commemorating the Emperor's conquest of Dacia. On the column, they saw conquered Dacians wearing the same long, brimless felt hats still worn by peasants in their own villages. When they returned, they introduced the Latin alphabet for their own language—which was, indeed, a Latin dialect. The doctrine spread that the Rumanians were descendants of Trajan's Legionnaires, who had taken Dacian wives and remained in the country even after the Emperor Aurelian withdrew the imperial garrison.

Goths, Scythians, Sarmatians, Slavs, and Turks had overrun the territory since then, so that the Magyars (among others) scoffed at "Daco-Roman" pretensions, called the Rumanians Vlachs or

Wallachians, and insinuated that they were merely low-grade Slavs or Gypsies. Phanariot Greeks from Byzantium continued to rule and rob the country on behalf of the Ottomans. But for Rumanians, from the nineteenth century onward, no vision was to be more inspiring than to be "Latins in a sea of Slavs." The vision was useful as well; Napoleon III helped promote Rumanian independence in 1856, just as General de Gaulle's later maneuvers within the Western alliance paralleled and reinforced Rumanian acrobatics within the Communist camp.

The Rumanians outwitted the great powers at the very moment of the creation of their state. The powers in 1856 decreed the formation of two autonomous principalities, Moldavia and Wallachia; the Rumanians elected the same prince, Alexander Cuza, to rule both. In the first World War, the Rumanian Conservatives favored Germany, the Liberals favored France; moreover, as Churchill recounted, "the King was not only pro-German but German. . . . The Heir Apparent was pro-French and his wife pro-English." Thus Rumania "could move in either direction towards alternative prizes . . . and in either case she would find a Party and a Royal Family apt and happy to execute her policy. . . . Each side bid for Rumania's favors and offered bribes for Rumanian intervention." The Allies won the auction, but the German Army quickly occupied Rumania to secure its oil and wheat. (When a German general complained that there were no toilets, a Rumanian reportedly replied, "If we had toilets, we would be invading Germany.") However, two days before the Germans signed the armistice, Rumania rejoined the Allied side—in time to crush the Hungarian Communist revolution and acquire Transylvania from Hungary and Bessarabia from Russia.

Despite its diplomatic victories and natural wealth, interwar Rumania was a scandal. There was corruption beyond belief in the pleasure-loving ruling class, grinding poverty among the peasants. Rumanian diplomats contrived a Little Entente and later a Balkan Entente against Hungary and greater powers. Rumanian intellectuals yearned for France and Italy, cultivated late-Roman worldliness, and modeled Bucharest after Paris, including an arch of triumph. From King Carol II (1930–40) on down, graft and profiteering were so pervasive that outsiders concluded that "with enough money and enough of an acquaintance, there was nothing in the country which was not for sale." * While the country's rulers were disporting themselves like the Phanariot Greeks of old, the peasants went begging. Between the privileged few and the destitute millions, there were hardly any Rumanians: Germans, Jews, Greeks, and Armenians did most of the business of the country, and the Jews ended up as the target of most of the Rumanian political parties.

When Hitler made anti-Semitism fashionable throughout Europe, Rumanians claimed to have invented it. Their claim was fairly solid: even at the Congress of Berlin (1878), the civilized European powers had been protesting Rumanian treatment of its Jews. In keeping with this tradition, the most authentic Rumanian mass movement before the war was the radical nationalist Iron Guard, which was anti-Russian, anti-Magyar, and especially anti-Semitic. (It might have been anti-German as well, except that Nazi Germany subsidized it.) The Iron Guard's handsome leader, Corneliu Codreanu, was half-Ukrainian, half-German; its slogan was *"Totul Pentru Tara,"* "All for the Fatherland." While idealistic youths of other nations fought to defend the Spanish Republic, Iron Guardists joined the Nazis and Fascists fighting for Franco. Two of their number received a spectacular funeral in Bucharest, and were later honored by Rumanian postage stamps (as was Codreanu, only a short while before King Carol had him murdered).

In World War II, Rumanian casualties were both absolutely and proportionally higher than those of the United States. It was not surprising, since the Rumanians fought on both sides. In the Germans' onslaught against Russia, the Rumanians were the toughest of the satellite armies accompanying them. They occupied large parts of the Ukraine and Crimea, and even briefly renamed Odessa after their "Conducator" (leader), General Ion Antonescu. From 1943 onward, however, Rumanian envoys

* Robert Lee Wolff, *The Balkans in Our Time* (Harvard University, 1955). Professor Wolff describes how the prewar Rumanian police "once jailed a newly arrived foreign newspaper correspondent because he attempted to change his money legally instead of patronizing the black market. He must, they concluded, have discovered a new racket of some sort, and they wanted him in safe custody until they could figure out what it could be."

were busily exploring means of abandoning the lost Nazi cause.

On August 23, 1944, with the Soviet Army crossing the Bessarabian frontier, King Michael finally arrested the German collaborators and changed sides. The Rumanian army joined the Russians fighting their way through Hungary. On route, they reclaimed the half of Transylvania which Hitler had awarded to the Magyars. Opposition politicians who had been carefully kept alive during the fascist years now formed a new government. Among them was the distinguished Communist lawyer, Professor Lucretiu Patrascanu. His friend, Ion Gheorghe Maurer, also a well-to-do jurist, had already secured the release of the Communist workers who had been jailed since the Grivita railway strike of 1933. One of the released prisoners, Gheorghe Gheorghiu-dej, was named leader of the revived Communist party. Another released prisoner, Nicolae Ceausecu (born 1918), the son of a shoemaker from Oltenia west of Bucharest, became head of the Communist youth. In prison, Ceausescu was remembered as "a skinny kid who rarely said a word. He didn't whine when they kicked him; he didn't smile when they fed him."

Patrascanu, Gheorghiu-dej, and Ceausescu were among the handful of ethnic Rumanians left in a Communist party that had never been popular (Maurer's father was of Saxon descent, while his mother was French). Between the wars, the party's leaders and policies were imposed by the Comintern, which sought to break up the Rumanian state by agitation among the Bessarabian Jews, the Magyars, and the Bulgarians from the Dobruja region in the Danube delta. Several of the party's most original thinkers (Christian Rakovsky, Marcel Pauker, Alexandru Dobrogeanu-Gherea) were shot in Russia during Stalin's purges.

Appropriately, it was the Moscow Trial prosecutor, Andrei Vishinsky, who accompanied the Soviet forces in Rumania and dictated the political changes which the country swiftly underwent. Vishinsky and the MVD brought with them the "Muscovite" leaders of the party—the Magyar Vasile Luca and the Bessarabian Jewess Anna Pauker—as well as the former Rumanian Army officer and security specialist, Emil Bodnaras, who acted as liason between the Soviet command and the various party wings.

Stalin treated Rumania like a conquered enemy. He annexed Bessarabia directly, under the name of the Moldavian Socialist Republic, and imposed the Cyrillic alphabet and Russification policies through such sturdy lieutenants as Leonid Brezhnev (who ruled the province from July 1950 to November 1952). Rumania itself was obliged to pay war reparations higher than those of Hungary or Bulgaria. Fifteen Soviet-Rumanian "mixed companies" were established to exploit Rumanian oil, timber, transport, and other resources. (The Yugoslavs called these companies "classic examples of imperialist plunder.") Tens of thousands of political prisoners were sent to build a Danube-Black Sea Canal, in imitation of the famous GPU canals in Russia; it became the most notorious slave-labor project in all Eastern Europe. A spelling reform and other cultural directives emphasized Rumania's Slavic affinities and rejected the Latin tradition. Patrascanu was arrested as a potential Tito on April 28, 1948—two months before the excommunication of Tito himself. His friend Maurer slipped into virtual obscurity for seven years.

In the course of 1952, Gheorghiu-dej and his "native" workers succeeded in ousting Anna Pauker, Luca, and other rivals. Gheorghiu-dej later claimed that this victory represented de-Stalinization in Rumania during Stalin's own lifetime. (More detached observers believe the purge was linked with Stalin's broader anti-Semitic campaign.) The Danube-Black Sea Canal was abandoned, and the mixed companies were dissolved, as part of the general Soviet "new course" after Stalin's death. It was a course which Gheorghiu-dej may have had reason to fear, as the Kremlin was not only changing policies but tampering with the leaderships of satellite parties, looking for figures less tainted by Stalinism, like Gomulka and Kadar. In April 1954, on the orders of Gheorghiu-dej, a kangaroo court condemned Patrascanu (after six years in prison) for high treason. As Ceausescu explained many years afterward, Patrascanu "was tried in a hurry and executed two days later, fast—shot in the back." Stalin's works remained required reading in Rumanian universities until 1961.

In retrospect, the most important event in the history of postwar Rumania was the withdrawal of the Soviet occupation army, which was decided upon at a Moscow conference in May 1958.

Precisely why and how the Russians were persuaded to withdraw their troops remains a mystery. The decision was accompanied by other moves to consolidate Eastern Europe—including the revival of Comecon as a means of coordinating the Communist economies. For Rumanian independence, Comecon was to play the role of Henry VIII's divorce. In struggling against Comecon "integration," the Rumanian Communist leaders discovered how to exploit Soviet weakness, and the world power balance, to their own advantage.

Stalin had created Comecon (the Council for Mutual Economic Assistance) in January 1949 as a propaganda counter to the Marshall Plan, but for a decade the organization barely functioned. Khrushchev chose to revive it when the Common Market in Western Europe posed yet another economic and propaganda challenge.

Khrushchev had abandoned direct plunder in Eastern Europe as well as the old economic line of 1948–52, with its frenzied concentration on preparations for a new world war. But each of the Communist economies was still styled on Stalinist lines, stressing "many-sided industrialization" and national self-sufficiency. Each of the party leaderships framed its own economic plan, determined to produce its "own" machine tools, trucks, and bathtubs. Each of them fixed their own prices, with little regard to the domestic or the international market. None of them would accept the currency of any of the others. Trade between them consisted of massive annual barter deals, with each side privately calculating approximate values in dollars.

This primitive state of affairs was hardly a basis for the "peaceful economic competition" with the West which Khrushchev had begun to preach. Although duplication in production was rampant, quality was low and shortages persistent everywhere. Integration of the various Communist economic plans seemed the obvious remedy, Comecon the natural agency to guide the new "socialist division of labor" and promote specialization.

With a minimum of good will, mutual trust, and common interests, Khrushchev's dreams for Comecon might have come true. Yet such qualities were hardly to be expected among nations which had historically despised one another, and political leaders who had been trained in the Stalinist school of general suspicion. Karl Marx may have considered the international division of labor to be inevitable, even progressive, but Communist leaders of the 1960s seemed more often guided by the sentiment formulated by Groucho Marx: "Any club that would have me as a member isn't worth belonging to." The more they saw of one another, and of one another's products, the more each of them felt cheated, and with reason. As Ceausescu later pointed out, Communists could keep on *saying* that their economic system was superior, but they would never be able to *prove* it so long as the West was producing better goods at lower cost.

Even had they been naïve by nature, which they assuredly were not, the Rumanians would have had grounds for suspecting any "grand design" for turning Comecon into an "integrated" Eastern Common Market. The Rumanians' national income per capita was less than half that of East Germany and Czechoslovakia, where education and industrialization had started many decades earlier. Ulbricht and Novotny were fervently pushing "specialization" in order to protect their own established, if inefficient heavy industries. Unable to compete in Western markets, they wished to ensure Balkan customers, at least, for their steel, machinery, and heavy equipment. But the Rumanians were hardly inspired by the vision of permanent dependence on East German, Czech, and Soviet machinery. Talk of joint Comecon investments and supranational enterprises made the Rumanians shudder; they had had their fill of "mixed companies."

Rumania had great natural riches—not only its oilwells and wheatfields, but barely exploited reserves of methane gas, timber, gold, silver, magnesium, and other metals. But in any "integration" limited to Communist Europe, Rumania would be merely the "gas station and sandwich shop" of a bloc that remained second-rate by world economic standards. "Why should we send our corn to Poland?" Maurer once asked. "So Poland can fatten its pigs and buy machinery from the West? We can sell the corn direct and buy the machinery we need ourselves."

When Comecon in 1958 began showing signs of life, the Rumanians played for time. Two years were spent reaching agreement on new statutes for the organization. The Rumanians made sure that the statutes pledged "respect for the national sovereignty and full equality of rights of each and all members." When Comecon committees began recommending that various countries discontinue making certain products, the Rumanians simply ignored the recommendations. (They were not the only ones who did so.)

While Moscow buzzed with theoretical talk of integration, the Rumanians were busy rediscovering the outside world. Once the Russian Army was out of the country, British, French, West German, and Italian businessmen began arriving at Bucharest's Baneasa Airport. In June 1959, a high Rumanian delegation headed by Alexandru Birladeanu went out to tour the golden West (France, Britain, Italy, Switzerland, Belgium, and Holland). The Rumanians liked what they saw, and numerous other delegations quietly followed, with a minimum of publicity and a maximum of cool-eyed observation.

The planners, traders, managers, and directors of Rumania's rapidly expanding economy were, increasingly, university-trained young engineers who were Rumanians and technocrats first, "proletarian internationalists" only on Communist holidays. As one such official observed, "We were lucky in not having a big Communist party before 1945. Otherwise we'd have had to give all the factory directorships to semi-literate party hacks, as the Czechs and the Yugoslavs did." Instead of trying to turn Communists into managers, the Rumanians passed their managers off as Communists.

Between 1958 and 1962, Rumanian trade with the West virtually tripled. The Rumanians bought whole factories, and Western engineers arrived in the Danube valley and Carpathian foothills to install them. By 1963, even the Japanese were scouting the terrain. "We are trying to sell anything to anybody," a Rumanian official told Le Monde, "provided the customer pays in dollars, pounds, marks or francs. We keep for the Comecon countries mostly what we cannot sell for hard currency."

Although the Rumanians had begun shifting their trade in 1958, they managed to delay an open conflict with Comecon for four years. By the time the conflict came in 1962 and 1963, the Rumanians had achieved the highest industrial growth rates in Europe and established firm commercial links with the West.

Khrushchev, Ulbricht, and Novotny, on the other hand, had foundered into deep economic troubles—and the Soviet struggle with China had passed the point of no return.

This sense of timing, the ability to tread water quietly while awaiting the most propitious political tides, became a hallmark of the Rumanian style. So was the sense of how far to go, how to frustrate their adversaries without provoking them to brutal confrontation.

The Comecon conflict centered on the Rumanian plan for a giant steelworks at Galati, near the mouth of the Danube. In this sleepy, deserted old town, the Rumanians proposed to erect Europe's greatest metallurgical combine, to consist of a steel mill, two hot rolling mills, two cold rolling mills, and other installations. The Galati combine would, by 1970, produce between four and five million tons of steel. Together with smaller plants, old and new, Galati would expand Rumanian steel production to five times the 1958 level.

The Galati plan was formally adopted by the June 1960 Rumanian party congress, which Khrushchev attended. The Soviet leader had come to Bucharest, however, not to ponder the virtues of Rumanian steel but to attack the Chinese. Needing allies, he cheerfully applauded the Rumanian plans while preparing for the larger conflict. But the East Germans, Czechs, and Poles soon realized that Galati would rival their own, older steel industries. The Magyars and Bulgarians ancestrally looked askance at anything Rumanian.

A quarrel like this among their East European comrades embarrassed the Soviet leaders (already divided by the U-2 incident and Chinese criticisms). They recognized the merits of "specialization," yet could not plausibly deny the Rumanians the right to do what they themselves had done before; "big steel" and heavy machinery was, after all, the Soviet prescription for happiness. Moreover, the quarrel over Galati erupted just as the Soviet leaders were on the eve of a new showdown with the Chinese.

On November 11, 1960—the very day on which the secret conference of eighty-one Communist parties opened in Moscow to seek a Sino-Soviet agreement—the Russians signed two new agreements with Rumania. They promised to supply about a third of the installations for Galati, with delivery to begin five years later. But the pressure for Comecon "integration" increased in the course of 1961. The Rumanians continued their shopping tours in the West, and began preparing their own party and people for possible trouble.

At the end of November 1961, the party Central Committee heard Gheorghiu-dej report on the Soviet 22nd party congress. He used the opportunity to rewrite the history of Rumanian Communism. He downgraded the role of the Soviet Army and blamed Anna Pauker and other "Muscovites" for all the country's troubles in the hard postwar years. According to the new line, these "alien elements" had been imposed by Stalin, but the native leadership of Gheorghiu-dej, Ceausescu (already the heir-apparent), and Maurer (who had become prime minister) would defend Rumanian interests.

In June 1962, Gheorghiu-dej and Maurer went to Moscow for a Comecon summit conference. The meeting adopted a wordy statement of principles which settled nothing. The Rumanians made sure that the principles included "national independence and sovereignty, full equality of rights, comradely help and mutual advantage." For Khrushchev, who was preparing the Cuban adventure, such verbal concessions meant little; but the Rumanians were thereafter able to cite these agreed "principles" endlessly.

First Khrushchev, then Ulbricht came to Rumania in the hot summer of 1962 in attempts to persuade Bucharest of the need for an integrated Comecon master plan for the region. Both failed. At working meetings of the Comecon executive committee, Birladeanu, representing Rumania, refused to budge. Meanwhile, Bucharest signed contracts with an Anglo-French consortium to install the first of the hot rolling mills at Galati. A few weeks after Khrushchev's humiliation in the Cuban missile crisis, the Rumanian Central Committee demonstratively endorsed Birladeanu's resistance to Comecon.

In February 1963, Birladeanu was summoned to Moscow again. He was asked to give up Galati and scale down Rumanian plans for rapid expansion of other industries.

The crisis was on, but the Rumanians were ready. In the first week of March 1963, another long Central Committee meeting was devoted to Comecon. This time, it was followed by propaganda rallies in factories and auditoriums all over the country, describing the party leaders' defense of "national independence and sovereignty," recounting the long series of economic injuries Rumania had suffered at Russian hands. But propaganda was not all the Rumanian leaders had in mind. On March 7, they announced a new trade agreement with Albania, thus abandoning the economic boycott which Khrushchev had imposed on Enver Hoxha. On March 28, the Rumanian ambassador returned to Tirana, thus ending the diplomatic boycott as well. On April 8, Bucharest announced a new trade agreement with China. The trade increase was modest (10 percent), but the hint of further political trouble for the Russians was formidable.

The Rumanians were not so naïve, however, as to stake their future entirely on the Chinese. On April 11, they announced a whopping new commercial agreement with Italy, providing for a 40 percent increase in trade. The contract for the major steel mill at Galati was offered up for bidding; Austrian, British, French, West German, and Swedish firms soon applied. One-third of Rumania's trade was now with the West.

After refusing for years to consider joint investments under Comecon auspices, the Rumanians now also concluded a pact with Tito's Yugoslavia for the biggest joint investment in Balkan history. This was the $400-million Iron Gates project to harness the Danube at the turbulent, impassable gorge on the border between the two countries. The massive project would not only provide 10 billion kilowatts of hydroelectric power for the two countries, but would open the Rumanian Danube to large-scale commercial shipping from the West for the first time in history. The project—to be completed in 1971—called for the use of Soviet turbines, but both Belgrade and Bucharest were ready to buy elsewhere if necessary.

Thus far, the Rumanians had been securing their economic future with a minimum of ideological pretense. When they reprinted Chinese and North Vietnamese attacks on Russia, however, a Soviet delegation led by Podgorny suddenly descended on Bucharest. The Russians stayed twelve days, but failed to heal the breach. On June 20, the Rumanian press published Peking's vitriolic twenty-five-point indictment of the Soviet leadership, which Khrushchev had suppressed elsewhere. One of the Chinese points stated the Rumanians' grievance more boldly than they themselves yet dared to do. "To impose one's will on others . . . in the name of the 'international division of labor' and 'specialization,'" the Chinese declared, was nothing less than "Great Power Chauvinism." Khrushchev, stung, called a meeting of the top party leaders in East Berlin for June 29. Gheorghiu-dej stayed home.

A month later, with the breach between Russia and China now wider than ever, Gheorghiu-dej and Maurer came to Moscow for yet another summit meeting. This time, they happily endorsed Khrushchev's conduct of the nuclear test-ban negotiations. Their price was Soviet abandonment of the grand design for Comecon, which even Ulbricht and Novotny now reluctantly agreed would have to continue lumbering along on the old basis of bilateral barter. When the disastrous Soviet harvest struck in September, the Rumanians quickly offered Moscow 400,000 tons of wheat to show they bore no grudges. The Russians soon promised anew that they would deliver the installations pledged for Galati.

By the fall of 1963, therefore, the Rumanians had won the struggle over Comecon integration. In the course of the struggle, however, the Rumanian Communist leaders had made two illuminating discoveries. On the one hand, they had successfully probed the pressure points at which Moscow was vulnerable— the divided leadership within the Kremlin, the conflict with China, the economic competition with the West. On the other hand, the Rumanian Communist leaders had discovered a bond with their own people. Their defense of "national independence" against Russia had evoked a more spontaneous popular response than anything they had done in twenty years. The prospect of popularity was irresistible.

In the course of 1963 and the first months of 1964, the Rumanians "de-Russified" with a vengeance. They ended the compulsory Russian classes in their schools (and 65 percent of the youth immediately opted for French). They closed down the Gorky Institute, the chief Soviet cultural institution in Bucharest.

They scrapped the Slavicizing spelling "reform" and went back to old Latin roots. They quietly renamed so many streets (most of them received their old prewar names) that there was no longer even a Lenin or Marx street to be found in Bucharest.

At the same time, the Rumanians ended the jamming of Western broadcasts and began quoting Western as well as Communist newspapers in their own party press. They rehabilitated the memory of scores of pre-Communist political leaders and intellectuals and reclaimed for the national heritage such modern artists as the sculptor Constantin Brancusi and the playwright Eugene Ionesco. By March 1964, the writers' union had formally legitimized virtually all the Western literature which Moscow, East Berlin, and Sofia were still forbidding as "decadent" and "formalistic."

Moscow viewed such Rumanian heresies darkly. In the first weeks of 1964, the Kremlin hinted at a possible future "encirclement" of Rumania, by promoting an unprecedented exchange of visits between Bulgarian leaders and officials of Soviet Moldavia (Bessarabia). The Rumanians soon showed that they could play an even deadlier "encirclement" game. During their March effort to mediate between Moscow and Peking, Maurer, Ceausescu, and Bodnaras won Chinese support for the Rumanian claim to Bessarabia. The Russians then attempted to recruit Bodnaras for a coup against his colleagues. Bodnaras rejected the offer and reported the plot.

From April 15 to 22, while Khrushchev was sadly celebrating his seventieth birthday in Moscow, the Rumanian Central Committee held an enlarged meeting in Bucharest, to which hundreds of the country's top officials, propagandists, army and police officers were invited. The meeting adopted a long policy statement which became known as the Rumanian "declaration of independence."

The statement recounted the Rumanian efforts at mediation between Moscow and Peking and assumed a pose of pious neutrality in the dispute. It condemned all attempts to dominate world Communism from a single center: the prewar Comintern for its interference inside Communist parties, the postwar Cominform for its campaign against Yugoslavia, Khrushchev's and Mao's campaigns to overthrow each other. The Rumanians declared it a "sovereign right" of each Communist party in power to "elaborate, choose or change the forms and methods" of its rule. They thus began to preach openly what Tito had long practiced.

"It is the exclusive right of each party," the Rumanians declared, "to work out its line independently. . . . There does not and cannot exist a 'parent' party and a 'son' party, parties that are 'superior' and parties that are 'subordinate.' "

The declaration of April 1964 set the Rumanian Communists firmly on a course they were to follow, with even greater dexterity, after Khrushchev's fall and the death of Gheorgiu-dej in March 1965. It was a course as different from the Chinese and Yugoslav deviations as it was from the Soviet model.

The essence of the Rumanian course was a combination of political discipline, economic sacrifice, and nationalistic self-assertion at home with an adroit diplomacy which wooed all of Russia's main adversaries while remaining formally part of the Soviet bloc. The Rumanian leaders conducted their affairs in the world with a subtlety and delicacy worthy of Byzantium, while ruling their own people in Roman fashion. Some called their policy "national Stalinism," others considered it glorified opportunism; the cruelest critics compared the new Rumanian Communism with the old Iron Guard.

There was an impressive professionalism not only in the Rumanian Communists' intricate maneuvers on a world scale, but in their development of the Rumanian economy as well. Plans for new industry elsewhere in Communist Europe were often equally shimmering, but reality was usually a shambles. Up went the factory—and then suddenly someone began to worry about the lack of raw materials, transport, workers' housing, storage, or repair facilities. By the time these problems were resolved, the machinery in the "new" factory was years behind the times. In Siberia in 1967, I saw an aluminum plant which had taken twelve years to build; its machinery appeared antediluvian compared with the French-equipped plant I had seen two years earlier at Slatina, Rumania.

Galati itself was a case in point. In March 1964, when the steel frame for the first hot rolling mill was just being erected, most of the road and rail connections had already been completed. Cement mills, foundries, power generators, toolsheds, warehouses, and administrative buildings were already neatly in place around the 1,800-acre site. Between the factory and the old town of Galati, a handsome new town center, with functional terraced apartments and glass-fronted shops, was already occupied. The manager and chief engineers at the plant itself could expertly describe the merits and demerits of various steelmaking processes from Osaka, Japan, to Gary, Indiana. Among them, they had personally inspected nearly every important steel mill in the world. Normal as such managerial competence might seem in the Ruhr, it was rare, indeed, in the Communist realm.

Visitors to Galati a year later found scores of British and French engineers already installing the rolling mill, with West German and Italian technicians on hand for the next stages of the combine. Some 20,000 Rumanian workers were employed on the site, and managers were describing the large new shipyard being built down-river to use the new Galati steel. By the end of 1965, Rumanian steel production was halfway to its 1970 goal.

Although Galati was Rumania's prime industrial showplace, it was not an untypical "Potemkin village." Numerous other factories displayed a similar professionalism—effectively combining the latest Western machinery, often automated or electronic, with auxiliary Rumanian or Soviet equipment. Although productivity remained low by Western standards, the factories were not overcrowded with redundant workers, as elsewhere in Communist Europe. Moreover, unlike their Yugoslav neighbors, the Rumanians had wiped out illiteracy and swiftly expanded polytechnic education, thus creating the basis for a skilled work force.

The Rumanians possessed the Latin visual sense as well as a feeling for proportions. The quality of their industrial design was often high, and Rumania's new modern architecture—ranging from airy, glass rural post offices to aluminum-stripped urban auditoriums—was light, graceful, and unpretentious.

In short, one was more inclined in Rumania than elsewhere to believe the standard Communist claim that the sacrifices of the present generation for rapid industrialization might ultimately be rewarded by a better life in the future—that, when the great key industries were developed, by the 1970s or 1980s perhaps, ordinary workers and farmers might begin to enjoy European living standards.

In the 1960s, however, sacrifice remained the order of the day. While neighboring Hungary and Yugoslavia slowed down industrial growth rates to permit popular consumption, the Rumanian economic plans adopted in 1965 and in 1969 retained high rates of investment, concentrated on heavy industry and power production. Clothing and other ordinary consumer goods were priced high; workers' wages were held at subsistence levels; managers lived well.

There was no shortage of food, and the Rumanian countryside only rarely offered the dispiriting Soviet spectacle of machinery rotting in the open fields. Nevertheless, many villages in Wallachia and Moldavia, with their oxcarts and hand pumps, appeared to have changed little since Ottoman times. The level was higher among the Magyars and Saxons in Transylvania, but it was clear that the peasantry were paying the bill for Rumania's shiny new factories and would continue to do so for a long time.

The results of such economic stress for the great mass of Rumanians were the same as elsewhere in Communist Europe. Between 1957, when abortion laws were eased, and 1966, when they were tightened again, the Rumanian birthrate plummeted from 22.9 to 14.3 per thousand *—a level nearly as low as in Hungary and the Czech lands, where there were fewer children than anywhere else in Europe.

Just as handsome Western-built factories contrasted with the poverty of Rumania's masses, there were two sides also to Rumanian Communist cultural policy. The attractive side was the opening to the West which swiftly followed "de-Russification." In the course of 1964 and 1965, a new monthly magazine called *Twentieth Century* was reintroducing Kafka, Camus, Joyce, Eliot, Proust, Lorca, and St. John Perse. Symphony orchestras were playing Schoenberg, Webern, and other modernists, while dance bands belted out the latest Italian pop hits. Theater troupes and moviemakers from Paris and Rome were receiving enthusiastic

---

* By way of contrast, in neighboring Yugoslavia, where abortion was easy but living standards were steadily rising, the 1966 birthrate was 20.2 per thousand.

welcomes, while Rumanian youths eagerly joined a new network of movie and jazz clubs. Dozens of talented young Rumanian writers, artists, scholars, and scientists were sent to study in Western countries.

But the opening to the West was largely one-sided: in 1965, more than 500,000 foreign tourists visited Rumania, but only 10,000 Rumanian tourists went abroad. Until 1966, there were Soviet-style internal "control posts" along all the country's main roads. At these posts, armed militiamen copied down all foreign license plates and stopped all trucks (to prevent smuggling, black marketeering, and private use of "socialist property"). Resident foreigners described the atmosphere of police control, over themselves and their Rumanian acquaintances, as oppressive and fearful. Officials remained formal and reserved, while Rumanian intellectuals seemed warier than their counterparts in Budapest, Prague, or Warsaw. Only at the very top—among such charmers as Maurer and Manescu—was there confidence, ease, and real zest.

The Rumanian Communist leaders showed that "de-Russification," and even a certain cultural relaxation, were by no means identical with political liberalization. As the historian Ghita Ionescu observed, Rumania's forced-labor camps "were closed, as they had been opened, in silence. More people were released, as they had been arrested, in silence." Many former political prisoners quietly reappeared as professors, editors, and writers; artists and writers were allowed to experiment in form and style. But content was another matter. Until the spring of 1968, even the slightest hint of an honest reckoning with the injustices of the past was strictly taboo. No poet was allowed to mourn the tens of thousands who had labored at gunpoint on the Danube-Black Sea Canal or, even later, among the marshy reeds of the delta.

Solzhenitsyn's *One Day in the Life of Ivan Denisovich* had been followed in 1963 by Joszef Lengyel's memoirs in Hungary, Ladislav Mnacko's *Delayed Reports* in Czechoslovakia, and other works elsewhere describing similar ordeals. In Rumania, no such literature appeared. Even Solzhenitsyn's novel itself was not translated. Asked about it in 1965, a prominent Rumanian editor replied angrily, "That book will never be published in this country. Never, never, never!"

Furthermore, Rumania's new nationalism held few blessings for the country's three major ethnic minorities, the Magyars, Saxons, and Jews. Jews were permitted to depart for Israel, but under conditions so demanding that diplomats remarked, "They are being sold for Jaffa orange juice." Saxons were permitted similar emigration to West Germany after Ruhr industrialists began extending massive credits to Bucharest. The Magyars, however, faced only the prospect of slow and steady "Rumanization." The old Hungarian University at Cluj had been merged in 1959 with the Rumanian university there, and gradually more and more "unnecessary" Magyar-language faculties were eliminated. Contacts between the Transylvanian Magyars and their relatives in Hungary were strictly controlled; there was no question of emigration, so long as life in Hungary was both freer and more prosperous.

Thus, there was little in the new Rumanian way of life to excite the admiration of neighboring peoples, let alone to shake the foundations of the empire as Hungary had done in 1956. From the Kremlin's viewpoint, Rumania's anti-Russian diplomatic maneuvers were annoying, but never provocative enough to compel a showdown. On the other hand, the internal order in Rumania— with its authoritarian party rule and centralized command economy—remained irreproachably orthodox. The Kremlin had reason to fear the Polish slogan of 1956, "No Bread Without Freedom, No Freedom Without Bread," as it later feared Czechoslovakia's demand for "Socialism With a Human Face." But the program of Rumania-first, "totul pentru tara," was never likely to ignite rebellious Russians, Poles, Czechs, or other non-Rumanians within the empire.

Indeed, by maintaining an orthodox Communist system while Khrushchev was experimenting dangerously with de-Stalinization and economic decentralization, the Rumanian party leaders may even have commended themselves to the rigid conservatives who succeeded Khrushchev. Without a doubt, Rumania's most daring act in foreign policy, its avowal of neutrality in the conflict between Russia and China, appeared in a different light after Khrushchev's overthrow. So long as Khrushchev was driving toward the isolation of the Chinese, the Rumanians seemed spoilers and saboteurs. But Rumania's friendship with Peking became an asset when Brezhnev, Suslov, and Kosygin sought a reconciliation with Peking in the winter of 1964–65.

Three weeks after Khrushchev's fall, Chou En-lai was again on the dais at the Kremlin Palace of Congresses, sitting at Brezhnev's right. In February 1965, Kosygin was dispatched to both Peking and Hanoi to solemnize the Kremlin's new, active support of Vietnamese Communist military operations (which Khrushchev had largely ignored). In March, the Soviets dismissed a preparatory meeting of nineteen Communist parties, which Khrushchev had originally called to arrange a larger anti-Chinese conclave. Later in the month, Mikoyan and Chou En-lai met briefly in Bucharest at the funeral of Gheorghiu-dej.

Although the Russians seemed willing to blame all past troubles on Khrushchev, the Chinese were wary of Soviet overtures, and their Albanian friends soon made clear that they distrusted Brezhnev, Suslov, and Kosygin as much as they had Khrushchev. Nevertheless, Brezhnev persisted in the attempt to appease Peking, hoping that the American bombing of North Vietnam would frighten Mao into his embrace.

Ceausescu deftly exploited this situation to enhance his own prestige a few months after Gheorghiu-dej's death. The forty-seven-year-old Rumanian leader offered his good offices in another attempt at mediation between the Russians and Chinese. Thus, the Rumanian party congress in July 1965 became the scene of the biggest international Communist gathering since the Moscow conference of November 1960. To a sweltering Bucharest, there came leaders of all the important Communist parties, fifty-two in all. They included Brezhnev and Teng Hsiao-ping, the secretary-general of the Chinese party.

Both Brezhnev and Teng arrived in Bucharest two days ahead of time. The parties known to favor Soviet appeasement of China (such as the East Germans, Bulgarians, and French) sent their highest leaders to aid the mediation effort. Nevertheless, when the congress opened on July 19, the division in world Communism was dramatized anew. The foreign guests filed onto the stage down two separate aisles. Brezhnev led one group, Teng the other. The two groups then sat at opposite ends of the stage, with the Rumanian leaders between them. When Ceausescu began calling the roll of foreign guests, and Brezhnev's name drew general applause, the Chinese and their allies kept their hands folded in their laps. Minutes later, Brezhnev, eager to please, applauded not only Teng Hsiao-ping but even the Albanian delegate. Ceausescu used the rest of the day to make clear, in polite but firm jargon, that Rumania would continue along its path of "independence, equal rights and non-interference."

The next morning, Brezhnev and Teng Hsiao-ping left the congress at the first recess. So did Bodnaras, Ulbricht, and several other key delegates known to favor a Sino-Soviet compromise. When, late that afternoon, Brezhnev addressed the congress, Teng applauded mildly at the beginning and end of his address.

Brezhnev's theme was the necessity for "unity of action" against the United States. "The need for unity," he declared, "is poignant today, when the United States perpetrates insolent aggressive actions against the Vietnamese people and against the Dominican Republic, brutally tramples underfoot the vital rights and interests of the Congolese people and of other peoples, and when in West Germany, with the assistance and encouragement of the same American imperialism, revenge-seeking plans are being hatched, threatening peace in Europe." *

Different Communist parties might have different views on some problems, Brezhnev said, but "these differences cannot and must not impede joint action" against the United States. What Brezhnev did not say was almost as important as what he said: in contrast to Khrushchev at the Rumanian congress five years earlier, Brezhnev paid only passing lip service to peaceful coexistence and the dangers of thermonuclear war; he made no mention of disarmament or the need for negotiated settlements with the West. He thus withdrew from the Soviet catechism the themes which had been arousing Peking since 1959.

It was not enough for Teng Hsiao-ping. The Chinese leader, light and trim in his black tunic, spoke with a high-spirited verve which made the portly Brezhnev seem all the more plodding.

---

* There had been no particular change in West German policy since Adzhubei had visited Bonn exactly one year earlier. What had changed in the meanwhile was that Brezhnev and Suslov had overthrown Khrushchev.

"Genuine unity," Teng exclaimed, was conceivable "only by defending the purity of revolutionary Marxist-Leninist theory"—that is, Peking's view of the pure faith. The Chinese, Teng declared merrily, were determined "firmly to combat modern revisionism"—Russia—"the main danger of modern times." Moreover, he added (with a look at the Rumanian delegates applauding him); "We are not isolated in our struggle."

The following day, Brezhnev, Teng, Bodnaras, Ulbricht, and other promoters of compromise were absent from the Congress virtually the entire session. They even missed a speech by the North Vietnamese delegate, Le Duc Tho—which would have been a diplomatic slight if Brezhnev, Teng, and the others had not been attempting to achieve "unity of action" in the Vietnam war. Le Duc Tho also left the hall later, presumably to add his voice to the pleas for Sino-Soviet unity.

The pleas all came to naught. Brezhnev was willing, and perhaps Teng Hsiao-ping privately was too; but Mao Tse-tung was not. When Mao launched the Chinese "cultural revolution" in June 1966, Teng was one of its first victims.* Thus, the chief beneficiary of the Sino-Soviet encounter at Bucharest—the last such high-level meeting for four years—proved to be Ceausescu. He used the July 1965 congress to assert his mastery of a party as disciplined as any, and to reaffirm Rumanian determination to fish for national advantage in Russia's troubled waters.

Like the Yugoslav party congress which Ceausescu had observed the previous December, the Rumanian congress was broadcast to the public and open to the foreign press, with simultaneous translations available in a half-dozen languages. (Soviet-model congresses were traditionally closed, with only carefully vetted texts or summaries of the speeches released hours later by official news agencies.) However, unlike the Yugoslav congresses, at which prominent Serbs, Croats, and Slovenes often sang distinctly different melodies, the Rumanian congress proceeded in

---

* The other main victims were Liu Shao-chi, who had negotiated the November 1960 Moscow compromise with Suslov; and Peng Chen, who had arranged the previous compromise with Khrushchev in Bucharest in June 1960. The victor in the purge was Marshal Lin Piao, who countered Brezhnev's appeals for "unity of action" (in which Soviet technology and resources would have been dominant) with the doctrine of "relying on one's own forces," and not on aid from outside.

an atmosphere of total unanimity and fervid self-congratulation. Ceausescu, Maurer, Bodnaras, and the other party leaders arrived at the Congress hall from their villas in chauffeured Cadillacs, Chevrolets, and Mercedes. Brezhnev and other foreigners were assigned Russian cars. The rank-and-file delegates were transported to and fro in Army buses and housed in second-rate lodgings. (Bucharest's three major hotels were reserved for hard-currency tourists.) The delegates did not seem to mind, perhaps because the congress hall was the only air-conditioned public building in Bucharest and the weather was so torrid. They dutifully shouted "Hoo-rah!" and provided standing ovations on cue, particularly when Ceausescu's name was mentioned.

At Ceausescu's suggestion, the party was renamed on the first day of the congress—from the Workers party (as it had been called since 1948) back to the Communist party. What began as the Fourth Congress of the Workers' Party instantly became the Ninth Congress of the Communist party. Literally overnight, thousands of placards and banners in Bucharest and elsewhere were replaced with new ones, featuring the new name and number. "Hail to the Rumanian Communist party" was the theme of most of the streamers; there was not a word about the Soviet Union, the world Communist movement, Vietnam, or American imperialism.

While some other Rumanian leaders at the congress spoke of the need for "collective leadership," Ceausescu spoke only of "collective work" and acquired Stalin's old title of party secretary general (thus anticipating Brezhnev's revival of the title in Russia by nine months). There was no particular homage to Gheorghiu-dej, who had died only four months earlier. (He was to be "exposed" three years later.) The new party statutes dropped previous tributes to the Russian Revolution and instead declared it the patriotic duty of all party members to defend the fatherland and its frontiers. During a week of speechmaking, few Rumanians bothered to mention Marx or Lenin. Rather, the air was filled with quotations from nineteenth-century Rumanian seers who had all, not surprisingly, preached that without steel mills and heavy industry Rumania would be "forever in bondage to foreign countries."

Much of this mythmaking the practical-minded Brezhnev could afford to ignore. Ceausescu's refusal to join in the attacks by Brezhnev, Ulbricht, and their friends on West Germany was a more serious matter. Here, the issue was not mere words about the past, but deeds in the present and future. For, while the Kremlin hierarchs had been quarreling over their policy toward Bonn, West Germany had become Rumania's second leading trade partner. In May 1965, an impressive West German industrial exhibition had been opened in Bucharest by one of Bonn's deputy foreign ministers, who had proposed establishing diplomatic relations between the two countries. Rumania was more than willing, although West German domestic squabbles delayed matters for nearly two years. Thus, in addition to its neutrality between Russia and China, Rumania was preparing to strike a balance between the two Germanies, which promised to be even more profitable. (By the end of 1965, the West German investment in Rumania was estimated at $50 million; trade between the two countries had quadrupled since 1959, and would expand even more substantially in the years that followed.)

However, Rumanian room for maneuver was limited when the great powers grew intransigent and sought to close ranks among their allies and clients. This was the case in the spring of 1966, as both Brezhnev and Mao hardened their positions. The Soviet 23rd Party Congress in April proclaimed a return to the cold war, with the United States and West Germany cast as the principal villains but China likewise beyond the pale. Mao responded with the "cultural revolution," which was as frenetically anti-Russian as it was anti-Western. The United States meanwhile, increasingly consumed by the Vietnam war, began judging European states largely by their attitude toward the Southeast Asian conflict. It was an unhealthy situation for the Rumanians, who swam best when the world situation was fluid, and dreaded situations in which they might be compelled to take sides.

General de Gaulle had similar fears, and when France withdrew from the NATO military command, the Rumanians thought the hour was striking for a concerted effort to loosen both the Soviet and American military blocs. In a speech on May 7, Ceausescu pointedly recalled how Rumanian progressives had sought to resist Hitler in 1939 and 1940, while Stalin and the Comintern were "arbitrarily placing fascist Germany on the side of the Soviet Union." Praising the architects of the prewar Little Entente and Balkan Entente, reaffirming Rumanian determination to expand collaboration with the West, Ceausescu concluded that military blocs, and military bases and troops on the territory of foreign states, were "incompatible with independence and national sovereignty." The world's ardent wish, he declared, was "to liquidate military blocs, to liquidate foreign bases, and to withdraw troops from the territory of other states."

In declaring an impartial plague on both NATO and the Warsaw Pact, Ceausescu miscalculated. General de Gaulle, for all his anti-bloc talk, gave Russia priority in his Eastern policy, while appreciating the shield provided by American forces in West Germany. Moreover, Ceausescu's speech brought Brezhnev to Bucharest on a hasty secret visit which immediately produced a "clarification" of the Rumanian line. Thenceforth, the Rumanians would (at least publicly) echo the Soviet proposition that the Warsaw Pact was necessary so long as the "aggressive NATO bloc" continued to exist. They instinctively sensed the limits beyond which it might prove dangerous to taunt the Russian bear.

These limits were demonstrated anew when Chou En-lai paid an eight-day state visit to Rumania in June. The visit seems to have been a Chinese idea, aimed at competing with de Gaulle's visit to Russia by showing that Peking was just as ready as Moscow to detach other people's allies. At first, it appeared that Chou would be content with publicizing the Chinese cultural revolution, which he announced would destroy "all the outdated culture, all the customs and traditions created in the course of thousands of years." At a Bucharest machine factory, he averted his eyes when passing West German, Italian, and British equipment, but cheerfully pronounced the plant "a revolutionary enterprise on a proletarian basis, a bastion of the dictatorship of the proletariat." Such rhetoric merely amused, rather than frightened, the Rumanians.

However, troubles began at Chou's first official lunch with the Rumanian leaders on June 17. His opening toast excoriated the "modern revisionists," as he called the Russians,* for a multitude of sins. Nearly 24 hours passed before the Rumanians finally released a heavily censored summary of Chou's toast—whereupon the Chinese news agency in Paris released the full text. Thereafter, Chou left the speechmaking to a subordinate, while day after day the communiqués on his talks with Ceausescu, Maurer, and other Rumanian leaders were blandly identical: a long listing of the participants ("down to the coffee-pourers," a Western newsman observed), concluding with the single pat phrase, "the talks proceeded in a cordial, comradely atmosphere."

There was a curious air of make-believe about the entire visit, even though both Chou and his Rumanian hosts politely went through all the approved motions. The Rumanians marshaled crowds to wave little Chinese and Rumanian flags and shout "Hoo-rah! Hoo-rah!" as Chou's cavalcade of Cadillacs and Mercedes went by. Peasants in colorful traditional costumes presented bread and salt. Rumania's smartest folk singers and dancers gave Chou a memorable concert; a Peking musical company in turn played "The East Is Red" with Chinese instruments and dramatized in ballet the all-conquering thought of Chairman Mao. While occasionally betraying a trace of nervousness, Chou generally remained inscrutable, even at the sight of West German tourist girls, in scanty bikinis, lining his route along the Black Sea resort coast. Maurer, who accompanied the Chinese premier to such high spots as Eforie Nord, amiably advised newsmen to expect "no dramas."

However, on the last afternoon of Chou's visit, June 23, the charade collapsed in dramatic fashion. A giant Chinese-Rumanian friendship rally was scheduled to open at 5 P.M. in the congress hall. The morning papers had announced that the meeting would be televised live. Rumanian officials disclosed that they already had the texts of speeches to be delivered by both Chou and Ceausescu and would distribute the texts as soon as they began speaking.

---

* Chou, a born Mandarin, was perhaps the last man to take such jargon seriously. He once began an interview with Western visitors to Peking by announcing that he would prefer to speak of "the Americans" and "the Russians" but that the transcript would have to read "the U.S. imperialists" and "the modern revisionists."

As home televiewers peered at a blank screen, the 3,200 invited guests in the Congress Hall waited—and waited—and waited—for the friendship rally to begin. A half hour went by, then an hour, with no sign of either Chou or Ceausescu. Nervous guests left their seats to smoke in the corridors. Foreign Minister Manescu, asked what was going on, smiled and shrugged his shoulders. At last, after a delay of more than two hours, Chou and Ceausescu appeared on the stage, both strained and angry. Neither read a text. Instead, each spoke extemporaneously, for less than ten minutes, expressing only the barest platitudes consistent with diplomatic protocol.

When Chou flew off the next morning for Tirana, there was not even the pretense of a joint communiqué on the eight-day visit and the twenty hours of formal talks he had conducted with Rumanian leaders. In Albania, the Chinese premier delivered the slashing anti-Soviet speeches which Ceausescu would not, and could not, permit him to deliver on Rumanian soil.

The Rumanians' restraint of Chou had been necessary to increase their leverage with Brezhnev and Kosygin, who arrived in Bucharest eight days after Chou's departure for a bloc summit meeting scheduled to open on July 4. Pressed by Ulbricht, Gomulka, and, doubtless, their own marshals, the Soviet leaders had been pushing for months to harden the bloc's policy toward West Germany. *Pravda* had been fuming continually about "resolute rebuffs" to the "aggressive designs" of the Bonn "revanchists" —hardly sweet music to Rumanian ears. Bucharest, as so often before, had played for time. In Moscow, Manescu had managed to stalemate a bloc foreign ministers' conference for two weeks before finally agreeing that the Bucharest summit meeting could take place.

Although Brezhnev and Kosygin had come to Bucharest two days early, they failed to persuade the Rumanians of the gravity of the new German menace. When the seven-nation conference formally opened, Ulbricht, Gomulka, Novotny, and the other satellite leaders watched the opening ceremonies in the old Royal Palace and then retired to their villas, leaving the Russians and Rumanians to argue it out alone for three hours. In view of the fact that American planes had begun to bomb the outskirts of

Hanoi, the Rumanians had an argument ready that was hard to beat. The main danger to peace, they said, had shifted from Europe to Southeast Asia, and therefore "American imperialism" was the only real problem. As for the West German "revanchism" agitating the Russians, that was limited to "certain circles" in Bonn who were being stimulated by the nasty Americans.*

After two days of haggling over adjectives and semicolons, the Russians wearily agreed to a declaration on European security which added nothing except length to previous statements on the German problem. The next day, the Rumanians happily subscribed to a declaration on Vietnam which condemned the United States. The fourth day of the conference, devoted to the sad affairs of Comecon, produced only a group photograph and a bland, brief communiqué.

At the end of the conference, Ceausescu threw his guests a lavish outdoor dinner at Lake Snagov. Musicians fiddled, Gypsies danced the hora, the wine poured plentifully. Brezhnev was already ruddy and Ulbricht tipsy when Ceausescu, in a finely phrased toast, deftly trimmed to Rumanian proportions what *Pravda* was already calling the "historic" Bucharest declaration on the German problem. It had been an interesting and useful "exchange of views," the Rumanian leader declared, a really comradely discussion, a contribution to the cause of "peace and friendship." As was well known, Rumania sought such friendship with all nations, regardless of their social systems, on the basis of national independence and sovereignty, equal rights, noninterference, and mutual advantage.

At the end of the banquet, Ulbricht was asked to respond to the toast. It was not one of his more coherent, or even grammatical, utterances. Foggy-eyed but cheerful, he too declared that the

---

* Ceausescu had been angry at the United States since the Firestone Rubber Company, in April 1965, was permitted by the Johnson Administration to renege on an agreement to build a synthetics plant in Rumania. However, he retained the keen Rumanian sense for discerning future possibilities. When a defeated American politician, generally regarded as a has-been, proposed to tour Eastern Europe a year later, the Poles refused him a visa, the Russians turned him over to petty civil servants, the Yugoslavs never bothered to answer his letter—but Ceausescu spent eight hours with him discussing the state of the world. The American, of course, was Richard Nixon, who remembered his friends of the dark days—and included Bucharest on his first world tour as President in August 1969.

conference had "achieved a great success—and I am not saying this because of the wine."

Barely six months later, a smiling Manescu arrived in Bonn to establish diplomatic relations, the first Communist foreign minister ever to visit the Rhineland lair of the wicked "revanchists."

CHAPTER 11

The Spoils of War

A popular East European joke of the mid-sixties found Lyndon Johnson and Leonid Brezhnev together, behind bars, in a Chinese concentration camp. "I kept telling you, Leonid," said Lyndon, "that Germany wasn't the only problem."

The anecdote expressed a growing weariness with the Kremlin's obsession with the German problem. Two decades after World War II, with the United States and Russia launching supersonic rockets into outer space, with China exploding nuclear weapons, the Soviet Union and its staunchest allies continued to portray West Germany as a major menace. Brezhnev, Ulbricht, Gomulka, and Novotny attacked the Bonn Republic as a hotbed of militarists and former Nazis, who were forever "lusting after nuclear weapons" and (as Brezhnev put it) "hatching revenge-seeking plans, threatening peace in Europe." Television screens in Moscow, Warsaw, and elsewhere featured an endless series of war films recalling Nazi atrocities, and cold-war dramas depicting West German officials, officers, spies, and scientists plotting new horrors.

The mystery was why Brezhnev and his colleagues remained so shrill after all the changes that had taken place in the world and in Germany itself. By 1965, more than half the West German population consisted of young people who had been born after 1933. Those of them old enough to remember Nazism recalled mainly the devastation it had wreaked on Germany itself. Increasingly, for West Germans of all ages, the dominant experience was the continuous postwar prosperity. If some senior Bonn officials still dreamed of atomic weapons and regaining lost territories, most of their countrymen cared far more about a cooperative apartment, a new Volkswagen, a charter flight to Ischia, Ibiza, or Corfu. From 1957 onward, they voted in increasing numbers for the anti-Nazi, anti-militarist Social Democrats. Pressed by public opinion as well as by their Western Allies, even conservative Bonn governments in the sixties began groping their way toward a dialogue with Communist Europe.

Nevertheless, Brezhnev, Ulbricht, Gomulka, and Novotny rejected any serious dialogue. They often acted as though a peaceful, prosperous, democratic West Germany were more dangerous than an aggressive, nationalist regime. There was a tone of glee in Soviet, East German, and other Communist periodicals when a West German neo-Nazi party, the NPD (National Democrats), profited from a brief recession in 1966–67 to win from 6 to 10 percent of the vote in various local elections. (In the 1969 national elections, the NPD received less than 5 percent.) It was as though life would be simpler in Moscow, East Berlin, and Warsaw if West Germany were really to become the bogey of their propagandist fantasies.

Why? Officially, the Communist answer was that the Bonn Government refused formally to recognize "the consequences of World War II" and therefore was really bent on overturning the postwar order. Yet, in fact, West Germany had done nothing to abet the June 1953 uprising in East Germany, to exploit the 1956 upheavals in Poland and Hungary, or to stop the building of the Berlin Wall in August 1961.

Strangely enough, the easiest place to acquire a certain sympathy with Communist anxieties was in Bonn itself. The political atmosphere in the "provisional" West German capital differed from that in the country's major cities—Hamburg, Frankfurt, Munich, or even Cologne and Dusseldorf just down the Rhine. In these cities, with their variety of occupations and interests, the overriding preoccupation of most West Germans with personal well-being was all too obvious. Bonn, however, like Washington and Brasilia, was a one-industry town. Its only real business was politics, and even its political life was limited, because in the decentralized Federal Republic many domestic issues were decided by provincial and local governments.

Thus, careers in the Bonn bureaucracy attracted Germans whose passion was foreign policy, "the German question." These included a goodly share of former civil servants and propagandists of the Hitler regime, restless scions of once-great Prussian military and landowning families, former *Volksdeutsche* who had been expelled from Bohemia and the Baltic coast, Silesia, and the Danube plain. A West Berlin city planner once remarked that he avoided Bonn like the plague because "all the old German nationalists have been reassembled there." Such aversion was shared even by many members of Parliament, who habitually fled Bonn on Thursdays to pass long weekends in more agreeable political climates. Like most West Germans, they were bored, if not repelled, by the zeal which senior Bonn officials devoted to keeping the German "question" alive.

For such officials, the "question" went beyond the crises in divided Berlin, beyond even the barriers which divided the 57 million West Germans from their 17 million "brothers and sisters" in East Germany. Indeed, what such officials called the German "question" closely resembled what the Communists called "the consequences of World War II."

As a result of the war, Germany had been stripped of its old eastern territories and effectively partitioned into two states, one democratic and the other Communist. Bonn's official doctrine held, however, that legally Germany remained a single nation whose fate could only be settled by a peace treaty. Until then, in the words of Bonn's "peace note" of March 1966, "Germany continues to exist within its borders of December 31, 1937."

Thus, official Bonn placed a question mark not only over the existence of Communist East Germany but also over Soviet occupation of the northern strip of East Prussia, including Koenigsberg (Kaliningrad); and the occupation and resettlement by Poland of the remainder of East Prussia, Pomerania, and Silesia east of the Oder and Lusatian Neisse rivers. Official maps, including the weather maps on West German television, continued to outline Germany in the 1937 borders. The territories east of the Oder-

Neisse line were shaded German but marked as under "provisional administration" by Poland and Russia.

Only on rare occasions, behind closed doors, could one encounter a Bonn official frank enough to state the hard reasoning behind such fictions. "German relations with the Slavs go back a thousand years," said one such official. "Twenty years is nothing in the long view. Who really knows what Eastern Europe will be like in 1980 or 1990? If the Soviet Union goes up in smoke, there could be a general move eastward. Why preclude it now?"

Few Bonn officials were so terrifyingly candid. Most asserted that they could not recognize the Oder-Neisse frontier because of "public opinion," as allegedly represented by the noisy organizations of expellees and refugees from the old Eastern territories.

The expellee organizations claimed to speak for 9 million Germans. However, the 1961 census disclosed that more than 3 million of these expellees were younger than twenty-five years of age—thus children, at most, when they left the Eastern territories. Moreover, the expellee organizations were anything but spontaneous. They were richly subsidized by Bonn government agencies, which also sponsored books, periodicals, films, rallies, and other demonstrations aimed at reminding West Germans of "our homeland in the East."

Expellee demonstrations resembled faded replays of the old Nazi newsreels of the 1930s. At the "Rally for Germany" on May 14, 1966, Bonn's largest expellee demonstration since 1958, most of the participants were men and women in their fifties and sixties. They seemed to have been frozen in prewar unstylishness. The men wore black fedoras or pink panamas with brims too wide; the women wore marcelled permanents and no lipstick.

Placards and banners were lettered in the old Gothic script, which post-Hitler Germany had abandoned for modern typefaces. Black flags bore the heraldry of lost provinces—including the Sudentenland in Czechoslovakia, as well as Silesia, Pomerania, and East Prussia. Speakers at the rally not only claimed the Oder-Neisse territories but asserted that "the strength of the Czech people" was "inadequate to maintain the once-blooming homeland of the Sudeten Germans as a Central European culture-region."

The expellees claimed, as one of the basic human rights, "the right to a homeland" (*heimatsrecht*)—that is, the right to resettle as Germans in their former territories. They also claimed the "right to self-determination." It was obvious that the two "rights" added up to a program for regaining the territories for Germany.

Such demonstrations were staged largely to persuade foreign diplomats that it was politically inopportune to recognize the consequences of Hitler's lost war. Yet by the mid-sixties, the act was wearing thin. The May 1966 expellee rally, officially sponsored, was countered the same day by a spontaneous demonstration of Bonn University students, at which leading professors, theologians, and television commentators condemned the expellees. Cabaret artists in Dusseldorf, Munich, and West Berlin satirized expellee pretensions mercilessly.

In contrast to the professional expellee lobbyists, many distinguished West Germans, themselves former expellees, pleaded tirelessly for German acceptance of Eastern realities. They included Klaus von Bismarck, a director of the West German radio and descendant of the Iron Chancellor; Countess Marion Doenhoff, once one of East Prussia's greatest landowners, now editor of *Die Zeit*, the country's most respected intellectual weekly; the novelist Günter Grass, who lovingly recreated his native Danzig in fiction, while campaigning politically against expellee demands; and numerous leaders of the Evangelical Church. Public-opinion polls showed that their views were steadily prevailing among young and educated West Germans.

After Khrushchev's fall, conservative Bonn officials and Soviet propagandists, each for different reasons, began spreading the tale that a dangerous "new nationalism" was rising in West Germany. Cool-eyed observers considered such agitation thoroughly spurious. In an interview early in 1966, Rudolf Augstein, publisher of the hard-hitting newsmagazine *Der Spiegel*, declared:

> I don't believe for a moment in all this nonsense about the new nationalism here—not an ounce of truth in it. It is impossible to overestimate the apathy, the non-political nature of today's Germany. . . . Not many people here really care about reunification at all. If it were

not for Berlin, they would have forgotten about it long ago. As it is, the shootings at the Wall every week disturb their bad consciences. . . . But the old nationalism is completely dead. When I was a student before the war, we really worried about the Polish Corridor. No schoolboy today pays the slightest attention to the Oder-Neisse line.

Even a few friendly gestures from the Soviet Union would thus have been sufficiently welcomed in West Germany to overcome the doctrinaire resistance of the Bonn old guard. Khrushchev had evidently realized this in 1964, and had sought through Adzhubei to enter realistic negotiations with Bonn. However, Khrushchev had been overthrown, partly in order to prevent such negotiations, and thenceforth Moscow's line was hard.

Brezhnev, Ulbricht, Gomulka, and Novotny posed difficult preconditions to West Germany without indicating any possible concessions in return. They asked Bonn to recognize the Oder-Neisse line, renounce nuclear weapons, recognize Ulbricht's German Democratic Republic (DDR) as a fully sovereign state in international law, and West Berlin as a "separate political entity" with no political ties to West Germany.

However, even if Bonn were ready to renounce all hope of German reunification, Khrushchev's successors offered no guarantee of freer Allied access to West Berlin, no hope of easier travel between the two Germanys, no promise of normal contact between West and East Berlin.* Moreover, when the West Germans or their Western allies accepted some Communist proposal, the Communists promptly withdrew it. Thus, Khrushchev had often proposed reducing the number of Allied and Russian troops in the two Germanys; when the West, after Khrushchev's fall, took up the idea, Brezhnev turned it down. Similarly, Poland's Foreign Minister Rapacki had declared in 1958 that "the reunification of Germany as a peaceful country is the condition for a complete normalization of the situation in Europe," but by 1965 Poland was demanding that Bonn recognize not only the Oder-Neisse line but the DDR as a fully sovereign German state.

* Telephone connections between the two halves of the city had been cut off as early as 1952. Calls had to be routed through Frankfurt am Main and Leipzig, and usually took hours. After 1966, even the special holiday visits which West Berliners had been permitted to make to relatives behind the Wall were prohibited.

Westerners found such intransigence difficult to understand, in light of the common view that conditions in East Germany and Poland had stabilized after the upheavals of 1953 and 1956 and the Wall crisis of 1961. Communist spokesmen emphasized that East Germany had become the world's seventh leading industrial power and that the Oder-Neisse territories were prospering mightily under Polish rule. To the extent that such claims were justified, Brezhnev, Ulbricht, and Gomulka should have felt more secure—and therefore capable of more flexible policies to take advantage of the evolution of West German public opinion.

The attitude of Brezhnev, Ulbricht, and Gomulka was considerably easier to understand for those who had actually visited East Germany and the Polish territories beyond the Oder-Neisse line. The picture they presented, two decades after World War II, helped explain some of the anxieties which lay beneath the Communist rulers' intransigence.

East Germany's worst days were clearly over by the mid-sixties. There had been, after the first nightmarish months of Russian occupation, a decade of systematic Soviet pillage of the East German economy—in the form of war reparations, dismantling of factories, compulsory deliveries, and "mixed companies." All these had lasted until 1955. Ulbricht himself estimated the toll at $22.5 billion; Western estimates were often higher.

Then, there had been Ulbricht's rash attempt in 1958 to imitate China's "great leap forward." His so-called "main economic mission" called for catching up with West Germany in per capita production by 1965. By 1961, this effort had failed as dismally as the Chinese "leap." Together with the various Berlin crises, and the brutally rapid collectivization of agriculture (carried out in ten weeks during the spring of 1960), Ulbricht's speedup provoked a rising outflow of refugees—which culminated in the building of the Wall.

Like their fathers and brothers killed in World War II, most of the 3.6 million refugees from East Germany between 1946 and 1961 were able-bodied young men. As a result, women accounted for 54 percent of the East German population and 47 percent of the work force. Moreover, one-fifth of the population were too old to work; for every four adults of working age, there were three old-age pensioners or children. With the birthrate steadily falling, East German statisticians did not expect a normal population pattern until the 1980s.

The manpower shortage made economic rationalization far more imperative in East Germany than in Russia, Poland, or the Balkan states. In July 1963, the DDR adopted a new system of economic management, based on principles which the party had summarily rejected as "revisionist" five years earlier. The new system stressed enterprise profits and gave broad management powers to some eighty industrial associations or cartels. Capital equipment was revalued, state subsidies were reduced, and by 1966 industrial prices became more flexible.

These changes improved both the quantity and quality of industrial production, which even in 1962 had been some three-fifths higher than the pre-Communist peak. Both output and incomes rose under the new management system. Although eastern Germany had formerly exported food and now had to import it, the standard of living in the DDR was higher than that of any other country in the Soviet bloc.

It always had been, of course. Before the war, what is now East Germany had accounted for more than 36 percent of the Reich's industrial production—including 40 percent of its textiles, cellulose, and paper products; more than 35 percent of its optical and precision instruments (the Zeiss works at Jena was world-renowned); 30 percent of its chemicals (in the Krupp subsidiaries at Leuna and Buna); and more than 20 percent of its machinery and heavy equipment, motor vehicles, and electrical products.

The Prussians and Saxons who inhabited Ulbricht's DDR had been industrious, disciplined, well-organized workmen since Marx's day. There had never been much reason to believe that Communism alone could transform efficient German workers, technicians, engineers, and scientists into Balkan peasants. Communist expansion of the East German school system produced the skilled personnel needed to operate advanced technology, and the Wall ensured that they remained in the DDR. East Germany was sophisticated enough to make effective use of computers while other Communist-ruled folk were still struggling with the abacus. The new economic system, moreover, despite the Marxist jargon with which it was explained, was distinctly in the German tradition of economic concentration.

By the spring of 1965, therefore, the worst was over in the DDR, and old hands who had known the country before the Wall noted various signs of economic improvement. However, for a Western visitor seeing East Germany for the first time, the DDR was a shock. In contrast to humming, prosperous West Germany, in East Germany a foreigner felt instantly: this is the country, these are the people, that lost the war. The immediate, overpowering impression was that time had stood still—that one was back in the first postwar years, or even in the gloom of the Great Depression. As John Dornberg, a sympathetic observer, summarized the difference:

> By West Germany's super-affluent standards, East Germany is drab, dull, dark, shabby, scruffy, somber, ragged, neglected and listless. Seen through Western glasses, a leaden, gray pallor hangs heavy over the country and East German life—from the appearance of its cities to the apparel of its inhabitants; from the lack of selection on the shelves, to the dirty, sooty stucco that cascades off the facades of older houses to which neither a painter nor a plasterer has laid brush or trowel in twenty-one years. . . .

Inside East Germany, one could understand not only why Khrushchev and Ulbricht had sought to strangle thriving West Berlin, but also why a Berlin pastor had despairingly observed that the DDR was God's chastisement of the German people for Nazism. The sense of defeat and humiliation among the human beings in the DDR was even more depressing than the decay of its buildings. Amos Elon, an Israeli journalist, compared the atmosphere to that of a penal colony. "The DDR," he remarked, "has a sobering effect on those who come to Germany with a bagful of resentments," on those who "want to see Germans in hair shirts, barefoot and covered with ashes. East Germany in its way changes this attitude. You think of the lonely people you meet there, of their perennial despair, of the young people who look so old. You think: for God's sake, enough! It is enough!"

This sense of a nation defeated arose partly from the wartime ruins. Unter den Linden and the Wilhelmstrasse in East Berlin, the great wastelands of firebombed Dresden, the gutted churches and palaces of Potsdam were—twenty years after the war—indescribably poignant. All the more so since Cologne, Hamburg, and other West German cities, which had been just as badly bombed, had long been flourishing as never before.

Yet, even apart from the uncleared rubble, the cities and towns of East Germany had a quaint, faded *Alt-Deutsch* (Old German) quality which had virtually disappeared in West Germany. Some West German visitors felt nostalgia for the scenes of their childhood. Foreigners felt as though they had walked onto the set of *The Blue Angel* with Emil Jannings and the young Marlene Dietrich. There was an eerie stillness in most of the towns as dark approached and life retreated behind shutters. There was no formal curfew, and yet it was true that (as Welles Hangen remarked) "in the DDR, it is always earlier than you think."

To be sure, the slow reconstruction of Unter den Linden in East Berlin had already begun in 1965, and there were master plans—mostly for completion in the early 1970s—for rebuilding Dresden, Karl-Marx-Stadt (formerly Chemnitz *), and other bombed cities. The plan for Dresden, with its high-rise hotels and glass-concrete shopping centers, would erect a kind of Marxist Miami on the site of what was once the baroque "Florence of the Elbe." Still, the functional architecture which began rising in major East German cities during the 1960s was an improvement on the pitifully meager construction, much of it Stalinist gingerbread, during the first postwar decades.

However, only one-fifth of the population lived in the eleven East German cities with populations of 100,000 or more. As Dornberg pointed out, the real DDR was still to be found in hundreds of small Saxon industrial towns, Thuringian villages, and Mecklenburg hamlets, where little had changed since the 1930s: "time and neglect have turned the aging facades, the bumpy cobblestoned streets, the cheerless veneer of petit bourgeois respectability into strongholds against time."

Many foreign visitors escaped only too gladly from this de-

* It was one of the few major German cities in which Marx had never been.

pressing, recent past into the happier, more remote past: the islands of great culture recalling so much of Germany's old glory. In Leipzig's St. Thomas Church, there were always fresh flowers at the simple stone crypt of Johann Sebastian Bach. In Dresden, at the renowned Zwinger Palace of the Saxon kings, there was one of Europe's greatest galleries—filled with Canalettos, Tintorettos, Titians, containing Rubens' incredibly sensual *Leda and the Swan* and Raphael's Sistine Madonna. In Weimar, there was the handsome little opera house in which the German National Assembly proclaimed the Republic of 1919. Before it, bronze arm-in-arm, stood Weimar's greatest sons, Goethe and Schiller, aristocrats of the spirit whose cosmopolitan universality transcended all the German history which followed them.

In Goethe's house, the master's books—from England, from Italy, from Paris an original edition of the great French Encyclopedia—testified to how deeply Eastern Germany was once part of a Europe united in spirit. Although Communist inscriptions in the house portrayed Goethe as an "anti-feudal bourgeois reformist," broader horizons were evident in the original manuscripts themselves, including the confident ode to the United States, "*Amerika, du hast es besser. . . .*"

Yet such retreats into happier tradition could never last more than a few hours. Across the square from the Goethe house at Weimar, there was a club for Soviet officers, and outside the town, on the road to Buchenwald, there was a huge Russian garrison. There were such encampments outside every major East German town—barracks encircled by watchtowers and searchlights, and often barbed wire as well. Along the autobahns radiating north, east, south, and west from Greater Berlin, there were vast parks of Soviet tanks and armored vehicles, ready to move quickly to put down any uprising as they had done on June 17, 1953.

At that time, the Ulbricht regime had been virtually overthrown in a single day by unarmed workmen, as East German police and soldiers stood idly by. Over the years, more than 30,000 East German soldiers, as well as several thousand border troops, had fled to the West—the highest desertion rate in the world. The essential foundation of the East German state remained the Soviet occupation force, comprising twenty divisions, or more than 250,000 men. In contrast to China and Albania, Yugoslavia and Rumania, where Communism had been successfully "nationalized," the harsh Ulbricht regime remained inconceivable without the Soviet Army.

The DDR's industrial products might well impress visiting Poles and Bulgarians, but the citizens of the DDR were neither Poles nor Bulgarians, but Germans. Their material conditions had improved after 1963, but their standards of comparison remained German standards: the memory of their own past, and the West German reality they could and did watch every evening on West Berlin television. One alarming feature of conversations with ordinary East Germans, as late as 1965, was the rather frequent recollection of the peaceful and victorious Nazi years (1933–42) as the "good old days." Old people recalled the era of Kaiser Wilhelm with even greater fondness. This kind of sentiment had died out in West Germany. When public-opinion polls asked which had been the best time in their country's history, most West Germans replied "the present."

The Berlin Wall remained mute testimony to the fact that East Germans, too, found Western reality attractive. The Wall, with its barbed wire, concrete, and cinderblock barriers, moats, tank traps, and electrified fences, extended nearly 100 miles encircling West Berlin, dividing it from East Berlin and the rest of East Germany. The "death zone" at the Wall was some 110 yards wide; it was manned by 14,000 East German border troops, stationed at or between more than 200 watchtowers and an equal number of bunkers and pillboxes, and aided by some 230 dog patrols. Some 110 miles west of encircled Berlin, the 856-mile frontier between the DDR and West Germany had been guarded with similar vigilance for years. Nevertheless, in the first five years after the Wall was built, some 25,000 East Germans successfully risked their lives to escape westward. There were more than a thousand reported incidents of border guards firing on East Germans attempting to escape, and 163 were reported to have been killed.

As border controls tightened, and East German economic conditions improved after 1964, the DDR authorities permitted several hundred thousand old-age pensioners (men over sixty-five, women over sixty) to visit relatives in West Germany. The regime had little to lose, as defections among these elderly people would have eased the DDR's high pension costs without affecting production.

Ulbricht was not tempted, however, to extend the experiment to East German citizens under sixty, for it had been the young, the able-bodied, and the professionally skilled who had led the great wave of defections before 1961. Moreover, the DDR prohibited virtually all but official travel to Yugoslavia when that country showed signs of becoming an escape route to the West. And when Czechoshovakia's western borders opened up after 1963, Ulbricht concluded a special agreement with Novotny under which Czechoslovak security police seized and repatriated thousands of East Germans attempting to flee westward.

Despite these and other security precautions, by August 1969 —the eighth anniversary of the Wall—more than a quarter of a million East Germans had managed to cross over to the West. Of this total, 126,911 were old-age pensioners or invalids who settled with Western relatives legally, with valid East German exit permits. But 127,276 had fled by crashing the Wall, swimming across border rivers and lakes, using false papers, jumping ship in foreign ports, or escaping by way of other Communist countries (such as Czechoslovakia, Rumania, and Hungary), where West and East German tourists mingled.

The plain fact was that, although daily life in most of East Germany was neither as dramatic nor as horrible as the scenes at the Wall, the DDR was a distinctly unappealing and unhappy society in the eyes of most Germans, East or West. It failed to attract even the families of its highest leaders. Ulbricht's sister preferred to live in West Germany, his brother in New York. The father and sisters of Erich Honecker, Ulbricht's chief deputy, similarly preferred to live in West Germany.

Although East German living standards remained 30 to 40 percent lower than those in West Germany, the unhappiness which permeated the DDR was less economic than political in origin. East Germany was not merely a country under foreign occupation, in a manner more tangible and visible than any other. Its Communist rulers were narrow, bitter fanatics consumed with hatred for everything Germany had ever been—not only Nazi Germany but, even more, the Germany of the Weimar Republic created by Social Democrats.

Ulbricht, the crafty survivor of numerous Stalinist purges of German Communism, personified this hostile spirit. Born in Leipzig in 1893, twice a deserter from the German Army in World War I, a professional Communist functionary since 1919, Ulbricht had followed the Comintern line in all the disastrous German Communist attempts to subvert the Weimar Republic. Between 1929 and 1933, as German democracy was struggling for survival, Ulbricht in the Reichstag was denouncing the social Democrats as "Social-Fascist agents of Big Business," "bedfellows of the Nazis," and "mortal enemies of the working class." A few weeks before Hitler came to power, Ulbricht had insisted that "now, as always, we must aim the main blow at . . .the Social Democrats."

In 1940, Ulbricht unhesitatingly preached the virtues of the Stalin-Hitler Pact, under which the NKVD was turning over many of his German Communist comrades to the Gestapo. "Not only the Communists but also many Social Democratic and National Socialist workers consider it their task to stand by the Pact," Ulbricht declared. Whoever opposed the pact, he said, " is an enemy of the German people and will be branded an accomplice of English imperialism. . . ."

Despite attempts in the 1960s to portray Ulbricht as an elder statesman, most East Germans—and many foreign Communists as well—continued to find his personality repulsive. One of the founders of German Communism, Clara Zetkin, once remarked of Ulbricht, "Look into his eyes and you will see how scheming and dishonest he is." Tito's contempt for Ulbricht, whom he had known since the 1930s, was legendary. When Ulbricht occasionally addressed a mass meeting in an East German public square, the area was cordoned off and filled with soldiers and security police.

Even Ulbricht's closest collaborators in the DDR found his presence chilling. One official described a birthday party at Honecker's, which was a gay, relaxed affair until Ulbricht entered: "The atmosphere curdled. . . . We felt like children caught with their hands in the cookie jar. . . We were almost paralyzed and I still don't know why. He is just one of those human beings whose very presence robs the atmosphere of gaiety."

Ulbricht shaped East Germany in his own image. The DDR managed to combine what was most offensive in Communism—sectarian fanaticism, paranoid hostility to outsiders—with rigid German traditions of military and bureaucratic authoritarianism. In Russia and elsewhere, daily life under Communism was often softened by inefficiency, inconsistency, corruption, laziness, and other human foibles. In East Germany, humorless thoroughness made the air even harder to breathe.

To Germans, East and West, the DDR often recalled the Nazi period. There were the goose-stepping soldiers of the East German Army, wearing the field-gray uniforms of the old *Wehrmacht*. There was the state within the state, the security police or *Staatssicherheitsdienst*, with its system of block wardens and informers. There was a censorship as deadly as any in history, a propaganda as shrill and pervasive (though not as skillful) as that of Dr. Goebbels. It preached a "heroic" compulsory optimism at home, hysterical hatred of the fiendish enemy abroad, narrow intolerance of "decadent" modern culture.

Khrushchev's efforts at de-Stalinization had had the least effects on East Germany. Solzhenitsyn's *One Day in the Life of Ivan Denisovich* was never published there. When Kafka was rehabilitated in Czechoslovakia, East German ideologists waged a campaign to prevent republication of his work elsewhere in the Soviet bloc. At the Wall, East German border guards pulled out the seats, and placed mirrors under the chassis, of every incoming car to search for Western books, magazines, and newspapers. (Such controls had long disappeared in Budapest, Prague, Warsaw, and Bucharest.) In 1963 and 1964, the party campaigned to prevent East Germans from watching West Berlin television or listening to West Berlin radio. The campaign failed, and most antennas in the DDR were pointed to West Berlin transmitters. But the DDR authorities showed that they were thinking ahead when, together with the Soviet Union, they adopted the French system for color television, which was incompatible with the system developed in West Germany.

More than in any other Communist country, conversations with ordinary citizens in the DDR tended to lead, with alarming rapidity, to violent expressions of contempt for their rulers. East Germans often expressed personal helplessness, passivity, resignation—but rarely a genuine acceptance of the regime. Thus, a Leipzig doctor explained, "We never thought you Americans would allow them to put up the Wall. That was a great shock, and I don't think we've recovered yet. What to do now? I suppose you must keep pressing the Russians with diplomatic notes, even if nothing comes of it. Maybe in twenty years things will change."

The doctor's young wife and children had been visiting Hamburg when the Wall was built. He had told them to remain there: "I can bear it here, but I do not want my children to grow up in this state." He made clear that his despair at life in the DDR was not based on material conditions, but on its totalitarian spirit.

A Jena student, barely in his twenties, put it even more plainly: "The issue isn't economics: capitalism or socialism. The issue is freedom. I visited West Germany before the Wall and, although there's lots wrong there, it's far better than here. I came back only because my parents are getting on and have nobody else. The new economic system here may be an improvement, but it's come a dozen years too late. We are all simply exhausted by this regime, tired of the same old exhortations and the same old functionaries.

"It is a question of confidence. Why should we work hard for them when they still don't let us read Günter Grass, they make us sign petitions approving the Wall, they jail people for conversations just like the one I'm having with you. . . . What we need is not new accounting systems in factories, but civil liberties and parliamentary democracy. Camus has explained it all quite clearly."

An East Berlin engineer in his forties expressed a more common attitude of adjustment. He hoped that the advance of modern technology would eventually transform both Communism and the West. He regarded German reunification as out of the question for the foreseeable future, but believed just as strongly that it was inevitable in the long run: "It may take twenty years, thirty years, maybe till the next century. But Germany is one nation, and Europe is too small to play the old games. Meanwhile, all we can do here is concentrate on our work."

Even among DDR officials, there was a unique defensiveness. Propagandists obsessively referred to divided Berlin as "Berlin, capital of the DDR" and to "the Soviet Union, the greatest friend of the German people." A deputy mayor of Dresden compulsively expounded the party line that the Allied firebombing which destroyed the city had been directed not against Nazism but as a warning to the Soviet Union (although Stalin had in fact approved the raid). Other officials felt compelled to describe the Wall as a great step for the "consolidation of peace." But in most such avowals there was a singular lack of conviction, and many such officials appeared to be lost, trapped men, profoundly ashamed of themselves. Even the handful of staunch dogmatists seemed defensive. Their manner was tight, resentful and sullen, with none of the ease or exuberant confidence to be found among Communists in Yugoslavia, Rumania, or occasionally elsewhere.

Among economic managers, there was frequently a certain pride in recent East German achievements. More often than not, however, the pride was in having made the best of a bad bargain —of having achieved as much as they had *despite* the Soviet occupation and the Communist system. In comparing their life with that of West Germans, few attempted to argue that the DDR was a superior, happier society. Rather, the most frequent theme was that West Germany had benefited from American aid, but that everything the East Germans had, they had been compelled to build with their own hands in the face of "all manner of difficulties" (that is, continuing exploitation by the Soviet Union).

The profound disaffection among even DDR officials was dramatized by the suicide of Dr. Erich Apel, the head of the East German state planning commission, on December 3, 1965. Apel, who was forty-eight years old, was the leader of the young technocrats who had introduced the new economic system two years earlier. He shot himself in protest against a new-five year trade agreement with Russia which was being signed that very day—a treaty whose unfavorable provisions he had been resisting for three months but which Brezhnev had come personally to East Berlin to impose.

Apel was not the first East German economic chief to take his own life. Gerhard Ziller, the Central Committee secretary for the economy, had shot himself eight years earlier for similar reasons. Both men had despaired of Ulbricht's policy of deliberately sacrificing East German economic welfare to the interests of the Soviet Union—in return for Kremlin support of his hard political line.

From Ulbricht's standpoint, such sacrifices were essential. The Kremlin would only maintain the walled division of Germany so long as he could make it pay—and pay better than the billions of dollars worth of credits and grants with which many of Bonn's statesmen ultimately hoped to "buy" reunification from Russia. Ulbricht, who had barely survived an attempt by Beria and Malenkov to undermine him in the spring of 1953, was in a much stronger position when Khrushchev made his ill-fated overtures to Bonn in 1964. By that time, more than half Russia's machine-tool imports came, at bargain prices, from the DDR. East Germany provided complex turbines, giant construction cranes, and numerous other industrial goods that were still beyond the capacity of Soviet industry.

"We did not lose our heads," Ulbricht later commented, "during the hostile campaign launched on the occasion of Adzhubei's visit to West Germany." Indeed, Ulbricht appears to have anticipated the overthrow of Khrushchev, and may have played a part in stimulating it. The East German press suddenly stopped all criticism of China two weeks *before* Moscow in its turn suspended attacks on Peking. Ulbricht had shown similar prescience in the weeks before the death of Stalin.*

Loyalty to the Soviet cause, and mastery of the corridors of Kremlin power, had made Ulbricht one of the most durable rulers

---

* Seven weeks before Stalin's death, a resolution of Ulbricht's Socialist Unity party quoted Georgi Malenkov several times at great length. On the other hand, Stalin himself was quoted only with a half-sentence dating from 1910. As Franz Borkenau, the Western Kremlinologist, explained, "Such a deliberate affront could have been offered only by people sure of the tyrant's approaching downfall, or else out of the reach of his retribution." On the basis of Ulbricht's resolution, Borkenau publicly predicted Stalin's imminent death.

of recent German history, twice as durable as Hitler. His achievement lay in persuading successive Soviet rulers that the spoils of World War II, in the form of a disciplined, dependent protectorate between the Elbe and the Oder, would be preferable indefinitely to the possible benefits of a broader Russian reconciliation with the real Germany. But he had failed to construct an order capable by itself of withstanding the tests and trials of normal international relations, a state that could live without the Wall and the Soviet Army.

The DDR had been a creation of the cold war; after twenty years, continuation of the cold war remained vital to its very existence. West Germans, who had long recognized the reality of another German-speaking state, Austria, might be ready to acknowledge the existence of still another, called the DDR. But East Germans would continue to hope for the freedom, ease, and mobility enjoyed by their countrymen west of the Elbe. Whether in one German state or two, they longed to live as normal human beings, rather than the inmates of a penal colony. Until they abandoned all hope, neither Ulbricht nor the Soviet leaders who shared his views could afford to relax.

To the east of Ulbricht's DDR, across the Oder and Lusatian Neisse rivers, there were Poland's "regained territories." It was claimed that Polish settlers had successfully built a bustling "new life" in the former German Pomerania, East Prussia, and Silesia.* Yet nearly everywhere, from Gdansk (Danzig) on the Baltic to Wroclaw (Breslau) on the Oder, not only did "the stones speak German," but even the state of the open fields proclaimed the existence of former boundaries. Driving north from Warsaw toward the Baltic, travelers could easily tell when they were crossing into the former East Prussia: dwarf plots and underbrush gave way to large, neatly landscaped estates,

---

* In 1939, the territories had a population of 8.8 million. Of these, 1.2 million (at the highest estimate) were Poles. By 1965, according to Warsaw, the territories once again had more than 8 million inhabitants. Nearly all of them were Poles, and almost half had been born there since 1945. Polish Government statistics also showed dramatic increases in coal, iron, steel, and machinery production since 1946. Even taken at face value, however, the production statistics lost much of their allure when compared with the postwar records in the rest of Europe, including East as well as West Germany.

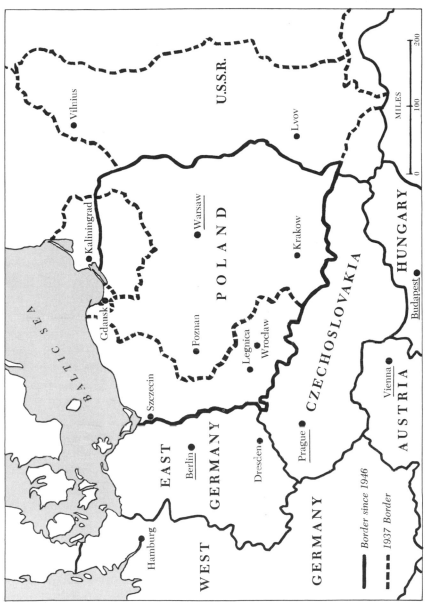

THE CHANGING POLISH FRONTIER

desultory wooden shacks to great stone manor houses, the roads and railways themselves improved. Such Baltic ports as Gdansk and Szczecin (Stettin), with their Gothic churches and town halls, their peaked roofs and open squares, resembled Bremen and Lubeck far more than they did Warsaw or Cracow.

On the whole, the "northern territories"—East Prussia and Pomerania—compared favorably in appearance with the rest of Poland. But they remained relatively underpopulated. In some districts, it was said, the population had regained prewar levels. In other districts, however, this was clearly not the case, despite the high Polish birthrate. Abandoned buildings and untended fields testified to the decline of what had once been Germany's great granary. (Poland was importing grain from the United States.)

On the old East Prussian *autobahn*, in a drive of nearly 100 miles from Elblag (Elbing) eastward to the Soviet frontier, on a prime June day in 1965 I encountered exactly one bus and three bicycles. On the same *autobahn*, driving westward toward Gdansk, there were a few more cars—but also mothers taking children to play on the deserted superhighway. We crossed the Vistula by the same "temporary" pontoon bridge that the advancing Red Army had erected twenty years before; the prewar bridge had not been rebuilt.

At the frontier station with the DDR, west of Szczecin, traffic in either direction was almost nonexistent. The eastern frontier with the Soviet Union, in the direction of Kaliningrad, could not be seen by a Westerner. It could only be approached through a series of security zones, in which the *autobahn* gave way first to paved village roads, then to dirt and gravel paths culminating in a series of barriers. Polish villages near this frontier were garrisoned by Soviet troops and among the civilians some of the new settlers seemed to be Russians and Ukrainians rather than Poles.

On the other hand, it was not difficult, in Prussia and Pomerania, to come upon German-speakers. Although officials maintained that there were fewer than 150,000 Germans left in Poland, Western intelligence estimates were four times as high. The statistical argument was largely pointless, however, since the population in these areas was traditionally bilingual, or spoke dialects which mixed German and Slavic; the Prussians themselves had been Germanized Slavs.

Silesia was even more dispiriting than the north. Twenty years after World War II, there was still a distinct air of transience in such cities as Wroclaw and Lignica (Liegnitz). Wroclaw's population was still far below that of the prewar Breslau (477,000 in 1966 as compared with 621,000 in 1939). A great deal of wartime rubble remained to be cleared, in Lignica as well as Wroclaw. New building and historic reconstruction were neither as massive in scope nor as intelligently conceived as in Warsaw and other central Polish cities. The most impressive site in Silesia, indeed, was the vast Soviet army base outside Lignica—a former *Wehrmacht* encampment strategically poised to strike at Prague or Berlin as easily as at Warsaw or Cracow.

There was, moreover, among the population in Silesia a desultory shabiness which contrasted unfavorably not only with Warsaw, Poznan, and Cracow but with Czech towns just to the south and East German towns 100 miles westward. Polish sociologists described the settlers in the "western territories" as a "melting pot: pioneers and scavengers, adventurers and the flotsam of war, the cream of the country's intelligentsia and simple workers and peasants." The intelligentsia had come largely from Lwow (now Lviv, in the Western Ukraine), whose university had been transferred to Wroclaw. But most of the new inhabitants of Wroclaw, Lignica, and similar cities were former peasants. Some of them had come from overpopulated areas of central Poland, but the largest proportion had come from the Carpatho-Ukraine, the old Eastern Poland, annexed by Russia. The unkempt peasant majority, transplanted from villages in the Carpathian mountains or the Pripet Marshes, seemed ill at ease in their Germanic urban surroundings. "They seem to be waiting for the Germans to come back and put things in order," one foreign visitor remarked.

One reason for the transient atmosphere in the Oder-Neisse lands was that the Polish Communists had only begun spending real money on the new territories after 1956. The "Muscovite" leaders before then understood that, for the Kremlin, the struggle for Europe was the struggle for Germany—and that Russia might yet tempt German nationalists with a revision of the German-Polish frontier.

Gomulka and the rising "Partisan" faction in the party invested greater efforts in developing the new territories, and defending them against West German "revanchism," real and imagined. The "enemy" in Bonn justified the need for Soviet "protection," and as time passed the defense of the Oder-Neisse frontier became the chief bond remaining between the Polish Communists and the population, which was otherwise becoming progressively disenchanted with Gomulka's rule.

After the optimism of the late fifties, the Polish economy had bogged down irreparably in 1962. "Veritable streams of all kinds of junk," one paper complained, "flow through our production halls and storerooms. . . . We face an avalanche of shoes and slippers made with leather hard and stiff as tin, shoes with unglued soles and wrinkled tips . . . electric soldering irons, heaters, transformers whose users are threatened with electrocution. . . ." The Oder-Neisse lands looked shabby, therefore, not only because of their neglect during the first postwar decade, but because of the general stagnation. For Poland as a whole, 1964 and 1965 brought no economic improvement over 1962 and 1963. Mass living standards remained low, and corruption spread.*

Since Khrushchev's wheat purchases from the West, there had been few illusions that Russia might yet provide poor countries like Poland with either massive infusions of capital or dynamic social ideas. Those in Eastern Europe who wished to modernize rapidly, like the Yugoslavs and Rumanians, were turning west-

---

* According to the Warsaw weekly *Tygodnik Demokratyczyny*, in October 1966 more than half the urban inhabitants in Poland had an income of less than 800 zlotys a month—$33 at the tourist rate of exchange, $8 at the black-market rate. Some 10 percent earned more than 1500 zlotys. Almost a third of those surveyed lived in one room. Only 59.8 percent had running water in their apartments, 58 percent had plumbing, 28.5 percent bathrooms, 9.1 percent central heating.

According to *Panstwo i Prawo*, Warsaw, September 1966, in the preceding four years there had been half a million "economic crimes," ranging from thefts of state-owned typewriters to large-scale racketeering. Most of the culprits were government employees or party functionaries. The extent of the crime was estimated at one billion zlotys a year.

ward—and especially to West Germany, which had become Europe's strongest economic power. Bonn for its part was no longer preaching unremitting cold war, but had begun to offer trade, aid, and "normalization" to Eastern Europe. Its conservative officials were still not ready to recognize the Oder-Neisse line without some progress toward reunification. However, Khrushchev and Adzhubei had shown in 1964 that, despite all the talk of Communist solidarity, the possibility of a Russian deal with Germany could never be completely dismissed. In the past, such deals had always been at Poland's expense.

By 1965, therefore, various Poles were drawing differing conclusions as to how their nation might avert the classic nutcracker. Gomulka had concluded that Communism in Poland was itself untenable without the Soviet Army. He saw Poland's only salvation in blocking any Russian rapprochement with West Germany —through continued solidarity with Ulbricht's DDR and with the Soviet marshals and military-industrial leaders who needed a West German "threat" to justify their swelling war budgets.

Outside Gomulka's entourage, on the other hand, thoughtful Poles, both Communist and non-Communist,* were drawing the opposite conclusion. They were gradually coming to believe that Poland's future might best be secured by attempting to reach an understanding with West Germany. For, without such an understanding, and without German economic aid on a large scale, all of Poland—including the Oder-Neisse lands—would be condemned to falling farther and farther behind Western Europe economically, while remaining at the political mercy of the Kremlin. Such Poles believed that, rather than join Brezhnev and

---

* "The dividing line in Polish society," wrote George J. Flemming early in 1967, "is not between party members and others, but rather between decent people and scoundrels, who are to be found among both. The present Central Committee is composed on the one hand of old campaigners—fewer and fewer of them—who once belonged to the pre-war Communist Party of Poland, and on the other hand of people who live on the dividends from Marx's *Capital*, of opportunists, yes-men, unabashed bootlickers and people who will undertake any job providing it is dirty. The nation itself has nothing to do with them. Poland's 32 million people are condemned to live with the party and the regime, but most live despite them and against them." It should be added that the number of both the "old campaigners" and the "decent people" in the party was significantly reduced in 1968.

Ulbricht in intensifying the campaign against Bonn, their country should sympathetically encourage moderate forces to gain influence in West Germany.

Among those who believed the time had arrived to seek a reconciliation with West Germany were the leaders of Poland's Roman Catholic hierarchy. Their expression of this belief provoked a major crisis, which began at the end of 1965 and gathered force through most of 1966. In the crisis, Brezhnev and Gomulka demonstrated that the Soviet interest in the DDR was more pressing even than an opportunity to invest the Polish Government with the prestige of the Pope.

The opening move came from West Germany in October 1965, and from Protestant leaders. In a thoughtful, forty-four-page memorandum, a study group of the German Evangelical Church declared that "a return to the previous status east of the Oder and Neisse would be impossible today without threatening the existence of the Poles. As a result of the behavior of the Germans toward their Polish neighbors during the war, the German nation is specially bound to respect the vital rights of the Poles."

The Evangelical Church document was sharply attacked by Bonn expellee lobbyists, and generally praised in Poland. However, the atmosphere changed radically when the Polish Catholic hierarchy attempted to broaden the dialogue a month later. On November 29, Cardinal Wyszynski and the thirty-five Polish bishops attending the Vatican Council in Rome published a letter inviting German Catholic bishops to attend the celebrations of the Polish Millennium—the thousandth anniversary of the conversion in 966 A.D. of King Mieszko I to Christianity.

Polish Catholics had been preparing for the Millenary Celebrations for a decade. The hierarchy planned months of religious observances and rallies to culminate on May 3, 1966, at the hallowed shrine of the Black Madonna in the Jasna Gora monastery near Czestochowa. Cardinal Wyszynski planned to invite cardinals and bishops from all over the world—including Pope Paul VI—to the solemn celebrations at Jasna Gora.

In their letter inviting the German Catholic prelates to the Millenary celebrations, the Polish bishops reviewed the "burden" of a thousand years of German-Polish history, and granted and asked forgiveness for past wrongs. After recalling the horrors of the Nazi occupation, the letter continued:

"The Polish Western border at the Oder-Neisse is for Germany, as we well understand, an extremely bitter fruit of the last war of mass extermination, compounded by the suffering of millions of refugees and expelled Germans (carried out in accordance with the inter-allied order of the victorious powers, Potsdam 1945). A large part of the population had left these territories out of fear of the Russian front and had fled westward. . . ." The Polish bishops recalled that "large sections of the German people" had also suffered under Nazism, and that "thousands of Germans, as Christians and as Communists, shared in the concentration camps the fate of our Polish brothers."

Nevertheless, the Polish bishops declared that for Poland, "which emerged from the mass murders not as a victorious power but utterly exhausted," the Oder-Neisse frontier was no mere territorial dispute but "is a question of existence." More than 30 million Poles could not be expected to live "without the Western Territories, but also without the Eastern Territories, from which millions of Poles were forced to stream into the Potsdam Western Territories."

"Only holy men, those who possess a pure thought and clean hands, can build bridges between peoples," the Polish bishops concluded. "We call to you: 'Let us try to forget.' No more polemics, no more cold war. Rather, the beginning of a dialogue. . . . Please also transmit, we beg you, our greetings and thanks to the German Evangelical brethren who, with us and with you, are trying to find solutions for our difficulties."

The Polish bishops' letter was part of a broader effort by the Roman Catholic Church to reconcile Germans and Poles. The text had been approved by a German committee composed of the Bishops of Essen, Eichstadt, and Meissen, and formally submitted to the Archbishops of Cologne, Munich, and Berlin ten days before publication. This enabled the German bishops to reply, in similar spirit, on December 5. The next day, the Polish episcopate formally hailed the German reply as "an immense step forward to a rapprochement . . . of the millions of Catholics on either side of the Oder and Neisse."

Pope Paul VI had made no secret of his desire personally to attend the Polish Millenary celebrations, and understood that he could do so only by coming as a guest of the Polish government as well as of the Polish hierarchy. He also indicated readiness to consider easing German acceptance of the Oder-Neisse frontier by raising the status of Polish bishops in the disputed territories. His very presence in Communist Poland—even if he did not visit the Western Territories (as some thought he might)—would have stimulated further soul-searching among German Catholics. Paul's predecessor, John XXIII, had already alluded publicly to the "inviolability" of the Polish frontier in October 1962, and had received Adzhubei in February 1963, as part of the new approach to Communism formulated in the encyclicals *Mater et Magistra* and *Pacem in Terris*. Khrushchev had cautiously welcomed the new Vatican approach, recognizing that it would aid not only the Italian Communist party but also his own plans for easing relations with the United States and West Germany.

The Polish bishops' letter was to demonstrate that Khrushchev's successors had other priorities. For eleven days after the publication of the letter in Rome, Communist Warsaw was silent as Gomulka's closest lieutenant, Zenon Kliszko, conferred with Brezhnev in Moscow. On his return, the Warsaw correspondent of *Le Monde* promptly reported that "the Soviet leaders let it be known . . . that they would appreciate it if the Polish Government adopted an intransigent attitude." On December 9, Soviet Foreign Minister Gromyko delivered a tough anti-German speech in Moscow, and the next day the Polish Communist press opened fire on the bishops, accusing them of having displayed "excessive humility" toward the Germans.

The clash between the Communist state and the Catholic Church mounted in intensity throughout the first half of 1966. The issues were clear to both sides: a Polish-German reconciliation based on German recognition of the Oder-Neisse frontier (as envisioned by the Catholic prelates) would undermine the Communist argument that Soviet hegemony in Poland was necessary to prevent German domination. As Gomulka put it on April 16, 1966, the bishops' concept of Poland as a "bulwark of Christianity" was "tantamount in our times to sowing discord between the Polish and Soviet people, to breaking up the Polish-Soviet alliance."

The Polish Communists first barred Cardinal Wyszynski from returning from Warsaw to the Vatican Council. Then they refused to permit Pope Paul, or other foreign bishops or cardinals, to attend the Millenary celebrations. All spring long, week after week, from Gdansk to Cracow, they staged concerts, soccer games, motorcycle rallies, folk-song festivals, and counterdemonstrations against the Catholic celebrations. "We shall never forget the Hitlerite crime of genocide! * We shall never forgive those guilty of such crimes!" was the theme of the Communist counterdemonstrations, in which General Moczar's security police assumed an active role.

On May 2 and 3, the Catholic Millenary celebrations reached their climax at the shrine of Jasna Gora. Despite police obstacles to travel, more than 300,000 enthusiastic pilgrims had reached Czestochowa. At one side of the huge outdoor altar, the papal throne sat empty, decorated with a portrait of Paul VI and a wreath of yellow roses.

The Communist authorities had sought to divide the Catholic clergy, but the Archbishop of Poznan hailed Cardinal Wyszynski in these words: "The Pope's absence was to humble you, but it has exalted you, for he has named you to represent him. . . . The Bishops and the nation are united with you as never before."

Although Communist posters proclaimed "We do not forgive!" the Archbishop of Wroclaw declared: "We forgive and we know how to forgive, and this is going to be our program for the future. Nobody can cram our faith into a narrow nationalistic ghetto."

In his sermon on the evening of May 3, Cardinal Wyszynski once more offered mutual pardon to the people of Germany and exclaimed: "We, the Polish Bishops and the whole nation of the children of God, say from here: 'We forgive. . . . At the threshold of the new millennium, we forgive.'"

"We forgive! We forgive!" the pilgrims chanted after him.

Eight weeks later, troops of police, swinging truncheons, were

---

* Two years later, an "anti-Zionist" campaign resulted in driving most of the 30,000 Polish Jews who had survived Nazi genocide out of the country.

beating up young Catholic demonstrators singing hymns outside Gomulka's office in Warsaw. In that same June of 1966, Marshal Tito—who had once been classed with Gomulka as a "national Communist," and who had even earlier tried the Cardinal of Zagreb for treason—was normalizing Yugoslav relations with the Roman Catholic Church while striking a decisive blow against the power of his own political police.

CHAPTER 12

Slavic Counterpoint

In July 1964, a few weeks after Josip Broz-Tito saw Nikita Khrushchev for the last time in Leningrad, a short, stocky young literary scholar, unknown to either of them, arrived in Moscow to spend a month among Soviet writers.

The young man, Mihajlo Mihajlov, not yet thirty years old at the time, was a Yugoslav citizen by birth who was seeing Russia for the first time. Yet he was Russian by blood, and Russian literature had become his lifework. His parents, like tens of thousands of other Russians, had emigrated to Yugoslavia during the famine that followed Lenin's Civil War.

Mihajlov himself had been born in Pancevo, on the left bank of the Danube opposite Belgrade. He had been educated in Yugoslavia (including the universities at Belgrade and Zagreb) and had served both in the Yugoslav Army and in the "youth brigades" building the *Autoput*. He became a university lecturer in Slavic Languages and Literatures at the Zadar (central Dalmatia) branch of Zagreb University and wrote for leading papers and magazines in Zagreb, Novi Sad, and Belgrade.

Mihajlov was a specialist on Dostoyevsky, but he had become increasingly absorbed by the new Soviet literature of de-Staliniization. Early in 1964, for the Belgrade monthly *Delo*, he had written an essay on "The Mission of *Novy Mir*," describing that

Russian magazine's sponsorship of Solzhenitsyn, as well as of Voznesensky, Yevtushenko, and the young poets, and explaining the significance of Alexander Tvardovsky's ballad "Tyorkin in the Other World." Mihajlov concluded that "the forces of the Russian renaissance are so strong that every attempt to retard the current development is only a hopeless attempt aimed at turning back the clock of history."

While Mihajlov was in Russia, the Zagreb monthly *Forum* printed his essay comparing Solzhenitsyn's *One Day in the Life of Ivan Denisovich* with Dostoyevsky's novel *The House of the Dead,* which had appeared exactly a hundred years earlier (1862) and which also described, from firsthand experience, the life of political prisoners at forced labor in Siberia. Mihajlov's article included a review of the history of concentration camps, which, he said, originated with the British in the Boer War (1899–1902). He cited original Soviet sources as well as International Red Cross reports to document the existence of forced-labor and death camps under Lenin.

Mihajlov expressed the view that "the most positive thing in Soviet society in the past few decades . . . is the fact that today Stalin's concentration camps are openly discussed and written about in the Soviet Union." For "until the last of the crimes committed during the last half century in the name of humanity has been traced and published, the most terrible consequence of 'labor-camp socialism'—fear, which implies a readiness for further slavery—will not have been removed."

On the other hand, Mihajlov wrote that, in defying Stalin "in the heroic year 1948, Yugoslavia herself showed how unlimited pressure gives birth to an unlimited power of resistance, and how this power of resistance alone guarantees that freedom shall not be lost. . . ."

This conclusion was identical with that of Milovan Djilas, whose *Conversations With Stalin* had warned that "those who wish to live and survive in a world different from the one Stalin created . . . must fight." Djilas had already spent two additional years in prison as a result of his book, which had been published abroad. However, not only was Mihajlov's essay published in the monthly magazine of the Yugoslav Academy of Sciences and Arts, edited by the celebrated Croatian novelist and prewar Communist Miroslav Krleza, but no obstacles were raised during Mihajlov's visit to Khrushchev's Russia.

In the course of a month in Moscow and Leningrad, Mihajlov met, spoke, and occasionally argued with many of the leading figures of the Russian "renaissance." They included such veterans as Ilya Ehrenburg and the venerable poet-aesthetician Victor Shklovsky; such younger poets as Andrei Voznesensky, Bulat Okudzhava, and Bella Akhmadulina; such novelists as Vladimir Dudintsev (*Not by Bread Alone*), Leonid Leonov (*The Russian Forest*), and Vladimir Tendryakov (whose story "Three, Seven, Ace" Mihajlov had translated into Serbo-Croatian). Mihajlov discussed Solzhenitsyn with *Novy Mir*'s deputy editor, Vladimir Lakshin, who reported to him the common Moscow saying "Tell me what you think of Ivan Denisovich, and I will tell you who you are." He discussed Dosyoyevsky and the literature of the Russian emigration with Moscow University professors and literary historians; tape-recorded concentration-camp ballads sung at parties of university students; visited theaters, movie houses, churches, Lenin's Mausoleum, and the grave of Boris Pasternak.

In all, Mihajlov found the air among Soviet intellectuals remarkably buoyant in July 1964. Dudintsev, among others, believed that "a new 1956" was on its way, confirming Mihajlov's own youthful optimism. Stimulated by his contacts, Mihajlov returned to Yugoslavia, to his one-room apartment at Zadar on the Adriatic, and wrote a literary travelogue in three parts, entitled "Moscow Summer." He was finishing the manuscript when Khrushchev was overthrown, and was circulating it to various Yugoslav magazines at a time when men far more experienced than he in the ways of Soviet politics were unsure as to what, if any, changes Brezhnev, Suslov, Kosygin, and their colleagues would bring.

The Soviet Central Committee in November 1964 vowed fidelity to the de-Stalinization proclaimed in 1956 and 1961, and the Russians sent an alternate Politburo member, Pyotr Demichev, to repeat the vow at the Yugoslav party congress, which met in Belgrade in the second week of December. Demichev's presence itself seemed a fair omen; this was the first Yugoslav party congress which the Soviet leaders had not chosen to boycott.*

Tito himself insisted (or pretended) at the congress that the main danger of "dogmatic conceptions and reversion to Stalinist methods" came from Peking. The Chinese, he declared, had expected the Kremlin leaders to abandon Khrushchev's policy and "revert to that of the Stalin period"—but "this expectation was not fulfilled." For this reason, Tito said, "Comrade Nikita Sergeyevich Khrushchev, who has submitted his resignation," continued to be the main target of Chinese attacks.

Like the Chinese, Tito attempted to identify Soviet policy as "Khrushchevism Without Khrushchev," although he doubtless realized that deeper changes were possible. He had taken Brezhnev's measure in 1962, and remembered Suslov's role in numerous Kremlin attacks on Yugoslavia between 1948 and 1960. While the Soviet press stopped all mention of Khrushchev immediately after his dismissal, Tito eight weeks later felt compelled to pay public tribute to the fallen leader:

> Although in the last few years Comrade Khrushchev did have certain failures and mistakes while heading the Party and Government, he played a great role in regard to de-Stalinization and in promoting freedom of expression, and also had great merits in safeguarding world peace . . . He deserves much credit for the normalization and improvement of relations between Yugoslavia and the Soviet Union. . . . Nor are his merits in this respect denied either by the leadership or the people of the Soviet Union.

At a news conference a few days later, Tito declined to enter more deeply into the nature of Khrushchev's errors or his merits, and sidestepped questions about his own possible future relations with the new Kremlin leaders. However, he offered Moscow at least two symbolic gestures. He announced that he would visit Ulbricht's DDR in the course of 1965 and that he would not, despite "many recent interventions," grant clemency to Djilas, the symbol of Yugoslav anti-Stalinism.

Thus, when the first installment of Mihajlov's "Moscow Sum-

---

* The only one thus far, since they later boycotted the 1969 congress.

mer" appeared in *Delo* at the beginning of 1965, it seemed that little had changed either in Russia, in Yugoslavia, or in the relations between them. Mihajlov's first article was published without incident, even though it was thoroughly unorthodox in spirit. It proclaimed Solzhenitsyn "the most popular Russian writer these days" and declared that "the basic characteristic of the Soviet literary mood" was "the expectation of a final liberation of literature and arts from all possible restrictions of dogmatic Marxism."

Mihajlov's first article was peppered with irreverent remarks about the queues at the Lenin Mausoleum (open only three hours a day, and not every day), the dullness of Soviet newspapers, the young girls in Moscow's forty open "overcrowded" churches, and the cult of Lenin ("strange, the way people do not notice that things frequently repeated lose their meaning").

Mihajlov also described the rising popularity among Soviet students of "the great and gifted Russian poet Nikolai Gumilev," the late husband of Anna Akhmatova, who had been shot as a "counterrevolutionary" in 1921 even though Lenin had promised Maxim Gorky that the poet's life would be spared. (Mihajlov noted without disapproval that Gumilev had in fact "actively fought against Soviet rule.") His first article concluded with a remark by the novelist Leonov that "people will be writing about Soviet concentration camps for the next eighty years."

In his second article, which appeared in the first days of February, Mihajlov returned to the theme of Soviet concentration camps. "A year ago," he recalled, "Khrushchev said that the editorial boards of literary journals had received about 10,000 novels, short stories and memoirs about life in the camps." Although only a few of these had been published, "Soviet magazines now remind one more and more of the annals of the misdeeds committed under the Inquisition of Philip II. . . ."

However, Mihajlov observed, this open exposition of the Stalin era posed a serious problem: "It is a question of the people who actively fought against Stalinsim before 1956, and told the truth about the situation in the Soviet Union. These people are still considered criminals and 'traitors.' . . . One the one hand, Stalinism is being condemned and proclaimed anti-national and criminal, while on the other hand anti-Stalinists are also being condemned. Sooner or later this abnormal situation must be resolved. . . ." It would be resolved in a manner Mihajlov did not foresee.

It was symptomatic, Mihajlov felt, that the Soviet press avoided comparisons between Nazi and Soviet concentration camps.

It is even understandable. The first "death camps" were not really established by the Germans, since they were founded by the Soviets. In 1921, in the vicinity of Archangel, the first death camp, known as Khomolgor, was formed with the sole purpose of physically exterminating the prisoners. . . .

Even with regard to genocide, Hitler was not the first to introduce it. On the eve of World War II, many small peoples from the border areas in the vicinity of Turkey, Iraq and Persia were deported to northern Siberia where, unused to the cold weather, they died like flies. It is therefore fully understandable that during World War II many units of the Red Army, composed of Kalmyks, Tatars, Cherkesses and other peoples who had been exposed to rude reprisals, escaped to the side of Hitler's criminals. . . .

Mihajlov noted other Soviet groups which had either fought at the side of the Germans or had become "third force" Partisans fighting both Nazi and Soviet troops. He then went on to quote several of the concentration-camp songs he had heard sung among Moscow university students, and declared that the prison songs, "will be sung, there is no doubt, for yet another century, the way Russian prison songs from the last century are still being sung today."

The theme of Soviet concentration camps was hardly new to Yugoslav readers, because a great deal of anti-Stalinist literature had been published in the country between 1948 and 1953. However, on February 6, 1965, Mihajlov's article became an international affair as the *New York Times* correspondent, David Binder, reported that it had "stirred the ire of the Soviet Embassy" in Belgrade.

On February 11, with the news of Soviet displeasure echoing around the world, Tito received a delegation of state prosecutors and declared:

You see what happened with that article in *Delo?* The public prosecutor ought to have banned it straight away, and made the decision known in public. . . . You ought to have instituted proceedings immediately against the person who wrote that article, and published your decision in the press. It was necessary to know that an indictment had been raised against him, that he was a reactionary who slandered a great event—the October Revolution. . . .

We must not permit instances of anyone in our socialist country defending Hitler's concentration camps, where living men were burned to death, where millions and tens of millions of people, children and old men alike, were destroyed. . . .

There have been other examples of the same kind. In such matters, you must take action immediately and energetically. . . . It is not only *Perspektive* from Slovenia which is in question here. We have such examples also in Zagreb, Belgrade, Novi Sad, Sarajevo, everywhere. I ask myself whether there is some sort of organization.* . . . It seems to me that this tendency, which we used to call Djilasism, is now assuming a new form.

That very day, a Belgrade court issued an injunction banning *Delo,* and more than a thousand copies of the magazine were seized by the police. A fairly calm criticism of Mihajlov in the party weekly *Komunist* was supplemented (evidently at the last minute) by a strong editorial note to the effect that "one cannot tolerate essentially anti-socialist outbursts." The editor who had accepted Mihajlov's article was dismissed from *Delo* and reprimanded by his Communist party cell.

Yet, after this—for more than two weeks—nothing happened. Tito's own remarks to the prosecutors were not published until three weeks later. There were rumors of a major struggle in the party leadership, among whom various divisions had been obvious at the December party congress. Then, on February 27, the Soviet ambassador, Alexander Puzanov, called on Tito. The Soviet envoy presented a message from Moscow which other Communist dip-

---

* *Perspektive* was a cultural review, popular among Ljubljana University students, which had been suppressed in June 1964; two of its editors were jailed but released after protests by eighty-five leading Slovene intellectuals.

Tito was accustomed to view political events, however spontaneous, as organized. At the 1952 party congress, when a rank-and-file delegate, discussing moral problems, accused Petar Stambolic (later premier) of having stolen his wife, Djilas proposed a board of inquiry. Tito cried "The enemy is in our midst!" and suggested that the outburst had been organized by the Cominform.

lomats were quick to characterize as "a veritable cannonade."

The next day, the Belgrade weekly *Nin* printed a long, un-signed attack on Mihajlov as a "White Russian *revanchist* and interventionist." His articles, *Nin* said, "have the mouldy smell of long-digested nastiness from the White-Russian kitchen . . . ma-licious claptrap." The style of the attack suggested that it may have been drafted in Moscow.

Mihajlov sought to reply, with a long open letter to *Nin* which he also sent to 290 other Yugoslav editors. None of them dared print it. Instead, on March 4, the daily newspapers published Tito's speech to the prosecutors for the first time. The same day, Mihajlov was arrested in Zadar. He was to remain in prison thirty-seven days before being released on parole.

While in prison, Mihajlov read some stories which had been published abroad by a mysterious Soviet writer who called him-self "Abram Tertz." At the moment that Mihajlov was discovering him, "Tertz" himself was appearing in *Novy Mir* for the last time under his real name, Andrei Sinyavsky. The forty-year-old Rus-sian critic had also just succeeded in arranging Soviet publication of an important new edition of Pasternak's poetry, with a sen-sitive critical introduction by himself. Sinyavsky and his writer friend Yuli Daniel, who had been published abroad under the pseudonym "Nikolai Arzhak," had been among the pallbearers who had laid Pasternak to rest in the grave at Peredelkino which Mihajlov visited.

The Yugoslav authorities first sought to prosecute Mihajlov on the same charge on which Djilas had been twice convicted—that of "hostile propaganda." However, there was no evidence, even remotely plausible, to suggest hostility toward Yugoslavia, as the law required. Instead, on March 26, Mihajlov was indicted on two counts: under Article 175 of the Yugoslav Criminal Code, "for damaging the reputation of a foreign state," and under Article 125 of the Press Law, for having mailed a copy of his manuscript to an Italian publisher after *Delo* had been banned.*

* Miloslav Mirkovic, the *Delo* editor, was also indicted on the first count, although (perhaps because he was a Communist party member) he was never arrested. However, after the indictment, he swore to the prosecutors that Mihajlov had insisted on the articles' publication without any editorial changes. The charge against Mirkovic was then dropped, and a few weeks later he was back at his old job at *Delo*.

In Zadar, an unsigned statement announced that Mihajlov had been suspended from his university post. However, someone—probably a student—also wrote on Mihajlov's office door: "*Ziveo Mihajlov! Ziveo Sloboda!*" (Long live Mihajlov, long live freedom). In Belgrade, liberal writers waited fearfully for signs of a general witch-hunt. The Nobel Prize novelist Ivo Andric advised them, coolly, that history rarely repeats itself.

Communist party stalwarts meanwhile informed visiting Westerners, "confidentially," that the publication of the Mihajlov articles had been a "Chinese-Stalinist provocation." However, other Yugoslav officials, some of them quite senior, frankly admitted, "They made a mistake." The "they" rather than "we" was indicative of how the Mihajlov case disturbed the more liberal Yugoslav Communists. They were disturbed on at least two grounds—first, because the frankly political prosecution of the young writer cast doubt on the constitutional and legal safeguards which Kardelj, the Croatian leader Vladimir Bakaric, and others had sought to build into the Yugoslav system; second, because the prosecution of Mihajlov seemed chiefly aimed at appeasement of the Soviet Union, a general policy of which they had become increasingly skeptical.

Mihajlov was brought to trial in the district court of Zadar on April 29 and 30. On the eve of the trial, he was expelled from the university as "morally undesirable." However, on the morning the trial opened, most of the 110 seats in the courtroom were occupied by young faculty colleagues and students, with almost as many standing in the back of the hall or in a small gallery. They were to remain throughout the five-hour hearing the first day, packed the hall a half-hour before sentence was pronounced the next day, and throughout the proceedings maintained a grave silence which could only be interpreted as sympathy for the defendant. After the verdict, many of them came to shake his hand.

Mihajlov was the only witness. Modest and mild-mannered, he was an intellectual of the type one often meets as assistant editors of Western literary magazines. His attorney, Dr. Ivo Glowatzky of Zagreb, was a Central European gentleman of the old school: half-Polish, half-Croat, lean, bald, gray-mustached, also deceptively soft-spoken. He took the case, he said, "as a matter of professional conscience."

Of the three judges, only one was a professional jurist: the presiding judge, Branko Novakovic, who attempted throughout to appear calm and unemotional. The other two, lay judges, were more colorful (one seemed out of a De Sica movie, the other out of a Montenegrin fresco), but neither ever said a word.

The public prosecutor, Zarko Kovacevic, was not particularly verbose either. He read his opening statement from a typewritten manuscript (its style recalled the astute draftsmanship of Belgrade diplomatic notes), intervened only three times thereafter, and seemed rather uncomfortable in doing so. Near the prosecutor sat three sunburned figures, the best-dressed men in the hall, whom nobody could identify. Some said that they were "other judges," others said they had come "from Belgrade." Most onlookers assumed that they were emissaries of the UDBA, Vice-President Rankovic's powerful security police.

The prosecutor's statement declared that Mihajlov had "abused the freedom of expression which exists in our country" by his derogatory references to the Soviet Union. When Judge Novakovic began to question Mihajlov, the defendant was swift to declare that "historical facts cannot constitute an offense." Mihajlov said he was "aware that by presenting such facts this would not be agreeable to the party concerned," but that he had not intended to defame the Soviet Union. Some 90 percent of the article was about literature, but one could not write about Soviet literature without discussing the camps—which had dominated that literature since the fall of 1962.

Why, asked the judge, did you feel it necessary to compare Soviet with Nazi camps? "It was not a coincidence. I consider Stalinism no better than fascism, and therefore made the comparison." But why had Mihajlov discussed Soviet camps *before* Stalin? "Because it is a historical fact. It may be painful but it is true." Mihajlov noted that all of his documentation had come from books in Yugoslav libraries. The court, however, at no point challenged the accuracy of Mihajlov's facts.

On the question of mailing his manuscript abroad, Mihajlov said that he was already in jail when *Delo* had been permanently banned (the first injunction had been temporary) and that he had made no commitment for foreign publication of "Moscow Summer."

Dr. Glowatzky, the defense attorney, argued that there was not a single precedent for the case in a Croatian court. He noted that Mihajlov's article in *Forum* on Dostoyevsky and Solzhenitsyn had produced no legal consequences. Of the seventy-two pages of the *Delo* articles, he said, the indictment had specified as offensive only four sentences scattered on three pages; this was hardly a way to go about being deliberately offensive to the Soviet Union. The *Delo* articles, moreover, were less specific than either the *Forum* article or than numerous books published in Yugoslavia on Soviet forced labor.

Summing up, Dr. Glowatzky said that Mihajlov had "felt deeply the patience and suffering of a great nation where, as Khrushchev himself said, some twelve million people have passed through the camps." The very week of the trial, he noted, the Croatian party newspaper *Vjesnik* had observed that, even now, no official light had been shed on the trials of the Old Bolsheviks. "Regardless of the circumstances which surrounded the inception of this case," Dr. Glowatzky concluded, "the court in its full independence should acquit the defendant."

Mihajlov, in his final plea, stressed that everything he had written was true. People had been offended by remarks about Lenin, "but nobody would claim that Lenin patented socialism. I have said that Yugoslav decentralization and self-management have prevented the development of Stalinist totalitarianism, or Leninist totalitarianism."

The next morning, the court pronounced Mihajlov guilty on both counts. All the evidence, the judge said, showed that Mihajlov's intention was "to belittle the endeavors of the present Soviet Government in the fight against Stalinism." This was an observation which Yugoslav Communists themselves would soon regard with wry irony. The sentence on Mihajlov was five months on each count—which the court combined into a single sentence of nine months, minus the thirty-seven days already served. Mihajlov could remain at liberty pending his appeal to the Croatian Supreme Court in Zagreb.

On May 8, 1965—barely a week after Mihajlov's trial—6,000 Soviet Communist party, Army, and KGB officials gathered in the Kremlin Palace of Congresses to celebrate the twentieth anniversary of Nazi Germany's surrender. Brezhnev delivered a two-hour speech embodying the new leadership's official view of World War II. In it, he referred to "the State Defense Committee headed by Stalin, General Secretary of the Communist Party of the Soviet Union." His brief reference provoked a storm of applause from the audience. The applause dramatized publicly how precious Stalin's heritage remained, despite Khrushchev's efforts, to the senior generation of the Soviet ruling class: the generation which had entered politics during the terror of 1936–39, and had reached high office at the time of Stalin's last party congress in 1952. *

This incident was to be only the beginning of a slow but determined effort, led by Brezhnev, to restore Stalin's "proper" place in Soviet history and to undo the effects of Khrushchev's attempt at open de-Stalinization in 1961. Eight weeks later, Brezhnev hailed as "an outstanding statesman and political leader" the late Andrei Zhdanov—whose "cruel eyes" and brutal threats the old political prisoner Dora Lazurkina had recalled at the 1961 congress, and who in 1948 had launched the Cominform campaign against Tito's Yugoslavia. These, then, were the dubious "endeavors of the present Soviet Government in the fight against Stalinism" which Mihajlov had allegedly belittled.

On June 23 in Zagreb, the Croatian Supreme Court reviewed the Mihajlov case and dismissed the first and more important charge against him—that of "damaging the reputation of a foreign state." The second charge, of mailing the banned article abroad, was upheld, but the prison sentence was suspended and Mihajlov placed on good behavior for a two-year period. However, Mihajlov was neither restored to his teaching post nor permitted to accept invitations to foreign universities. This enforced obscurity

---

* Thirty-five of the Soviet party Central Committee chosen in 1952 remained full members at the beginning of 1970, constituting the senior sixth of the membership. The "class of 1952" included six of the eleven members of the 1970 Politburo and numerous other high officials, from the chief state planner to the editor of *Pravda*. The statistically "average" Central Committee member was born in 1910, and thus spent more than half his adult life in the period of Stalin's greatest horrors.

and unemployment, after the experience of having been briefly a world figure, eventually drove the young scholar into political activities which he otherwise might never have contemplated.

The ruling of the Croatian Supreme Court nevertheless demonstrated, in several respects, how Yugoslavia by 1965 had come to differ from the Soviet Union and its vassals. The relative independence shown by the Court, in throwing out the very accusation which Tito had been first to make against Mihajlov, would have been unthinkable in Russia, the DDR, or similar states. The dignified conduct of the open trial in Zadar, as well as the appellate ruling in Zagreb, also showed the degree of autonomy which the Croatian authorities had wrested from the central government. The Zagreb court dismissed the "anti-Soviet" charge against Mihajlov when Tito was actually visiting Russia.

The entire course of the Mihajlov affair, with its obvious hesitations on the part of the regime, was symptomatic of larger uncertainties besetting the Yugoslav Communist leaders. While the outsider Mihajlov was never a major issue among them, the Soviet Union was—and the controversy over Yugoslav policy toward Moscow was crucially linked with the struggles over economic and social reform, the nationalities question, and the rising power of Rankovic.

Kardelj, Bakaric, and other Slovene and Croat leaders had agreed reluctantly to abandon the path of reform as part of Tito's rapprochement with Khrushchev in 1962–63. But Tito's pro-Soviet turn had failed to save Khrushchev or to prevent his successors from attempting to woo Peking. Tito had failed to obtain Soviet economic aid of any consequence, while arousing suspicion among the Western creditors from whom Yugoslavia had borrowed nearly a billion dollars between 1955 and 1962. More than $200 million of this debt was up for repayment in 1965 and 1966, and Yugoslavia was unable to meet the charges. Inflation had been gathering force since 1963, cutting the value of the dinar in half by March 1965, when prices were frozen by decree. The farmers had been slaughtering calves since 1964 and a series of floods early in 1965 guaranteed that the year's grain harvest would be poor—increasing the need for American wheat. Machinery in the factories was being operated at only 54 percent of capacity because of the inefficiency of the recentralized system, with its cumbersome curbs on imports and enterprise funds. Some 180,000 workers—two-thirds of them Croats, most of the rest Slovenes—had already left the country to work in West Germany, Austria, and other lands with higher wages. Other workers, particularly in Slovenia, had been staging wildcat strikes and stoppages in protest against declining living standards.

In March 1965, Tito observed that people in Yugoslavia "feel the bad effects of various shortcomings, increased prices, low salaries, etc. They put the blame on us, on the Central Committee, on myself. They say that no one listens to me any longer. They criticize our party, our League of Communists. . . ."

In Zagreb and Ljubljana, the Croat and Slovene reformers blamed the crisis on Belgrade's heavy taxation of efficient northern enterprises to support high investments in the backward south as well as a growing federal bureaucracy. At the December 1964 party congress, the reformers called for lower taxes on enterprises, decentralization of banking and credit, higher wages for workers, and a return to the aims of the abandoned 1961 reform: a stable convertible currency, a market economy, and an opening to the West.

Rankovic and his followers rarely opposed such aims frontally, but succeeded in sabotaging them behind closed doors through their control of the UDBA and the Serbian party organization. The 1964 congress produced a paper commitment to renewed reform, but when Bakaric was asked when he expected the reform to be fully implemented, he replied, "Practically speaking, never."

Nearly every issue between the two factions was tied in some manner to relations with the Soviet camp. For example, Bakaric and others had long argued that Yugoslav agriculture could never regain its prewar self-sufficiency so long as the regime continued to discriminate against private farmers. Rankovic and his followers blocked the sale of machinery to private farmers, among other reforms, until 1965—partly on the "theoretical" ground that such measures would be a departure from pure "socialism," partly on the practical ground that a pro-peasant policy would offend the Soviet leaders, for whom Stalin's collectivization remained sacrosanct.

In June 1965, Tito visited Czechoslovakia, East Germany, and the Soviet Union in an attempt to obtain new credits for the strained Yugoslav economy. Some old debts were deferred, but no new money was obtained. Brezhnev was unwilling to revive the Yugoslav negotiations for a long-term Soviet loan, negotiations which had been inspired by Khrushchev but had been dragging since the beginning of 1965. The Soviet chief may also have indicated to Tito his determination to seek "unity of action" with the Chinese.

On Tito's return from the East empty-handed, Yugoslav officials moved swiftly to contact the International Monetary Fund and other Western agencies which had helped Yugoslavia in 1960 and were willing to do so again provided that serious reforms were implemented. Symbolically, the Yugoslav leaders finally decided to embark on a radical new economic reform—Tito called it a "surgical knife"—during the very week that Brezhnev was unsuccessfully wooing Teng Hsiao-ping in Bucharest.

The Yugoslav economic reform, adopted on July 24, 1965, devalued the dinar from 750 to 1,250 to the dollar; slashed state taxation of enterprises from 49 to 29 percent of net income; shifted turnover taxes from producers to consumers; replaced arbitrary import controls with a rational tariff system; drastically reduced state subsidies and premiums to industry; guaranteed higher procurement prices for farmers; raised rents, transport, and utility charges to more economic levels; and pledged a fully convertible currency, market prices, and the shutting down of economic enterprises which could not compete profitably.

The reform was thoroughly deflationary. It cut the real living standards of most Yugoslavs by some 30 percent. It promised no overall economic growth for at least three years. It frankly counted on large-scale unemployment and further migration of workers to Western Europe. Such drastic measures were necessary, as Tito admitted in November, to remedy the effects of years of political mismanagement:

We have built factories regardless of whether they could survive. We have been depriving those who work well and efficiently in order to invest elsewhere, regardless of economic consequence. We have been wasting funds on projects whose sole purpose was political ambition, and we have been propping them up with enormous state subsidies. . . . Today we are paying dearly for the balance sheet of our own mistakes.

Yet, beyond the painful austerity of the early years, the reform promised Yugoslavia a new economic and social system—a radical departure from the Soviet model of centralized political-bureaucratic command. In the new Yugoslav system, the state was to regulate rather than rule the economy. The enterprises—and the managers and workers in them—were to be largely responsible for their own success or failure; higher productivity would mean higher profits and higher wages, not only for the large socialized enterprises but for private farmers and artisans. The enterprises would have to compete, in quality and price, in the world market, to which Yugoslavia was now opened. The consumer would be the ultimate arbiter. Western investment was invited and private enterprise encouraged in the service sector, from taxicabs to rooming houses and restaurants. Workers, technicians, and specialists who wished to earn higher wages—and gain needed experience—in the West were encouraged to do so; the border was open, and the reformers were confident that most of their earnings and new skills would return to Yugoslavia. The counterpart of an open economy would be an open society.

The significance of the reform extended far beyond the frontiers of Yugoslavia. Its progress was watched anxiously by economists and managers throughout the Soviet empire. The more ignorant party spokesmen still pretended that the Stalinist economic model was viable: in the caustic words of Professor Yevsei Liberman of Kharkov University, "a cock sitting on a dunghill imagines that there is no better dunghill than his, and that everyone else wants to sit on it as well." But, after the industrial and agricultural failures of 1962–64, most East European economists recognized that fundamental changes were necessary, and that the modest adjustments being proposed in Moscow, East Berlin, and elsewhere scarcely went beyond changes Yugoslavia had already made a dozen years earlier.

In no country was the Yugoslav reform of July 1965 observed

with greater interest than in Czechoslovakia, in which the depression of 1962–63 had compelled Novotny to authorize the elaboration of a "new economic model." Such economists as Eugen Loebl, Radoslav Selucky, and especially the able team surrounding Professor Ota Sik at the Economic Institute of the Czechoslovak Academy of Sciences were inspired by the boldness openness, and confidence of the Yugoslav reformers. "The best evidence of the hopefulness of the Yugoslav reform," one Czech economist remarked, "are the glowing faces of the Yugoslav economists themselves. Just compare them with the Russians or East Germans—or us, for that matter."

In Yugoslavia itself, however, Rankovic and his followers attempted to sabotage and discredit the reform. Everywhere they argued that the reform would discriminate against Serbia and the less developed republics, that it would victimize the working class, that it would undermine party control. On November 7, 1965, Tito complained publicly that "while reforms are being strictly implemented in one republic, the people in another continue to work as they did before."

By midwinter, there had been strikes in many factories, as well as nationalist student demonstrations in Zagreb and Ljubljana, reflecting broad discontent with policies which seemed to have brought only austerity with no real change in the social climate. Tito convened the party central committee on February 25, 1966, and reported a growing "lack of confidence in us Communists" and local nationalism "even stronger than twenty years ago." He warned that "there is no place in the League of Communists for those who do not carry out its decisions. They should get out." Yet the Central Committee meeting produced no decision, and had to be adjourned until March 11. The March meeting produced a ringing new resolution forwarding the reform; but Rankovic and his followers had survived many resolutions.

Disillusion within the party continued to mount. In a series of newspaper articles, Bogdan Crnobrnja, Tito's long-time *chef de cabinet*, declared flatly that "there is in fact no self-management in the economy and society today," in effect blaming the UDBA and the party machine for thwarting democratization since 1952.

Surveying the world scene, Yugoslav Communists expressed

uneasiness at the changes which had taken place since the period when Tito could lead a large "non-aligned" bloc and at the same time get on with both Kennedy and Khrushchev. A succession of neutralist leaders had been overthrown—Achmed Ben Bella in Algeria, Joao Goulart in Brazil, Kwame Nkrumah in Ghana, Sukarno in Indonesia. The United States had become absorbed in the Vietnam war.

Yugoslav Communists were most disturbed by the evolution of Soviet foreign and domestic policies. In March 1966, a secret Soviet letter to Communist parties around the world disclosed that after Khrushchev's fall Brezhnev and Kosygin had presented a "far-reaching program" for rapprochement with Peking, on the party as well as state level, and that they had continued to press through most of 1965 for "unity of action" with the Chinese. At the 23rd Soviet Party Congress which began on March 29, 1966, Brezhnev and his colleagues formally proclaimed policies of "sharpening the international class struggle," increasing military spending, and tightening discipline over the Soviet bloc— which they increasingly referred to as the "world socialist system" or the "socialist commonwealth."

Soviet policies at home were equally discouraging to the Yugoslav reformers. Although there had been much talk in Russia of economic reform, the most substantial change made in 1965 was the abolition of Khrushchev's decentralized regional economic councils and the restoration of Stalin's old central economic ministries in Moscow—the very system from which the Yugoslavs had been moving away since 1950. Suslov had proclaimed as early as June 1965—and the 23rd Congress confirmed his view—that military spending would continue to take priority over consumer needs.

On September 8, 1965, the KGB arrested Andrei Sinyavsky and, four days later, Yuli Daniel. Young writers and students who demonstrated in their behalf in December were likewise detained. In February 1966, Sinyavsky and Daniel were tried—in a court from which even Communist journalists were barred—and condemned to seven and five years respectively at hard labor, to be served at the Potma concentration camp in the Mordvinian region on the Volga. The regime rejected the appeal of sixty-three

Moscow writers (including Ilya Ehrenburg, Bulat Okudzhava, Bella Akhmadulina, and Victor Shklovsky) to release Sinyavsky and Daniel in their surety.

Furthermore, Brezhnev had been restrained from a full-scale rehabilitation of Stalin at the 23rd Congress only by wide-ranging protests from the Soviet elite, including Russia's best-known nuclear physicists.* The congress was silent about Stalin, as about numerous other issues, but the direction in which Brezhnev was moving was all too clear. Just before the congress, Tvardovsky's "Tyorkin in the Other World" was withdrawn from the Moscow theatre repertory. At the congress, the Moldavian party chief, Ivan Bodyul, sharply attacked Solzhenitsyn, and at its close Tvardovsky was removed from his alternate membership in the party central committee.

The new trend in Russia was particularly disturbing to the Yugoslav reformers because, with the special relationship between Tito and Khrushchev at an end, Rankovic appeared to be emerging as Moscow's man in the Yugoslav party. The UDBA under his supervision had been cooperating in various ways with the KGB since 1962. Rankovic had visited Moscow on his own in February and again in May 1966. He had attempted unsuccessfully to replace Tito as party secretary general at the December 1964 congress, and his agents had continued afterward to spread rumors of Tito's advanced age (seventy-four in 1966) and declining health. His single term as vice-president was to expire in the spring of 1967, but meanwhile in the fall of 1966 Tito was planning a two-month voyage to India and Japan which would leave Rankovic acting chief of state, as well as master of the UDBA and the party machine. The Yugoslavs remembered how easily Nkrumah had been overthrown while traveling in the Far East.

Exactly when Tito, Kardelj, and Bakaric decided to remove Rankovic remains a mystery. Some of his positions in the party,

* The most famous protest against Stalin's rehabilitation, an open letter to Brezhnev from twenty-five leading figures in Soviet life, was signed by the nuclear physicists Pyotr Kapitsa, Igor Tamm, Andrei Sakharov, Mikhail Leontovich, and A. A. Artsimovich. Other signatories included Maya Plisetskaya, prima ballerina of the Bolshoi Theatre; Igor Smoktunovsky, the Soviet film *Hamlet;* Ivan Maisky, Russia's wartime ambassador to London; and such writers as Konstantin Paustovsky, Boris Slutsky, and Vladimir Tendraykov.

army, and UDBA began to be pared away as early as the December 1964 congress. It was only in the spring of 1966, however, that Tito set the KOS—the military intelligence—against the UDBA. According to some accounts, he did so after Rankovic had mentioned something in conversation which Tito had discussed only with his own wife. When the KOS experts discovered that the UDBA had planted listening devices in the homes and offices of all the Yugoslav leaders, including Tito's own residences at Brioni and Zagreb, Tito decided to act.

At a secret meeting on June 16, the Politburo confronted Rankovic with the evidence assembled against him. This included not only the listening devices and disclosures of UDBA attempts to suborn Serbian generals, but the systematic efforts of Rankovic and his followers to sabotage the economic reform. It is likely that Rankovic's links with the Soviet Union were also exposed, although Yugoslav officials confirmed this only in vague terms.

Rankovic was caught by surprise. He had underestimated the conspiratorial abilities of such intellectuals as Kardelj and Bakaric, and had concluded prematurely that Tito was senile. He had counted on support from Serbian, Montenegrin, and Bosnian Communist leaders so long as the issue was merely economic reform. When UDBA microphones in their own apartments became the issue, however, Rankovic found himself isolated. At the secret Politburo meeting, he offered to resign his party and government posts.

Tito and the reformers moved swiftly to neutralize counteraction before the news was made public. Trusted general staff envoys took over all the important Army garrisons. Slovenian regiments were sent to Belgrade. Dozens of UDBA chiefs were removed and placed under house arrest. On July 1, when the Central Committee met formally at Brioni to remove Rankovic and his leading associates, the political stage was set. Army units had already voted unanimous condemnation of Rankovic's activities. Tito delivered the main indictment of his disgraced Dauphin, but most of the speakers who followed were Serbs, and prominent Serbs were named quickly to fill the various party and government posts vacated by Rankovic.

In contrast to the Soviet Central Committee meetings which had removed Malenkov in 1957 and Khrushchev in 1964 but had made no changes in the Soviet political system, the Brioni plenum which deposed Rankovic thrust open the floodgates for political as well as economic reform in Yugoslavia. The committee vowed openly to break the power of the UDBA as a "state within the state" and to reorganize the Communist party itself.

For weeks on end, the crimes of the UDBA were exposed in the press and at meetings throughout the country. The charges ranged from the torture of Albanians by the Serb UDBA officials hitherto ruling the "autonomous" Kossovo region to rape, police brutality, smuggling, forced labor, and a hundred forms of corruption and special privilege. The exposure of the UDBA quickly uncovered links with party functionaries, government officials, directors of factories and other enterprises. A sweeping purge affected the entire society. In the first set of reelections for factory directors in Serbia, for example, 70 of the 546 directors were removed. Most of them were primitive, inept old Partisan warriors who had survived on their party and UDBA connections; they were replaced mainly by professionally qualified younger men. The UDBA itself was sharply reduced in size to become a compact security service under firm government control. Most of its functions were transferred to civilian police or local government officials.

Freed from UDBA interference, the processes of Yugoslav government became more spontaneous and decentralized. Even before the ouster of Rankovic, Yugoslav legislative bodies had been manifesting increasing independence, criticizing the executive branch, rejecting or amending government proposals, and voting along lines of regional and economic interest. It was no longer unusual, by the summer of 1966, to see the Federal Assembly adopt an amendment by a vote of 68 to 51, with 13 abstentions. The ouster of Rankovic encouraged even greater independence. The new tendency was dramatized in December when the Slovenian Cabinet resigned after the Slovenian legislature had rejected a government health-insurance bill. Under the new system, too, the powers and funds of the central government in Belgrade were sharply reduced and Yugoslavia's six constituent republics moved toward a status approaching confederation.

Most important, however, the ouster of Rankovic led the Yugoslavs to resume their efforts, suspended during the Tito-Khrushchev affair, to rethink the theory and practice of their own Communist party. At the Brioni plenum, a blue-ribbon forty-man commission was named to restudy the party's organizational structure and its role in society. At the commissions's very first meeting, a Macedonian theoretician asked why, after twenty-one years of power, the party should still be organized in the same way as the underground Russian Bolsheviks of 1903. The commission challenged Lenin's principle of "democratic centralism," under which Communist parties everywhere had been organized along the lines of tight military hierarchies. "The mechanism works from the top down," observed one Central Committee member, "but it is worse than useless in bringing ideas, opinions and new talent from the bottom upwards."

The commission's work in the autumn of 1966 led to a series of important changes. The number of professional party functionaries was sharply reduced. The party organization was separated from the government as such, by limiting individuals (with the exception of Marshal Tito) to positions in one or the other. New rules were adopted for choosing delegates to the party congress, permitting democratic elections by rank-and-file members. (Previously, delegates were more or less hand-picked, as in Russia, by the central "cadre department.")

The "confederation" approach to the Yugoslav nationalities was at last applied within the party. Party congresses in the six republics were to be held before, rather than after, the federal congress, so as to clarify local views, rather than transmit a predetermined "general line." Some observers felt Yugoslavia already had, in effect, a six-party system as the six republican party organizations increasingly reflected local interests and aspirations.

On the theoretical level, the Yugoslav reformers recognized the need for constructive disagreement, and the new party rules (ultimately adopted at the March 1969 party congress) formally legitimized the right of dissent, the right of minorities within the party to continue to argue their views in the hope of gaining a majority. Here was the first formal break in the history of the

Communist movement with the principles of "party unity" which Lenin had imposed on the Russian Communist party in 1921 and which all other "Leninist" parties had accepted. Indeed, as time passed, the Yugoslavs spoke less and less about Lenin, drawing their inspiration partly from Marx but more often from their own experience. The ultimate Yugoslav aim, Kardelj theorized, was neither a "monolithic" one-party system of the Stalinist type nor a Western multiparty system. Instead, the aim was a "nonparty system" of "direct democracy" based on federalism, decentralization of government, and "workers' self-management" in enterprises. Belgrade University philosophers soon criticized the notion of "direct democracy" as a "new myth," while historians noted the resemblance to traditional doctrines of anarchism, which had always been strongest around the Mediterranean.

Like the economic reform of 1965, the Yugoslav political reforms in 1966 aroused great interest in the Soviet empire. *Pravda* and other Kremlin organs warned openly against any dilution of "the leading role of the party." Under Brezhnev, Soviet policy toward Yugoslavia was, in its most benign moments, suspicious, reserved, and formally correct; just as often, it was openly hostile. However, the Yugoslav political innovations exercised considerable influence beneath the surface—particularly in Czechoslovakia, whose citizens by the thousands had, in the summer of 1965, begun returning for the first time since the war to their traditional vacation spots on the Yugoslav Adriatic. In the course of the mid-sixties, Czech and Slovak reformers were learning from Novotny what their Yugoslav counterparts had learned over so many years from Rankovic—that economic reform alone could not succeed without broad political change as well. Czech and Slovak Communists found merit in Yugoslav federalization, in the separation of party and government offices, in the independence of legislative bodies, in the replacement of "democratic centralism" by broad inner-party discussion. These and other Yugoslav innovations were widely discussed among Czechoslovak Communist theoreticians in the course of 1966 and 1967, and were to be embodied in the Prague "action program" of April 1968.

In Yugoslavia itself, the removal of Rankovic and the reforms which followed—along with the vigorous pursuit of the economic reform measures previously stalled—soon produced a dramatic change of atmosphere. 1966 proved to be the most important milestone in the country's history since 1948. New hope, idealism, and critical thinking were stimulated among sincere Communists long discouraged by bitter compromises. Social groups long demoralized by petty UDBA tyranny and party dogmatism took advantage of new economic incentives. In the summer of 1966, for example, Yugoslav farmers produced a record harvest—the clear result of freer prices, lower taxes, and new credits for fertilizer and machinery. From then on, the major Yugoslav agricultural problem would no longer be (as it had been since 1948) how much wheat to buy from the United States, but rather how much surplus meat could be sold in Western Europe in the face of Common Market tariff barriers.

The improvement in the quality of Yugoslav life, as well as the quality of Yugoslav products, did not need to be advertised by dubious propaganda or selective statistics. It was dramatically visible to all who wished to see it. By 1969, nearly 5 million foreign tourists were vacationing in Yugoslavia and more than a million Yugoslavs were traveling in the West each summer. In terms of living standards and amenities, there was little difference between Slovenia and Austrian Carinthia across the frontier. The gap between Serbia and neighboring Bulgaria, on the other hand, widened steadily.

In terms of civil liberties, too, Yugoslavia came to resemble the open societies of the West more than the "monolithic" police states of the Soviet empire. (Some foreigners thought Yugoslavia most resembled Spain, another dictatorship born of civil war which mellowed and modernized during the 1960s.) Western newspapers, magazines, books, and films were freely available and hugely popular. So were Russian works repressed by Soviet censorship, such as the later novels of Alexander Solzhenitsyn.

There were limits, however, beyond which the Yugoslav Communists were not prepared to go. While elections more often offered some choice of candidates, nearly all the candidates were Communist party members. Although the Yugoslav press was the most informative in Communist Europe, it continued to be hampered by various taboos when it came to internal policy. Despite open discussion within the party, religious freedom, and cultural diversity, there was no question of permitting organized opposition movements.

The limits of the new Yugoslav Communist tolerance were tested, almost immediately after the fall of Rankovic, by young Mihajlo Mihajlov. Unable to teach or write within the Yugoslav system, in May 1966 he wrote an article for a Russian émigré magazine published in West Germany hailing the imprisoned Djilas as "the symbol of liberty within the framework of a socialist system" and urging Yugoslav evolution toward a "free, democratic multi-party system."

A month later in New York, Mihajlov's sister Marija released the prospectus of a magazine, to be called *Free Voice*, which the young scholar hoped to found as the nucleus of an opposition party. The magazine would oppose Marxism and materialism (Mihajlov was an admirer of Nikolai Berdyayev and other Russian religious philosophers). The magazine would seek support among "the cultural and technical intelligentsia, religious people of all denominations, ideological opponents of Marxism within the top strata of the cultural elite, followers of Christian personalism in Slovenia, the champions of the nationalist aspirations of the Croatian people and the Serbian nationalists in Serbia. . . ." The appeal to Croat and Serb nationalists was not so much dangerous (although it was these forces that the party, and a large part of the country, feared most) as naïve, because such nationalists would not sit with each other, let alone heed the "Russian" Mihajlov.

Early in August, Mihajlov invited the Western press to what he said would be a public founding meeting of the new magazine in Zadar. The invitation promised that leading cultural figures from all six Yugoslav republics, as well as representatives of European Social Democratic parties, would also attend. However, only seven young men, nearly all from Zadar and Zagreb, answered Mihajlov's call—and the most impressive member of the group, Daniel Ivin, a thirty-four-year-old historian, indicated that he had come "not because of Mihajlov but because of Djilas." In the course of his research at the Institute for the History of the Workers' Movement in Zagreb, Ivin had studied the Yugoslav Communists' ideological break with Stalinism in 1949 and come to the conclusion that Djilas had been the chief inspirer of the new course. His dissertation on this thesis had been prohibited by party officials.

Mihajlov was arrested before his group could assemble, and his collaborators canceled the plan for a public meeting when police told them they would be held responsible for any disturbance of the peace. Their attempt to launch the magazine was blocked by the official refusal to grant them the necessary license. Partly as a result of police threats, partly as a result of general indifference to their efforts, the members of the group gradually resumed their individual lives. The indifference reflected an observation which Djilas himself had made during his parole in 1961–62: namely, that there was much "Djilasism" in the Yugoslav air, but very few actual "Djilasites." By the fall of 1966, the Yugoslav Communists themselves had accepted many of the ideas which Djilas had originally attempted to foster in 1953–54, although rejecting the call for a multiparty system he had made later.

Mihajlov was determined personally to confront the contradictions of the regime. Released briefly on parole early in September, he told foreign visitors that he had refused to migrate abroad, although he could have, and that even his imprisonment would be a victory for freedom: "If I am convicted, then the authorities will be admitting that they identify socialism with a single-party system."'On September 22, he was tried and sentenced in Zadar to a year in prison for "defaming Yugoslavia's Communist society at home and abroad." Before he had served half the term, he was on trial again for new articles which he had sent abroad attacking Yugoslavia's "totalitarian" system. This time he was tried in Belgrade, on April 19, 1967, and sentenced to four and a half years in prison.* In an able defense, he noted the limits of Yugoslav freedom by observing that since July 1, 1966, the press had been "unanimously" against Rankovic and the UDBA, but that there had been no criticism of either before then.

For those who knew him personally, Mihajlov's fate seemed virtually predestined. As an admirer of Dostoyevsky and Solzhen-

* He was released in February 1970.

itsyn, a singer of songs from concentration camps, a religious "Russian" among the flexible South Slavs, he seemed drawn to martyrdom as much by his nature as by the reluctant prosecution of the Yugoslav authorities. In "Moscow Summer," Mihajlov himself had described his argument with Ilya Ehrenburg, who "eventually said that I was cut out to be a fanatic—'the same as our dogmatists are, except that you stand on different ideological ground.'" Ehrenburg's observation was less kind than the broader conclusion drawn (without direct reference to Mihajlov) by the old Croatian Communist novelist Miroslav Krleza, who had first published Mihajlov's reflections on Dostoyevsky and Solzhenitsyn. "The ideal man," Krleza wrote on January 1, 1967, "exists only in medical encyclopedias," and Communism had not much changed the human condition. "Under socialism liars lie, scoundrels and rascals cheat, gangsters kill, and the lovers of truth die for their ideals." *

It was not as a result of Mihajlov's publicizing of his views, but as a consequence of Rankovic's fall, that Milovan Djilas was released from prison on the last day of 1966. Tito and his colleagues had decided, after several months of deliberation, that there would be no criminal charges brought against Rankovic and his lieutenants. Removal from political office would be their only penalty; otherwise they would be free men. With Rankovic, accused of a "struggle for power," at liberty, the continued imprisonment of Djilas—whose only offense lay in his writings—was indefensible.

A decade had passed since the gray November afternoon in 1956 when six agents of Rankovic's UDBA had arrested Djilas for having criticized Tito's ambivalence toward the Soviet intervention in Hungary. Djilas had spent nearly nine years of that decade in prison. He emerged, at fifty-five, alert, sovereign, self-contained, with his vivacity and lively humor unimpaired, his intellectual brilliance tempered by a new flexibility. It was easy for those who met him to understand why he had been the most

* Krleza himself quit the Communist party a few months later in an angry Zagreb-Belgrade dispute over Croatian and Serbian language rights. The dispute tended to confirm the Yugoslav Communists' view that, if they were ever to permit opposition parties, the first such parties would probably be Serbian, Croatian, and other nationalist organizations.

popular of the young Partisans, and why he had been held hostage for Tito's attempt at reconciliation with post-Stalinist Russia. He was the only Yugoslav leader, apart from Tito, who thought instinctively and imaginatively in world terms—beyond not only the spiritual barriers between the Yugoslav nationalities but beyond the limitations of Balkan power politics to the larger destiny of Communism and freedom.

In prison, reading the Yugoslav newspapers, Djilas had been impressed by the accounts of a fresh new spirit among Soviet youth and intellectuals, but remained disturbed by the darker continuities of Russian history, from Ivan the Terrible to Stalin. "I have the feeling," he said a few days after his release, "that the present government is the best Russia has had since Lenin died—maybe because they are not trying to do too much. But being a great power makes it more difficult for Russia to evolve democratically than for the smaller countries of Eastern Europe."

Barely twenty months later, Djilas would be traveling in the West—with Tito's permission—to rally support for their country against the threat of Soviet invasion. In Communist Europe's greatest crisis since 1956, Djilas would defend Mihajlov, criticize but also praise Tito, and reserve his greatest scorn for "the country and party that is the private property of a most sinister and unscrupulous band of men"—the "unimaginative, faceless" rulers of the Soviet party machine, committed to "strengthening Stalin's imperial heritage."

CHAPTER 13

Jubilee

Red banners everywhere proclaimed the *veliki praznik,* the great holiday. Not a day, but a jubilee year—1967—"the Glorious Fiftieth Anniversary of the Great October Socialist Revolution." From all over the world, pilgrims streamed toward Russia—Communists out of devotion, tourists out of curiosity, journalists and scholars to draw a balance sheet of Soviet rule.

Visitors returning after an absence of four or five years generally remarked that conditions had improved: there was more food, better clothing, some modern architecture. Visitors returning after ten or twenty years, however, were depressed: "Fundamentally," they said, "nothing has changed"—and pointed to the army garrisoning every city, the ubiquitous police, the bureaucracy, censorship, propaganda, and suspicion, the fatigue and indifference locked on almost every human face.

Wherever one looked, there were signs of material improvement. Yet behind, beneath, or alongside them, there were portents to justify the deepest pessimism. A tour of the Soviet Union in the Jubilee Year 1967 was an exercise in contradiction, an endless series of "yes—buts." Yes, life was better than in 1952 or 1937— but was it better than in 1964? That was a matter of values. For visible material accomplishments contrasted with unspoken, intangible traumas just as real: a horrible past unmastered, an uncertain present, an uncharted future.

283

At Bratsk in the wilds of Siberia, the most powerful hydro-electric station in the world had been completed. How much did it matter that the industries which its capacity was designed to serve were yet to be built, and their workers yet to be conscripted from the Dnieper and the Dniester, the Don and the Volga, to the frozen north? Did it matter more, perhaps, that the construction of the great power station had been begun by slave labor? And if more "volunteers" kept leaving Siberia each year than stayed there, might forced-labor camps perhaps swell there again, or would the great power station stand one day abandoned like the ruin of Ozymandias?

Everywhere one looked, there were such questions, and no clear answers.

In Moscow, oranges were now available. Dacron shirts, British sweaters, and other rarities appeared in the shops. Women began to wear eye shadow, and some even sported miniskirts and patterned stockings. Glass and aluminum architecture had finally arrived, most strikingly in the dozen skyscrapers whose facades were being rushed toward completion on Kalinin Prospect, the capital's new showplace thoroughfare. As the great *praznik* approached, these and other new buildings (such as the mammoth Hotel Rossiya opposite the Kremlin) were ringed with colored light bulbs and illuminated with floodlights. At the sites of unfinished buildings, the festive bulbs were placed to outline giant construction cranes.

But 40 percent of Moscow families still lived in communal apartments, where five or six families—a single small room each—shared a common kitchen and bath. *Pravda* cursed the "Judas" Trotsky (who had led Lenin's 1917 coup) and the "anti-Leninist" Bukharin (whom the dying Lenin had called "the favorite of our entire party"). Two dozen Chagalls remained in the padlocked cellars of the Pushkin Museum. A brilliant young director, Andrei Tarkovsky, completed a great film, *Andrei Rublyov;* the censors barred it from movie theaters.*

In Leningrad, the city of Peter and Catharine, the "Venice of

---

* The head of the State Cinematography Committee, Alexei Romanov, was the very man who, as a military intelligence officer in 1945, had denounced Captain Alexander Solzhenitsyn and thus doomed him to nine years in forced-labor camps.

the North" had not looked as comely in decades. The baroque and neoclassical palaces built by Rastrelli, Rossi, and Quarenghi glistened with fresh gold, pale-green, and cherry-red paint. The city's third subway line was completed, with all the cleanliness and precision of the Moscow lines but without the capital's Stalinesque station decor. A handsome new concert hall was opened for the nation's finest orchestra, Eugene Mravinsky's Leningrad Philharmonic. In hotels and restaurants, Finnish drinkers, escaping their country's prohibition against vodka, jostled Western art-lovers flocking to the Hermitage. Each day, Leningraders brought flowers to the well-tended mass grave of the million victims of the 900-day siege in World War II.

But in the Smolny Institute, where Lenin had directed the struggle for power, only paintings and drawings depicted the great events of the Revolution. The authorities continued to suppress the thousands of photographs showing Lenin with his closest colleagues, Trotsky, Bukharin, Zinoviev, and Kamenev, all of whom Stalin had murdered. In the former Maryinsky Palace, the city's tough mayor, Alexander Sizov, scoffed at the pre-Communist Russian intelligentsia (Stravinsky, Chaliapin, Leontief, Nabokov. . . .); they had "run away," he said, "because they didn't want to work." In contrast to Khrushchev's days, there was silence now about the terror which had so often ravaged the city, about the murder of Kirov in 1934 and the "Leningrad case" of 1948. There were no official honors for Leningrad's greatest poet, Anna Akhmatova (1889–1966), whose husband, Gumilev, had been shot under Lenin and whose son had been imprisoned by Stalin. In her "Requiem," Akhmatova herself explained why Stalin's heirs could not accept her:

> Because even in blessed death I am afraid
> To forget the rumbling of the Black Marias,
> To forget the banging of the hateful door,
> And how the old woman wailed like a wounded beast. . . .

In Tashkent, the Russified capital of Uzbekistan, workers from fourteen Soviet republics and forty cities struggled to rebuild a city one-third destroyed by the earthquake of April 26, 1966.

More than 300,000 persons had been rehoused, mainly in new housing projects of the periphery. There were plans for a subway, a new Intourist Hotel, a nineteen-story administration building, a circus, and a special new boulevard, 40 yards wide, for military parades.

But only half a dozen mosques were open for the city's 800,000 Moslems. The Asiatic Uzbeks and the European Russians still lived in separate quarters of the city. The economy of Uzbekistan was harnessed by Moscow planners to a single crop, cotton. The alphabet was Russian. And, in a lovely film called *Tenderness*, made by a twenty-five-year-old Uzbek director, Elyor Ishmuk-hamedov, the young Uzbek hero could fall in love with—but could not dream of wedding—the Slavic beauty from Leningrad.

In the model "Academic Village" outside Novosibirsk, Siberia, a scientific community of 30,000, embracing twenty specialized institutes, had been set up in a decade, mainly by professors from Leningrad. The young scientists were housed in neat four- and five-story apartment buildings, while their professors dwelled in a lovely section of individual cottages called "Golden Valley." *But* at Shelekhova, outside Irkutsk, some 5,000 young workers lived four-in-a-room in two large barracks near an aluminum plant that had been under construction for fourteen years. Most of the workers had been sent to Siberia by the Communist youth organization in Orel, south of Moscow.

In Irkutsk, Siberia's old tsarist capital, the population of the province had increased by 250,000 since 1960 as a result of Communist youth "mobilizations." In Khabarovsk, 10,000 new residents were arriving each year. Local officials pretended that the migration had nothing to do with China; and, to show foreign visitors that all was quiet, they took them to the Ussuri Sanatorium for cardiovascular and nervous patients, barely twenty miles from the Chinese frontier. Its therapeutic facilities included a bird room, in which patients were expected to relax as canaries flew over their heads.

But the woods outside the Sanatorium were state farms operated by men in uniform—soldiers of the Soviet Army and the KBG security forces; and when foreign visitors were not present in Khabarovsk, Soviet marshals harangued the troops with proud memories of the secret border wars of the 1920s and 1930s, wars whose very existence Moscow denied until they were well over.

From Riga to Alma-Ata, from Kishinev to Yakutsk, across the empire of a hundred nationalities filling one-sixth of the earth's surface, visitors encountered the same banners and slogans: *"Fulfill the Decisions of the 23rd Party Congress!"* *"Long Live the Leninist Foreign Policy of the Soviet Government!"* *"Glory to the Soviet Armed Forces!"* *"The Party and the People Are One!"* *"The Five Year Plan—Ahead of Time!"* This was Soviet Russia—strident and assertive—as its latest masters, Brezhnev, Suslov, Kosygin, and their peers, wished it to be seen. But beneath the surface, eternal Russia remained, and a new Russia struggled to be born in the minds of Soviet youth.

Long before the Jubilee Year 1967 arrived, the Kremlin had begun preparing to make it a memorable year—a demonstration of stability and power at least as impressive as the 300th anniversary of the Romanov dynasty, celebrated in 1913, which senior Soviet leaders were old enough to remember. At the very least, Brezhnev and his colleagues wished it to be a year without scandal or bad omens—a year in which few inside or outside the empire would be driven to doubt either Russia's progress or the legitimacy of their own rule.

Their major preparations were economic, and dictated by necessity. Reacting against Khrushchev's impulsive experimentation, they sought tranquility and order, predictability, security, continuity. There had been much talk of reforms; they made adjustments.

Agriculture came first. In March 1965, Brezhnev promised Soviet collective and state farmers a new deal: reasonable and stable delivery quotas over the next five years; guaranteed procurement prices, higher than those of Khrushchev's day; and a doubling of investment in land-improvement, chemical fertilizers, tractors, trucks, and agricultural machinery. The promises came too late to avert a poor harvest in 1965, and Russia once again bought wheat from the West. However, the 1966 harvest broke all Soviet records. It was as much a triumph for Brezhnev as the 1958 "virgin lands" harvest had been for Khrushchev; in

Soviet Russia, as in the time of Catharine the Great, "one good harvest makes up for ten years of misrule." The bumper crop of 1966 ensured that the anniversary year 1967 would not be marred by the food shortages that had plagued Khrushchev from 1962 onward.*

In September 1965, the new party leaders compromised the long debate over industrial-management reform which Khrushchev had inspired. The new system, while strengthening central control, promised a new emphasis on cost-accounting methods and a modest degree of incentive for factory directors to improve quality and reduce labor costs. The new management methods were to be introduced gradually—at first in light and consumer industries, then after a few years in construction and heavy industry.

At the 23rd Party Congress in April 1966, Brezhnev and Kosygin presented sober economic plans for the years 1966–70. Khrushchev's ambitious 1961 party program, with its twenty-year schedule for the "building of communism" by 1980, was quietly buried. The new leaders scaled down most of the targets which had originally been set for 1970 and which were clearly impossible of fulfillment. Instead, they set lower growth rates which would be easier to attain. Unlike Stalin and Khrushchev, they made no promises of overtaking the United States, Western Europe, or Japan. Men like Kosygin realized, although they never said so publicly, that the real problem was to prevent Russia from falling even farther behind the developed countries than she had been at the beginning of the century. While cruder Soviet agitators boasted that Russia was surpassing the United States in the production of coal, pig iron, and cement, scientists like Academician Andrei Sakharov observed that "we are now

* However, the 1966 harvest also encouraged the Politburo to abridge the reforms promised in 1965 and revert to old habits. Early in 1967, Dmitri Polyansky noted publicly that already "several comrades are beginning to argue that collective and state farms can now develop with less substantial help and that it is possible now to cut back. . . ." By October 1967, the 1965 promise of increased investment in agriculture had already been cut back by 24 percent. Investments in the fertilizer and farm-machine industries were similarly reduced. Meanwhile, Communist party activists got around the fixed delivery prices and quotas set in 1965 by campaigns forcing "voluntary" plan increases and "gifts" to the state.

catching up with the United States only in some of the old, traditional industries which are no longer as important as they used to be for the United States (for example, coal and steel). In some of the newer fields, for example, automation, computers, petro-chemicals and especially in industrial research and development, we are not only lagging behind but growing more slowly. . . ." *

At the 1966 party congress, Brezhnev and his colleagues also promised that, toward the end of the five-year plan, Soviet consumer-goods production would—for the first time since 1928—begin to increase at a slightly higher percentage rate than heavy industry. This pledge hardly betokened a major shift in Kremlin priorities, toward consumer goods and away from heavy industry; for a mouse growing at an annual rate of 6.2 percent would not, in anybody's lifetime, outstrip an elephant growing at an annual rate of 5.8 percent. However, along with the promises of better food supplies, continued housing construction, and a five-day work week (introduced in 1967), the increased consumer-goods production would assure a modest rise in living standards for the postwar babies now entering the labor force (half the Soviet population in 1966 had been born since 1940).

To revive the long-neglected consumer industries, the new leaders contracted for the purchase and installation of whole factories on credits from the West. The most celebrated of these

* Statistical comparisons involving the Soviet Union (and most other Communist countries) are difficult to make primarily because, in the words of the Russian-born economist Naum Jasny, "Soviet statistics are an amalgam of falsified, distorted, misleading and correct statistics." Apart from deliberate distortion, many major economic figures have long been Soviet state secrets (including production of shipping and nonferrous metals, wages in manufacturing, consumer price indices, the money supply, etc.) Of 64 standard indicators employed by the United Nations in 1964, the Soviet Union supplied only 21.

Despite the deficiency of reliable data, most economic and social indices in 1967 showed that, on a per capita basis, the 19 or 20 countries which ranked higher than Russia in 1900 also ranked higher in 1967. In mass education, the area of Russia's greatest achievements since 1908, she still ranked 39th among 124 countries for which data was available.

In 1967, Russia had about as many computers as Britain, West Germany, and Japan, but each of these countries outstripped her within the next year or two, just as they and several other countries moved ahead in the production of atomic power for peaceful purposes (which Russia had pioneered in 1954).

As for mass living standards, few statistics speak as eloquently as Khrushchev's response when invited in 1963 to compare Russian living standards with those of semideveloped Yugoslavia (see Chapter 4).

contracts called for Fiat to build a new automobile plant at Togliatti (formerly Stavropol) and for Renault to reequip the plant at Gorki (formerly Nizhni-Novgorod) which Ford had originally constructed in the thirties. When completed sometime in the 1970s, these installations would ultimately enable the Soviet Union to produce a total of 800,000 automobiles a year— nearly as many as Japan in 1966, or one for every fifteen Soviet Communist party members. In addition to Western credits, Brezhnev and his colleagues called on East Germany, Czechoslovakia, and other members of Comecon to step up deliveries of modern equipment and to invest in ambitious projects for extracting raw materials in Soviet Asia.

The modest economic adjustments approved in 1965 and 1966 could not be expected to produce startling results for the Soviet consumer—particularly since Brezhnev and his associates were firmly committed to "strengthening the defense capacity of the socialist commonwealth." Their military program included accelerated rocket production, experiments with anti-missile missiles and orbital bombs, expansion of the fleet, and the formation of new units of paratroopers and fleet marines. They were also committed, by 1966, to dispatching an estimated billion dollars in armaments annually to maintain the Communist war effort in Vietnam.

However, to assure a memorable Jubilee Year for Soviet citizens weary of living on promises, the Kremlin leaders commandeered special train loads of bright consumer goods from the West, East Germany, and Czechoslovakia to stock the shop windows of Moscow, Leningrad, and other showplace cities.*

While assuring bread and preparing circuses for the Jubilee Year, the new leaders also took steps to ensure political order. On July 26, 1966, after a decade of experiments with local and volunteer police forces, the Kremlin recreated the old state gendarmerie—at first under the new title of the Ministry for the

* The broadest selection of such imports was to be found in the revived hard-currency stores (known under Stalin as *Torgsin* shops, closed under Khrushchev, reopened as *Beryozka* shops). They were open to Westerners and to those members of the Soviet elite possessing dollars, pounds, West German marks, and other "*valuta*." These and other, more discreet special shops sold not only Western imports but rare and higher-quality Soviet products (ranging from caviar to Latvian transistor radios) at prices one-fourth of those in ruble shops.

Protection of Public Order. Its powers were roughly similar to those of the old Ministry of Internal Affairs (MVD), and in 1969 it regained its old name as well. Reestablishment of this "ordinary" state police complemented the unceasing activities of the KGB, the political security police.

On September 16, an unpublicized decree added two new articles to the criminal code—prohibiting "group activities disturbing public order," as well as "oral or written statements derogatory to the Soviet system." The new measures were confirmed in December despite protests by the composer Dmitri Shostakovich, the nuclear physicists Igor Tamm and Andrei Sakharov, the historian Pyotr Yakir, and other Soviet liberals. The new regulations would soon be used to punish the kind of demonstrations which Moscow youths had staged in favor of Sinyavsky and Daniel, as well as the spread of underground literature (popularly known as *samizdat,* or self-publishing).*

Other preparations were made as well, at home and abroad. New statues of Lenin were commissioned. The Stalin museum at Gori in Georgia—closed since 1961—was reopened, and would receive 186,000 visitors in the course of the Jubilee Year. A television series of fifty programs was prepared for the anniversary, one for each year of Communist power; Stalin appeared twelve times, Khrushchev not once. Stalin's death was marked by the narrator with the Delphic comment: "The death of a man one knows always leads to mourning. All the Soviet people knew Josef Stalin well."

So too, Alexander Niekrich's history, *June 22, 1941,* which had exposed Stalin's costly blunders before the Nazi invasion, was now condemned. A program of public lectures by Solzhenitsyn was canceled in November 1966. His last story had appeared in *Novy Mir* in February of the same year. The KGB had impounded several of his manuscripts in the summer of 1965. As the Jubilee

* The most common form of *samizdat* was the typewritten manuscript, usually single-spaced, on onionskin paper to permit the maximum number of carbon copies. The recipient of one such copy then retyped a half-dozen new copies, and so on. However, mimeographed literature and (later) photocopies also appeared. The early *samizdat* publications were largely cultural in content: novels, stories, poems banned by the censorship. In the late 1960s, however, *samizdat* became ever more political: protest petitions, trial transcripts, accounts of arrests and persecutions, translations of foreign anti-Communist books, resistance manifestos.

Year began, copies of *Ivan Denisovich* began to be removed from libraries. In the Ukraine, police arrested intellectuals protesting Russification. Elsewhere, they moved against leaders of the Evangelical Baptist sect.

Abroad, the attempt to conciliate Mao Tse-tung had failed, but for Brezhnev, Suslov, and their colleagues West German "revanchism" remained a principal foe. Prohibition of the Pope's visit to Poland in the spring of 1966 had blocked one movement for reconciliation with West Germany. In the autumn, when the Social Democrats entered the German government for the first time since 1930 and proclaimed more flexible policies, new hopes rose, and Rumania quickly normalized relations with Bonn. But Brezhnev and Ulbricht soon prevented Hungary, Czechoslovakia, and others from following suit.

In November 1966, Brezhnev journeyed again to Prague, as he had in 1962, to attend the Czechoslovak party congress. Here too, "order, stability, continuity" were enforced. Novotny remained in power, economic reforms were delayed, a new censorship law was adopted, and a plea at the congress by Professor Ota Sik for political liberalization went unrecorded in the Czechoslovak press.

Looking outward, the Soviet press in the autumn of 1966 launched a new campaign. The state of Israel and the "imperialists," Moscow charged with increasing insistence, were plotting to overthrow the "progressive" military dictatorship of Syria.

The Soviet anniversary year was blessed by magnificent weather. In Moscow, spring was early and sunny, with temperatures in the 70s; a long Indian summer was clear and fair with temperatures in the mid-50s well into November, when harsh snows usually blanketed the capital. Yet, despite the climate and all the regime's preparations, a spiritual pall hung over the land. Even the party's best-rewarded propagandists seemed glum and dyspeptic. The new leaders had corrected some of Khrushchev's "harebrained schemes"; they had shunned his personal self-glorification and avoided his impulsive adventures, global dramas, and utopian promises. They had calmed the "cadres"—the professional functionaries of the party machine, the KGB, and the

Army, the ministers, managers, propagandists, and censors—who
had been threatened by Khrushchev's radical maneuvers. They
had sought to seal the Pandora's Box which Khrushchev had
rashly pried open. In so doing, however, they had already stifled
many of the hopes which Stalin's death and dethronement had
aroused.

In the midst of the jubilee year, an American visitor who had
known Russia intimately since 1933, observed, "When I was
here in 1955, all my Russian friends thought that this country
was really on its way at last—the sky was the limit. Even in 1959,
lots of people still thought Russia would make it after all. Now,
the same people just shrug their shoulders."

The gloom was to thicken as the jubilee year unfolded, for
neither the wisdom nor the fortune of the Kremlin leaders proved
equal to the occasion.

The anniversary year began with a two-month delay in the
publication of *Novy Mir*. The delay was caused by the censorship's prohibition of the war memoirs of Konstantin Simonov,
a veteran novelist and in his time one of Stalin's ablest propagandists. Now, however, Simonov refused to delete or alter his sharp
criticism of Stalin's wartime leadership. The memoirs remained
unpublished.

On January 17, the Moscow KGB arrested Yuri Galanskov, the
twenty-eight-year-old editor of an underground magazine called
Phoenix 66. This mimeographed 379-page anthology, like other
underground publications, had sought to fill the spiritual and
intellectual vacuum caused by the tightening censorship and the
increased political pressure on *Novy Mir* and other legal journals.
The contents of *Phoenix 66* had included a penetrating essay
by Sinyavsky on Yevtushenko; a study of the "Russian Path
of Transition to Socialism" by the late economist, Academician
Eugene Varga; an account of the Writers Union meeting which
had condemned Pasternak; excerpts from the debates between
party ideologists and Old Bolsheviks on a new party history; a
case study of religious persecution at the Pochaevsky Monastery
near Kiev; and an open letter by Galanskov himself in defense of
Sinyavsky and Daniel. Within the next two days, three of
Galanskov's collaborators in *Phoenix 66* were also arrested.

At 6 P.M. on January 22, some thirty young Muscovites gathered in Pushkin Square to demonstrate for the release of Galanskov and his associates and for repeal of the laws against "anti-Soviet agitation." Many of the youths had previously demonstrated against the arrest of Sinyavsky and Daniel and the rehabilitation of Stalin. This time, KGB plainclothesmen seized their homemade posters and arrested five of the demonstrators (Vladimir Bukovsky, Vadim Delone, Victor Khaustov, Yevgeny Kushev, and Ilya Gabai).

The day after the Pushkin Square demonstration, police arrested Alexander Ginsburg, thirty, who had compiled a "White Book" of documents on the trial of Sinyavsky and Daniel. In it, he had included an anonymous "Letter from an Old Friend," recalling the abortive de-Stalinization of 1961: "At the 22nd party congress, it was promised that the victims of Stalin's arbitrary rule would be posthumously rehabilitated and their names inscribed on an obelisk. Where is that obelisk? Where is the marble slab in the Union of Writers, on which the names of those who perished in Stalin's time were to have been engraved in gold letters?"

On February 11, Academician Sakharov, who was widely regarded as the father of Russia's hydrogen bomb, appealed to the party Central Committee to dismiss the case against Ginsburg and Galanskov. His appeal received no reply. Instead, four days later, one of the Pushkin Square demonstrators—the young worker Khaustov—was suddenly brought to trial and condemned to three years at hard labor.

Some time later, KGB interrogators persuaded one of Galanskov's imprisoned collaborators, Alexei Dobrovolsky, to swear that Sakharov and another distinguished nuclear physicist, Academician Mikhail Leontovich, were part of a "single anti-Communist front" embracing the accused writers, Moscow University poets, and other dissidents. According to Sakharov, this threatening amalgam was inspired by the bumptious KGB chief, Vladimir Semichastny, who had once called the poet Boris Pasternak "worse than a swine" and had more recently promised the Politburo that he could guarantee "order" in Soviet society if authorized to arrest 1,000 to 1,500 intellectuals.

But the party leaders shied away from a mass purge affecting atomic scientists. A more cautious policy of selective intimidation and political pressure was adopted. The other Pushkin Square demonstrators were held in prison until the end of August, Ginsburg and Galanskov until the following year. Semichastny was removed and replaced at the head of the KGB by Suslov's old collaborator Yuri Andropov (the Soviet Ambassador in Hungary during 1956). Foreign visitors arriving to publicize the anniversary year were told "confidentially" that—if only the West refrained from embarrassing protests—Sinyavsky and Daniel might be amnestied in November.

What the Politburo wanted most of all in 1967 was quiet. Yet the spring brought a series of unpleasant surprises—each in its way casting new doubt on the authority of the Kremlin leaders and the competence of their policies.

First, on March 6, Stalin's daughter, Svetlana Alliluyeva (whom Kosygin had permitted to visit India), sought refuge in the American Embassy in New Delhi. By the end of April, she had obtained political asylum in the United States. The flight of Stalin's only surving child—and Stalin had ruled the Soviet Union for twenty-five of its fifty years—was a bitter commentary on the "glorious anniversary," as well as on Brezhnev's efforts to rehabilitate her father.

Next, at the beginning of April, the Soviet military provided a striking demonstration of its generally unsuspected political power. The occasion was the death, after a long illness, of Marshal Rodion Malinovsky, the defense minister since 1957. Communist party spokesmen promptly informed foreigners that his successor would be a civilian, Dmitri Ustinov, the veteran boss of the Soviet defense industry. Ustinov, they said, would be "the Soviet McNamara"—a reference to the American civilian who had put the Pentagon generals and admirals in their place. So said the party spokesmen. The Soviet marshals had other ideas. After more than a week of official silence, it was announced on April 12 that the new defense minister would be the senior marshal, Andrei Grechko. Never before in Soviet history had the Army been able to dictate the choice of its minister.

Two weeks later, on April 24, a Soviet cosmonaut, Vladimir

Komarov, burned to death in the first human test of the new Soyuz-1 spaceship.* This disaster set back the Soviet space program more than a year, and doomed Politburo plans for a space "spectacular" to mark the fiftieth anniversary as dramatically as Khrushchev had marked the fortieth anniverary with the first "sputnik."

The Politburo's next unpleasant surprise came barely three weeks later. After many delays, the first Soviet Writers Congress since 1959 had been summoned for the end of May. The scenario called for a glowing show of unanimity behind the new party line. But on May 16, when it became clear that liberal writers would not be allowed to speak at the congress, Alexander Solzhenitsyn addressed a bold open letter to his fellow writers which soon reverberated around the world. Solzhenitsyn urged, first of all, that the congress discuss the "no-longer tolerable oppression, in the form of censorship, which our literature has endured for decades."

> A survival of the Middle Ages [Solzhenitsyn wrote], the censorship has managed, Methuselah-like, to drag out its existence almost to the 21st century. [Novels, stories, poems, and plays that] might express the mature thinking [of the Russian people] are proscribed or distorted by censorship on the basis of considerations that are petty, egotistical, and—from the national point of view—shortsighted.
> . . .
> Even Dostoyevsky, the pride of world literature, was at one time not published in our country (even today, his works are not published in full); he was excluded from the school curriculum, made unacceptable for reading, and reviled. . . . For decades, the immortal poetry of Akhmatova was considered anti-Soviet. . . . For a long time, the name of Pasternak could not be pronounced out loud.
> . . .
> Our literature has lost the leading role it played at the end of the last century and the beginning of this one, and it has lost the brilliance of experimentation that distinguished it in the 1920s. . . .
> I propose that the Congress adopt a resolution which would de-

---

* Soyuz-1 was the first major spacecraft produced after the death in January 1966 of Sergei Korolev, Russia's chief space designer. Korolev was by all accounts a man of genius (as well as a former victim of Stalin's prisons). Brezhnev and his colleagues had replaced the strong-willed Korolev with a committee.

mand and ensure the abolition of all censorship, open or hidden, of all fictional writing, and which would release publishing houses from the obligation to obtain authorization for the publication of every printed page.

Solzhenitsyn's open letter next turned to the character of the Union of Writers, which since the early 1930s had been an instrument of regimentation in the hands of Stalin and his heirs. Solzhenitsyn recalled how "many writers have been subjected to abuse and slander," or "exposed to violence and personal persecution." The Union not only failed to defend such writers but its officials were "always first among the persecutors. . . ."

> The leadership of the Union cravenly abandoned to their distress those for whom persecution ended in exile, labor camps and death. We learned after the 20th party congress that there were more than 600 writers whom the Union had obediently handed over to their fate in prisons and camps. However, the roll is even longer. . . . It contains the names of young writers and poets . . . whose talents were crushed in camps before being able to blossom, whose writings never got further than the offices of the state security service . . .

Solzhenitsyn urged that the writers' congress adopt clear guarantees for the defense of persecuted writers. His open letter then demanded that the congress discuss his own case: the seizure by the KGB in 1965 of his novel *The First Circle* and other literary papers; the ban on his novel *The Cancer Ward;* the prohibition or rejection of various plays, screenplays, and stories; the cancellation of his public readings; and an official slander campaign insinuating that Solzhenitsyn (a decorated war hero arrested in 1945 for criticizing Stalin) had collaborated with the Germans.

"Will the Congress defend me—yes or no?" Solzhenitsyn asked. More than a hundred leading Soviet writers took up his cause—including Paustovsky, Ehrenburg, and Tvardovsky among the older generation, and Voznesensky, Yevtushenko, and Aksyonov among the younger writers. But party pressure was severe, and most other writers shared the view of Anatoly Kuznetsov, who remarked that "Solzhenitsyn is asking me to commit suicide with him" and decided simply to stay at home during the congress.

Solzhenitsyn's open letter was not read at the Soviet Writers Congress—but it was read publicly a month later at a Congress of Czechoslovak Writers in Prague, where intellectuals were now readier to defy the regime. And, even in Moscow, despite the party managers' "victory" at the Writers Congress, Solzhenitsyn was greeted with a huge ovation when he appeared at a public literary meeting on May 31.

That same day, Brezhnev, Kosygin, and Marshal Grechko left Moscow for a four-day inspection tour of the Soviet fleet in the Arctic Sea. The heads of the Soviet party, government, and armed forces left the capital at the height of an international crisis in the Middle East—a crisis which their policies had helped to create and which brought them their most fateful surprise of the Jubilee Year.

Russian ambitions in the Eastern Mediterranean went back to the tsars. Stalin had asked Roosevelt and Churchill for "trusteeship" of Libya in 1945, and in 1948 had helped Zionists in Palestine overthrow the British mandate and establish the State of Israel. But when Israel's first ambassador to Moscow, Golda Meir, was greeted enthusiastically by Russian Jews, Stalin turned violently against Israel, and in 1949 he launched the bloody anti-Semitic purge which culminated in 1952 with the grisly Slansky trial in Prague. Stalin could not, however, develop much enthusiasm for the Arab leaders of the time, who were nearly all traditional Moslems as well as anti-Communist.

It was Khrushchev who discovered the "progressive" Arabs in the form of the Egyptian Colonel, Gamal Abdel Nasser, and the radical Ba'ath party in Syria, whom he hoped to utilize against the Middle Eastern states still under Western influence. But after a number of crises between 1955 and 1958, the area had become relatively peaceful, with United Nations forces stationed on the Egyptian border with Israel. Khrushchev's attention had turned to Cuba, China and Berlin.

Brezhnev and his colleagues, however, saw a new chance for a breakthrough in the Middle East, in the form of the radical regime which had taken power in Syria in February 1966. The

Communist party was represented in the new regime, which seemed dynamic as well as "progressive": that is, it was not only violently anti-Western, but also encouraged a Palestinian guerrilla group, Al Fatah, to launch raids and terrorist actions against Israel.

Three months after the new Syrian regime came to power, Kosygin visited Cairo and persuaded Nasser to sign a military alliance with the "progressives" in Damascus. By October 1966, Soviet propaganda had begun to charge, at least once a month, that Israel was concentrating troops on the Syrian frontier and planning to overthrow the shaky "progressive" regime in Damscus.*

The Israeli border with Syria, in the open plains beneath the Golan heights, was only a dozen miles wide, and United Nations observers regularly reported that there were no Israeli troop concentrations. However, when the Israeli premier, Levi Eshkol, offered to drive the Soviet ambassador to the Syrian frontier to see for himself, the Russian envoy replied, "I know best what is there and what is not."

At the end of April 1967, an Egyptian delegation led by Anwar as-Sadat came to Moscow and met with various Soviet leaders (including Kosygin on April 29). As Nasser disclosed later, "Our Soviet friends informed Anwar as-Sadat that the invasion of Syria was imminent." In fact, what Syria faced at this point was not an external threat but domestic turmoil—partly accentuated by the humiliation of the Israeli reprisals which inevitably followed the terrorist raids of Al Fatah. Instead of stopping the raids, the Syrians—in consultation with Moscow—called in Nasser.

According to Nasser, on May 13 both he and the Syrians received definite information that Israel was concentrating a dozen brigades on the Syrian frontier. Such "information" could only have come from the Kremlin; nobody else saw or imagined such concentrations then or later. On May 14, however, the Egyptian Army began moving into the Sinai peninsula, and within a week 80,000 Egyptian soldiers and hundreds of Soviet-built tanks were massed along the Israeli border. On May 16, Nasser requested the

---

* In his definitive study *The Road to War 1967*, Walter Laqueur cites numerous examples of this charge, starting on October 12, 1966. The myth of Israeli concentrations against Syria was spread not only by *Pravda, Izvestia*, and Moscow Radio, but in official notes of the Soviet Government.

withdrawal of the United Nations contingents which had been separating the Egyptian and Israeli armies since 1957. On May 19, he privately informed U.N. officials of his intention to blockade the Straits of Tiran entering the Gulf of Aqaba, in order to close the Israeli port of Eilat to all shipping. On May 22, after receiving a secret letter from the Soviet party central committee and government, Nasser publicly announced his decision to blockade the Straits.

An international crisis had begun. The Kremlin's contribution to the crisis was immediately to intensify anti-Israeli propaganda and threaten Russian intervention. On May 23, the Soviet news agency Tass asserted that the Israeli Cabinet had received "special powers to carry out war preparations against Syria. Israeli forces concentrating on the Syrian border have been placed in a state of alert for war. General mobilization has also been proclaimed." There was not a word of truth in any of this. The Soviet statement also threatened that "whoever ventured aggression in the Middle East would encounter not only the united strength of the Arab countries, but also resolute resistance to aggression on the part of the Soviet Union. . . ." Kosygin made a similar threat in a cable to President Johnson.

On May 24, Egyptian forces prepared to blockade the Straits, and the next day the Egyptian defense minister, Shams ed-din Badran, arrived in Moscow with a ten-man delegation to confer with the Kremlin leaders and the Soviet marshals. In Cairo, Nasser's chief spokesman proclaimed jubilantly that "an armed clash with Israel is inevitable," a clash in which Israel would now be forced to strike the first blow. Nasser himself declared that "the battle will be a general one, and our basic objective will be to destroy Israel." In Tel Aviv, Eshkol offered to fly to Moscow to explain the Israeli position, but the Kremlin leaders were not interested in seeing him. At the United Nations, diplomats sought a compromise, but *Pravda* declared firmly that the Straits of Tiran "cannot, under any United Nations decision, be regarded as Israeli territorial waters."

On the morning of May 27, Soviet ambassadors in Cairo and Tel Aviv routed both Nasser and Eshkol out of bed to warn each against striking the first blow. However, that evening, Marshal

Grechko threw a farewell party for the Egyptian military delegation headed by Shams ed-din Badran. In a joyful toast, the Soviet
defense minister declared that "the U.S.S.R., her armed forces,
her people and Government will stand by the Arabs and will continue to encourage and support them. . . . On behalf of the Ministry of Defense and in the name of the Soviet people, we wish
you success and victory!"

When Shams ed-din Badran returned to Cairo on May 28,
Nasser disclosed publicly the next day, "he handed me a message
from the Soviet Premier Kosygin, saying that the U.S.S.R. supported us in this battle and would not allow any power to
intervene. . . ." The same day, May 28, the heads of the Syrian
Government arrived in Moscow and held long talks with Brezhnev, Kosygin, and the Soviet marshals. When they returned to
Damascus, the Syrians declared that the Russian leaders had
shown "profound understanding" of their views. Some months
later, however, the Syrian prime minister disclosed that the Soviet
military chiefs had been considerably more hawkish than the
civilian political leaders. The marshals had privately advised the
Syrians to pursue an even more militant line toward Israel in
order to prove to skeptical Politburo members that they were
really "serious."

On May 29, while the Syrians were receiving such counsel in
Moscow, *Pravda* was gleefully reporting that Israeli and American
ships had ben turned back from the Straits of Tiran. The next
day, the Soviet press joyfully hailed a joint military pact linking
Jordan with Egypt and Syria. On May 31, as Brezhnev, Kosygin,
and Marshal Grechko left for Murmansk and Archangel, the first
of ten Soviet warships steamed through the Dardanelles into the
Eastern Mediterranean. That same day, Ceausescu in Bucharest
publicly pleaded for direct negotiations between Israel and the
Arabs; the Kremlin ignored his plea. On June 1, Moscow also
formally rejected General de Gaulle's appeal for an emergency
Big Four meeting.

By the time Brezhnev, Kosygin, and Marshal Grechko returned
from the Arctic on June 4, Iraqi troops had crossed the Jordan
River and were moving toward Jerusalem. Israel had mobilized,
and Nasser that day declared on Cairo Radio, "We are facing you

in the battle and are burning with desire for it to start."

The next morning, Israeli planes knocked out the Soviet-built Arab air forces, and within six days Israeli soldiers occupied the Sinai peninsula, the left bank of the Jordan, and the Golan Heights—destroying or capturing millions of dollars worth of Soviet armaments. As soon as the war started, Kosygin used the "hot line" to the White House to assure the United States that —despite his earlier threats—Russia would not intervene. Once Arab defeat was obvious, Soviet representatives at the United Nations quickly accepted resolutions calling for a cease-fire. When the war ended, it was clear that Moscow had suffered its most serious international defeat since the Cuban missile crisis.

As Michel Tatu observed, the Soviet gamble in the Middle East —in fanning up the Syrian war scare and encouraging Nasser to move into Sinai and the Straits—was "a miniature Cuban operation," "meant to help the so-called progressive camp to alter the balance of power." The Soviet leaders may not have wished a war, but they were "unable to resist the pleasure of helping Nasser win a diplomatic victory and later claiming credit for it." Moreover, Brezhnev and his colleagues proved themselves incapable of gauging the consequences of their own actions: "In 1962, Khrushchev miscalculated; in 1967, it would be more accurate to say that no one calculated at all."

The Soviet leaders found it easier to restore Russia's international position after the Six Day War than to contain the effects of the shock within their own empire. Brezhnev summoned two emergency summit meetings of Communist leaders, the first to break off relations with Israel, the second to pledge new arms to the Arabs. Ceausescu boycotted both meetings, but Tito (an ally of Nasser's since 1952) attended them. Podgorny was dispatched to Egypt, Syria, and Iraq to promise that Soviet, Czech, and East German arsenals would swiftly replace the armaments destroyed or captured by Israel.

Kosygin was sent to the United Nations to demand a resolution calling for Israeli withdrawal from the occupied territories. The resolution failed, but Kosygin met with President Johnson in Glassboro, New Jersey, to assure the American Administration that Russia sought peace. The Glassboro meeting was broadly publicized in the West, where Kosygin got favorable marks for good intentions, but it was barely mentioned on the inside pages of the Soviet press, and immediately forgotten.

In his first speech after the Six Day War, an address to graduating military cadets, Brezhnev ignored the Glassboro meeting. Instead he publicly compared the Israelis to the Nazis, blamed the war on the United States and Britain, and declared that "the arrogance and perfidy of imperialist reaction" required even greater efforts to strengthen Soviet military might. The defense budget was sharply increased. The official figure (representing the tip of the iceberg) was to show a 17 percent rise for 1968 over 1967. Funds previously earmarked or promised for agriculture, consumer goods, and housing * were cut back accordingly.

At the same time, Communist propaganda launched a virulent campaign against "Zionism," officially linked with American "imperialism" and West German "revanchism." The tone resembled the similar campaign of Stalin's last years, which had also been supervised by Suslov. The propaganda was fiercest in such traditionally anti-Semitic regions as the Ukraine and Moldavia, but even in cosmopolitan Leningrad measures were taken to exclude Jews from sensitive positions.

The "anti-Zionist" campaign was all the more shrill because it was so artificial. It went against the grain not only in Russia but, even more so, among peoples who had rarely been anti-Semitic —notably the Czechs. There was little affection anywhere in Communist Europe for the Arabs, considerable admiration for Israel's David-vs-Goliath triumph, and, often, barely concealed satisfaction at the manner in which the Soviet leaders' bluff had been called.

In Moscow, when Arab students demonstrated angrily at the Israeli and Western embassies, they aroused no sympathy from

* The 1961 party program had promised to end the acute Soviet shortage (three people per room) by 1970 and to provide each Soviet family with its own apartment by 1980. To achieve this goal, Khrushchev said that the volume of housing construction would increase from a planned annual average of 135 million square meters in 1961–65 to 400 million meters by the late seventies.

Actual Soviet construction in the late sixties was below Khrushchev's promises for the early sixties, and showed a tendency to decline: 1966–102.1; 1967–104.5; 1968–102.1; 1969–(est.) 103. This amounted to about a square foot a year per Soviet citizen in new construction (without calculating substantial demolition or disintegration of pre-1917 housing).

either Russian passersby or the Soviet troops controlling them. When, on the fifth day of the war, a few busloads of Soviet Communist militants were dispatched to demonstrate outside the Israeli Embassy, onlookers were either detached or openly critical. "Why don't you go home and leave these people alone?" cried one old Russian woman. "Do you want us to get involved in that war, too? Haven't we suffered enough from the last war?"

Even before the war had ended, Moscow was full of jokes mocking the Arabs and the Kremlin. (According to one tale, Arab strategy had been letter-perfect by Russian military standards, but unfortunately Brezhnev had failed to supply snow.) Barely a month after the war's end, scores of Russians were linking arms with foreign tourists at Moscow's Uzbekistan Restaurant, as the band played a rousing hora, a traditional Jewish and Israeli folk dance. A few minutes later, by popular request, the band played the strictly Israeli "Hava Nagila" ("Let us rejoice")—and at least a dozen of the dancing Russians sang the Hebrew words. And, despite decades of anti-American propaganda, after the dance was over a Soviet airforce captain told a pretty American tourist, "I flew one of your bombers during the war—Wright Cyclone motor, Bendix radio. America saved us in the war. You are our friends, and we know it."

Six months after the war, in the monthly magazine *Moskva*, a Russian-Jewish translator of Islamic classics, Semyon Lipkin, published a poem which said:

> I'm told that overseas in Asia
> There's a people by the name of "I."
>
> Just think: birth and death,
> Childhood days, a plot of land and home,
> Rejection of falsehood, and the concepts
> Of compassion, fearlessness and kindness,
>
> The breadth and joy and sadness
> Of all our human race
> Are condensed and powerfully united
> In this small tribe of "I."
>
> And when in a captured temple

My mother is led to the sacrifice
All the louder, for the world to hear,
Do I speak, together with her, of myself . . .

Mankind would come to grief and cannot be
Without this people by the name of "I."

Such sentiments, contrasting sharply with the official propaganda assailing "international Zionism" and "Western imperialism," were by no means confined to the 3 million Soviet Jews
or to the liberal, Western-minded Moscow and Leningrad
intellectuals. Similar feelings were strong among veteran Communists in Eastern Europe who had joined the movement in the
period of anti-Nazi struggle and among those who uneasily
recalled how similar "anti-Zionist," "anti-imperialist" hysteria had
forshadowed terror in Stalin's last years.

The Kremlin leaders, sensing the unpopularity of their policies,
intensified their efforts to maintain "discipline" among their subjects. And the effort to assert "discipline" in turn provoked new
incidents and scandals, which led the Kremlin to further insecurity and repression, in a vicious cycle. The immediate aftermath
of the Middle East war brought the Kremlin new conflicts with
liberal Russian intellectuals, and the first rumblings of approaching thunder in Czechoslovakia.*

The first Russian casualty of Brezhnev's Mideast defeat was a
poetry reading which Andrei Vozesensky had been invited to give
in New York. In the long history of Communist torment of
Russian writers, the incident was relatively minor, but it cast a
revealing light on the style of the collective leadership over
which Brezhnev presided—illustrating in microcosm the psychology and methods which, on a larger scale, had helped produce the
Middle East fiasco and were also evident a year later in Czechoslovakia. The new style differed sharply from that of Khrushchev.

* The events in Czechoslovakia between June 1967 and January 1968, between
the revolt at the writers' congress and the fall of Novotny, will be described
in the next chapter. However, it should be borne in mind throughout the remainder of this chapter that the steady erosion of despotism in Prague during
these months was closely watched in Moscow; it worried Kremlin doctrinaires,
and encouraged Soviet liberals.

Khrushchev had blustered and bragged, fumed and raged, blown hot and cold. But he had personally dominated the scene, he relished publicity, and he had an irrepressible urge to bring matters out into the open at large meetings, formal and informal. Many of his statements later came back to haunt him, but he spoke his mind often, and at his best strove to call things by their proper names.

Under Brezhnev, however, there was a return—in matters both great and small—to the instinctive secrecy and deliberate hypocrisy which had distinguished Stalin's statecraft. The collective leaders themselves traveled little, at home or abroad. They made few public speeches and saw few outsiders privately. The powerful, anonymous agencies of Kremlin control, from the party secretariat through the Army and the KGB to the Writers Union, felt little compulsion to explain—or even disclose—their actions to anyone. The tendency was to manage all of Soviet society, and Russia's activities in the world, on the kind of "need to know" principle of restricted information which traditionally governed the clandestine operations of security-conscious espionage agencies.

Such secrecy facilitated the return of the old Stalinist technique of "orchestrating" different lines—and different lies—at different levels to different audiences.

Systematic lying had, of course, been openly recommended by Lenin; Trotsky as well as Stalin was a master of the art; and few who have not lived in Soviet Russia can imagine to what extent lying had long become a daily norm, an automatic reflex. However, as in other spheres of Russian life, fifty years had eroded intellectual as well as moral standards. Lenin and Trotsky had lied in the grand manner, with skill, sophistication, selectivity, and purpose. In contrast, the hallmark of the Brezhnev administration was a systematic duplicity which was cynical but inept, so crude that the lies often defeated, rather than advanced, the purposes of their fabricators. Such was the case with Voznesensky's reading.

The poet was to have appeared at the Lincoln Center festival in New York on June 21. The performance had been advertised for six months; some 3,000 tickets had already been sold a week before the performance. However, following the Mideast War, party leaders saw an opportunity to punish Voznesensky for his approval of Solzhenitsyn's open letter, and for his nonconformist behavior during a previous visit to the United States.

On June 16, four days before the poet was to depart for New York, Writers Union officials notified Voznesensky that his trip was "inadvisable" and compelled him to cable New York that he could not come. The reason officially given to the poet was that relations with the United States had deteriorated in the wake of the Six Day War (although that had not prevented Kosygin from leaving for New York the same day).

When Moscow correspondents and the American Embassy inquired as to what had happened, they were officially told that Voznesensky was ill. This was difficult for anyone to believe, since he had been seen publicly in perfect health. Word quickly reached the West that Voznesensky's voyage had been prohibited on political grounds.

The Soviet Foreign Ministry, seeking to dampen the scandal while Kosygin was in New York, then quietly sent Voznesensky's passport (which it had been holding for three weeks) to the U.S. Embassy in Moscow, so that an American visa could be inscribed. Ministry officials told foreign correspondents that there was now no obstacle to Voznesensky's trip. But the Ministry said nothing to the poet. On the contrary, at the very same time, Writers Union officials were telling Voznesensky that the prohibition still stood. It was only from foreign radio broadcasts that he learned that his passport had ever reached the American Embassy. By that time, it was already too late to catch the last plane for New York.

On June 22, Voznesensky sent an angry letter to *Pravda* recounting the episode. "For nearly a week now," he wrote, "I have been living in an atmosphere of blackmail, confusion and provocation." He denounced "the lying and total lack of scruples" of Writers Union officials "who tell one lie to me and another to the world at large. . . ."

"I am a Soviet writer, a human being made of flesh and blood, not a puppet to be pulled on a string," Voznesensky wrote. "Clearly the leadership of the Union does not regard writers as human beings. We are surrounded by lies, lies, bad manners and lies. I am ashamed to be a member of the same Union as these people. That is why I am writing to your newspaper, which is called 'Truth' (*Pravda*)."

Voznesensky's anguished protest was ignored by both *Pravda* and the Writers Union. The poet left Moscow for the country-side for a week. He returned to attend the hundredth perform-ance, on July 2, of a staged adaptation of his verse, "Anti-Worlds," at the Taganka Theatre. The theater was packed with bright-looking young men and girls; scores of others jammed the sidewalk outside, unable to obtain tickets. At the end of the per-formance, a wave of applause summoned Voznesensky to the stage. He read a few of his older poems, and then a new one:

> They've taken out our sense of shame
> As an appendix is removed. . . .
>
> How shamefully we hold our tongues,
> Or at the most we hem and haw.
> I'm ashamed of things
> I've written myself. . . .
>
> It's scandalous
> that censorship's been introduced
> —in Greece—
> so that all the newspapers look alike.
> It's scandalous
> when Vietnam becomes a pawn to be played with,
> It's scandalous to lie and lie. . . .
>
> You so-called intelligentsia,
> Caught in the tissue of your lies,
> You read Herzen
> While you bare your backside for the lash.

Two days later, Voznesensky was summoned to the Writers Union, where fourteen officials berated him, censured him formally, and threatened him with expulsion from the Writers Union (which would mean the end of legal publication of his works). In August, when Voznesensky's letter to *Pravda* was published abroad, he was summoned by that newspaper's editor, Mikhail Zimyanin, a veteran of Stalin's 1952 Central Committee.

As Zimyanin confided to Soviet journalists later, "I told him that he might get off with a reprimand the first time, but if he ever did it again, he would be ground to dust. I myself would see to it that not a trace of him remained."

A similar combination of secrecy and duplicity characterized the trial August 30 and September 1 of three of the youths who had demonstrated in Pushkin Square seven months earlier. The trial was closed to all but witnesses and the immediate families of the defendants: Vladimir Bukovsky, twenty-six, Vadim Delone, twenty, and Yevgeny Kushev, nineteen. Bukovsky was sentenced to three years in a forced labor camp; the other two received suspended sentences of one year each.

The only Soviet newspaper ever to mention the case was the Moscow local evening paper, which falsely claimed, three days after the trial, that all three defendants had pleaded guilty and that Bukovsky had a long record of "antisocial acts of hooliganism." The paper, *Vechernaya Moskva,* gave no indication that the purpose of the demonstration was to demand the release of Galanskov and Ginsburg.

All three defendants admitted taking part in the demonstration, but refused to regard it as a criminal act. Each made plain that he had been harassed for his political views. Bukovsky boldly turned the trial into an indictment of the regime. "It was in 1961," he explained, "that I first asked myself whether in fact the democratic liberties guaranteed by the Constitution are a reality in the Soviet Union." At that time, three of his friends were tried as criminals for producing a handwritten periodical.

Ever since then, Bukovsky said, "I have been opposed to the atmosphere of oppression and concealment which exists in our country." At a poetry reading in Mayakovsky Square, he had been attacked and beaten by young Communist vigilantes. For photostating sections of Milovan Djilas's book *The New Class,* Bukovsky was arrested and sent for twenty-one months to the Leningrad Prison Mental Hospital.

Now, after seven months in Moscow's Lefortovo Prison, Bukovsky remained unrepentant. "We know," he concluded his defense, "that freedom of speech and of the press is, in the first place, freedom to criticize. No one has ever been forbidden to praise the Government. . . ." When it came to free speech, he observed, there was "a touching unanimity" between Soviet law and that of Fascist states.

"You accuse us," Bukovsky declared, "of trying to discredit the KGB by our slogans, but the KGB has discredited itself so effectively that there is nothing we can add . . . I absolutely do not repent of having organized the demonstration. I believe it has done its job and, when I am free again, I shall organize other demonstrations. . . ."

Here, then, was a conscious rebel against the dictatorship who had gone even farther than Sinyavsky and Daniel in defending himself with unequivocal vigor. Bukovsky's friends were outraged when *Vechernaya Moska* portrayed him as a "hooligan" who had pleaded guilty.

One of Bukovsky's friends bore a name famous in the Soviet Union. He was Pavel Litvinov, a twenty-seven-year old physics instructor at a Moscow institute of chemical technology and the grandson of the Old Bolshevik and anti-Nazi Soviet foreign minister, Maxim Litvinov. Pavel Litvinov's aunt, Tatyana Litvinova, a daughter of the late foreign minister, had been among the defense witnesses at the trial. So had Alexander Yesenin-Volpin, mathematician and writer, son of the late poet Sergei Yesenin, and Anatoly Krasnov-Levitin, a Christian Socialist philosopher who had spent seven years in Stalinist labor camps. All were people of broad education and independent outlook, with deep sympathy for what had begun to emerge as an informal "democratic movement," whose members were prepared to struggle actively on behalf of civil liberties in Russia. Together with relatives of the defendants, they were able to reconstruct the testimony at the Bukovsky trial—just as Yuli Daniel's wife Larissa and others had reconstructed the Sinyavsky-Daniel trial, a record which formed the basis of Alex Ginsburg's "White Book" on the proceedings.

Pavel Litvinov's own disillusion with the Soviet system had begun with the Sinyavsky-Daniel trial; Ginsburg, as well as Bukovsky, was among his friends. On September 26, Litvinov was summoned to the main headquarters of the KGB and warned that, if any record of the Bukovsky trial were to be circulated, he would be held criminally responsible. Litvinov objected that there was no law against circulating nonsecret documents. "You know perfectly well what we are talking about," the KGB official replied. "We are only warning you, but the Court will find you guilty. . . . Imagine if all the world were to hear that the grandson of the great diplomat Litvinov was involved in such a thing—it would be a blot on his memory."

"Well, I don't think he would blame me," Pavel Litvinov answered. A week later, he sent a transcript of the Bukovsky trial, as well as a record of his own interrogation by the KGB, to four Soviet and three Western Communist newspapers. The documents compiled by Maxim Litvinov's grandson were published abroad shortly after the appearance of *Twenty Letters to a Friend*, by Stalin's daughter, Svetlana Alliluyeva.

Alexander Solzhenitsyn posed a more formidable problem to the Kremlin than any of the other Soviet dissidents and liberals disturbing the planned joyousness of the Jubilee Year. Unlike Vladimir Bukovsky and Pavel Litvinov, relatively unknown youths, Solzhenitsyn was world famous, the very symbol of Khrushchev's final effort at de-Stalinization. Unlike Andrei Voznesensky, who was only twenty at Stalin's death and a golden success before he reached thirty, Solzhenitsyn had been hardened by four years as an artillery captain in World War II, eight years in Stalinist prisons and camps, three years of forced exile, and a painful personal struggle against cancer. Having already experienced the worst, Solzhenitsyn could not be intimidated; nor could he simply be disposed of as a "hooligan" or "schizophrenic," the epithets being applied by the KGB to the lesser-known rebels it was clapping into prisons, labor camps, and psychiatric wards.

Moreover, like other veterans of Stalinist persecution, Solzhenitsyn had developed an expert knowledge of the limits and pitfalls of Soviet law. He was determined not to be maneuvered into committing—or even appearing to commit—such a "crime" as sending his manuscripts abroad, as Sinyavsky and Daniel had done. On the contrary, he pressed all the more urgently for speedy publication of his works in Russia itself, partly because he realized that the KGB might well "plant" his manuscripts abroad and then use their foreign publication against him.

Solzhenitsyn's novel *The Cancer Ward* had been submitted to *Novy Mir* in the summer of 1966 but had been in a state of limbo for nearly a year. Tvardovsky, *Novy Mir's* editor, wanted to publish the novel but was reluctant to do so without some word from higher authority. The party leaders would neither authorize nor prohibit its publication. Meanwhile, typescripts of *The Cancer Ward,* and later of an even more powerful novel, *The First Circle* (which the KGB had seized among Solzhenitsyn's papers), had begun to be circulated in ever broader Moscow circles— increasing the likelihood that copies would soon find their way abroad. This tension had partly prompted Solzhenitsyn's open letter to the Writers Congress, and the publication of Solzhenitsyn's letter abroad (May 30) had increased the tensions.

On June 12, the Monday after the Six Day War, Solzhenitsyn appeared at a meeting of Writers Union officials which he later described as "quiet and peaceful." Four high officials agreed that it was the Union's duty to refute the slanders on Solzhenitsyn's war record and promised to "examine the question" of approving *The Cancer Ward* for early publication in *Novy Mir*. Tvardovsky produced a draft communiqué aimed at ending the deadlock. He proposed that the Writers Union weekly, *Literaturnaya Gazeta,* publish extracts from *The Cancer Ward* with an announcement that the full novel would appear in *Novy Mir*, and that Solzhenitsyn's short stories be published in book form, with a biographical introduction that would in effect refute all the slanders against him. Konstantin Fedin, the seventy-five-year old chairman of the Writers Union, agreed to the compromise and helped edit Tvardovsky's draft communiqué. Solzhenitsyn returned from Moscow to his home in Ryazan, 120 miles to the southeast, satisfied that he had made "some progress."

By the end of the summer, however, Solzhenitsyn realized that there had been no progress at all. Foreigners arriving in Moscow were being told that *The Cancer Ward* and the short stories would be published. But at meetings of party activists and army instructional seminars, the old slanders against Solzhenitsyn continued and new rumors were spread—that he had run away to

Britain or the United Arab Republic. Copies of *Ivan Denisovich* continued to be withdrawn from the library shelves, and the novel was no longer available even in the public reading room at Ryazan, where Solzhenitsyn lived. Solzhenitsyn's very name could no longer be mentioned in the press.

On September 12, Solzhenitsyn sent an angry letter to the Writers Union, recounting these and other incidents and insisting that *The Cancer Ward* be published without further delay. Otherwise, he feared, "we cannot prevent its unauthorized appearance in the West."

Ten days later, on the afternoon of September 22, the Secretariat of the Writers Union confronted Solzhenitsyn at a meeting which lasted five hours. Some thirty of the forty-two secretaries of the Union—as well as a representative of the party Central Committee—were present. Tvardovsky and Konstantin Simonov supported Solzhenitsyn, but it soon became apparent that the official tide was running against him. Fedin, the aging Union chairman who had agreed to a compromise in June (and who had similarly turned against Pasternak in 1958), now suddenly demanded that Solzhenitsyn first issue a statement denouncing the publication of his open letter "by our enemies in the West." It was with such a recantation, Fedin told Solzhenitsyn, that his "acquittal" would have to begin.

Fedin was echoed by other party literary watchdogs, including Alexei Surkov, who had led the campaign against Pasternak. "The works of Solzhenitsyn," Surkov now declared, "are more dangerous to us than those of Pasternak. Pasternak was a man divorced from life, while Solzhenitsyn, with his animated, militant, ideological temperament, is a man of principle."

Solzhenitsyn refused to repudiate his open letter, since none of the grievances raised in it had been corrected. He also noted bitterly that three months earlier he had been assured that the communiqué drafted by Tvardovsky and approved by Fedin would be printed without further ado, "and yet today conditions are posed. What has changed?" There was no answer.

The meeting ended in a deadlock—with no decision taken on whether the Union would approve or disapprove *Novy Mir*'s publication of *The Cancer Ward*. Tvardovsky now attempted to force a decision. The first eight chapters of *The Cancer Ward* were set in type, scheduled for the December issue of *Novy Mir*, and approved by Solzhenitsyn in galley proofs. On November 1, just a few days before the "glorious fiftieth anniversary" of the revolution, the page proofs of *Novy Mir* containing the first installment of Solzhenitsyn's novel were approved by Tvardovsky and submitted, as required, to the censors.* Tvardovsky realized that, on an issue so important, the censor would doubtless consult the Central Committee secretariat, headed by Brezhnev.

In 1962 Khrushchev had personally forced through the publication of *One Day in the Life of Ivan Denisovich* after four years of delay. Once more, Tvardovsky needed a political decision to publish *The Cancer Ward*.

But Brezhnev was not Khrushchev. While he wished to avoid an untimely scandal, he had led the movement to close the book on Stalin's crimes, reassert his "virtues," and restore the old "discipline." On the very eve of the Jubilee celebration, the Government demonstratively awarded the Order of Lenin to the judge (L. N. Smirnov) who had condemned Sinyavsky and Daniel. A few weeks later, after a meeting between Brezhnev and Fedin, the order went out to destroy the type of the first eight chapters of *The Cancer Ward*. The issue of *Novy Mir* which Tvardovsky had completed on November 1 was remade and did not finally clear the censorship until December 29—long after all the foreign and provincial visitors who had come to celebrate the great Jubilee in Moscow had gone home.

At the height of the celebrations, however, visitors to the Soviet capital could read a new panegyric to Stalin by the poet Sergei Smirnov, who recounted reverently how "we made of him a living icon to whom we turned and prayed." To the disgust of numerous readers, Smirnov was rhapsodic even about the Muscovites who had been trampled to death at Stalin's funeral ** : the "hundreds

---

* Officially, censorship does not even exist in Russia; no published Soviet law contains any mention of *Glavlit*, the censorship organization embracing thousands of officials throughout the country, as well as resident censors in every newspaper, magazine, and publishing office in Moscow. *Glavlit's* main headquarters are on the sixth floor of the Ministry of Electric Power building on Chinese Lane, roughly halfway between the Kremlin and KGB headquarters.

** Yevtushenko, an eyewitness, has provided the best description of this disaster in his *Precocious Autobiography*.

of souls of the citizens crushed underfoot," he wrote, had "fashioned a funeral wreath" for the mighty Stalin.

In keeping with the post-Khrushchev style, nobody could ever prove that Brezhnev personally had either approved Smirnov's poem or forbidden Solzhenitsyn's novel. It was merely that the party of which Brezhnev was general secretary had (in Mao's phrase) "leaned to one side."

But Brezhnev did noticeably dominate the five-day jubilee celebration, including four days of massive speechmaking in Moscow and Leningrad. He presented a four-hour report to open the festivities in Moscow and also delivered the major speech in Leningrad. In reviewing fifty years of Soviet power, Brezhnev avoided any reference to Trotsky, Stalin, or Khrushchev. He defined "Marxism-Leninism" as "the science of how to win."

All year long, party and trade union agitators had been pressing workers to fulfill their 1967 production targets before the November 7 anniversary. Brezhnev was thus able to announce that industrial production had increased by 10.5 percent. (As a result of the strain of doing so, however, growth rates began declining a few months later and continued to do so throughout 1968 and 1969.) The harvest was also above the modest 1965 plan, although 18 million tons below the record 1966 crop.

Brezhnev's greatest achievements, however, were evident in the military parade through Red Square on November 7. There, the Soviet armed forces displayed new units of "Red Beret" paratroopers and "Black Beret" marines, and no less than five new rocket systems, one for each class. They included a submarine-launched missile larger than the American Polaris, and a 120-foot intercontinental ballistic missile, capable of launching nuclear bombs into orbit from where they could be fired at any time by ground control.

The thousands of militants who followed the armed forces through Red Square with floats and flags had been mobilized at 8 A.M. or earlier at special points around the city. Some six hours later, all the weapons had been sheathed and the floats, flags, and banners returned to the party *agitpunkts*. That night, there were special fireworks for the tens of thousands who poured into the downtown streets and squares, which had been specially lit. The crowds at night were unorganized—a few of the men drunk and raucous, but most of the people quieter than the disciplined militants of the parade. Men, women, boys, and girls strolled and gazed at the illuminated portrait of Lenin floating over the Kremlin, peered at shop windows, jammed theaters and concert halls, queued up at restaurants. Loudspeakers kept blaring revolutionary songs, with little echo.

That evening, the thirty-seven-year-old Soviet writer Anatoly Kuznetsov wrote in his diary:

> November 7, 1967. The 50th anniversary of the founding of the Soviet state. . . . The 50th anniversary of the nightmare. Illuminations on the streets. From morning till night, formal meetings with Niagaras of speeches and boasting. Inspiring military parades. The disciplined "celebrations" of the people. The military parade of death-dealing instruments for intimidating mankind. . . .
>
> Shout hurrah, clap your hands. Otherwise they will notice at once that you are not "reacting" and they will ask you why . . .
>
> I am getting stupider. I am gradually turning into Ionesco's Rhinoceros. I feel the hardening on my forehead. I feel sick. . . .

A few weeks after the anniversary of Lenin's coup, the Soviet leaders festively celebrated the fiftieth anniversary of the Cheka-KGB, and, a few weeks after that, the fiftieth anniversary of the Red Army. In the second week of 1968 (which the United Nations had proclaimed Human Rights Year), the KGB was at last ready to try Yuri Galanskov, the editor of *Phoenix 66,* and Alex Ginsburg, compiler of the "White Book" on the Sinyavsky-Daniel trial. Two other defendants had been imprisoned with them for nearly a year: Vera Lashkova, who had typed some of their manuscripts, and Alexei Dobrovolsky, a contributor to *Phoenix 66* who had agreed early in the KGB interrogations to turn state's evidence.

They were tried in a half-empty courtroom to which only seven relatives of the defendants were admitted, and from which witnesses were dismissed after their own testimony. The other spectators, supplied by the KGB, jeered at the defendants and prevented their relatives from taking notes in court.

Dozens of friends of the defendants as well as foreign newsmen, both barred from the courtroom, were permitted to gather during the January daylight hours in a tawdry-looking corridor at the other end of the courthouse and a floor below the room in which the trial was held. This waiting room was blocked off by uniformed militia and filled with alert young eavesdroppers who identified themselves as young Communist volunteers but were doubtless KGB employees. On the first day of the trial, they removed the corridor's feeble light bulbs and put in stronger wattage so that they could photograph the defendants' friends. Outside the courthouse, plainclothesmen soon prevented newsmen from speaking with the defendants' relatives as they arrived and left for the day. And, after 5 P.M. each day, the waiting room was cleared; both friends and newsmen were thrust out to wait on the frozen pavement (in temperatures that sank 15 degrees below zero) for two or three hours until each day's trial session was over.

The defendants' friends, men and women of various ages, were united only by a certain solidarity which was visible and tangible. Most were nameless, but not all; some bore famous Russian names, and others were to become well known as doughty leaders of the nascent democratic movement.

The tall, handsome young man in a brown leather, fur-trimmed coat was Pavel Litvinov, who had already been dismissed from his lectureship in physics for having published Bukovsky's final plea.

The vivid, bright-eyed man with the well-trimmed black beard, who insisted on speaking French even to foreigners who knew Russian, was Alexander Yesenin-Volpin. An eminently lucid, dedicated, and civilized man, he had been thrust into mental homes for his frequent protests against injustice under Khrushchev. When, six weeks after the Ginsburg-Galanskov trial, he was again seized and placed in a lunatic asylum, an immediate protest by ninety-five Moscow University mathematicians (including a dozen Lenin and State Prize winners and two dozen full professors) forced his release.

The restless, alert, stocky figure in a fatigue jacket, then wearing a bristly, unshaven "Cuban" beard, was the historian Pyotr Yakir. He had been arrested at the age of fourteen and spent seventeen years at forced labor as the son of the Red Army hero General Iona Yakir, executed by Stalin in 1937.* Since 1966, he had been a leader in the struggle against the rehabilitation of Stalin.

The ramrod-straight, balding man with the cane was Pyotr Grigorenko, former major general of the Soviet Army, wounded veteran of the Civil War and World War II, professor of cybernetics at the Frunze Military Academy until 1964. In that year, he was arrested and charged with "anti-Soviet activity" for criticizing Khrushchev, clapped into mental homes, stripped of his rank and deprived of his pension. He was now working as a construction foreman, and still considered himself a "Marxist-Leninist."

At last, on the third day of the trial, there came a woman in a blue cloth coat, with a thin scarf around her head, who could not control her shivering as night fell and whose friends had to press against her to keep her warm. She was quiet, soft-spoken, simple, and direct in manner, not at all conventionally handsome. Yet, through her wan face and deep-set eyes shone qualities of the last century, of the martyr-women of the legendary People's Will which had fought tsarism. This was Larissa Daniel, and when asked why she was outside this trial, when her husband Yuli was already in a camp, she answered quietly, "I cannot do otherwise."

The trial itself was in an old tradition of Moscow trials. Not the tradition of confessing Old Bolsheviks, doing the party a last service, but the tradition of unrepentant non-Communists from the Socialist Revolutionaries of 1922 down to Sinyavsky and Daniel. Both Galanskov and Ginsburg defended themselves firmly. The typist Vera Lashkova admitted typing the manuscripts but considered that this was no crime. Only Dobrovolsky went along with the prosecution, but his testimony was obviously considered

---

* "I knew Comrade Yakir well," Khrushchev told the 22nd party congress (October 27, 1961). "I knew (Marshal Mikhail) Tukhachevsky too, but not as well as Yakir. In 1961, during a conference in Alma-Ata, his son, who works in Kazakhstan, came to see me. What could I tell him? . . . When Yakir was shot, he exclaimed: 'Long live the party, long live Stalin!' . . . When Stalin was told how Yakir had behaved before his death, he cursed Yakir."

Shelepin had previously told the same congress how Yakir had appealed, the day before he was shot, to Marshal Voroshilov to protect his family, "helpless and quite innocent." Voroshilov had sneered at the request, Shelepin disclosed. These public disclosures in 1961 did not prevent the post-Khrushchev Politburo (of which Shelepin was a leading member) from harassing Pyotr Yakir and staging a great state funeral in 1969 for Voroshilov, at which even the discredited Molotov was an honor guard.

insufficient, for the KGB had to produce a last-minute "mystery witness" who could not even claim ever to have seen any of the defendants. This was Nicholas Brocks Sokolov, a twenty-one year old student of Russian extraction, German birth, and Venezuelan citizenship, whose arrest by the KGB had been publicly announced a month earlier on his arrival in Moscow from the University of Grenoble. He was said to be an envoy of an émigré group, the NTS (Popular Labor Alliance), which had given him "very incriminating" photographs of "so-called writers" whom that group supposedly wished to defend.

Outside the courtroom, a black-bearded young KGB agent recounting this tale said that there were five photographs: of Ginsburg, Galanskov, Dobrovolsky, Sinyavsky, and Daniel. However, when *Izvestia* finally discussed the case a week later, there were still five photographs, but only three names cited. In the wave of protests reverberating among Moscow intellectuals, it was no longer prudent to mention Sinyavsky and Daniel.

The protests had started before the trial, with a petition from thirty-one writers, artists, and scientists (among them Vassily Aksyonov, Bella Akhmadulina, and Lenin Prize mathematician Igor Shaferevich) demanding an open trial and testifying that "all of us who know Alex Ginsburg personally do not doubt his honesty and decency." The petitions and letters continued day after day, through the trial and beyond it, and ultimately involved literally more than 700 artists, writers, scientists, social scientists, and engineers, including forty-six scientists from Novosibirsk. The protesting writers included such venerable figures as Konstantin Paustovsky and such younger figures as Novella Matveyeva (whom some considered the most promising woman poet in Russia).

The most important protest, because it summed up what the relatives saw and heard inside the courtroom, was signed by Pavel Litvinov and Larissa Daniel. They branded the proceedings "a witch trial . . . no better than the celebrated trials of the 1930s which involved us in so much shame and blood that we still have not recovered." They accused Judge Lev Mironov, Prosecutor Gennady Terekhov, and the hand-picked audience of "a wild mockery, unthinkable in the twentieth century." They charged

Mironov with browbeating the defendants, their attorneys, and the witnesses, and with permitting only testimony "which fit in with the program already prepared by the KGB investigation." They asserted that the audience was filled with "specially selected people, officials of the KGB," vigilantes who laughed and insulted the defendants and the witnesses. They reported that witnesses were "shoved out of court in a depressed state, almost in hysterics" (a charge supported by a petition signed by thirteen witnesses).

The protests failed to influence the verdict. Vera Lashkova was given a one-year sentence, which she had virtually served, and was quietly released a fortnight later. Dobrovolsky received a two-year sentence. Alex Ginsburg was sentenced to five years at hard labor, Yuri Galanskov to seven. They joined Sinyavsky and Daniel at the Potma concentration camp.

Surprisingly, on the last freezing night of the trial, more than a hundred strangers joined the friends, journalists, and police agents awaiting the sentences outside the courthouse. Ordinary Russians, they had heard from Western radio broadcasts where and when sentence was expected. Extra militia arrived to prevent a demonstration. They were powerless to prevent one, for it was silent, spontaneous, and eloquent. When the prosecutor, judge, and court officials left the building, the crowd parted to let them pass without a word. When the four defense attorneys emerged, each was presented with red carnations. Then came the relatives, including Ginsburg's aging mother, a retired economist, and Galanskov's handsome wife, whose broken ankle was in a cast. Pavel Litvinov and Alex Daniel, the sixteen-year-old son of Yuli and Larissa, came up the steps for Olga Galanskova and lifted her high on their shoulders. They carried her—dazed but radiant —down the steps, across the small courtyard and the frozen street into a taxi. The crowd followed her mutely, step by step; it was, somehow, a triumphal procession.

Four days after the trial, in the magazine *Znamya*, there was a poem by Yevtushenko curiously titled "Smog" (the name of an underground literary group to which several of the persecuted young writers had belonged). In Yevtushenko's poem, American writers were made to say:

Darkness is descending,
Darkness!
This is the smell of outer hell.
There is no excuse for those
Who can breathe in this stench!
In a world of moral vacuum,
In a world of fog and chaos,
The only halfway decent person
Is he who suffocates.

. . . There will be still more burnings at the stake
By Inquisitions. Smog
Is the smoke of stakes to come.

In a memorandum on "Progress, Coexistence and Intellectual Freedom" that began circulating four months later, Academician Sakharov, the nuclear physicist, condemned as "disgraceful" the censorship of Solzhenitsyn and other writers; the trials of Sinyavsky and Daniel, Khaustov and Bukovsky, Ginsburg and Galanskov; "the persecution, in the best witch-hunt tradition, of dozens of members of the Soviet intelligentsia" who had protested; the efforts to "rehabilitate Stalin, his associates and his policy."

Despite his condemnation of these alarming trends, Sakharov was not as pessimistic in the late spring of 1968 as Yevtushenko had been in winter. For, although developments in Russia were deeply disturbing, there was a new hope on the western horizon. "Today," Sakharov wrote, "the key to a progressive restructuring of the system of government in the interests of mankind lies in intellectual freedom. This has been understood, in particular, by the Czechoslovaks, and there can be no doubt that we should support their bold initiative, which is so valuable for the future of socialism and all mankind."

Czechoslovakia too had an anniversary to celebrate—the fiftieth anniversary of the independence and democracy created by Thomas G. Masaryk in 1918. In its jubilee year, Czechoslovakia found its soul—and an empire lost hope.

CHAPTER 14

March Revolution

Revolution was in the air, tangible and vibrant, the dream of liberation and renewal come alive with spring. It was a time for poets, orators, and lovers, a time of euphoria, hope, openness, and youth. Historians might compare it with Petrograd in March 1917, or Warsaw and Budapest in early October 1956. But Prague in the spring of 1968 was unique: there were no tanks, no troops, no armed confrontations or violent demonstrations; the only police to be seen were guiding traffic. Formally, nothing had changed—and yet everything had changed.

Sad old Prague, whose stones told of tragedies since 1618, a city humbled by twenty years of submission to Stalinism, suddenly glistened with the bright eyes of young boys and girls thronging to great mass meetings to demand truth, justice, freedom. On the streets, people who had formerly shuffled now strode with purposeful pace. Men and women who had waited obediently at traffic lights now jaywalked merrily. In restaurants and cafés, the old suspicious silence and cautious whispers had given way to hearty shouts and jovial laughter. On trams and buses, good humor and manners returned; there was no more of the old sullen shoving. Huge crowds swooped down on newspaper vendors. Excited groups gathered around transistor radios. A city which had so recently seemed mute and monolingual suddenly turned out to be filled with people, young and old, only too delighted to explain the great events to foreigners in English and German. The revolution was peaceful, civilized, and extraordinarily good humored: a happy national reconciliation symbolized by the shy smile of the young Slovak, Alexander Dubcek, who sought nothing more—nor less—than "socialism with a human face."

How had it happened? Why had the Novotny system broken down at the end of 1967? Politically, the worst had ended for Czechoslovakia in 1955, with the last of the rigged trials. Economically, the low point had been the winter of 1962–63. On the surface, Czechoslovakia between 1964 and 1967 seemed to outsiders to be in the process of a slow, controlled "liberalization." The country was far from the proud, elegant republic of the Masaryks firmly based on the rule of law. Yet, by the conventional standards of Communist Europe, it was not doing too badly. The economy, to be sure, was going nowhere, but living standards remained high above those of Russia, Poland, and the Balkan states. Culturally, only Hungary seemed as tolerant.

Yet such comparisons were misleading, for Czechoslovakia moved to its own internal rhythms. What seemed to outsiders to be a controlled "liberalization" was, in fact, the result of countless compromises—of fitful daily struggles at nearly all levels of Czechoslovak society. These were not only struggles between Novotny's Old Guard and new forces pressing for change. They were also struggles within the minds of three generations of Czechs and Slovaks. The older generation remembered Masaryk's Republic but was haunted by the shame of 1938–39: the Western betrayal at Munich, the Czech failure to fight the Nazis, the Slovak quisling state. The men in their thirties and forties, and especially the Communists among them, were haunted by the shame of the 1950s: first the trials, and then Czechoslovakia's failure in 1956 to support Hungary and Poland. The youth, free of the complexes of 1938 and 1956, were impatient with their elders and resentful of the gray mediocrity and mendacity to which the Novotny system seemed to be condemning them.

On the surface, Czechoslovakia seemed calmer during 1965 and 1966 than it had been in 1963. Abstract painting and sculpture were being exhibited. Twelve-tone music was being performed in concert halls and "big beat" jazz almost everywhere else. Czechoslovak films made an extraordinary renaissance and captured the imagination of critics throughout the world. Tourists poured in from Austria and West Germany.

After two decades of neglect (and a series of fatal accidents caused by crumbling cornices and building stones), the authorities had at last begun to repair and restore the old glories of Prague, Brno, Bratislava. Everywhere, there was scaffolding bracing up castles, churches, and towers, archways and arcades. There was sandblasting here, fresh paint there, cobbled streets torn up and replaced by asphalt; brighter goods in shop windows. In Hradcany Castle, the throne room of Maria Theresa was reopened. The Wallenstein Gardens were refurbished. A Gypsy orchestra played in the elegant new restaurant opened in Bratislava Castle.

These and other signs of revival in Czechoslovakia in 1966 seemed to resemble what had happened in Hungary during the last years of Khrushchev—the emergence of a live-and-let-live compromise between the regime and the population.

But, while outsiders noted the little signs of "liberalization," Czechs and Slovaks resented its petty pace: "We Czechs," a young film director remarked in the summer of 1966, "live in a country where almost everything ends in a lousy compromise, in hollow words and stupid slogans, in good intentions gone sour, energies wasted, hot blood unspilt. I am a member of a political party in whose ideas and actions I have long ceased to believe. . . . I live in a city of gray-faced men and women who hardly ever smile, who travel in screeching, ramshackle streetcars to unwanted destinations, who feel safer walking in the gutters to escape the falling plaster. . . . All this twenty years after the war. . . ."

The young director thought that the situation had been better ten, even five years earlier. "We had hopes then for progress, for more meat for those who cared, and for more freedom and respect for those who found they could not live without them. Nothing came of it. Things got worse. Or if they didn't get worse they stayed the same. And the whole thing lasted too long to be funny, or even interesting.

"You may think I'm talking about politics or ideology; I'm not. We're past that. By now we'd be willing to accept any label and pay lip service to almost any system if it would only work. . . . The problem lies elsewhere. . . . Mediocrity has triumphed and established its imperturbable, iron rule—a stupid, vulgar, arrogant, heartless and brainless mediocrity. . . . One can fight it, cheat it, kick it, prick it here and there on its enormous bland surface, and even get some results in the direction of sanity—but what an effort! What a waste of time and energy, what a discrepancy between the outcome in terms of actual achievement and the input of energy and nerves, the cost in plain human decency!"

Compromise had been tried, in almost every sphere of life, and failed. Leading Communist victims of the Stalinist trials had been partly "rehabilitated," but men who put them in jail remained in power. The Slovak uprising of 1944 had been vindicated, but Slovaks continued to resent Prague's centralized rule. Economic reform had been discussed interminably, then introduced in stages, with numerous delays and compromises. The reform had led to new tensions, while disclosing for all who cared to see the heart of the old problem: people simply did not want to work. They had almost forgotten how under the old system, which offered them so little reason to hope that their work would make any difference.

Intellectuals had waged a continuous running battle with party ideologists and censors: "We write, they criticize, and then we write again." The absurdity of the entire system was dramatized in biting plays by Vaclav Havel, novels by Ludvik Vaculik and Milan Kundera, films and television dramas—but the system failed to change. Novotny issued stern warnings, but repression did not follow. "They are putting the screws on again," a writer remarked in 1965, "but the screws are broken."

Slowly but surely, the failure of Soviet-inspired Communism in Czechoslovakia had eroded the confidence not only of Communist intellectuals, but of many party leaders. Since 1962, there had no longer been a coherent majority in the party Central Committee, where Stalinists, anti-Stalinists, and fence-sitting careerists had been evenly balanced. Since mid-1963, Slovakia under Dubcek had been a tolerant sanctuary for reformers, but Novotny in Prague had the police, the national treasury, and the confidence of Moscow. Since Khrushchev's fall in October 1964, the economists' reform plans had run athwart Brezhnev's new foreign policies—arms for North Vietnam and a hardening line toward West Germany, both of them costly for the Czechoslovak economy.

Wary of criticism, facing increasing resistance among party and state officials, aping the post-Khrushchev trend in Moscow, Novotny from 1965 onward increasingly sought to concentrate power in the hands of a narrow circle of trusted cronies. As two official Communist historians * later explained:

> The party center, led by Novotny, expended an enormous amount of political energy not only on making centralized decisions on a great number of problems, but on an increasing effort to suppress any demonstration of criticism. . . . Problems were shelved and remained unsolved. . . . This mode of procedure excluded from management first the state and economic organs, and in the course of time also the party agencies. . . . Between the beginning of 1965 and October 1967, the party Central Committee did not even once discuss the political situation in the country. . . . Unconsidered approval, rather than real discussion, was the order of the day.

According to these official historians, Novotny's stage-managed October 1966 party congress, which Brezhnev attended, was "the spark" that set off the crisis among the Communist leaders themselves. It persuaded many such leaders that compromise could lead nowhere—that economic and social changes would be impossible without a "sharp internal political conflict," aimed at ending Novotny's personal power.

Thus, by the middle of 1967, Novotny faced opposition from a variety of sources. There were the Slovaks seeking national rights. There were the victims of Stalinist persecution, demanding full rehabilitation and the repudiation of Stalinist men and Stalinist methods. There were economists and managers urging a market economy, price reform, the end of wage leveling, trade with the West. There were disillusioned Communist intellectuals (and vindicated non-Communist intellectuals) seeking an end to censor-

* Professor Vojtech Mencl and Dr. Frantisek Ourednik: "What Happened in January"—a series of six articles published between July and September 1968 in Zivot Strany, a biweekly magazine of the party Central Committee.

ship and police rule, constitutional rights, democracy.

Among the party leaders, there were a few radicals who urged sweeping changes. There were many intelligent conservatives who realized that Novotny, by blocking even minor reforms, was risking the collapse of the entire system. And there were careerists who feared that, in any new crisis, Novotny would sacrifice them to appease public opinion—as he had turned on Barak in 1962, and sacrificed Siroky and Bacilek in 1963.

Above all, there was the youth—and especially the students. They were, by and large, the children of the great majority of non-Communist Czechs and Slovaks. They had been born and bred under Communism—and they were simply fed up with a regime that they considered stupid, inefficient, dishonest, repressive, and unworthy of the traditions of Hus, Comenius, and Masaryk. Each May Day starting in 1962, there had been clashes between students and police, riots, and arrests. The clashes in 1966 had been the most serious.

In the historic turns and trials of 1968 and 1969, the students were to stand, along with a handful of non-Communist thinkers, on the radical left of the revolutionary spectrum. Next to them would be the Communist intellectuals and journalists, mediating through the communications media between power and the streets, articulating both the desires of the students and the tactical necessities of the party leaders. In the very center, there would be the party reformers—who knew that the students and writers spoke for the nation, who were anxious to found a new system on their enthusiasm, and yet were compelled constantly to look to their right and to the east. Between the reformers and the Kremlin which was to determine their fate, there would stand the relics of Novotny's party machine: conservatives both moderate and extreme, compromisers by tactical instinct or political conviction, men who for varying reasons were unwilling to contemplate either the dissolution of the Soviet model of Communism or an unequivocal confrontation with Soviet power.

The men, women, and youths who were to embody these differing tendencies in 1968 were virtually unknown, even to most Czechoslovak citizens, in 1967. The Novotny system still appeared to be functioning. The population seemed plunged in its habitual resignation. Opposition was fragmented as Novotny divided and ruled. He played the workers off against the economic reformers and intellectuals, the Prague bureaucracy off against the Slovaks. Police repression disciplined the students. Intrigue and manipulation kept the party machine off balance.

The Arab-Israeli war was the shock which galvanized the opposition, and set off the train of events which doomed Novotny. Unlike the Poles, Magyars, and Rumanians (or even the Slovaks), the Czechs historically had little sympathy for anti-Semitism. As Hitler's first foreign victims, they felt a common bond with Jews exposed to Nazi genocide. Czech arms had helped create the state of Israel in 1948. But only a few years later the "anti-Zionist" hysteria of the Slansky trials had become the badge of Czechoslovak shame under Stalinism. The Stalinist trials (which had made Novotny's career) had made no discrimination between Jews and non-Jews, Czech liberals and Slovak nationalists.

The survivors of those grim persecutions had emerged after long years in prison and disgrace. Some of them were of Jewish origin, like Professor Eduard Goldstuecker and the economist Eugen Loebl. But many more were not—and they included such important figures as Josef Smrkovsky, the leader of the Prague anti-Nazi uprising of May 1945; Gustav Husak, a leader of the Slovak uprising of August 1944; and General Ludvik Svoboda, commander of the Czechoslovak forces formed in Russia during the war. Moreover, the former prisoners were not the only Czechs and Slovaks to recall the shameful fifties. There was a general revulsion when Novotny eagerly echoed the Kremlin's new attacks on "Zionism" and pledged new Czech armaments to the Arabs, thus imposing yet another burden on the sick Czechoslovak economy.

On June 27, 1967, the Fourth Congress of Czechoslovak Writers opened in a torrid hall in Prague. Novotny's ideological spokesman, Jiri Hendrych, was on hand to read the party line to some 300 writers. Instead, he heard the opening salvos of the Prague spring. The very first speaker, Milan Kundera, declared that a quarter-century of Nazi occupation and Stalinist rule had been a "tragedy," which had reduced Czech letters to banal propaganda. To survive at all, Czech civilization required freedom. "I know," Kundera said, "that when freedom is mentioned, some people get hay fever and reply that every freedom must have its limits. . . . But no progressive period has ever tried to fix its own limitations. Only in our case is the guarding of frontiers still regarded as a greater virtue than crossing them."

This was only the beginning. Later that day, the playwright Pavel Kohout openly attacked Novotny's policy in the Middle East and defended Israel. Then, to the general surprise, he began to read the full text of Solzhenitsyn's open letter to the Soviet Writers' Congress. Kundera later described what happened:

"When. . . . Pavel Kohout began to read Solzhenitsyn's letter, in which this great heir of Tolstoy described the tragic lot of Soviet literature under Stalinism and under neo-Stalinist conditions, Jiri Hendrych turned purple in the face, rose from his seat in the first row on the dais, put his coat on over his white shirt adorned with suspenders, and perspiringly left the hall." On his way out, Hendrych told liberal writers: "You have lost everything, everything!"

Yet the writers were beyond intimidation. Speaker after speaker —Ivan Klima, Eduard Goldstuecker, Antonin Liehm, Jan Prochazka, Alexander Kliment—each emphasized the general disillusion and called for greater freedom.

The most memorable speech was made by Ludvik Vaculik, the son of one of the founders of the Czechoslovak Communist party, and himself a Communist since 1946. Vaculik was a stormy petrel who believed frankly that "literature is significant only insofar as it leads men toward revolution." His speech to the Writers Congress on June 28, 1967, forshadowed the even more fateful "Two Thousand Words" manifesto which he was to write on June 27, 1968.

A thousand years of human experience, Vaculik told the Writers Congress, had taught mankind certain "traffic rules" of democracy. These democratic safeguards were not "bourgeois" but simply humane. They were "biased in favor of the ruled, but when the government falls, they protect it against being shot." Democracy does not produce very strong government, "but only the conviction that the next government might be an improvement on the preceding one. Thus, the government falls, but the citizen stands renewed. On the other hand, where the government stands for a long time, the citizen falls." Even selective political terror "is followed by the fall of perhaps the entire nation into fear, into political indifference and resignation, into petty daily cares and small desires, into dependence on gradually tinier and tinier overlords, into a serfdom of a new and unusual type. . . ."

Vaculik described how the Novotny system had destroyed independent institutions, intimidated individuals, spread mistrust and mediocrity. "Everything good that men have done or created in our country," he said, had been achieved literally in spite of the rulers. There were no guarantees of justice, legality, or personal security, no guarantees against a return of the Stalinist past. Freedom, Vaculik said, "exists only in places where one does not need to speak of it. The regime is annoyed because people talk about what they see. But, instead of changing what people see, the regime wants to change their eyes. . . ."

It was necessary to understand, Vaculik concluded, that "in the course of twenty years not a single human problem has been solved in our country—starting with the elementary needs, such as housing, schools and prosperity, and ending with the finer requirements of life which cannot be satisfied by the undemocratic systems of the world: the feeling of full value in society, the subordination of political decisions to ethical criteria . . . the need for confidence among men. . . . Our republic has lost its good name."

Hendrych denounced the rebel writers at the congress. The police redoubled security precautions to prevent Vaculik's speech from reaching the outside world. A young writer named Jan Benes was condemned to five years imprisonment for contacts with Czech refugees abroad. Novotny told graduating military cadets that the writers had been set off by Professor Sik's appeal for democratization at the 1966 party congress.

These pressures only angered the writers further. In August, Ladislav Mnacko, the popular Slovak novelist and journalist, fled to Israel in protest against Novotny's policy toward the Middle East. Mnacko, who was not Jewish, was the author of the book *Delayed Reports*, which had symbolized the de-Stalinization of 1963–64.

On September 15, Jan Prochazka, who had once been Novotny's cultural adviser and was an alternate member of the party Central Committee, paid public tribute to Thomas Masaryk on the thirtieth anniversary of his death. The tribute was published on the front page of *Literarni Noviny*, the Writers Union weekly. Prochazka praised precisely those qualities of Masaryk which were most alien to Novotny. Masayrk, said Prochazka, "proclaimed honorable principles and, surprisingly, acted on them." He was "esteemed even by his enemies" because of his "respect and tolerance for opinions with which he did not agree"—a respect "now no longer known."

On September 26 and 27, Novotny struck back at a Central Committee meeting which party historians later described as "very nervous and tense." The meeting finally backed Novotny's proposals, but only after he had claimed to possess proof that "the Writers Congress was prepared in Paris" by enemy agents. No such proof was ever produced, and Dubcek in Slovakia—among other high party leaders—never said a word against the rebel writers. Nevertheless, Prochazka was suspended from the Central Committee; Vaculik, Klima, and Liehm were expelled from the party; and *Literarni Noviny* was transferred from the Writers Union to the Culture Ministry, under the supervision of a Stalinist engineer, Karel Hoffman.

The repression backfired. All the leading writers refused to write for the purged *Literarni Noviny* (which became popularly known as "The Tales of Hoffman"). Even street vendors in Prague competed for the honor of who could sell the *fewest* copies. The weekly had had a circulation of 130,000; street sales now declined to a few hundred.

Attempting to crack down during August and September, Novotny further antagonized opponents within the party. At meetings of the party Presidium, he criticized Dubcek for leniency in Slovakia and fulminated against Sik and the economic reformers. At conferences with regional party leaders, he managed to alienate liberal party officials in northern Bohemia and Moravia as well as Slovakia. He also sent an alarming personal directive to the Central Committee's Security Department, which was headed by his protégé Miroslav Mamula and which controlled both the police and the Army. The directive urged the security agencies to discover which positions "the ideological enemies have occupied or intend to occupy, where their blow will fall, and what they intend to use in their support." This was precisely the sort of language which had been used in Czechoslovakia in 1949 to prepare the Stalinist purges.

On October 30 and 31, the Central Committee met in Hradcany Castle to discuss the general political situation. Various party commissions, local and regional organizations, and research institutes had submitted a flood of suggestions for reform—including separation of party and government offices, home rule for Slovakia, streamlined economic management. "Unfortunately," party historians later noted, "all this rich material went practically unused." The first draft of a resolution based on these grass-roots and expert suggestions appeared "too bold" to Novotny. "Virtually overnight," another draft was substituted, ignoring the reform proposals. The new draft emphasized instead that "the state must exercise an indispensable repressive function toward all internal and external anti-socialist forces and negative manifestations in society."

It was Dubcek who suddenly balked. The documents which had been submitted to the Central Committee, he declared, differed from those that had been agreed on in the Presidium. This kind of cheating was typical of Novotny, especially when Slovakia was at issue. Dubcek cited statistics showing how Slovakia had been deprived of promised investment funds. He went on to attack the resolution itself.

Novotny and his friends, Dubcek said, were confusing effects with their causes. "Neither the émigrés nor the imperialist agents can create major problems for us," Dubcek said; it was misrule that fed their propaganda. Instead of dictating to society, the party should lead it. It was time to end the concentration of power at the Prague center, to separate party, government and economic management.

Changes in organization, Dubcek implied, would inevitably mean changes in personnel. "It is natural," he said, "that in the party and in society conflicts still occur between the old and the new, between the progressive and what is conservative and routine. The supporters of the one and the other are always individual people." Dubcek concluded by suggesting blandly that the Central Committee examine "the cumulation of party and state offices"—a suggestion aimed squarely at Novotny, who combined the posts of party first secretary and president of the Republic.

Novotny's men rejected Dubcek's criticisms, and at first his suggestions for democratization were supported only by a few Czech liberals—notably the physician Frantisek Kriegel and the young Brno leader, Josef Spacek. But then Novotny committed a decisive error. He ordered the hall cleared of nonmembers of the Central Committee and delivered a sharp, emotional attack both on Dubcek's ideas and on his person. "We have had enough of democracy in life," Novotny declared. Moreover, he said, he had already warned Dubcek that the Slovak leader was overly influenced by "narrow and national interests"—in other words, by Slovak nationalism.

Novotny's speech united the Slovak Communists, liberal and conservative, around Dubcek. The conservative Vasil Bilak, second secretary of the Slovak party, reminded the audience of how Clementis, Husak, and other Slovak Communist leaders had been condemned as nationalists in the fifties. "Now again we hear that what the Slovak Communists all say here is in conflict with the party line . . . and Comrade Dubcek is even described as a nationalist."

By simultaneously rejecting democratization and attacking Dubcek as a Slovak nationalist, Novotny had brought the Slovaks and the Czech liberals together for the first time. Even together, however, they did not constitute a majority in the Central Committee, which had been selected at the 1966 party congress under Novotny's control. But there were, as always, numerous fence-sitters waiting to join the winning side.

The October 31 meeting ended in an uneasy compromise. Novotny's resolution was passed, but a new Central Committee meeting was scheduled for mid-December. Novotny, together with Lenart and other loyalists, left for Moscow, to attend the Soviet fiftieth anniversary celebrations and to seek Kremlin backing. Novotny's week in Moscow and Leningrad had ironic consequences. Brezhnev had neither the time nor the inclination, in the midst of the Jubilee, to discuss Czechoslovak problems. Novotny himself, after numerous outdoor ceremonies and copious Kremlin banquets, came down with the flu. In Prague, meanwhile, with Novotny and his leading aides absent, his Slovak and Czech liberal opponents had an opportunity to plan their next moves in a crisis which continued to deepen.

Prague's students soon provided a new impulse for Novotny's critics. On the very evening that the Central Committee had been closing its discussions in Hradcany Castle, nearby in the Strahov dormitories student council leaders were receiving journalists to complain of erratic lighting and insufficient heating in their buildings. At 9 P.M., in the midst of their talks, the lights went out again.

More than 1,500 students, many carrying candles, began marching toward the Castle, crying "We want lights!" Police squads arrived to disperse them. Tempers flared, and the police began using tear gas and clubs. They chased the students back to their dormitories and beat up girls as well as boys. Twelve students and three policemen were taken to the Petrin hospital, two of the students suffering from severe concussions. At a doctors' meeting the next morning, the chief surgeon declared that the police had gone too far, but the newspapers the following day distorted the incident, and officially inspired rumors began to circulate that the demonstrations had been "organized by foreign agents."

The police brutality at Strahov, and the regime's response, reverberated throughout the Prague student body. On November 8, students at the Philosophical Faculty of Charles University held a five-hour protest meeting. They discovered that they had considerable support among the faculty. The regime, however, took the line that the students had been provoked by Western propaganda and the speeches at the Writers Congress. On November 20, there was another mass meeting at the Philosophical Faculty, this one lasting nine hours, in which the rector, Oldrich Stary, and the deputy rector, Eduard Goldstuecker, participated. The meeting ended with an ultimatum to the Government to meet student demands by December 15.

The university crisis, in which not only the students and most faculty but nearly all the educated citizens of Prague were ranged against the regime, heightened the determination of Novotny's foes in the party leadership. The Central Committee had originally been scheduled to meet on December 12, and in the first week of December, Dubcek and his allies pressed for change at meetings of the party Presidium. Within that leading body, Novotny and his friends now agreed "in principle" that the highest party and state offices should be separated. However, they suggested that Novotny should retain the party leadership and instead cede the presidency at the appropriate time—that is, after the National Assembly elections due in the summer of 1968. However, this obvious attempt at delay failed. Of the ten Presidium members, at least five (five, six or eight, according to various accounts) at this point favored Novotny's resignation as party leader.

Novotny now telephoned Brezhnev, and on December 8 the Soviet leader arrived on a flying visit to Prague. Although the papers announced that he had been invited by the Central Committee, in fact even Presidium members were surprised by his arrival. According to Hendrych, Brezhnev's visit constituted "an intervention in favor of Comrade Novotny." Other accounts state that Brezhnev succeeded in turning a 6–4 (or 8–2) majority against Novotny into a 5–5 deadlock. However, Brezhnev failed to intervene decisively in Novotny's favor. Instead, the Soviet leader contented himself with insisting that whatever changes were made should take place in a gradual, quiet, "orderly" manner—in other words, so as not to arouse hopes of radical change. Whichever of the two offices Novotny might give up, he should retain the other to preserve stability. Apart from these general principles, Brezhnev was reported to have said, "*Eto vashe delo, tovarishchi*"—"That is your affair, comrades." *

The Central Committee meeting scheduled for December 12

---

* Numerous reasons have been adduced for Brezhnev's passivity. According to Hendrych, he was simply "not too intelligent a man," and the Soviet leaders generally were "weak and fearful of any change, scenting danger in any concession." However, Novotny's foes at this time included Hendrych, Drahomir Kolder, and other conservatives whose devotion to the Kremlin had been exemplary. The highest party and state offices had been split up in Russia itself in 1964, and more recently in Hungary, without serious repercussions.

was now postponed a week, while the Presidium tried to resolve its 5–5 deadlock. By this time, foreign press reports on the leadership conflict were being beamed back to Czechoslovakia by foreign radio, even though provincial Central Committee members still had not been officially informed of the issues by party headquarters.

On December 15, in the midst of the deadlock, the Government report on the student disorders was published. A compromise document, it acknowledged that the students' grievances were largely justified and that the police had used "unduly harsh methods." However, none of the police would be punished. The report failed to satisfy the students completely, but it gave them a new sense of their potential political strength.

The party Presidium was still deadlocked when the Central Committee assembled on December 19. Lenart opened the plenary session with a bland report on economic problems. Then Novotny spoke. He attempted to excuse his criticism of Dubcek and the Slovaks in October and tardily explained his invitation to Brezhnev. However, according to Novotny, "the activities of the enemy" were the party's main problem. He suggested postponing any discussion of separating the two highest offices for two or three months. Even then, Novotny said, the problem would require "thorough examination . . . in its internal as well as its international connections." This was a hint that the Russians should again be consulted; later, one of Novotny's protégés made the hint explicit.

Novotny, however, had misjudged the temper of the Central Committee. No sooner had he finished than Frantisek Vodslon, a rank-and-file member, protested:

Comrades, what do you think we are? . . . I should like to ask why we have to hear about controversies within the Presidium from other sources, and not from the Presidium itself. . . . I read in the papers that Comrade Brezhnev was invited by the Central Committee. Then, the next day, I read that the invitation was extended by the Presidium. . . . Don't you see what the situation is among the people, among the party members? It is time for us to face all this, because this way we are steadily losing the people's confidence.

Professor Sik delivered a long speech which, in effect, was to be the program of the reformers in the weeks that followed. He had three main proposals. First, "we must eliminate the extreme accumulation of power in the hands of certain comrades, especially those of Comrade Novotny." He accordingly proposed that Novotny resign immediately as party leader.

Second, Sik proposed the selection of a special commission, composed of independent-minded Central Committee members, to nominate a new party leader as well as to add new members to the deadlocked Presidium.

Third, Sik urged that the new Presidium move immediately to adopt fundamental measures for the democratization of the party, from top to bottom, and to begin drafting a short-term political and economic "action program" to deal with the nation's problems.

Novotny's men attacked Sik's proposals and also claimed that Novotny's presence was necessary to ensure the support of the workers and the confidence of the Soviet Union. However, the conservative counteroffensive on the second day of the plenary session failed. Once again, as in October, the Slovaks were united against Novotny. Bilak declared that Novotny had been anti-Slovak since 1963 and disclosed how Novotny at that time had attempted to save Bacilek and had delayed publication of the news of Dubcek's election as Slovak leader.

On the third day, December 21, Novotny spoke first and announced, "I am putting the office of First Secretary . . . at the disposal of the plenary session. . . . I shall accept any decision which the Central Committee deems fit to make." Dubcek, who was presiding, then announced that the Presidium had agreed to accept Novotny's suggestion, but that the leadership proposed to adjourn the discussion for the Christmas-New Year holidays and reassemble the Central Committee on January 3.

A heated, confused and prolonged debate followed, but as the day dragged on, it was clear that there would be no immediate solution. It was decided to name a consultative group of regional leaders who, together with the Presidium, would propose solutions to the Central Committee on January 3.

Novotny had good reason for accepting the "compromise" in

which his possible resignation might be discussed, but not until two weeks later. Since Brezhnev's failure to intervene openly in his behalf, Novotny had been preparing another type of intervention: by the Army and security police. The key figures in the conspiracy were Novotny's crony Mamula, at the head of the Central Committee Security Department, which ruled both the Army and police; General Jan Sejna, a personal favorite of Novotny's, who was chief of the Communist party organization in the Defense Ministry; and General Vladimir Janko, a deputy defense minister.

During the December Central Committee meeting, Sejna had already begun informing leading generals that "a hostile faction" was conspiring to remove Novotny and that the Army would have to help him "smash" the opposition. Sejna's remarks alerted reform-minded officers, led by General Vaclav Prchlik, chief of the Political Administration of the armed forces. It was these officers who ultimately foiled the plot.

The conspiracy called for a tank brigade to move on Prague at night, while security police rounded up Novotny's critics. Mamula drew up more than a thousand arrest warrants, which were dutifully countersigned by the interior minister and state prosecutor, both of them Novotny creatures. The warrants bore the names of Dubcek, Smrkovsky, Sik, Spacek, and other party reformers, General Prchlik and other liberal officers, and hundreds of writers, artists, journalists, and student leaders.

On January 2, General Janko summoned various commanding officers to Prague on the eve of the crucial Central Committee meeting. However, the plotters received no signal from Novotny, who still hoped to win by political means. Indeed, on January 3, the special consultative group which had been appointed before Christmas seemed as deadlocked as the Presidium; both were now inclined to postpone a decision on Novotny's future for another few months.

When the Central Committee met, first Lenart, then Novotny urged postponement and further "reflection." They hinted that the Soviet Union would be displeased by Novotny's removal. Smrkovsky protested strongly against any delay. The present conflict, he declared, would "decide for a long time whether the party will progress or petrify." On behalf of the Czech reformers, he rejected Novotny's slurs on Dubcek and the Slovaks. He also attacked suggestions that the Russians be consulted again. Smrkovsky called for Novotny's immediate resignation and the addition of four or five members to the Presidium.

Smrkovsky had apparently been advised by General Prchlik of the plot being hatched by Mamula, General Sejna, and General Janko. For he concluded his speech by declaring:

> . . . among the comrades there prevails a feeling of uncertainty as to what will happen if, after all the criticism that has been expressed, everything remains as before. I say openly—and I feel that someone has to say it without mincing words—that many comrades are afraid (and, in view of past experience, not without reason) that there could be a return to the fifties, to the hard repression of opponents within the party . . . to the use of the security organs. . . . This would be the most serious danger for the entire Republic.

It appears to have been on the night of January 3 that the Presidium confronted Novotny with the evidence gleaned by General Prchlik about the plot. Novotny denied any part in it, and—under pressure—gave orders which made military action impossible. However, the incident also broke the deadlock in the Presidium and the consultative group. For, on the morning of January 4, Deputy Premier Oldrich Cernik, a moderate reformer, informed the Central Committee that the leadership had agreed that a decision would have to be taken at this session. While the Central Committee debate continued, therefore, Novotny was to work out proposals with the consultative group, to be presented to the Presidium that evening.

The debate itself now showed a strong majority for Novotny's immediate replacement. Agreement on a successor proved more difficult. During the negotiations, which lasted deep into the night, Novotny firmly turned down Sik, Smrkovsky, and other liberal foes. The liberals vetoed Novotny's suggestions, such as Lenart. The bargaining then turned to centrists, who offered some hope of reuniting the divided party. The first one suggested was Lubomir Strougal, a tough young party secretary who had helped Novotny oust Barak in 1962. Strougal declined, for reasons not yet clear.* The second centrist suggested was Cernik, an engineer and state planner, who preferred to become prime minister. Cernik also declined—and suggested Dubcek.

Novotny did not reject the nomination. He may have calculated that, as president of the Republic and with the support of hardliners and Soviet agents in the police, army, and party apparatus, he would be able to outmaneuver Dubcek, who had not been an assertive personality. (Hendrych considered him "an honest man, but indecisive.")

Dubcek himself was reluctant. He had always viewed affairs in a purely Slovak framework and, as he explained much later, would have preferred to have become second secretary. ("I like my work, but I don't like sitting on a throne.") However, because the inner-party crisis had already lasted ten weeks, and the negotiations with Novotny had already lasted into the early morning hours, Dubcek accepted.

When the Central Committee reassembled on January 5, Novotny formally submitted his resignation as first secretary and announced the Presidium's unanimous nomination of Dubcek as his successor. At the Defense Ministry that morning, Generals Sejna and Janko had drawn up a petition by high-ranking officers demanding Novotny's retention in office. By the time their emissaries reached Hradcany Castle, however, the debate was over. Dubcek, at forty-six, had become the youngest party leader in Communist Europe. That night, Brezhnev sent a telegram congratulating him "from the bottom of my soul."

A new era had begun. Or had it? For most Czechs and Slovaks, January and most of February passed without any obvious change in the sullen atmosphere of the country. Indeed, outside Prague, Brno, and Bratislava, it was not until April that Dubcek began to sense "an echo" from the people at large. Yet, even among the political leaders, intellectuals, journalists, and youth of the major

---

* Strougal was a notorious womanizer, which gave rise to many tales of what he and Novotny supposedly said to each other on this occasion. ("My hands may have held many lovely women's bottoms, Comrade Novotny, but there is no blood on them," etc.) However, Strougal may simply have preferred to see whether Novotny could succeed in stalemating the negotiations and then routing his foes through a coup. (Strougal became prime minister in 1970.)

cities, the first six weeks of Dubcek's administration appeared to have brought little change.

Later, Dubcek and his colleagues would loosely refer to their reforms as "the post-January policy" or "the line of the January plenum." Yet in fact the Central Committee in January, while appointing Dubcek first secretary and adding four members to the Presidium, had neither proclaimed a new program nor decisively altered the balance of power within the regime.

Dubcek's appointment was announced in a resolution that Sik considered "toothless," and for the broad public scarcely differed from dozens of previous boring official communiqués. Novotny continued to occupy the presidential palace at Hradcany. His appointees remained defense minister, interior minister, prosecutor-general, foreign minister. Even the conspirators Mamula, Sejna, and Janko remained in place. Moreover, among the 110 members of the Central Committee, no more than 40 were ever to be considered reformers. There were just as many Novotny loyalists. The balance was held by conservatives and careerists who had become disgruntled with Novotny but remained wary of radical change.

Dubcek spent most of January briefing himself on the party files, then began a round of meetings with Soviet and satellite leaders. In Moscow on January 29 and 30, he met with Brezhnev, Marshal Grechko, and other Soviet leaders. The joint communiqué after their meeting claimed "complete agreement" on all issues and an atmosphere of "cordial friendship, sincerity and comradly understanding." ° Early in February, Dubcek met with Kadar near the Hungarian border and then with Gomulka near the Polish frontier. These meetings also appeared routine, as did the invitations to Brezhnev, Gomulka, and the others to attend cele-

---

° Eight months later, *Pravda* claimed (August 22) that already at the January 29–30 meetings Dubcek was warned of the danger of "rightist, revisionist elements" (as represented by the writers and such reformers as Sik) and that he assured the Soviet leaders that he would "take the necessary measures to stabilize the atmosphere." There may be some—although not necessarily much—truth in this retrospective claim. The Soviet leaders were indeed nervous about "revisionist" intellectuals in late January, when the protests over the Ginsburg-Galanskov "witch trial" were at their height. However, it would appear just as likely that Dubcek and Brezhnev exchanged vague generalities, amid much vodka and caviar, with neither very clear about what he himself or the other had in mind. Each probably heard what he wished to hear.

brations on February 22–23 marking the twentieth anniversary of the Communist coup in Prague.

For the reformers, the situation in mid-February appeared both frustrating and precarious. Virtually nothing had been done to implement or even to propose concrete reforms. In the provinces, various "mini-Stalins" continued as before, ignoring eloquent but isolated appeals on the press and radio by Smrkovsky, Husak, and Goldstuecker for democratization. Novotny's men meanwhile were telling Czech workers that the Slovaks and the Jews were taking over and that the economic reform would be at the expense of workers' living standards.

Moreover, the Czech and Slovak reformers were conscious of the anti-intellectual wind that was blowing in Russia itself, as well as in Poland and East Germany. The Ginsburg-Galanskov trial in Moscow had been followed by secret trials of professors and students in Leningrad. In Minsk on February 14, Kosygin (perhaps reacting against the appeals for democratization by Smrkovsky, Husak, and Goldstuecker) made a tough speech attacking "false democratic phraseology." A few days later in Kiev, Pyotr Shelest, the tough party boss of the Ukraine, demanded "revolutionary vigilance" and the inculcation of "hatred of imperialism and the bourgeois way of life."

For Czechoslovak Communists with a memory, both the internal and external situation recalled what had happened in Hungary after July 1953. At that time, the good-humored reformer Imre Nagy had become premier and vowed a new course, but the Stalinist Rakosi had remained party leader, with his cronies and Soviet agents controlling the police. Nagy was systematically undercut by the Stalinist party and police apparatus and then abandoned by the dominant faction in the Kremlin. The result was a Stalinist comeback in 1955—and the explosion of 1956.

The Czech and Slovak reformers were determined not to permit Dubcek to become another Nagy—nor another Gomulka. To avert a Novotny comeback, they had to move to consolidate the victory, thus far only symbolic, that they had won on January 5. To remove dangerous Novotnyites from key posts, in the face of the conservative majority in the Central Committee, the reformers had to mobilize outside pressure. Such pressure could only come from the people of Czechoslovakia. But the masses of Czechs and Slovaks, party members included, remained plunged in deep apathy. There were, as Husak remarked early in February, some new hopes, but there was also "much old skepticism," born of bitter experience.

There is little evidence on what happened behind the scenes, among the party leaders, in the icy mid-February of 1968. Yet clearly, between February 15 and 22, there was a decision, or a series of decisions,* to break the ice of compromise: to move against the Novotnyites and to bid for popular support by freeing the press and radio.

Symbolically, for many ordinary Czechs and Slovaks, the Dubcek era began (as it would end) with a hockey game. On the night of February 15, in Grenoble, France, a previously uninspired Czechoslovak team defeated the Soviet Union, the world champions, by a score of 5 to 4. For millions of Czechs and Slovaks who watched the game on television, the victory seemed a portent. "Novotny would never have let us win," was the almost universal sentiment.

That weekend, however, Novotny made a demonstrative tour of Prague's largest factory, the CKD machine plant, in an obvious bid for workers' support. This may have been the signal that sparked the reformers. For two days later, on February 19, it was announced that Mamula had been removed as chief of the Central Committee Security Department and replaced by General Prchlik.

In the next two days, the reformers took the offensive. Bratislava radio, followed next day by the Czechoslovak news agency CTK in Prague, announced the first broad outlines of the party's coming "action program," including a government "fully responsible" to the National Assembly. On Radio Prague, Loebl made the first reference to Czechoslovakia's "unequal trade relations" with

---

* It remains unclear whether these were conscious, active decisons taken by Dubcek and perhaps other responsible party secretaries; or whether Dubcek and his associates merely assented to initiatives undertaken by Smrkovsky, Sik, and other reformers; or whether the old constraints simply crumbled, leaving a vacuum of power which the reformers, the new leaders of the Writers Union, and determined individual journalists decided to fill, emboldening others as they did so.

Russia. Sik, also on radio, described how "some comrades" were visiting factories and "spreading lies" to incite the workers against "radicals." Goldstuecker and Liehm, in a press conference at the Writers Union, denounced similar conservative agitation, including anti-Slovak and anti-Semitic appeals. They also announced that within a week, the writers and editors whom Novotny had removed in September from *Literarni Noviny* would publish the first issue of a new weekly, to be called *Literarni Listy*. In a Czechoslovak press that within a few weeks was to be as free and exciting as any in the world, *Literarni Listy* would provide intellectual leadership of the highest order.

On February 22, Brezhnev, Shelest, Ulbricht, Gomulka and other bloc leaders arrived in Prague for the twentieth anniversary ceremonies. Dubcek used the occasion to assume publicly—for the first time since his accession to office—the leadership of the reform movement.

Dubcek criticized Novotny's centralist 1960 constitution, and promised a new deal for Slovakia. He denounced the "false suspicion" and judicial frameups of the 1950s, "from which not only Communists suffered." He called for "true rehabilitation of the dignity of all those who honestly served the republic during the first and especially the second world wars"—in other words, all the non-Communists who had fought for the ideals of Masaryk and Beneš in the Czech Legion, the R.A.F., and the underground resistance, but who had been cruelly persecuted after 1948.

"We must remove . . . all the injustices done to people," Dubcek declared, "and we must do so consistently and without reservations." With this bland statement, offering reconciliation to hundreds of thousands of non-Communist victims of Stalinism, Dubcek went far beyond anything Khrushchev had done in eight years of fitful de-Stalinization.

Dubcek then repudiated Novotnyite harassment of writers, artists, scientists, filmakers, and other intellectuals. "We are dealing with educated people," he said, "whose work requires deep understanding and appreciation. . . . We must eliminate everything that tends to hamstring scientific and artistic creation, everything likely to breed tensions."

"The enthusiasm of the youth," Dubcek continued, "cannot be

restricted to constantly praising our achievements. Our young people want to have achievements of their own, bring their dreams and ideas to reality." Youth should be enabled "to develop its own initiative, work for its own goals. . . ."

Finally, Dubcek denounced "the old view" of the Communist party as a force which "decides minor issues in an authoritarian way," throttling public initiative. He pledged "to create the necessary preconditions for the growth of creative initiative, to provide greater scope for confrontation and exchanges of opinion, to make it possible for every Communist to be informed thoroughly, objectively and in good time about events in his own country and abroad." The 1.3 million rank-and-file party members "should participate not only in implementing but in framing the party's policy." Dubcek called for developing "more, and above all, deeper democratic forms"—especially at the grass roots.

Dubcek had thus summoned the support of all the groups Novotny had so long sought to suppress, and he had done so, despite his cool bureaucratic terminology, under the banner of free speech and democracy.

The very next day, the Czechoslovak Army weekly hinted for the first time that Novotny had attempted a military coup at the turn of the year. Two days afterward, on February 25, Major General Jan Sejna, his son, and a young girl drove across the border into Hungary in an official car and made their way, through Yugoslavia, Italy, and the C.I.A., to the United States, where their arrival was announced on March 5.

Sejna's flight was a scandal, and Czechoslovak newspaper, radio, and television reporters competed with one another in exposing it. As the story unfolded in the first week of March, Czechs and Slovaks learned that Sejna had embezzled some $20,000; that he was an intimate of Antonin Novotny, Jr., the President's son; that Sejna, his son, and the girl had left Czechoslovakia on diplomatic passports. More important, General Prchlik disclosed Sejna's role in Novotny's plot for a military coup.

The Czechoslovak reporters probed, digged, named names. They publicly implicated Novotny and his entire coterie, and compelled such high officials as Defense Minister Bohumil Lomsky to account for their actions on live television. Nothing like this had ever happened in any Communist country. Czechoslovak citizens no longer needed foreign broadcasts. Their own press, radio, and television were telling them more, and telling it more quickly.

The March days also brought a cascade of resolutions and spontaneous meetings. The resolutions—from groups as diverse as the Prague medical students, the General Staff, the anti-Nazi resistance fighters—demanded the resignations of Novotny, General Lomsky, and all others implicated in the Sejna affair. Spontaneity became a habit, and the discussions and resolutions soon went beyond the Sejna case. A real public opinion began to express itself with increasing boldness. Czechs and Slovaks demanded a clear reckoning with the entire past.

On March 6, the weekly newspaper *Student* raised the issue of the Stalinist trials—listing the names of all the judges, prosecutors, and "defense" attorneys who had participated in the frameup. "Where are all these people today? . . . What are they doing, how do they earn their living? Do they hold themselves responsible for their role at that time?" Beyond these court functionaries, *Student* asked, who were the political architects of the trials? "Who signed the death sentences—not the official ones but the secret ones, i.e., the decisive ones? Does the public know these names, or does it know only the names of the puppets?"

March 7 was the birthday of Thomas G. Masaryk. Sunday, March 10, was the twentieth anniversary of the tragic death of his only son, Jan Masaryk, who had been found dead in the courtyard of the Foreign Ministry a fortnight after the Communist seizure of power. The official verdict in 1948 had been "suicide," but many doubted it.

Both Masaryks, father and son, were buried near the family home at Lany, twenty miles outside Prague. For years, brave individuals would bring flowers to their graves but police and party militants would take the flowers away. The Stalinists had torn down the statues of the founder-president which had stood in most Czech towns. Until 1966, it had been forbidden to mention his very name.

Now, in March 1968, the Czechoslovak press paid respectful tribute to the Masaryks, and all weekend long, in driving snow, workers, students, and simple citizens of Prague made the pilgrimage to Lany. Late Sunday afternoon, a delegation of 3,000 Charles University students arrived. They carried a giant wreath and unfurled two banners reading *"Jan, we will not forget you!"* and *"The truth will prevail—even here!"* While a girl played a folk melody on a flute, a bearded youth delivered a brief eulogy:

> We stand at the grave of a man who died an unusual death twenty years ago, a great son of a great father. . . . Let us remember this man at this crucial time in which we hope people of the quality of Jan Masaryk will lead our nation.

A few days later, a bookstore in downtown Prague placed Thomas Masaryk's picture in its window. Passersby stopped, stared, and sometimes wept. Before the week was over, the Czech film corporation released a documentary on the life and work of President Masaryk "as a philosopher, political thinker, statesman and above all as a citizen." Viewers emerged from the theaters, after seeing it, with eyes swollen from deep emotion long repressed.

By mid-March, the revolution was in full flow. Each day brought startling news. On March 12, the Interior Ministry formally apologized to the Prague University students for the police brutality of the previous October and announced that henceforth policemen would wear identification badges. The same day, the three top leaders of the Stalinized trade unions resigned—the beginning of what became a flood of resignations. March 14, General Janko shot himself—the first of several dozen suicides among old Stalinists.

The next day, March 15, brought a brief announcement which, in its way, epitomized the peaceful revolution. The announcement came from the Communists at the so-called Central Publications Board—an organization which previously could not even be mentioned, because it was the Censorship itself. Now, the censors themselves passed a resolution declaring that the entire system had been illegal, that their board was "headed by senior security officials who operated by a system of orders" and who had "created an atmosphere unbreathable even for the censors."

The Communist censors therefore demanded that "preventive political censorship should be abolished."

Almost every day, the press, radio, and television brought similar announcements—men and women, individuals and groups, from all walks of life, breaking with the shameful past, calling for a new future. Yet the March days were, most memorably, the days and nights of the great Prague public meetings.

On the night of March 13, the meeting was at Slavonic House. Thousands of youngsters, fresh-faced boys and bright-eyed girls, attempted to press their way up the stairs into an old dance hall, long jammed beyond capacity. The crush was unbelievable, but the students were patient. They laughed and joked, sang and chanted, while waiting for a relay loudspeaker to be set up on the street.

"This is Prague, March 1968," Neal Ascherson reported to the London *Observer:* the "meeting hall jammed with excited men and women, suffocation-tight all the way down the stairs and out to the pavement; questions on little screws of paper coming down like snowflakes from the galleries; speakers talking like free men. A woman, long imprisoned, denounces President Novotny for his part in the show trials. A playwright says that the public prosecutor has eleven judicial murders on his conscience. A novelist says the Defense Minister has the mentality of a half-educated corporal. . . ."

The playwright was Pavel Kohout, who had read Solzhenitsyn's letter to the Writers Congress. The novelist was Jan Prochazka, who had honored Masaryk. The woman long imprisoned was Maria Svermova, whose husband, a veteran Communist, had died in a Stalinist jail. There were others—and first among them Josef Smrkovsky. It was at this meeting, and those which followed, that Smrkovsky emerged as the popular tribune of the Prague spring.

Smrkovsky, a Communist since 1932, had been imprisoned for nationalist "deviations" from 1951 to 1955. Politically "rehabilitated" in 1963, he had at last in 1966 become minister of forestry. Lanky and slow moving, still boyish in manner, the fifty-seven-year old Smrkovsky spoke with a deliberate drawl, in plain words free of jargon. His speech combined hope, gravity, and wry humor. In the months which followed, he was the man whom, even more than Dubcek, the Czechs trusted instinctively to tell them the truth.

The great meeting at Slavonic House was not one for set speeches; it was a night for answering questions, no holds barred. The students laughed, applauded, interrupted, and when they did not like an answer, they stamped their feet. *"What was Brezhnev doing here in December—who invited him, Novotny?"* Smrkovsky answered, describing how Brezhnev had come but had declined to intervene. Smrkovsky thought a new era of genuine partnership with Russia had begun.

Many of you may think that the relationship between us and the Soviet Union is not one of equals. . . . You thought that here, in our Republic, the Soviet Union was in the driver's seat. If anybody is still thinking that, my young friends, he's terribly wrong. Those times are behind us. . . .

We very often see young people giving way—especially at ice-hockey matches—to their dislike of the Soviet Union. Well, look here: to love, not to love, that's everybody's private affair. Nobody can force that on you. But . . . look at the map, look at the frontier, who our neighbor is . . . in Germany. . . . If it were not for the Soviet Union, I would be afraid for the future of our country. . . . And as for our various sins, doing everything after "the example of the Soviet Union," cleaning one's teeth a certain way and so on—for that, the Soviet Union is not responsible. . . .

Maria Svermova was surprised by the many questions about the Stalinist purges, coming from youngsters who had not lived through the dark fifties. She answered as best she could, describing the atmosphere of terror and hysteria, the role of Gottwald, the dogmas of Stalin. *"You are talking about rehabilitations,"* came a question, *'but so far only about Communists. What about Milada Horakova?"* Yes, Svermova answered, we are trying to rehabilitate all the innocent victims—yes, definitely including Milada Horakova, the Socialist woman deputy who had been hanged.

The meeting lasted until well after one in the morning. The final resolutions called for the ouster of Novotny, thorough democratization, and solidarity with students who had begun to demonstrate in Poland a few days earlier "for the same objectives." The next morning, there was yet another great meeting at the Law Faculty of Charles University. Some 3,000 students jammed the great indoor courtyard and its five rectangular stone balconies. Behind the podium was a huge, hand-printed poster with a quotation from Comenius:

> *I believe that, after the storm of wrath which we brought upon ourselves by our own sins, my nation will again be able to assume the responsibility of ruling itself.*

The leaders of the meeting were unknown students, and everything seemed improvised. The chairman announced that Dubcek had sent his "full support." Ota Sik called on the students to overcome the "conservatives who for so long have used repression and suppression to silence new ideas," the "men who wish to keep the workers down while they themselves keep their own influential posts." However, he urged the students to "exercise caution" and avoid "reckless steps."

Eduard Goldstuecker, the University's deputy rector and now also chairman of the Writers Union, declared that the meeting reminded him of another in the same place when he was a student: one of the first great anti-Nazi demonstrations in 1934. "The whole world is waiting to see," Goldstuecker declared, "whether the Czechoslovaks are capable of achieving what has never been done in human history: produce a socialist society linked to personal freedom—*which it should have been from the very beginning!*" The applause lasted five minutes, with the students chanting "Goldstuecker, we love you!"

Other speakers—professors, students—followed in the same vein. Once again, there was a resolution voicing solidarity with student demonstrations in Poland.

Meanwhile, each day the newspapers were exposing new scandals, reporting new resignations and resolutions, airing new ideas. The radio and television were presenting unrehearsed and sharp discussion, grilling old Stalinists under the cameras. Boys and girls manned the Prague Radio telephones to accept calls of congratulations, to relay listeners' questions to panelists. Thousands of letters poured in, expressing appreciation for the new freedom.

On March 20, more than 10,000 students gathered in and around the Congress Hall in Fucik Park for the largest of the great March meetings. Smrkovsky, Husak, Sik, Goldstuecker, Prochazka, and Selucky were among those on the platform. The meeting lasted six hours and concluded with resolutions demanding abolition of censorship, freedom to travel abroad, the right of free association, "legal guarantees of democracy," and "the whole truth about our economy."

However, at this meeting, notes were sounded which disturbed the Communist reformers. The rebel student leader Lubomir Holocek expressed youth's support for the party's current efforts under Dubcek, but declared that this support "is not our final demand or our last word." Other students urged an investigation of the death of Jan Masaryk, removal of the Communist star from the state coat of arms, renewal of diplomatic relations with Israel, a review of Czechoslovak arms deliveries to Vietnam and the Arabs. In a resolution, the students demanded a new foreign policy which "would respect Czechoslovakia's location in Central Europe"—the old dream of a bridge between East and West. When Smrkovsky reproached the students for failing to include a pledge of allegiance to the Soviet Union, there were whistles and catcalls. It was only with great difficulty that Smrkovsky and Husak persuaded the students to add a phrase to their resolution urging "equal relations with all socialist countries, especially with the Soviet Union."

The students again demanded, as they had at the two meetings the week before, a resolution voicing solidarity with the continuing student demonstrations in Poland. This time, however, Smrkovsky pleaded with them, in the higher interests of the Czechoslovak state, to forego any commentary on the events in Poland.

Here, on March 20, was the first foretaste of many incidents and dramas to come, in which Dubcek, Smrkovsky, and other Communist reformers sought to maintain what proved to be an impossible balance. On the one hand, there were the rising demands of the awakened Czech and Slovaks, and especially their youth. They wanted democracy and national independence, an end to the Soviet model of Communism imposed on their country and all the injustices, burdens, and lies that had gone with it. Their support—the support, that is, of more than 90 percent of the nation—was the Communist reformers' strength, but Dubcek, Smrkovsky, and the others were reminded again and again that they could retain that support only by striving for a new Czechoslovakia.

On the other hand, the farther Czechoslovakia advanced in peaceful civil liberty, the greater were the hopes aroused among the other peoples of the empire that they, too, might aspire toward "socialism with a human face." And thus the fear grew among their rulers—Brezhnev, Ulbricht, Gomulka, and the others—that the spark of Czechoslovak freedom could ignite a forest fire that might engulf them all.

The Soviet, East German, and Polish press had begun censoring news from Czechoslovakia from the first January days when Smrkovsky, Husak, and Goldstuecker had made their first pleas for democratization. But, as the Czechoslovak revolution gained force and depth in March, there could be no concealing it from alert intellectuals and students in Moscow, Leningrad, and Kiev, Warsaw and Cracow, East Berlin and Budapest. Apart from foreign broadcasts, Czechoslovak, Yugoslav, and Italian Communist papers were available in these cities. More important, Russian, Polish, Hungarian, and East German cultural, scientific, economic, and tourist delegations kept moving in and out of Prague, Bratislava, and other Czechoslovak centers. They came, they saw and —returning home—reported to their countrymen.*

Ulbricht, the ever vigilant, was the first to register concern. In the early days of March, when Soviet news media were largely silent about Czechoslovakia, East German press and radio coverage were distinctive. There were no direct attacks on the Prague reformers as yet, but the East Germans made a point of publicizing statements being made by obscure Novotnyites warning against various potential "dangers."

* In late March, returning from Prague to Moscow for a few days, I was struck by how avidly Soviet intellectuals were following events in Czechoslovakia. How did they know so much about what was happening? Partly through foreign broadcasts—but mainly because a Moscow theatrical group had just returned from an engagement in Prague, and the actors had immediately informed their fellow actors, directors, writers, friends, relatives. . . .

Indeed, Ulbricht's Stalinist antennae had scented danger in Czechoslovakia more than five years earlier—when East German ideological commissars fought to prevent Goldstuecker's revival of Kafka. (Both Ulbricht and Goldstuecker, from opposite viewpoints, recognized Kafka's work as a prophecy of the moral atmosphere of Stalinism.) Yet in the Kafka case, as with Ulbricht's periodic warning against the Yugoslavs, Rumanians, and other heretics, the Russians had not hesitated, when they saw fit, to set Ulbricht's counsel aside.

In early March, the Soviet leaders were preoccupied with other matters—with Rumanian opposition to their planned "world Communist conference," and with the final negotiations for a nuclear nonproliferation treaty with the United States, a pact which would bar West Germany from atomic weapons. On March 6 and 7, Brezhnev and Kosygin attended a bloc summit conference in Sofia to discuss these matters. Dubcek and Lenart were on hand for Czechoslovakia, and there was not the slightest sign that all was not well between them and the Russians.

The next day, however, the student demonstrations began in Warsaw—and within a fortnight helped bring on the first of a fateful series of Soviet-Czechoslovak confrontations.

The situation in Poland had been deteriorating steadily since the Catholic-Communist conflict of 1966. Wages had been frozen for two years, but food prices had continued to rise. The Six Day War had brought a denunciation by Gomulka of "Zionism" as a "fifth column," stirring anxiety not only among Poland's surviving 30,000 Jews but among liberal intellectuals. Foreign visitors in 1967 feared that Poland was "at the mercy of an incident," with repressed hatreds, frustrations, and resentments building up increasing tensions. To contain these pressures, Gomulka's regime had been continuously strengthening the "organs" of repression —the UB or secret police; the Militia or regular police; the Militia Reserve, comprised of "workers" who were in fact a privileged force of Communist storm troopers.

All of these forces were under the supervision of Colonel Mieceszlaw Moczar, the ambitious, nationalistic leader of the "Partisan" faction. Behind Moczar, there stood a rising group of young functionaries who blamed Poland's troubles on Gomulka and his aging coterie—and on the Jews. With living standards declining, and a party congress due in the fall, the Moczar forces were preparing to bid for supreme power. Their increasing influence further disconcerted the country's educated liberals.

The crisis began at the end of January, when Gomulka (allegedly at the prompting of the Soviet ambassador) closed down Warsaw performances of Adam Mickiewicz's classic (1832) anti-Russian play *Dziady*. Audiences had been demonstratively applauding such lines as "Polish history is conducted in a prison cell" and "Everyone sent here from Russia is either a jackass, a fool or a spy."

The ban on the play provoked a brief student demonstration at Warsaw University on January 30 and then a series of protests by writers and students against censorship. There were meetings at the Writers Union, petitions, discussions—to no avail. Two of the students who had demonstrated on January 30 were expelled from the University.

On March 8, some 4,000 students gathered on the Warsaw University campus to demand the readmission of their two expelled colleagues. Suddenly, Militia Reserve units—the so-called "workers"—stormed onto the campus grounds and fighting broke out. Almost immediately, twenty-five truckloads of steel-helmeted regular Militia arrived and began swinging billyclubs to disperse the demonstrators.* Their brutality enraged students throughout the city.

On March 9, Warsaw Polytechnic Institute students joined in solidarity with their colleagues from the University. Now, some 10,000 students moved out into the streets. The Militia attacked them with truncheons and tear gas. The students screamed "*Gestapo!*" at the police, but they also shouted "*Constitution!*" "*Liberty!*" and—"*Long Live Czechoslovakia!*"

March 10 was a Sunday, and quiet; it was the Sunday on which Prague students were honoring Thomas and Jan Masaryk. In Warsaw, however, the party leaders were preparing to blame

---

* Many Warsaw observers believe that these circumstances indicated a deliberate provocation by the Moczar forces—to demonstrate that the universities were a source of subversion and that Gomulka was incapable of maintaining "order."

student unrest on the "Zionists" and "revisionists"—that is, on Jews and liberal intellectuals.

The March 11 morning newspapers infuriated the students. *Trybuna Ludu,* the party organ, printed a long list of student "troublemakers," most of them with Jewish names, and also chose to identify their parents, many of whom were liberal officials. Another paper openly blamed "Zionists" for the troubles. Within a few days, the campaign against "Zionists" was to reach an anti-Semitic pitch unknown in Europe since Hitler's Third Reich.

On March 11, the student revolt spread across the nation. In Warsaw, young workers, teen-agers, and high-school students took to the streets, carrying Polish flags, marching toward Central Committee headquarters. Among the youths' banners were *"Long live Czechoslovakia!"* and *"We want a Polish Dubcek!"* Moczar's police were out in force, with truncheons, clubs, and tear gas. Wild clashes lasted more than eight hours.

In Cracow, 10,000 students gathered the same day to pass a resolution of solidarity with Warsaw. There were similar meetings in Lublin and Poznan. The demonstrations that day in Cracow and Poznan were peaceful, but there was violence in Lublin. The violence spread the next day to Poznan and to Cracow, where police used rubber truncheons against some 3,000 students (beating up the University's rector and deputy rector as well).

On March 14, there were new demonstrations in Poznan, Lodz, Wroclaw, and Katowice. In Katowice the following day, police used water hoses and clubs against a demonstration of 10,000 students, workers, and other citizens. Here, too, not far from the Czechoslovak frontier, students shouted *"Long Live Czechoslovakia!"* as they were being clubbed by police.

Everywhere the police struck, there were arrests as well as beatings. Gomulka later disclosed that there had been 1,200 arrests in the first week of the disturbances. In the face of such force, the students at the major universities shifted tactics—to passive resistance, sit-ins, and boycotts of classes. Wherever the students gathered, there were transistor radios bringing news of the Prague spring, of Dubcek's pledges of the "broadest possible democratization."

On March 18, there was an omen which doubtless terrified hard-line Communists in Poland and elsewhere. At Nowa Huta, the pride of the Stalinist steel industry, a group of young workers joined in a solidarity demonstration with Cracow students. The police went after them with water hoses, truncheons, and vicious dogs. More than a hundred were reported hospitalized, many of them with dog bites.

The next day, Gomulka—who had been silent while the police and anti-Semitic rabble-rousers had been dominating the scene—finally spoke to the nation. He did so at a rally at the Congress Hall in the Warsaw Palace of Culture donated by Stalin. The hall was filled with loyal party activists, police, and the "workers" of the Militia Reserve.

It was a measure of the atmosphere which Moczar's propagandists had aroused that Gomulka's speech was to be called relatively "moderate." This was because Gomulka did not blame the student troubles exclusively on Jews, but directed his main attack at "reactionary, anti-Soviet intellectuals." Among those he denounced were the philosopher Leszek Kolakowski, the economist Wlodomierz Brus, the aging poet Antoni Slonimski, the former Catholic deputy Stefan Kiselewski (who had been badly beaten by thugs a few days earlier). The men whom Gomulka now attacked had been among the intellectual leaders of the "Polish October" of 1956, which had returned Gomulka to power and which had briefly made Poland "a case history of hope."

When Gomulka made his first mention of "Zionism," wild shouts resounded through the hall. The hysteria of his audience prevented him from continuing for several minutes. The reaction reminded some foreign witnesses of the blood-curdling cries which used to greet the word "Jew" at Nazi rallies. Gomulka divided Poland's Jews into three categories. Convinced "Zionists," he said, should leave the country. Other Jews who could not fully support party policies would be removed from positions of influence. However, those Jews ready to support the party line 100 percent—including the campaign against "Zionism"—would not be harmed.

Gomulka's speech (reprinted in full in Moscow's *Pravda*) helped steal some of the thunder of Moczar's Partisans. It led, in the months which followed, to the emigration of not only most of Poland's remaining Jews, but of many distinguished non-Jews as well. (The philosopher Kolakowski, for example, went to Canada; the playwright Slawomir Mrozek, who was already in Paris, decided to stay there.) Gomulka failed, however, to calm the students. For more than two weeks afterward, there were sit-in strikes and demonstrations in Warsaw, Cracow, and other cities. The regime responded with new arrests, massive expulsions from the universities, and the discharge from their jobs of the parents of students who continued to demonstrate. The UB, the Militia, and the Militia Reserve took over the country, creating a climate of fear which recalled the grim days of Stalinism and which lasted for more than a year.

In October 1956, a wave of free speech and peaceful demonstrations in Poland had inspired Hungary to violent revolution. In March 1968, a similar danger seemed imminent, except that Poland's role had been reversed. For, while Czechoslovak youth were engaging in cheerful dialogue with their new reformist leaders, Poland—which had remained disciplined in 1956—seemed on the verge of an explosion, possibly equal to the bloody anti-Russian insurrections of the nineteenth century.

It was on March 20—as the demands in Prague for Novotny's ouster reached their peak, and after the Nowa Huta steelworkers had struck in solidarity with the Cracow students—that the first Soviet troop movements were reported in the western Ukraine, near the Czechoslovak and Polish frontiers.

This was why Smrkovsky, at the great meeting that night in Fucik Park, had pleaded with the Prague youth to express their allegiance to the Soviet Union and especially to withdraw their resolution of solidarity with the Polish student demonstrators. It was also why Dubcek the previous day had sent two special envoys (Cernik and General Egyd Pepich) to Moscow. The Czechoslovak envoys explained to Soviet political and military leaders that the speedy ouster of Novotny as president was imperative, so that a united party leadership might reassert control and direct popular emotions into orderly channels.

The Russians had little choice but to approve Novotny's removal. A month of free political struggle in Czechoslovakia had shown that Novotny was a used-up, played-out figure; Sejna's appearance in the United States was the last straw. Besides, Marshal Ivan Yakubovsky, the Russian commander of the Warsaw Pact, had previously obtained Czechoslovak approval for maneuvers of Soviet, East German, and other Pact military units on Czechoslovak territory later in the spring. If necessary, these maneuvers could (and would) be used to maintain control.

Moreover, in the twin-pronged crisis developing to Russia's west, Czechoslovakia remained orderly and peaceful; it was Poland in which violence had erupted. At this point, the Soviet leaders were probably less anxious about the mild-mannered, idealistic Dubcek than about General Moczar, the tough Polish nationalist. In Moczar's steely personality, and in his notorious willingness to exploit anti-Russian sentiment, there were the makings of a Polish Ceausescu.

For Brezhnev and his colleagues, therefore, it was more urgent to bolster the loyal Gomulka, against both the masses and Moczar, than to essay another futile attempt to maintain Novotny in office. However, Gomulka himself was by now thoroughly alarmed by the winds of freedom blowing northward from Czechoslovakia. For hundreds of years, the Poles had looked down on their southern neighbors as docile and craven. Now, the libertarian exploits of the Czechs and Slovaks were a standing rebuke and challenge to the pride of Poles who considered themselves the nation of heroes.

Thus, Gomulka joined Ulbricht as an irreconcilable foe of the Czechoslovak reformers. Their fears were shared by an increasingly influential member of the Soviet Politburo: Pyotr Shelest, Communist party chief of the Ukraine.* Shelest, whose brutal,

---

* Besides the general concern over the possible "infection" of freedom from Czechoslovakia, Shelest had specific reasons to be alarmed. Part of his domain in the western Ukraine had been the interwar Czechoslovak province of Ruthenia, and many of its inhabitants doubtless remembered the Masaryk Republic as a golden age. Under Dubcek's new freedom, the Ukrainian minority living in Slovakia quickly demanded all kinds of new rights, discussing them on uncensored Ukrainian-language broadcasts. Most important, there was Dubcek's promise of "federalization" of the Czechoslovak state—in which Slovakia would not only enjoy domestic home rule but would be guaranteed constitutional parity with the Czech lands (even though the latter were twice as populous) in conducting their joint affairs. If 4 million Slovaks gained genuine national autonomy as well as political liberty, 46 million Ukrainians—with a rich territory larger than France—could hardly be expected to remain indifferent.

porcine visage made even Brezhnev seem refined by comparison, had been struggling to suppress nationalist unrest in the Ukraine for more than two years. In February, Shelest had already sounded the first call for "revolutionary vigilance." In mid-March, he forced through a purge of Ukrainian party officials suspected of insufficient toughness.

Shelest, Gomulka, and Ulbricht were not only among the earliest, but they remained the most determined, opponents of the Czechoslovak reformers. They were not, however, the only ones. Differing opinions within the Soviet Politburo were apparent (then, as well as later) in the gingerly, contradictory treatment given Czechoslovakia in the Russian press, even if Czechoslovak, Yugoslav, and Rumanian Communist reports of the specific individual Russian viewpoints are largely discounted.* Soviet troop movements in East Germany and Hungary, reported on the very day Novotny's resignation was accepted (March 21), probably indicated concern in the Soviet military command as well as among political circles.

Such early danger signals were hardly apparent, however, to the great mass of Czechs and Slovaks, who were turned inward, concentrated on their own affairs. When Novotny's resignation was announced on March 22, a thrill of joy went through the nation—a joy deepened by the satisfaction that the former dictator had been removed without violence.

Even before the announcement, the antifascist resistance veterans, student organizations, journalists, and other groups were proposing candidates to succeed Novotny as president. Four men were mentioned most prominently. They were Smrkovsky, the Slovak novelist Laco Novomesky, Cestimir Cisar, and General Ludvik Svoboda.

---

* Kosygin and Suslov were mentioned most consistently as sympathetic to the Czechoslovak reforms, or at least wary of brutal action to halt them. Among other high officials, Ponomarev and Andropov usually followed Suslov; Polyansky often echoed Kosygin. On the other hand, Andrei Kirilenko (who had risen in the Ukrainian party machine with Brezhnev, and had become Suslov's rival in the Secretariat) was considered hostile by the Czechs at a very early stage. So was Konstantin Katushev, the young provincial whom Brezhnev had brought to the Prague anniversary celebrations in February and who was promoted to the Secretariat in April. Podgorny's influence was generally discounted; Shelepin seemed to be playing a waiting game until the final stages, when he aligned himself with Kosygin and Suslov.

Cisar had been a popular minister of education whom Novotny had exiled as Ambassador to Rumania in 1965. Svoboda, seventy-two, had commanded the Czechoslovak Brigade attached to the Soviet Army in World War II, had been defense minister between 1945 and 1950, and had been imprisoned in 1952 and remained in disgrace until Khrushchev personally insisted on his rehabilitation in 1958.

Novomesky was out of the question because he was a Slovak; a Czech was needed to balance Dubcek in the party leadership. Cisar, who was forty-eight years old, was the choice of students who favored youth on principle and wanted "a Czech Kennedy." Svoboda enjoyed respect as an honorable patriot and a victim of Stalinism. But liberal Communists worried about his age and political determination, while non-Communists had not forgiven him for keeping the Army neutral during the Communist coup of February 1948.

Of the four men, therefore, the most popular choice—had Czechoslovakia been completely free to choose for itself—would probably have been Smrkovsky, who had voiced the aspirations of the Prague spring most clearly.

On Saturday morning, March 23, an unexpected news bulletin hit Prague with the sting of a cold shower. Dubcek had been summoned to Dresden, East Germany, to meet with Brezhnev and other bloc leaders—for the third time in a month. Even the first announcements of the Dresden meeting were disquieting. The meeting had been called in a hurry, as was shown by second-string representation from Bulgaria (whose highest leaders were abroad). The Rumanians were absent, although they had attended the Sofia conference two weeks earlier; Rumanian spokesmen soon indicated that Ceausescu had refused, on principle, to discuss the internal affairs of other parties. Ulbricht and Gomulka, however, were on hand; and from the Russian side Brezhnev and Kosygin were flanked by Shelest and the conservative Andrei Kirilenko.

The communiqué which followed the Dresden meeting produced profound irritation in Prague. It not only called in the usual stale language for "vigilance" against "imperialist subversion," but made it obvious that Czechoslovakia had been the principal subject of discussion. In a long, murky paragraph, the communiqué pretended that the January 1968 turn in Czechoslovakia had been aimed merely at "realizing the policies defined by . . . [Novotny's 1966] party congress." The communiqué concluded by expressing confidence that "the working class and all the toilers of Czechoslovakia, under the direction of the Czechoslovak Communist party, will insure the further socialist construction of the country"—in other words, that orthodox Communism would prevail.

In fact, Brezhnev, Ulbricht, Gomulka, and their associates at Dresden had sharply criticized the manner in which the Novotnyites were being forced out by the press and free public meetings. They had vetoed the plans drawn up by Professor Sik and other economists to seek a $500 million loan from the West. They had strongly condemned the conduct of Smrkovsky—and they had insisted that only General Svoboda would be acceptable to them as President of Czechoslovakia.

None of this, however, became known to the people of Czechoslovakia, or even to wider circles in the party leadership, until a year later. For, returning from Dresden to Prague, Dubcek and the colleagues who had accompanied him decided that it would be wiser to conceal the evidence of such flagrant intervention in Czechoslovak affairs. Dubcek admitted publicly on his return that the Dresden conferees had expressed "a certain concern" that "antisocialist elements should not take advantage of the democratization process." But Dubcek chose to accentuate the positive: namely, to stress the vague hints given by Kosygin that Russia might consider extending Czechoslovakia economic aid.

Dubcek's initial reassurances were not accepted. Most Czechs believed that he should not have gone to Dresden at all. On the night of March 26, a cable signed by 134 prominent Prague writers and artists urged Dubcek to "make clear that, in spite of international solidarity toward the socialist states, you hold yourself to be solely responsible to this country and to this people." Thirty-six hours later, Dubcek felt obliged to state that "at the Dresden meeting, we have not discussed, either officially or unofficially, the changes in the leadership of our party and our state." Which was not true—but calmed the public.

From the Dresden meeting onward, Dubcek was repeatedly confronted, in ever new forms, with the same dilemma: It was impossible fully to satisfy both the people of Czechoslovakia and the reactionaries who ruled Russia and its most strategic dependencies. What overjoyed Czechs and Slovaks infuriated Brezhnev, Shelest, Ulbricht, and Gomulka. What reassured the Kremlin frustrated the deep desire of Czechoslovakia for democracy and national independence.

There were only two possible ways to resolve this dilemma. One was to take arms against the sea of troubles, and by opposing, end them, but for many reasons—the most basic of which lay in the Czech national character *—preparation for an armed conflict was never seriously considered by the party leaders. The overwhelming majority of the Czechoslovak reformers agreed, from March to August and beyond, that "physical resistance is out of the question." Only the students, some of the bolder writers, and a handful of individuals like General Prchlik, dared even to think otherwise. They were more than outweighed by the conservatives in the party leadership and by the Soviet agents still embedded in the police and Army.

The other path open to Dubcek was to attempt to square the circle: simultaneously to reassure both the Kremlin and his people of his own good will, of the ability of Czechoslovakia to elaborate a free society which did not threaten the existing order in Russia, Poland, and East Germany.

The Hungarian experience of 1956 was on everybody's mind, and Dubcek and his colleagues were determined not to repeat what they regarded as the Magyars' two principal errors: namely, to withdraw from the Warsaw military pact, or to permit popular

* The rational explanations for the Czechs' unwillingness to consider armed resistance are obvious. Similar rational calculations had applied in 1938, during the war, and in 1948. Indeed, Marx had even criticized the Czechs for their passivity in 1848, which also had its reasons. The sad fact was—as numerous Prague liberals freely conceded in 1968—that the Czechs had had their warrior instincts burned out of them by the Thirty Years War and the Counter-Reformation. They had become (and this was part of their glory as well) an eminently peaceful, civilized, reasonable people with a genuine repugnance for violence. As one Czech explained, only "half-savage tribes" like the Yugoslavs were instinctively ready to fight to the death against insuperable odds. Or, as a Yugoslav in Prague put it mournfully in July 1968, "Everything here would be completely different if there were only 10,000 Montenegrins in the mountains of Slovakia. But there are not even one thousand. . . ."

revenge against Stalinist police and party officials. Therefore, throughout the Prague spring, fidelity to the Soviet alliance was vowed daily, and the most that was asked of even the police torturers of the Stalinist period was that they find other employment. As time went on, and the Kremlin demanded concessions, Dubcek and his colleagues granted them, whenever possible, in the hope of preserving "essentials" and persuading Moscow that Prague was reasonable and reliable.

Within a few weeks after Dresden, for example, it gradually became clear that there could be no question of starting new political parties, reviving the old Social Democratic party, or even invigorating the three petrified pseudoparties which still formed part of the Communist-dominated National Front.

Such concessions were aimed only partly at influencing sympathetic foreign Communists—notably the Yugoslav, Rumanian, Italian, and Hungarian parties. They were aimed mainly at bolstering forces of caution and moderation within the weak, divided Soviet "collective leadership." The Czechoslovak Communists knew that people like Shelest were irreconcilable, but they hoped that men like Kosygin could be won over and shaped their tactics in order to do so. The choice of General Svoboda was, to a large extent, a deliberate olive branch extended to the marshals of the Soviet Army, who knew and trusted the old soldier.

However, with all the good intentions and tactical finesse displayed by Dubcek and his colleagues, it was impossible to dam up the rush of profound feeling being expressed by hundreds of thousands of Czechs and Slovaks, liberated at last after their long nightmare. Indeed, Dubcek, Smrkovsky, and the genuine reformers did not even wish to suppress such feelings. For, as they toured towns and villages, factories and farms, the spontaneous affection with which the people greeted their promises of democratization inspired and strengthened them in the resolve to create a new society, whatever the difficulties. The Communist reformers recognized the necessity to bring alleged "antisocialist elements" under control. But they believed that their own popularity and leadership, rather than police repression, constituted the most effective possible control. In this belief, they were thinking like democrats, as sons of Masaryk rather than of Stalin.

It was even less possible for Dubcek and his associates to prevent provocations from across the borders—words and deeds by dogmatic foreign Communists which incensed Czechs and Slovaks determined to end outside interference. Dubcek had barely calmed the Czechoslovak population after Dresden, for example, when Ulbricht's chief ideologist, Kurt Hager, made a speech charging that statements by Smrkovsky and various Czech writers were playing into the hands of West German reactionaries. Hager's statement produced outrage in Prague almost as great as that provoked by the Sejna affair. There was a flood of angry denunciations and resolutions and even a formal diplomatic protest.

The anti-Hager outburst released emotions pent up since Dresden, and made it easier for the liberals to accept the nomination of Svoboda as president by the party Central Committee. Smrkovsky now entered the party Presidium, and soon became National Assembly president; Cisar became the new party secretary for education and culture. Ignoring the party decisions, some 5,000 young workers and students demonstrated for Cisar as president. They snakedanced and chanted their way for hours through Wenceslas Square, through Reformation Square, through the arcades and courtyards. There were no police to bother them.

Finally, the students arrived at the Central Committee building, and Dubcek came out to greet them. Where was the guarantee, the students asked, that the old days would not come back? "You yourselves are the guarantee—you, the young . . . There is only one path, and that is forward."

On March 30, a day as warm as May, Svoboda was formally elected president in the Vaclav Hall of Hradcany Castle. He was, clearly, a very old man. He walked slowly, and his hands sometimes trembled. But he had a strong, ruddy soldier's face, and his wife was a Renoir miniature: petite, sympathetic, refined. Along with the National Assemblymen electing him, the hall was filled with officials, diplomats, scarlet-robed clergy, writers—and also recent political prisoners (notably Jan Benes, whom Novotny had jailed the previous August), uniformed veterans of the Czech Legion of World War I (repressed for twenty years), and Boy Scouts (also rehabilitated at last).

The election was followed by a joyful reception in the castle's elegant Spanish Hall. Dubcek led Svoboda through one packed reception room after another, shaking hands right and left. Light and springy, Dubcek was informal, affable, all smiles. He laughed easily as men grabbed him by the shoulder or elbow and ladies leaned up to kiss him. He smiled happily as Svoboda spoke briefly to the thousands of students assembled in the courtyard below.

It was a sunny day of national reconciliation. But the same day's papers brought another reminder of the dark past that had yet to be fully surmounted. It was an interview with Professor Richard Slansky, brother of the executed Rudolf, who had himself been a prisoner for seven years. In the first month of interrogation, Slansky recalled, he had lost forty pounds:

> Can you imagine what it is not to sleep for five or six nights, to have to walk up and down the cell without being allowed to sit, to be hungry with a fever and almost in delirium after nights spent in a freezing cell with wide-open windows—and then to be dragged to the interrogators constantly to discuss one's "guilt." . . . I think that Dante must have seen some medieval trials to write the *Inferno*.

Early Sunday morning, March 31, there was a meeting of a new organization which had been announced in a few newspaper squibs. The meeting was called to found a new club, "K-231." The number was that of the so-called Law for the Defense of the Republic covering subversion, treason, and other "antistate" activities. Some 70,000 persons were condemned under this law after 1948, most of them to the Leopoldov prison and the Jachymov uranium mines.

The meeting was held at a hall on Slovansky Island, which was packed with at least 3,000 people—standing in the aisles, leaning from the balconies, crowding in from overflow rooms. Behind the platform, there was a red and white banner reading *"Aby se to neopak"*—"Let it never happen again." In a corner stood a small secular altar with a memorial flame for the political prisoners who had not survived.

The men and women on the platform were easily recognizable as old Social Democrats and Czechoslovak Socialists (the old

Beneš party). They included, for example, the gentle law professor Zdenek Peska, who had been jailed by the Gestapo during the war, who had helped draft Czechoslovakia's 1945 constitution, and had been imprisoned for eleven years, from 1949 to 1960, as an independent Social Democrat. The others—former Attorney-General Frantisek Trzicky, Professor Karel Negrin, General Vaclav Palacek, and many more—had similar histories.

The chairman read a touching letter from Goldstuecker, who was hesitant even as to how to address these non-Communist prisoners. Twenty years ago, he said, "most of you did not want to be my friends"; yet he could hardly call them comrades, "because you would not like that." Nevertheless, they shared the deep bond of their common suffering. "Is it possible completely to efface what we have gone through? . . . You can give a person back his freedom, civic rights and work—but you cannot ever completely eradicate the scars left on his dignity as a man."

A professor named Krupicka then announced that "we have not met for any individuals to vent their anger or desires for revenge." If there were any such individuals present, they should leave at once. He went on to speak of democracy as "a form of political life which stands above any sort of [economic or social] content." The rights of man, civil liberty, alone make human society different from a pack of wolves.

A physician, who was imprisoned by the Gestapo and the Stalinist police for the same reason (friendship with Beneš), recalled the students who had been deported by the Nazis on October 17, 1939. They had returned after the war to found a new university; yet, under Stalinist rule, many were arrested, and others were forced into factories and were still the object of discrimination. It was regrettable but true, the doctor said, that the democrats who had led the resistance against Hitler had been the first to suffer after 1948. On arriving in prison (where he remained twelve years), he was told, "We are sick of you people—you are professional resisters. We must liquidate you first."

Coming to the present, the physician concluded that the authorities would have to realize that "if something is not Red, that does not make it Black." If "we are guaranteed human dignity, a chance at prosperity and real freedom, we don't care about isms.

... We belong to this nation and want to work for it. But we want our country to be a home, and not a place where relations are based on zoological principles."

Already, 184 people had asked for the floor; the chairman asked speakers to be brief. A young woman quickly announced herself as acting secretary of a newly formed Society for Human Rights, a voluntary society open to all. She was the first speaker to quote Thomas Masaryk—*"Democracy is discussion"*—amid strong applause.

A Slovak described the wartime partisan movement and the anti-Nazi uprising in 1944. "Just as the uprising started in Slovakia, so now we are starting with Dubcek from Slovakia."

A worker described the resistance to Stalinism in the factories. "Those gentlemen up there know very well what went on in the factories in 1956, '57, '58—what the workers really thought." When he was imprisoned, he was told, "You have come here to die. Your wives and daughters will become prostitutes."

A blonde lady spoke movingly of the thousands of women who had labored and suffered in the concentration camps. "If we survived, it is because we were sustained by our love for President Masaryk and President Beneš, and our faith in their teachings."

Josif Just, a Communist in 1945 and still a young man, had known all the political leaders "when democracy was reborn here—and then buried." He said that he had tried to warn Gottwald, but that Gottwald had called him "naïve."

Colonel Ladislav Bedrich, a wartime deputy of General Svoboda, recounted how he had gone to see the general in January, when it was first rumored that he might become president. "Nobody has officially spoken to me," Svoboda had said, "but if they ask, I have one serious condition—the complete rehabilitation of all the innocent victims and their families."

Dr. Trzicky, who had been Czechoslovakia's attorney general in 1945, described the legal difficulties of the former prisoners' situation and urged them to be patient despite the outrages of the past. "We have been faithful to Masaryk under the Nazis and later, in the concentration camps," he said. "Now, I don't like strong words, but I believe we will go forward ... to honor, honesty and justice!"

The 3,000 former prisoners rose for a moment of silence to honor the memory of Milada Horakova. Then they sang the Czechoslovak national anthem, many with tears in their eyes. A telegram was sent to Dubcek "expressing our esteem for the manner in which you are restoring the dignity of human life."

This was the founding meeting of "K-231," the club which Soviet propagandists were soon to brand as a dangerous "counterrevolutionary," "antisocialist" organization. According to their perverse definitions, the heirs of Stalin were right: for the tortures which had been inflicted on scores of thousands of Czechs and Slovaks over two decades paled in comparison with the sufferings experienced by tens of millions of Russians in a half-century of Soviet power. Although Alexander Dubcek, whose hands were clean, could extend them in reconciliation with Stalinism's innocent victims, the men who had imprisoned Andrei Sinyavsky and Yuri Galanskov, who had sought to silence Solzhenitsyn, could hardly be expected to do so.

For five months, as Czechoslovakia basked in the moral splendor of the Prague spring, the great question was whether the ghost of Stalin would triumph once more, or whether—as Academician Sakharov and so many others hoped—events might compel at least one of Stalin's heirs to resume the work that Khrushchev had started and to step forward as a Soviet Dubcek.

CHAPTER 15

The Sheathed Knife

"*Someone must have been telling lies about Joseph K. for with-out having done anything wrong he was arrested one fine morn-ing. . . .*" So begins the greatest work ever written in Prague, Franz Kafka's *The Trial*. The innocent bank clerk Joseph K. is led through bewildering and menacing interrogations by anony-mous magistrates, officials, assessors, and advocates, all attempt-ing to obtain his confession of guilt to crimes never specified. All the while, Joseph K. is not imprisoned, but is able to continue seeing friends and working at the bank.

The Trial ends on the night before Joseph K.'s birthday, when two "pallid and plump" men with "fat double chins," who remind him of "tenth-rate actors," come to his lodgings and lead him off to a deserted quarry on the outskirts of town:

"*Then one of them opened his frock-coat and out of a sheath that hung from a belt girt around his waistcoat drew a long, thin, double-edged butcher's knife. . . .*" An "*odious ceremonial of courtesy began: the first handed the knife across K. to the second, who handed it across K. back again to the first. K. now perceived clearly that he was supposed to seize the knife himself . . . and plunge it into his own breast. But he did not do so, he merely turned his head, which was still free to move, and gazed around him. . . .*

"*Was help at hand? Were there some arguments in his favor*

that had been overlooked? Of course there must be. Logic is doubtless unshakeable, but it cannot withstand a man who wants to go on living. Where was the Judge whom he had never seen? Where was the High Court to which he had never penetrated? He raised his hands and spread out all his fingers. But the hands of one of the partners were already at K.'s throat, while the other thrust the knife into his heart and turned it twice . . ."

For nearly five months, between April and August 1968, Czechoslovakia experienced the last night of Joseph K. The logic of its situation was unshakeable—in the superior power and rising enmity of the plump, pallid men who were Stalin's heirs. But logic "cannot withstand a man who wants to go on living." The nation "searched for arguments in its favor that had been overlooked," hoped for divine help, and refused to plunge the knife into its own breast.

It was easy, in retrospect, to judge the Czechs and Slovaks—and especially Dubcek, Smrkovsky, and the other Communist reformers who led them—as naïve, optimistic, and trusting with regard to the masters of the Soviet empire. They were neither more nor less naïve than Master Jan Hus, who accepted an Imperial safe-conduct and commended himself into the hands of the Council of Constance—which, unable to force him to recant, burned him at the stake on July 6, 1415.

Although they were trained as Communists rather than as Christians, most of the leaders of the Prague spring were, like Hus, in a state of exaltation that placed them beyond strategy, tactics, and cold calculation. They were caught up, between April and August, not merely in the renaissance of their own country, but in the enthusiastic belief that they were bearing a new truth that was universal. In striving to create "socialism with a human face," they believed that they were serving not only Czechoslovakia but the entire Communist realm—and especially Russia, which needed that truth most. *Pravda vitezi, Veritas vincit*—Truth Will Prevail: this was not only the national motto but the national conviction.

The Czechoslovak reformers had committed no crime; they had spilt no blood. They counted on the moral power of their example to radiate throughout the empire, and to melt the ice of suspicion and fear in which they too, so recently, had themselves been locked. They had seen in their own country how tens of thousands of Communists, who had formerly done the bidding of Stalin and Novotny, had undergone, in a few weeks or months, an astonishing metamorphosis which could only be described as a moral conversion. The leaders of the Prague spring refused to believe, therefore, that all the rulers of the Soviet empire were beyond redemption. If a thorough metamorphosis among Stalin's heirs was not possible, the Prague reformers hoped at least for their toleration.

As the weeks passed, and crises ebbed and flowed, the Czechs and Slovaks seized upon every sign, argument, or trend that might vindicate their hopes. And there were many such. The Yugoslavs, the Rumanians, the Italian Communists were for them; so, too, in large measure, were the Hungarians (although they could not often say so publicly). A delegation of Soviet writers—none of them rebels, all pillars of the system—visited Czechoslovakia in May. The head of the delegation, Konstantin Simonov, declared: "The Czechoslovak experiment is important from the viewpoint of socialist unity, and we desire its success." A colleague, Boris Polevoi, the hard-boiled editor of *Yunost*, added, "What is good for you, is good for us too."

At about the same time, a group of senior Soviet marshals toured the country to celebrate the anniversary of its liberation from the Nazis. One of them, Ivan Konev (next to Marshal Zhukov the leading Soviet commander of World War II), went back to Moscow and wrote a long article with high praise for General Svoboda and for Dubcek's personal courage in the Slovak national uprising. Another marshal, Kiril Moskalenko (who was said personally to have arrested Beria, the dread police chief, in 1953), publicly assured an audience that Russia would not intervene in Czechoslovakia's internal affairs.

In the midst of Soviet propaganda attacks on Prague's free press, Kosygin came to Karlovy Vary and privately expressed a contrary view. Asked by a Czech reporter for his off-the-record opinion of the activities of Czechoslovak journalists, Kosygin clasped the reporter's hands warmly and said, "I wish you all success in the noble work you are doing." Kosygin's remark was never made public.

In June, however, a Czech delegation did report on its two-hour conversation with Brezhnev in the Kremlin. According to Josef Zednik, a vice-president of the Czechoslovak National Assembly, "Leonid Brezhnev, while recognizing certain faults committed by the Soviet side, energetically affirmed that in no case could there be any attempt to influence our affairs. . . ." Brezhnev, "profoundly moved," vowed that the Soviet attitude toward Czechoslovakia remained "unchanged, cordial and warm."

"I never expected to see tears in the eyes of such a high official and former soldier," Zednik reported and quoted Brezhnev as having said:

> The Soviet Union is ready to justify itself, even before an international tribunal, against the unjust insinuations which appear in connection with events in Czechoslovakia. The Soviet Union has never wished to influence the internal policy of its neighbors. It hasn't done so in Poland, why should it do so in Czechoslovakia? What happened in your country was the fault of your own leaders, you can't blame the Soviet Union for it.

In June, too, Academician Sakharov's plea to support Czechoslovakia's "bold initiative" was published abroad. Coming from such an eminent leader of the Soviet scientific community, which was generally presumed to be acquiring heightened influence in the Kremlin, Sakharov's plea further encouraged the Czech and Slovak leaders in the belief that, somehow, help was at hand and their cause would prevail.

Later, fellow Communists would blame Dubcek for the excessive optimism which was part of his character, and even in the March days there were tough-minded Prague observers who predicted that his trusting nature would be his undoing. But, from April onward, the euphoria of the Prague spring gradually dissolved the reserves of even the most pessimistic Czech and Slovak temperaments. By summer, faith in a miracle was virtually universal. So strong was that faith that it persisted for many months after the die had been decisively cast.

It was not until the Soviet and Czechoslovak leaders were locked in grim confrontation, at the end of July, that a few cold, realistic voices were heard, defining the nature of the challenge which Czechoslovakia posed. Thus, Jiri Hochman, a former Washington correspondent, wrote in the Prague *Reporter* on July 31:

> We have in fact not committed any of the sins we are being accused of, and we were not engaged in any deliberate and perfidious liquidation of socialism. . . . Nevertheless, we are introducing to the scene something else. . . . which is the real crux of the matter.
> We have introduced the spectre of liquidation of the absolute power of the bureaucratic caste, a caste introduced to the international scene by Stalinist socialism. . . . We are heading toward the breakup of the power of this, now almost hereditary, caste which has been bound by a thousand threads of mutual corruption and mutual interests with foreign counterparts. Such is the extent of our sin. We do not endanger socialism; to the contrary. We endanger bureaucracy, which has been slowly but surely burying socialism on a world-wide scale. For this we can hardly expect bureaucracy's brotherly cooperation and understanding. . . .

Even in this warning, the term "bureaucracy," which could conjure up visions of mild British civil servants or fussy Swiss customs inspectors, was a euphemism. For the Czechoslovaks in 1968 were dealing with a Soviet ruling class which had been created in the bloody 1930s—a caste (in Bukharin's words) "of professional bureaucrats for whom terror was henceforth a normal method of administration." Nonetheless, even the occasional sober warnings which appeared in the *Reporter*, *Literarny Listy*, and other intellectual journals were submerged in the oceanic faith of 14 million Czechs and Slovaks that virtue would somehow triumph. It was the faith of Joseph K. in "the Judge whom he had never seen. . . . the High Court to which he had never penetrated."

However, the March days had so transformed the moral atmosphere of Czechoslovakia, had carried its people and leaders so far in spirit from the Soviet system, that a stable compromise between the two was difficult to conceive. Conflict between them could only be averted by radical change in one or the other. While the Czechs and Slovaks (echoed by the Polish students, Academician Sakharov, and countless others) prayed for a change in Russia, the Soviet rulers attempted to compel Dubcek to "normalize" the situation in Czechoslovakia. In view of what the Kremlin regarded as "normal," it was an invitation to Dubcek "to seize the knife himself . . . and plunge it into his own breast."

The chasm which had opened between Czechoslovakia and Soviet Communism was dramatized during the first fortnight in April, when each party held a plenary meeting of its Central Committee. The contrast between the two was striking.

The Czechoslovak plenum lasted a week, with scores of speakers expressing a wide variety of viewpoints. Even Novotny made a forty-minute speech in self-defense, and the text was carried *in extenso* by all the major newspapers.

Each night at the Prague Journalists Club, amidst klieg lights, microphones, tape recorders, and Turkish coffee, Dr. Jiri Hajek (soon to become foreign minister) and other Central Committee officials described the committee sessions to hundreds of Czech and foreign reporters. They then answered dozens of sharp questions in numerous languages. (Dr. Hajek spoke English, French, German, Spanish, and Norwegian as well as Czech.) The final evening, Hajek was joined by Cestmir Cisar, a breezy, confident man with the gift of soft irony. "Now, of course," he explained, "nobody in the Central Committee claims to have ever been a conservative." Describing the rehabilitation of the rebel writers expelled by Novotny in September 1967, Cisar observed that the writers had merely "expressed too early standpoints with which we all now agree." The Central Committee meeting, Hajek stressed, had "begun the process of having differences and has decided to continue having differences."

Among the speeches at the Central Committee itself, there was no uniform "monolithic" line. For example, there was now more or less general agreement that the victims of the 1950s should be rehabilitated. But Jan Nemec noted:

A few years ago, Solzhenitsyn's book *One Day in the Life of Ivan Denisovitch* greatly disturbed the people, and today we read about such Solzhenitsyns every day and in all magazines. Today, unfortunately, we find that even in the sixties there were still methods of interrogation at variance with humanist concepts.

Bohumil Sucharda, the finance minister, stated the essence of the reformers' program most succinctly. "Without democratization," he said, "we shall solve no social problems, nor even any major economic problems. In this sense, the intensification of socialist democracy is the most effective investment." Other speeches were equally provocative.

The Central Committee removed a score of Novotnyites, repealed the resolutions condemning the rebel writers, demanded the rehabilitation of all those illegally condemned between 1949 and 1954. It postponed national and local elections so that a new election law could be written. It called for speeding preparations for a new party congress, new party statutes, and a new constitution for the Republic which would guarantee civil liberties for all and federal status for Slovakia. It formally suspended the censorship and called on the National Assembly to draft a new press law.

At the same meeting, the Czechoslovak Central Committee nominated a new government. Cernik became premier; Sik and Husak were among the deputy premiers. Two former victims of Stalinism, Josef Pavel and Martin Dzur, became the ministers of the interior and defense respectively. Frantisek Kriegel, a liberal physician, became president of the National Front.

At the close of its meeting on April 5, the Czechoslovak Central Committee adopted its famous "action program." Despite numerous compromises, loopholes, and qualifications, it was the most democratic document in the history of Communism. The action program promised freedom of speech, press, assembly, and religious worship; the autonomy of parliament, the courts, and government administration; sweeping economic reforms aimed at a convertible currency; and workers' participation in industrial management.

"We are seeking our own Czechoslovak way of building socialism," the Central Committee resolution declared. "This is our internal affair which will be decided by the supreme will of our people and their honest work."

This was the Czechoslovak "April plenum," which with a single burst had gone far beyond even the reforms achieved by the Yugoslavs in twenty years of cautious evolution. ("Of course, the Czechs must assume the leadership now," a Yugoslav Communist observed. "After all, one out of every thousand of them is an Academician, while among us 500 are practically illiterate.")

The Soviet "April plenum" followed five days later. It was held in utter secrecy. Not a single one of the speeches delivered at the two-day meeting was ever published. There was only a communiqué listing the names of the speakers, and a bitter, cryptic resolution. Brezhnev was the main speaker, with a report on the "international situation and the struggle of the Soviet Communist party for the unity of the international Communist movement." The contents of Brezhnev's report could be inferred from a speech he had made earlier, declaring war on "nationalist and revisionist tendencies," defending the literary trials, and warning that "renegades should not count on remaining unpunished."

Shelest followed Brezhnev immediately to the Central Committee tribune, the only other Politburo member to speak. (He was to assume the same role at the other Central Committee sessions that year, in July, October, and December.) Among the other speakers, ideological watchdogs were most prominent—men like Zimyanin, the editor of *Pravda* who had threatened to ground Andrei Voznesensky into dust.

The resolution adopted by the Soviet April plenum offered no "action program" to deal with the ills of Russian life. Instead, as in the days of Stalin and Zhdanov, it called for an "intransigent struggle against enemy ideology," a campaign of "vigilance" against enemy attempts to "undermine socialist society from within." It demanded "active intervention" against efforts by writers or artists to introduce "alien conceptions."

In the weeks that followed, the Soviet party expelled from its ranks and dismissed from their jobs dozens of prominent writers, artists, and historians who had protested the rehabilitation of Stalin, the persecution of Solzhenitsyn, the trials of the writers. At local party meetings held throughout the country to "implement the resolution of the April plenum," the most prominent speakers were the local heads of the KGB and MVD, followed by cultural commissars. A general crackdown in the arts closed a Chagall exhibition planned by scientists in Novosibirsk, ended rehearsals of a play by Voznesensky, withdrew Western films from movie theaters. Contacts with foreigners were sharply curtailed. The "historic April plenum" brought fear and suspicion such as Russia had not known in nearly a decade.

The Soviet Central Committee meeting was followed swiftly by the first open attempts to intimidate the Prague reformers. On April 12, *Pravda* carried a delayed, tendentious report on the Czechoslovak Central Committee sessions which had adopted the "action program." No details of the program were given. Nor was there a hint of Dubcek's profound conviction, expressed at the meeting, that "democracy is the only way to establish a true and conscious socialist discipline."

Instead, *Pravda* reported the views of Novotnyites, who had observed that "under the cover of the slogans, 'Democratization' and 'Liberalization,' antisocialist elements. . . . attack the party," that there had been "strange, demagogic demands for a return to the Czechoslovakia of Masaryk and Benes." *Pravda* concluded by citing a demand for "a resolute rebuff" to such dangerous elements.

The veiled threats concealed in such jargon were apparent to initiated Communists in Prague and Bratislava, as well as in Moscow. But the Czechs and Slovaks were weary of jargon, weary too of hanging on every Soviet word and nuance. Dubcek and his colleagues might preach the need for prudence, but broad circles of public opinion, long silenced, were determined to obtain a reckoning with the crimes of the past and to guarantee that such crimes could never be repeated.

In *Literarni Listy*, the young playwright Vaclav Havel, who had never been a Communist, argued calmly for the creation of a second political party, to work with the Communists in a system of coalition, cooperation, and mutual control.* Soon afterward,

* Havel's essay, published on April 4, was a common-sense exposition of basic democratic principles. He said the second, non-Communist party should not be based on class or special economic interest, but should be bound by agreement to the reformed Communist party "on the fundamental aim—humane, socially just and civilized self-awareness on the part of the nation via democratic socialism." Havel's basic appeal was for "moral-political recognition of the non-Communist viewpoint," recognition by the Communists that "Communist error other non-Communists, less calm than Havel, announced the creation of a "Club of Engaged Non-Party Members"—known by its Czech initials as KAN—which sought to become the nucleus of an opposition party. It soon attracted thousands of members across the country and tens of thousands of followers among the Prague youth. KAN began staging open meetings and demonstrations which demanded "democracy, not democratization."

In the newspaper *Student,* meanwhile, the philosopher Ivan Svitak urged a new inquiry into the death of Jan Masaryk, citing a variety of evidence that pointed to murder arranged by agents of the Soviet secret police. The Czechoslovak Government soon promised a new investigation of Masaryk's death. The party newspaper *Rude Pravo* interviewed Josef Urvalek, who had presided as chief judge at the 1952 Slansky-Clementis trial. He placed most of the blame on Gottwald, Novotny, and other Czechoslovak leaders, but he also indicated that Soviet security officers had collaborated in the tortures which had led the defendants to "confess." Other Czechoslovak officials also mentioned the presence of Soviet "advisers," but named only two of them—henchmen of Beria whom the Soviet leaders themselves had executed in 1954.

At the end of April, however, a reporter for the Slovak youth daily *Smena* got to Karol Bacilek, who had been national security minister when the great trials were prepared. Bacilek not merely disclosed that there had been twenty-six Soviet "advisers" in his Ministry; he declared that Slansky's arrest had been directly ordered by Stalin, who had sent Anastas Mikoyan to Prague to enforce the order on a reluctant Gottwald. Slansky's widow soon comfirmed that her husband had been arrested on the night following Mikoyan's arrival. (Mikoyan was still a member of the Presidium of the Supreme Soviet.)

Here were thrusts at the very vitals of the Soviet rulers. The

---

is not fundamentally different from non-Communist truth." His conclusion merits quotation in full:

"If many a non-Communist recognized Communist error even when the Communists did not have the slightest inkling that a fallacy existed, then those non-Communists must be given credit, however unpalatable that might be. For if this is impossible, it would mean that Communists are a special type of supermen who—in principle—are always right even when they have made a mistake, while non-Communists—in principle—are always in error, even when they are right . . . . . If Communists have a right to err from time to time, non-Communists have a right to be right sometimes; otherwise no useful purpose can be served."

Czechoslovak Communist reformers—not merely Dubcek and his colleagues, but the writers and journalists supporting him—had deliberately refrained from ascribing their nation's ills to its twenty-year vassalage to Moscow. The Prague reformers had tried to pretend (even to themselves) that the tragedies of the past were things of the past, the work of Czechoslovak leaders dead or disgraced and of "Beria's gorillas," whom Russia itself had repudiated after Stalin's death. They had pretended, too, that their own Czechoslovak "renaissance" was perfectly compatible with fidelity to the comrades of the "fraternal" Soviet party.

This pretense might have been tenable had the Russians, indeed, carried through to the end the de-Stalinization which Khrushchev had attempted first in 1956, then in 1961. But Khrushchev's attempts had been checked. The Soviet party had gone in the opposite direction instead, and intimate collaborators of Stalin's last vicious years had returned from obscurity to high office.

Moreover, the Czechs and Slovaks were not the only peoples pressing for a reckoning with the past, with the crimes committed by Stalin's associates throughout the empire. Barely a week after Prague agreed to investigate the death of Jan Masaryk, Ceausescu in Rumania called his Central Committee together to rehabilitate a whole series of Communists purged between 1936 and 1954. The most prominent figure rehabilitated was Lucretiu Patrascanu, who had been arrested in 1948 and killed in 1954. Ceausescu placed the blame on Gheorghiu-Dej, rather than on Moscow, but he made clear that Patrascanu's real "crimes" had been patriotism and opposition to Stalin.

Ceausescu also rehabilitated the leading Rumanian Communists who had been executed in Moscow during the Stalin terror between 1936 and 1938. Careful readers of Ceausescu's report noted that only "some of these men" had been exonerated by Soviet tribunals during Khrushchev's initial effort at de-Stalinization. The Rumanian leader was not telling all that he knew—not yet; but he might well do so in the future if the Czechs and Slovaks continued to make their accusations with impunity.

Furthermore, in Moscow itself, although the party and police retained overall control with an iron hand, a handful of courageous anti-Stalinists, among them Pyotr Yakir and the writer Lidya Chukovskaya, were framing open letters and petitions against the revival of Stalinism, documents which soon found their way abroad. These protests, apart from their moral eloquence, disclosed numerous details on the manner in which, under Brezhnev, Communists who had been officially rehabilitated by Khrushchev were now again being classed as "traitors." Such details, broadcast back to Russia by foreign radio, were having an incalculable effect on millions of Soviet families which had been scourged by Stalin and given some new hope under Khrushchev. The Russian protesters—like the Polish students, like Ceausescu in his way—drew strength from the Czechoslovak revolution.

May Day provided an even more startling contrast between Prague and Moscow than had the two Central Committee meetings of early April. In Moscow, as usual, admission to Red Square was by special pass, verified by successive cordons of police. The Politburo members and Red Army marshals mounted the Mausoleum through Stalin's old secret entrance. There was the usual grim parade of awesome rockets, rumbling tanks, and goose-stepping soldiers, followed by disciplined herds of party militants carrying official banners and portraits of the Politburo. Powerful loudspeakers provided prerecorded "enthusiasm."

In Prague, on the other hand, for the first time in twenty years, May Day was spontaneous. Nobody was compelled to demonstrate, and there was hardly a policeman in sight. As a result, 400,000 Praguers demonstrated, the largest turnout ever. The parade lasted seven hours. The marchers included uniformed veterans of the R.A.F. and other Allied forces, of the Spanish Civil war, of the old Czech Legion of 1919; there were Boy Scouts, and athletes of the historic Sokol physical culture organization—all of these groups reemerging in the May sunlight after two decades of suppression. There were the members of K-231, the political prisoners' organization, and of KAN, the opposition group, carrying portraits of President Masaryk. There were students and hippies, parents and children. Most of the demonstrators carried flowers or or the Czechoslovak flag. But one group carried an American flag, another an Israeli flag. The placards and posters were homemade. Some of them read *"Make Love, Not War," "Truth Prevails—But It Takes Some Doing," "For the First Time—Of our own Free Will!*

On the platform, Dubcek, Svoboda, Smrkovsky, Kriegel, Sik beamed with delight. Hundreds thronged freely around them, offering Dubcek sandwiches and cake, seeking his autograph. One citizen offered Dubcek a camera; he took it, snapped a photo of Svoboda, and returned it to the happy citizen. "Poppies, roses, tulips, fragrant stalks of lilacs and lillies of the valley were tossed toward the tribune," *Rude Pravo* reported. "It is the spring of our new existence."

But, that same night, 300 students demonstrated against anti-Semitism outside the Polish Embassy. Next day, Prague publishers announced that they would issue Boris Pasternak's *Doctor Zhivago.* On May 3, thousands of students gathered around the statue of Hus in Old Town Square for a meeting which turned strongly anti-Communist. "We have been rabbits long enough!" cried an engineering student. Another read excerpts from Karel Capek's biting 1924 essay "Why I Am Not a Communist." Still another read the KAN group's opposition program. There were denunciations of Polish anti-Semitism and banners with such slogans as *"With the Soviet Union Forever—But Not a Day Longer!"* Police did not interfere. Late that Friday night, Dubcek was suddenly summoned to Moscow.

On May 4, Dubcek, Cernik, Smrkovsky, and Bilak conferred in the Kremlin with Brezhnev, Kosygin, Podgorny, and other Soviet chiefs. The essence of the meeting remains somewhat obscure to this day. The official communiqué at the time was vague, describing a "frank . . . exchange of opinions." Months later, *Pravda* disclosed that the Russians had demanded that Dubcek and his colleagues "take the necessary measures" against anti-Communists. *Pravda* also claimed that the Czechoslovak leaders had promised to do so.

The months of May and June were filled with mixed signals, shifting tactics, contradictory developments—all pointing to divergent views among both the Soviet and Czechoslovak Communist leaders. In Prague, while many old Novotnyites had retired, a new conservative faction had regrouped around such men as Bilak and Alois Indra. These conservatives urged compliance with Moscow's demands, curtailment of the freedoms granted in March, and "normalization" of Czechoslovakia somewhat along the lines of Kadar's Hungary. Dubcek, Smrkovsky, Kriegel, Cisar, Sik had larger visions; and they also knew that only by retaining popular confidence could they hope to deal with the Russians as equals.

The differences among the Czechoslovak leaders were obvious; they were being publicly expressed. Differences within the Soviet leadership, which maintained its habitual secrecy, were less apparent but quite as real.

The division in the Kremlin was not between saints and fiends —between men who genuinely wished Czechoslovakia to become a democratic country (there were no such men) and other men who wished to return Czechoslovakia to the terror of the 1950s (this was impossible). The Soviet leaders, civilian and military, broadly agreed that Czechoslovakia should be "stabilized" at, more or less, the Hungarian level—that is, the level of a moderate police state. The Russians differed, however, over the methods to be used in achieving such a result. One group expected the Czechoslovak Communists themselves to restore "order." Such a course would cause least repercussions in the world Communist movement and would avert the risk of provoking unforeseeable reactions on the part of the United States. The second group, however, profoundly mistrusted Dubcek and his colleagues, considered the situation already out of hand, and pressed for Soviet military intervention.

There were divisions, too, among the East European Communist leaders. On April 28, Marshal Tito passed through Moscow, en route home from a trip to Japan, and warned Brezhnev in an angry quarrel to leave Czechoslovakia alone. Ceausescu had made clear his support for Prague even earlier, by refusing to attend the Dresden meeting. On May 8, four days after their meeting with Dubcek, the Soviet leaders summoned the other satellite chiefs to Moscow. Ulbricht and Gomulka urged drastic action, but Kadar counseled caution.

Thus, the week between May 8 and 15 saw a bewildering series

Marshal Grechko and Brezhnev, 1967

Pavel Litvinov

Gen. Pyotr Grigorenko

Larissa Daniel

General Svoboda and Dubcek, April 1968

Soviet and Czechoslovak leaders enter the Junction Club at Cierna-nad-Tisou, July 29, 1968, for crisis conference

August 1, 1968: In Prague's Old Town Square, Smrkovsky (left) defends the Cierna compromise to students (below)

At Bratislava station, after the compromise, August 3, 1968

Prague students at the funeral of Jan Palach, January 21, 1969

of mixed signals. While Polish and East German papers criticized Prague daily, most (but not all) Soviet papers treated Czechoslovakia kindly. To be sure, Tass on May 8 issued an angry denial of Soviet complicity in the death of Jan Masaryk, and on May 14 *Sovietskaya Rossiya,* the most Stalinist of the Soviet dailies, viciously attacked Thomas G. Masaryk as an "absolute scoundrel" who had subsidized attempts to murder Lenin. But on May 9, and for several days afterward, *Pravda, Izvestia,* and other papers were printing long articles by Cernik, Svoboda, and other Czechoslovak leaders expounding, in moderate terms, the essence of their program.

On May 9, the world trembled as Soviet tanks in southern Poland began moving toward the Czechoslovak frontier. Their movement was well advertised by the Polish police, who prevented Western diplomats from leaving Warsaw that day. The same day, however, Marshals Konev and Moskalenko began their tour of Czechoslovakia, pledging eternal friendship. As they toured, the Soviet Army paper, *Krasnaya Zvezda,* provided warm descriptions of how well they were being received by the friendly Czechs and Slovaks. On the other hand, in *Pravda* on May 14 Marshal Yakubovsky—in words obviously addressed to Prague— insisted that the Warsaw Pact countries "have carried out, are carrying out, and will carry out joint maneuvers of the united military forces." *

In the general confusion, there was obviously no common ground between the two extremes: the Czech and Slovak anti-Communists on one side and the Soviet and East European Stalinists on the other, ready to repeat in Prague what had been done in Budapest in November 1956. However, neither the Czechoslovak Communists nor, apparently, most of the Soviet leaders in May belonged

* Numerous other examples of such "hawk-dove" contradictions could be cited during this period. Similar contradictions appeared at later phases of the crisis, well into 1969. Briefly, there were times when the Soviet leaders seemed united on a hard line, other times when they seemed agreed on restraint or compromise, and still other times when they were clearly divided, with no firm majority for any coherent policy. The fever chart of their vacillations is a study in itself. Certain attitudes were fairly clear in May and June—Kosygin among the moderates; Shelest, the KGB, the censors, and cultural vigilantes "hard," with Brezhnev usually leaning their way. Other attitudes—notably, among the marshals—were contradictory and variable, although certain factional lines could be discerned.

to these two extremes; and there *was* common ground between the more cautious Soviet leaders and the Czechoslovak Communist conservatives. The result of this common interest was what was later loosely termed "the Kosygin compromise," because it followed a totally unexpected visit by the Soviet premier to Czechoslovakia May 17–25.

Kosygin arrived suddenly, announcing that he was coming to take the waters at Karlovy Vary (Karlsbad). He came alone, only a few hours after the arrival in Prague of the Soviet defense minister, Marshal Grechko, and his political commissar, General Alexei Yepishev. After a series of talks in Karlovy Vary and Prague, the compromise emerged which became known in official jargon as "the line of the May plenum," from a Czechoslovak Central Committee meeting held between May 29 and June 1.

The compromise was military and political. The Czechoslovak leaders agreed formally to Warsaw Pact military maneuvers on their territory. On May 21, it was announced that these would be "small-scale staff exercises," with no date given for their commencement. But on May 30, to the apparent surprise of the Prague Defense Ministry, some 3,000 Soviet troops began crossing the frontier from East Germany into western Bohemia. Other units were flown directly from Russia to Milovice, just north of Prague. Before long, more than 27,000 Soviet troops were dispersed along the country's main communications routes. When the May plenum of the Czechoslovak Central Committee began, teams of Soviet security agents had also arrived in Prague.

Politically, the May Central Committee meeting saw the crystallization of a majority of old conservatives, neoconservatives, and hesitant reformers. Smrkovsky, Sik, and others continued to stress democratization, and it was decided to prepare for an extraordinary party congress on September 9, which would choose a new Central Committee. However, Dubcek himself felt compelled to condemn "antisocialist forces" as the principal danger to the country. Conservative speakers did so even more strongly. The session heard sharp attacks on the Czechoslovak press, radio, and television, against the K-231 club of political prisoners and the KAN opposition group.

After the plenum, Indra, Bilak, and other conservatives began stirring up the so-called People's Militia—the party's private army—against the "antisocialist elements" in journalism and cultural life. Anonymous letters were circulated denouncing Goldstuecker, Kriegel, and Sik in anti-Semitic terms. Meanwhile, the reformers traveled abroad attempting to reassure the orthodox Communist chiefs that the line would be held against extremists: Dubcek went to Budapest, Smrkovsky to Moscow, Hajek to East Berlin.

The "Kosygin compromise" broke down within a month. Despite the presence of Soviet troops in Czechoslovakia, and the compromises of the Prague party leaders, the Stalinists abroad were not reassured, and in Czechoslovakia the wave of democratic feeling was too high * to permit a neoconservative "restoration" under men like Indra and Bilak. Although Czechoslovak radio, television, and newspapers were more prudent, Soviet, East German, Polish, and Bulgarian dogmatists were combing their every word—and using every possible occasion to "expose" heresies and attack offending heretics. The Czech and Slovak intellectuals replied in kind. Some went further: *Student* denounced the Soviet repression of Solzhenitsyn and reprinted the defense pleas made by Yuri Galanskov and Alex Ginsburg at the January trial. *Literarni Listy* published a long memorial tribute to Imre Nagy, the leader of the Hungarian Revolution, on the tenth anniversary of his execution (June 17).

By the last week of June, it was clear that the compromise had satisfied neither the Prague progressives nor their foes abroad. Both were uneasy about the summer and the preparations for the September 9 Communist party congress. The Warsaw Pact maneuvers, which had formally begun on June 18, were scheduled to end June 30. Afterward, there would be no legal excuse for Soviet troops to remain in Czechoslovakia. If the Soviet Army left, the Stalinists feared that Czechoslovakia might well resume the revolutionary tempo of the March days.

The Prague liberals, on the other hand, worried about the possibility of popular complacency during the summer vacation period—when scores of thousands of Czechs and Slovaks were

---

* One example among thousands: a *Rude Pravo* poll taken in June showed that 90 percent of the country—including 50 percent of Communist party members—favored the creation of opposition parties.

planning to use the new freedom to travel abroad, and when the students, who had been the democratic revolution's driving force, would be absent from the cities. Conservative functionaries still controlled much of the Communist party machine. The liberals feared that, unless public opinion were mobilized anew, a conservative majority might yet emerge at the September party congress.

June 27 marked the turning point in both Moscow and Prague. In Moscow, Soviet Foreign Minister Gromyko launched a campaign to remove the principal inhibition which had been restraining the more cautious Politburo members—namely, the fear that Russian military action in Czechoslovakia might provoke counteraction from the United States, producing a world crisis.[*] In a speech to the Supreme Soviet, Gromyko suddenly answered "yes" to a question to which Washington had been vainly seeking a reply for sixteen months. Gromyko announced Soviet willingness to consider opening negotiations with the United States to limit the strategic armaments race.

Over the next three weeks, similar Soviet gestures followed, one after another. Kosygin signed the nuclear nonproliferation treaty and proposed new disarmament measures. The Supreme Soviet ratified a consular convention with the United States, which had been held up two years. A cultural-exchange agreement with Washington, which had been stalled for many months, was now signed. The Kremlin even agreed finally to begin airline service between New York and Moscow, after negotiations that had lasted ten years.

The campaign launched by Gromyko's speech on June 27 was a triumph of Soviet diplomacy: when the Czechoslovak crisis reached its peak, the President of the United States was eagerly seeking a summit conference with the Kremlin leaders.

[*] Such counteraction was never seriously considered in the United States for a variety of reasons (partly because the Prague reformers themselves advised Washington to look the other way). However, the Kremlin leaders could not be *sure* of how Americans might react in the stress of an election year. Moscow had been unpleasantly surprised twice by U.S. reactions which most experts (Western as well as Soviet) would not have predicted: in 1962, by Kennedy's ultimatum in the Cuban missile affair, and in 1965, by Johnson's unprecedented decision to start bombing a sovereign Communist state, North Vietnam, while Kosygin himself was visiting it.

Meanwhile, in Prague on June 27, four morning newspapers published a statement entitled "2,000 Words to Workers, Farmers, Civil Servants, Scientists, Artists, and Everyone." It was written, at the request of Czech scientists, by Ludvik Vaculik—and its seventy signatories ranged from machinists and sow-breeders to Olympic prize athletes, distinguished stage and screen artists, respected surgeons, mathematicians, and educators.

The "2,000 Words" reviewed the failures of the Novotny system, praised the Communist reformers' effort since January, and warned against any attempts "to conduct some sort of democratic revival without the Communists or possibly against them." However, the manifesto was clearly a response to the "fears . . . expressed that the process of democratization has stopped." It called for popular "initiative and determination" in the weeks ahead, when "we can be certain . . . that our adversaries will not indulge in summer recreation, that they will mobilize those who are obliged to them. . . ."

The "2,000 Words" urged no pressure on the highest party and state leaders: "We must give the new people . . . time to work." However, on the local level, "Let us demand the resignation of people who have misused their power, damaged public property, behaved dishonestly or cruelly. We must find ways and means to induce them to resign—for instance, through public criticism, resolutions, demonstrations, collecting contributions for their pensions, strikes, boycotts of their office doors. However, we must reject illegal, rude, coarse methods because they would be used to influence Alexander Dubcek. . . ."

The manifesto suggested various other kinds of civic pressure to defeat the conservatives' efforts within the country. It also dealt with the menace of Soviet intervention:

> Faced with their superior forces, all we can do is remain politely firm and not start trouble. We can assure the Government that we shall stand behind it, even bearing arms if necessary, as long as it carries out our mandate; and we can assure our allies that we will fulfill our treaties of alliance, friendship and trade. . . .
>
> This spring, just as after the war, a great chance has been given us again. We have the opportunity to take up a common cause, which for all practical purposes we call socialism, and shape it to

correspond with our former good reputation and the fairly good opinion we once had of ourselves. This spring has just ended and it will never return. In the winter, we shall know everything.

The "2,000 Words" infuriated conservatives in both Prague and Moscow. At the Prague Central Committee, Indra immediately sent a telex message denouncing it to party headquarters throughout the country. A few hours later, the Soviet leaders telephoned Dubcek, demanding drastic action against the "counterrevolutionaries." The next day, Dubcek personally, the party Presidium, the Government, and the National Assembly all formally condemned the "2,000 Words."

This hasty attempt to appease the Kremlin offended most Czechs and Slovaks, including Communist reformers. Kriegel, Spacek, Cisar, Smrkovsky, and others soon indicated varying degrees of sympathy for the "2,000 Words." Some 70,000 letters and resolutions poured into Prague radio, newspaper, and party offices supporting it. A spot poll of more than 1,000 workers at the Tesla electrical factory outside Prague showed 75 percent support.

Moreover, as *Pravda* made clear later, Dubcek's "verbal condemnation" of the "2,000 Words" failed to appease the Soviet leaders who had demanded "tangible measures." Events now began to move swiftly. The Czechoslovak Communist leaders had issued their condemnations in the course of June 28. The Warsaw Pact maneuvers in Czechoslovakia were to end on Sunday, June 30. In Moscow that Sunday evening, as in capitals of other Pact states, the official news agency issued a formal announcement that the maneuvers had been concluded. On Monday, July 1, however, Tass issued a new bulletin annuling the announcement it had issued the previous day. The Soviet troops remained in Czechoslovakia.

On July 3, Brezhnev and Kadar, who had come to Moscow, addressed a rally at the Kremlin Palace of Congresses. Both made ominous references to the Soviet military repression of the Hungarian Revolution. Brezhnev declared that "we cannot be and never will be indifferent to the fate of socialist construction in other countries," and that the Warsaw military pact "offers sufficient possibilities for reliably defending the positions of socialism." Kadar asserted that, while persuasion sufficed in normal times, once Communist rule was threatened "it is our right and duty also to use force to defend the cause of socialism."

A massive propaganda inside the Soviet Union, vowing support for the Czechoslovak conservatives, had been under way even before the "2,000 Words." (The campaign took the form of pledging solidarity and "all necessary aid" to the Czechoslovak Communist "People's Militia," which had held an antireformist rally June 19.) The propaganda campaign was intensified as the Soviet and satellite leaders decided to summon Dubcek and his colleagues to another meeting of the Dresden type.

The Russian, East German, Polish, Hungarian, and Bulgarian leaders each addressed formal letters to Dubcek proposing a conference, letters which Prague received July 5 and 6. Brezhnev phoned Dubcek demanding a meeting in Warsaw at the end of the following week. Dubcek said the Czechoslovak Presidium would meet on Monday, July 8 to discuss the Soviet request. In Kiev, meanwhile, on July 5, Shelest publicly prodded unnamed colleagues who seemed ready to give Dubcek another chance. "We cannot agree," Shelest said, "with *those who seek excuses* for theoreticians" propagating "ideas of so-called democratization and liberalization."

On July 8, while the Czechoslovak Presidium was discussing the five-power invitation, Brezhnev addressed graduating military cadets in the Kremlin. He directed most of his speech to the United States, criticizing American "hawks" who claimed that Russia was increasing its military budget. But Brezhnev also observed that the Soviet Army had been charged with "protecting the achievements of the revolution" against "all enemies of the people." Moreover, this "decisive" role of the Russian armies had been confirmed by "the historical experience of *world* socialism" (that is, in East Germany in 1953, and Hungary in 1956).

The Czechoslovak Presidium played for time. On July 9, it issued a calm statement declaring that Prague welcomed all opportunities to "exchange experiences" with its allies. However, without formally rejecting a six-party conference *à la* Dresden, the Czechoslovak leaders proposed, instead, bilateral talks with each of its allies.

The next day, however, *Literaturnaya Gazeta* * in Moscow published a fierce attack on the "2,000 Words," the newspapers which had printed it, and the political leaders who had expressed sympathy. The manifesto was branded "provocative, inflammatory, anti-Communist, and counterrevolutionnary."

Pravda followed suit on July 11, comparing the Czechoslovak reformers to "the counterrevolutionary elements in Hungary . . . in 1956." The *Pravda* article, in great detail, laid the ideological groundwork for military intervention. However, it also expressed "confidence that the Czechoslovak Communists . . . will succeed in dealing a decisive rebuff to the reactionary, antisocialist forces." Obviously, elements in the Soviet leadership still hoped that the Prague conservatives could gain control on their own.

That day, Kosygin departed for what was scheduled as a three-day visit to Sweden. The same evening, a Warsaw Pact communiqué formally announced the successful conclusion of the maneuvers on Czechoslovak territory, noting that the Soviet and other Pact troops were "gradually" returning to their respective countries.

Pravda the next morning published the Pact communiqué prominently. *Krasnaya Zvezda*, the Soviet Army paper, went much further, printing a glowing front-page editorial which contrasted sharply with the denunciations elsewhere of "counterrevolutionary forces." The Soviet Army paper effusively described the friendly welcome Russian soldiers and officers had received everywhere they went in Czechoslovakia. There was not a word about "antisocialist elements." Moreover, *Krasnaya Zvezda* declared that the Warsaw Pact countries reached agreement through "free and creative exchange of opinions": "There are no partners without equal rights, and *there is no place for dictation on any question whatever*." To some observers in Moscow, it appeared that the Soviet marshals had ranged themselves with Kosygin and other Politburo moderates.

---

* *Literaturnaya Gazeta*, the Writers Union weekly, was the most shrill foe of the Czechoslovak reformers throughout all the crises of 1968 and 1969. The reason was obvious: Czech freedom of the press was a direct challenge to the cultural vigilantes who were then struggling to suppress Russian liberals. Two weeks previously *Literaturnaya Gazeta* had published a lengthy, anonymous indictment of Solzhenitsyn, implying criminal collusion with Western agents in the publication of his works abroad.

However, tensions within the Soviet leadership were high. At a press conference in Stockholm on Saturday, July 13, Kosygin was obviously nervous and deeply troubled. Four times, he accidentally said "Czechoslovakia" when he meant to say "Sweden." With visible emotion, he emphasized the decades of Soviet-Czechoslovak friendship. Then, the Soviet premier cut short his Swedish visit by twelve hours in order to fly back to Moscow. For while he had been talking in Sweden, Brezhnev, Shelest, and Podgorny had already arrived in Warsaw for a summit meeting with Ulbricht, Gomulka, and the other satellite chiefs. Kosygin only joined them next day, after the meeting had already begun.

The five-power Warsaw meeting lasted two days, July 14 and July 15. On the night that it ended, a brief communiqué announced that the conferees had discussed Czechoslovakia and had "sent a joint letter" to Prague. The Warsaw "joint letter" was not made public for another two days. But, even before the Warsaw meeting had ended, cries of protest reverberated throughout Communist Europe.

Ceausescu, speaking at the Galati steelworks, denounced "those who are alarmed over what, allegedly, is happening in Czechoslovakia and would like to intervene." The Rumanian leader attacked the use of the Warsaw Pact to "justify interference in the internal affairs of other states," expressed "full confidence" in Dubcek and his colleagues, and wished them "total success from the bottom of our heart."

The Belgrade newspaper *Politika* asserted that the Warsaw conferees were frightened "not by the prospect of the failure of socialism in Czechoslovakia, but by the prospect of its success." In East Berlin, the Marxist philosopher Robert Havemann declared himself "horrified and outraged by shameless slanders" directed at Prague, and "the attempts at Stalinist interference." French and Italian Communist party leaders flew to Moscow, appealing to Suslov in the Kremlin while the Warsaw meeting was still in progress.

In Prague on July 15, General Vaclav Prchlik—the man who had foiled Novotny's plot for a military coup in January—held a memorable press conference. His subject was the Warsaw Pact. He recalled that the Treaty prescribed "mutual respect and independence, and the principle of noninterference in internal affairs." It did *not* authorize foreign troops to be stationed on the territory of a member-state without its consent. Nor did it authorize actions by some Pact states against others. Furthermore, Prchlik disclosed that the Joint Command of the Warsaw Pact consisted "entirely of Soviet marshals, generals and officers"; the other allies only had liaison officers with no powers of decision.

Prchlik was to be removed ten days later for these remarks, and, much later, in retrospect, criticized for antagonizing the Soviet marshals who had until then seemed sympathetic to Czechoslovakia. Yet Prchlik, as chief of the entire Czechoslovak intelligence and security apparatus, was one of the few men aware of the danger in which Czechoslovakia stood on precisely that day. It had been learned that Brezhnev, on arrival in Warsaw, had strongly advocated immediate military intervention. There were still more than 15,000 Soviet troops in Czechoslovakia, as well as at least 150 heavy tanks. Larger units were available just across the frontiers in East Germany and Poland.

Moreover, as Kenneth Ames later reported to the *Washington Post* (his report was based on information provided by high Czech communications officials):

> Prague and other major Czechoslovak cities had been quietly surrounded. . . . Plainclothes "tourists" came in, mostly quietly by night, loaded on buses with Soviet license plates. The tourists were distinctive for their uniform gray suits; they were mostly young men, and they avoided the more obvious tourist attractions. . . .
>
> Television and radio transmitters throughout the country were surrounded. Several thousand alternative transmitters, including mobile short-range equipment, had been installed. It would have required only minutes to silence all Czechoslovak programs and substitute alternative ones.
>
> The Soviet Embassy in Prague . . . had recruited a large number of imported fluent Czech-speakers; . . . and was utilizing a printing plant to prepare leaflets calling for cooperation with the Soviet forces. . . . Leading figures in Czechoslovakia's peaceful revolution regularly had their homes and offices searched.
>
> At various times on July 15 and 16, there were inexplicable breakdowns in telecommunications between Prague and the outside

world. This was the period when Brezhnev and the Politburo were poised on the verge of brinkmanship.*

"Sometime between July 16 and 17," according to Ames's authoritative account, there was a reversal of orders in the Kremlin. When Brezhnev returned to the Kremlin on July 16, he phoned Prague ordering Dubcek to fly immediately to Moscow. According to a witness, Dubcek "picked up the telephone . . . and roared at Brezhnev in unambiguous Russian," refusing "to accept an invitation to an inquisition."

The Czechoslovak Party Presidium that day adopted a temperate communiqué, stating that it had received the Warsaw Letter, was preparing a reply, and was still willing to discuss matters bilaterally with the Russians or any of the others. At the Warsaw meeting, Kadar had opposed immediate intervention. In addition to Ceausescu's open support of Dubcek, Tito had cabled a strong private warning to the Kremlin. The French and Italian Communists had threatened Suslov with a boycott of the world Communist conference under preparation. The attitude of the United States was still uncertain; in May, Washington had publicly expressed "interest and sympathy" in the Czechoslovak democratization.

These factors apparently induced the Politburo majority to restrain Brezhnev. Undaunted, the General Secretary hastily convened a Central Committee meeting for the next day. However, the Central Committee left the essential decision in the hands of the Politburo.

The text of the Warsaw Letter was made public late on the night of July 17. It was an ultimatum, the like of which had not been seen since Stalin's excommunication of Yugoslavia in 1948. (A Belgrade paper promptly headlined the text "Comimform 1968.")

"We cannot reconcile ourselves," the five-power letter declared, "with the fact of hostile forces pushing your country off the road of socialism. . . . This is no longer your concern. It is a common concern. . . ."

---

* It was also the period whose lessons enabled Czechoslovak Army intelligence, radio, and telecommunications personnel to prepare the countermeasures which startled the world between August 21 and 27.

Apart from the vague charge that Prague was "flirting" with West Germany, the Warsaw Letter's basic assault was on freedom of speech and the press in Czechoslovakia. According to the letter, the Communist party had become "a discussion club" through the "weakening of the party leadership." "Antisocialist and revisionist forces have gained control over the press, radio, and television." A "moral terror" was being waged against "honest and devoted" Communist cadres. The "2,000 Words" constituted "an organizational-political platform of counterrevolution." The Czechoslovak information media were "sowing suspicion and hostility" over the continued presence of Russian troops in the country. All this was "absolutely unacceptable."

The Warsaw Letter concluded with four demands, phrased in opaque jargon.* Their meaning, however, was clear. Brezhnev and his allies demanded (1) police action against militant liberals, (2) prohibition of all non-Communist political activity, (3) the reimposition of censorship, and (4) the defeat of the reformers within the Communist party itself and restoration of orthodox policies and discipline.

The Czechoslovak Presidium's reply was published next morning. It was polite but firm. Once again, there were lengthy assurances of fidelity to the Russian alliance, and recognition that the party leaders disapproved of extremist actions. But the Presidium emphasized that the crisis had arisen because of the "distortions of the 1950s" and the later policies of Novotny. Under his leadership, "on the outside, it seemed that everything was in order in Czechoslovakia. . . ." But "inside, problems were growing, whose real solution was suppressed by forceful means. . . ."

"Any indication of a return to these methods," the Prague leaders declared, "would evoke the resistance of the overwhelming majority of party members, workers, cooperative farmers and

---

* "A determined and bold offensive against the right-wing and antisocialist forces, by mobilizing all the defensive means of the socialist state; a cessation of the activity of all political organizations coming out against socialism; seizure by the party of the media of mass information—the press, radio and television—and their utilization in the interests of the working class. . . ; cohesion of the ranks of the party itself on the basis of the principles of Marxism-Leninism and democratic centralism, struggle against all those who, by their activity, assist hostile forces."

intelligentsia." The Czechoslovak Presidium would proceed on the principle that "political leadership cannot be imposed by the old administrative and power structures."

"We know," the Czechoslovak reply concluded, that extremist activity "is facilitated by the abolition of censorship in our country, and the enactment of freedom of speech and of the press. What had been spread before in the form of 'whispered propaganda' can now be expressed openly." But "if we ask ourselves" whether this constitutes an abandonment of Communist leadership, "we reach the conclusion that this is not so."

The Czechoslovak Presidium's reply was not published or broadcast in Russia, Poland, East Germany, or Bulgaria. But it was broadcast that same evening by Radio Budapest, and summarized in all Hungarian newspapers afterward—a sign both of Hungarian sympathies for Prague and of the lack of a firm decision in the Kremlin.

That night, Dubcek addressed the nation on television. "Dear friends, dear citizens," he began:

> We are determined—and we are counting on public support—to continue the policy we adopted in January . . . a policy desired and supported by the Czech and Slovak nations. We wish to create a socialism which has not lost its human face.
>
> We have paid dearly for the old practice of taking decisions without consulting the people. The masses were dissatisfied with the previous leadership. The Communist party cannot change the masses; but it can change its leadership. After long years of silence, everyone here can express his opinion in a dignified manner; socialism is starting to become the concern of the entire people. . . ."

Mistakes were unavoidable, Dubcek continued, but "who can judge the needs of the Czechoslovak people better than this party, which works here, than the government of this country?"

The people had been rightly shocked, Dubcek declared, by the Warsaw meeting and the Warsaw Letter. "I should like to think that we shall surmount this test, not only before our own nation but before the entire Communist movement." Czechoslovakia did not wish "to impose our way" on other Communist states. "But we want socialism to take firm root here, a socialism in accord with the socialist conscience of our people. What we need is support, the confidence of our people, their wisdom and self-discipline which will not succumb to any hysteria or passionate actions."

Thus, on July 18, the lines were drawn between Czechoslovakia's new democratic socialism and the half-century Soviet model of Leninism, as clearly drawn as in the time of Hus and the Holy Roman Empire.

In New York the same day, U.S. Secretary of State Dean Rusk firmly denied reports that Washington had warned Moscow against military intervention in Czechoslovakia. "We have not involved ourselves in any way in the Czech situation," he said. Later that week, he privately reassured the Soviet ambassador to the same effect.

CHAPTER 16

The Trial

On the morning of July 19, the Czechoslovak Central Committee assembled in the Spanish Hall at Hradcany. There were still some fears that conservatives, ready to compromise with Soviet demands, might gain the day. But Dubcek had also invited to the session dozens of progressives who had been newly elected as regional delegates to the coming party congress. Just outside, in the corridors, journalists and intellectuals gathered, piling up the hundreds of letters, telegrams, and resolutions of support for Dubcek.

The Central Committee gave Dubcek a clear vote of confidence. Within a few hours, the Soviet Politburo—formally and publicly—made an unprecedented proposal. It called for a bilateral meeting, three or four days later, between "the full memberships" of the Politburo and the Czechoslovak Presidium. The proposal reflected both Kremlin hopes of dividing the Czechoslovak leaders and the divisions within the Politburo itself.

The Russians proposed that the meeting be held on Soviet territory—in Moscow, Kiev, or Lviv. But the Czechs remembered all too well the fate of Hus at Constance—and of Polish wartime underground leaders and others, who had gone to Moscow on Stalin's invitation and perished at the hands of the NKVD. Prague insisted that the meeting be held on Czechoslovak soil. Three days later, the Soviet Politburo agreed in principle, but nearly a week was spent in further bargaining over a precise time and site.

It was a week of high tension in both Moscow and Prague. In Moscow, the Defense Ministry announced that the Red Army had begun what it called "logistics" exercises in the Western Ukraine, Byelorussia, Latvia, and Western Russia. The announcement noted that, in addition to regular army units, "reservists and civilian motor vehicles are involved." Later bulletins reported that "a sea of oil" had arrived in the maneuver area—which in fact extended to southern Poland and East Germany.

The propaganda campaign against Prague was intensified. *Krasnaya Zvezda* now attacked General Prchlik, and, along with other papers, reported the alleged discovery of "secret arms caches" in Czechoslovakia, purportedly American in origin. (On investigation, the arms proved to be East German and Russian, but the charges produced new American "reassurances" of disinterest.) In a major speech, Podgorny promised the "true Communists" in Czechoslovakia that "all Soviet people" would give them "every type of aid and support."

All Soviet people, however, did not share Podgorny's outlook. A thirty-year-old worker, Anatoly Marchenko, who had spent six years in a forced-labor camp, wrote a bold open letter which General Pyotr Grigorenko and another friend delivered publicly to the Czechoslovak Embassy. Marchenko noted that the Kremlin leaders had continually assailed "the bloody terror" in China, but they made no threats of "aid and support" to "true Communists" in China. Such threats were made only against the "basically peaceful development of democracy in Czechoslovakia." Why, Marchenko asked. Fear of China's power was only part of the answer.

> Compared with the regime in China, our present regime is not one of terror but merely one of suppression—it is almost liberal, almost as liberal as that of the 19th century. But if Czechoslovakia should really succeed in organizing democratic socialism, then there would be no justification for the absence of democratic freedoms in our country. . . .

Marchenko recalled the "moral terror" which the Warsaw

Letter said was being used against "honest Communists" in Czechoslovakia—"honest Communists" such as Dr. Urvalek, the chief judge at the Slansky trial:

> It is understandable why our leaders hasten to intercede for the likes of Urvalek and Novotny: the precedent of making party and government leaders personally responsible before the people is a dangerous and contagious one. What if our own leaders should suddenly be required to account for deeds that have been shamefully termed "errors" and "excesses," or (still milder and more obscure) "difficulties experienced in the heroic past"—when it was a matter of millions of people unjustly condemned and murdered, of torture in KGB dungeons, of entire peoples declared to be enemies, of the ruin of the nation's agriculture and similar *trivia.* . . .

Marchenko feared that the Kremlin propaganda campaign was "paving the way for intervention under any pretext that may arise or be artificially created." Sadly he recalled how tsarist armies in 1830 had "drowned the Polish insurrection in blood. I am ashamed for my country, which is once more assuming the shameful role of gendarme of Europe. . . ."

Marchenko was arrested on the day his letter was delivered. Even before then, Academician Sakharov's essay urging support for Prague's "bold initiative"—a letter which had been circulating in Moscow for months—was sped to the West with a request for immediate publication.

In Prague that week, radio and television reporters stopped dozens of Russian, East German, and Polish tourists on the streets, asking them if they saw any signs of "moral terror," "anti-Soviet propaganda," or "counterrevolution." To a man, these tourists—including a few members of official delegations—replied that, on the contrary, everything was calm and peaceful; they were having a fine time; their Czech and Slovak hosts could not be friendlier. Moreover, hundreds of East Germans were seen in Prague signing the powerful appeal which the Czech liberals had drawn up urging their Presidium to stand firm at the coming meeting with the Soviet Politburo.

The appeal, published July 26 in a special issue of *Literarni Listy,* was written by Pavel Kohout, who thirteen months earlier had read Solzhenitsyn's open letter to the writers' congress. Now he was to appeal to Dubcek and his colleagues:

The moment has come when after centuries our country has again become the cradle of hope—not only for ourselves but also for others. The moment has come when we can prove to the world that socialism is no mere emergency solution for underveloped countries but the only true alternative for all civilized mankind. . . .

[Instead,] we are accused of crimes we did not commit. We are suspected of intentions we never had and do not have. The threat of an unjust punishment hangs over us. And, in whatever shape it may materialize, it may rebound like a boomerang also on our judges. . . .

Comrades, it is your historic task to avert this danger . . . to convince the leaders of the Soviet Communist party that the process of revival must proceed. . . . Tell them that we need freedom, peace and time. . . .

It is possible that not all of you hold the same views on everything, [but] it would be tragic if the personal feelings of any one of you should prevail over the responsibility that you bear at this moment for 14,261,000 people. . . . Think of us, write on our behalf a fateful page of the history of Czechoslovakia. Write it with deliberation, but above all with courage. We trust you. At the same time, we appeal to all citizens who agree with us to support this message.

Once again, the students were first to respond. Volunteers quickly set up tables for collecting signatures throughout Prague, and the movement quickly spread to Bratislava, Brno, Olomouc. Evening television programs showed long lines waiting to sign the appeal even in small villages. Within three days, the appeal had been signed by more than a million Czechs and Slovaks. On Sunday morning, July 28, the nation's churches witnessed the rare spectacle of solemn prayer for the leaders of its Communist party, as the Presidium departed for its meeting with the Russians.

The meeting was one of the stranger encounters of recent history, held in the midst of one of the most exotic regions in Europe—a region where almost every place had at least three names and had changed hands at least four times in a half-century. Borders had been drawn and redrawn, but it was a form-

less, polylingual plain of wheat fields and rolling hills, where
Eastern Slovakia merged imperceptibly eastward into Ruthenia
(or *Podkarpatski Rus*) and the Western Ukraine, southward into
the Hungarian *puzsta* where the Tokay grapes were grown, south-
eastward into northern Transylvania, northward into Galicia.

Dubcek and his colleagues arrived first at Kosice, which was
(more or less) indisputably Eastern Slovakia, although the
Hungarians who had held it still called it Kassa and the thousands of Jews who had fled it called it by the German name, Kas-
chau. A town of some 80,000 inhabitants, whose center remained
Hapsburg in character, Kosice was now the site of a massive but
notorious steelworks—notorious because the original proposal to
build the steelmill was one of the "crimes" for which Rudolf
Slansky had been hanged, because Novotny had later gone
ahead and built it anyway, and because the costly mill's sole purpose was to turn *Soviet* iron ore and coal into steel and send it
back to Russia. The mill's director, Emil Rigo, was a Gypsy, and
a member of the Czechoslovak party Presidium.

Kosice's main square had once been named after Milan
Stefanik, the Slovak aviator and hero of the French Army, who in
1918 had been a co-founder, with Thomas Masaryk, of the Czechoslovak state. The Stalinists had named the square after Lenin.
But when Dubcek and his colleagues arrived in Kosice, a bust
and photographs of Stefanik were mounted on a pedestal in the
center of the square. Beneath and beside the pedestal were gar-
lands of flowers and a stark black-and-white poster: *"We Demand
That Soviet Troops Leave Our Country."* A group of workers
nearby was asked whom they preferred, Stefanik or Lenin.
"Stefanik! Stefanik!" they replied.

At dawn on the morning of July 29, Dubcek, General Svoboda,
and the members of the Presidium boarded a bright blue electric
train for the meeting site: Cierna-nad-Tisou, a sleepy village of
some 2,500 souls (most of them Magyars), with white geese and
brown cattle, a few paved streets, modest brick peasant homes,
and resplendent flower gardens. Cierna, a few hundred yards
from the postwar Soviet frontier, had become a railway junction
to handle the Russian iron and coal for the Kosice steelworks;
and it was in their blue train in the railyards that the sixteen

Czechoslovak leaders were to sleep, caucus, and eat all their meals.

The Russians arrived at 9:52 A.M. aboard a diesel with fifteen dark green cars, their bulletproof windows masked with curtains. Each night, the special train would return a mile across the border to the Ukrainian village of Chop. In addition to the thirteen Soviet leaders,* there were black-suited KGB agents to control security around the conference room.

Earlier, Czechoslovak railway guards, border troops, uniformed police, and plainclothesmen had drawn a cordon of roadblocks around Cierna itself, up to the neighboring hamlet of Biel, a half-mile from the Cierna station. The Czechoslovak officers were relaxed and good-humored, and dozens of journalists slipped repeatedly around the roadblocks and into Cierna—where they were quickly discovered and politely driven back to a roadside café in Biel just outside the cordon.

Within the cordon, groups of Soviet signal troops were dispersed around camouflage-netted communication trucks, as well as other electronic and radio gear. Individual Russian soldiers meanwhile patrolled Cierna's weedy backyards, awing the curious village children.

Despite these and other precautions, a delegation of Kosice steelworkers, whose cars were turned back one morning at the Biel roadblock, steamed into the Cierna railyards later that day aboard a freight train. Draped on the train were banners in Russian reading *"Eto nashe delo"*—"This is our affair," an echo of Brezhnev's words when he had failed to save Novotny eight months earlier.

When Dubcek boarded the Soviet train to welcome the Russians, Brezhnev was furious at the sight of Czechoslovak photographers outside. The Soviet leaders had demanded that the meeting be held in total secrecy. When Brezhnev emerged from the train, he hugged and kissed General Svoboda in the traditional Russian style, but there were only cool handshakes for the other Czechoslovak leaders.

* Nine of the eleven full members of the Politburo, two alternate members, and two senior party secretaries. The two Politburo members who remained in Moscow were Andrei Kirilenko, Brezhnev's deputy in the party, and Dmitri Polyansky, first deputy prime minister under Kosygin.

Together, the two delegations walked the hundred yards from the railroad tracks, past police barriers restraining curious villagers in the station, to a two-story, tin-roofed, yellow-stucco building called the Junction Club, a social center for railwaymen. To the right of the entranceway, there was Cierna's only movie theater, which the night before had shown Jean-Luc Godard's science-fiction anti-Utopia, *Alphaville*. To the left, on the second floor, there was a banquet hall, fitted with a large glass-topped, baize-covered table across which, with the aid of six microphones, the trial of Czechoslovakia's leaders began.

"I know the Soviet comrades," Smrkovsky had said before leaving Prague, "and I can't believe they are capable of anything bad." But, on the very first day of the Cierna conference—as fifteen Soviet divisions moved toward Czechoslovakia from East Germany, Poland, and the Ukraine—Brezhnev presented an angry, four-hour indictment. He repeated all the attacks that had been made over the weeks on Cisar, Sik, Selucky, Goldstuecker, Kohout, and the heretics of press, radio, and television. He repeated the four demands of the Warsaw Letter—reimposition of censorship, suppression of the political clubs, arrest of the anti-Communists, a purge of the party liberals. He also repeated a demand which had been diplomatically omitted from the Warsaw Letter but which the Kremlin had long been pressing privately: that Czechoslovakia accept the permanent stationing of Soviet army garrisons on its territory.

Dubcek attempted to explain that democratization in Czechoslovakia would threaten neither its revived Communist party nor its alliance with Russia. He urged the Soviet leaders "not to stay in Cierna but walk around the country at your leisure and see how much your fears are illusory." But Stalin's heirs understood perhaps better than Dubcek the nature of their fears. Tempers soon flared on both sides; there were loud shouts and heated interruptions. At 10:30 that night, the Russians stomped out of the Junction Club, angry and alone. For more than fifteen minutes after the Soviet train had left Cierna, onlookers feared that the talks had ended. Finally, a weary Smrkovsky emerged from the Junction Club to say that the Russians would return.

After midnight, Dubcek, unable to sleep, paced the station

platform. "Take care of yourself, we need you," a railwayman advised him. "Don't worry, everything will end well," Dubcek replied, but continued his wandering until 3:30 A.M. Finally, he had to find an attendant to open the door of his railway coach, which had already been locked.

It was General Svoboda, on the second morning of the talks, who succeeded in persuading the Soviet leaders to think twice. He was the Czech they respected most, because of his wartime service alongside the Soviet Army. Politely but firmly, he insisted on Czechoslovakia's national sovereignty and criticized the indignity of Soviet troops remaining on its territory. Svoboda's speech doubtless impressed some of the Soviet leaders, but it did not prevent further angry quarrels. The Ukrainian Shelest was particularly brutal. When the two delegations broke for lunch, they again left the Junction Club separately—the Russians first, looking purposeful and somber, the Czechoslovaks afterward with the dispirited air of an American baseball team which has just lost for the third straight time in the World Series.

Prague officials had insisted from the beginning that the conference would last a day, or a day and a half at most *; it had been announced that Marshal Tito would arrive in Prague next day. The talks were utterly deadlocked, while a deputy commander of the Soviet "logistics exercises" surrounding Czechoslovakia declared that they were "among the largest ever staged."

Uneasiness spread throughout the country. Slovaks in Kosice recalled the pressures exerted by Nazi Germany on Czechoslovakia during the Munich crisis thirty years earlier. Radio Prague compared the situation "to that of a hospital operating theater during a heart transplant."

Dubcek and his colleagues had little choice but to continue talking. The afternoon session of the second day was less turbulent but equally indecisive. Both sides were exhausted, and the session broke off early, with agreement to continue a third day. Prague announced that Tito's visit had been postponed.

When the Soviet train arrived next morning, Brezhnev did not emerge from his compartment. Although there were reports that

* However, Cierna villagers all said, right at the start, that security officers had commandeered lodgings and facilities for three days.

he had suffered a mild heart attack, his indisposition was probably political. While the other members of both delegations gathered in the Junction Club, Dubcek boarded the Soviet train to see Brezhnev. They talked for two hours, and precisely what they said remains their secret. They evidently agreed, however, that no useful result could be achieved by further debates, with twenty-nine Communist leaders shouting at one another in the presence of dozens of members of their staffs; that neither side was prepared to yield unconditionally but mutual concessions were possible; and, therefore, that a face-saving compromise should be sought by private bargaining between a small group of top leaders.*

When Dubcek rejoined the conference at the Junction Club, the atmosphere relaxed immediately. At noon that day, the two delegations strolled around Cierna together, talking to the villagers, smiling for photographers, patting children's heads. It was made known that, after lunch, the negotiations would be entrusted to four top leaders of each side (Brezhnev, Kosygin, Podgorny, and Suslov for the Russians; Dubcek, Svoboda, Cernik, and Smrkovsky for Czechoslovakia).

So optimistic were the Czechoslovak leaders that at 3 P.M. a call went out to Kosice for newsmen and cameramen. They were told that the conferees were polishing up the final communiqué, that Dubcek would make a television statement and hold a news conference sometime after 5, and that there would be a ceremonial banquet for the two delegations at 8. At the roadside inn in Biel at 5:30, kitchen personnel were slaughtering suckling pigs

---

* According to accounts stemming from Czechoslovak liberal sources, Brezhnev realized by this time that he had been unable to split the Czechoslovak leadership and was also influenced by the threat of eighteen Western Communist parties to condemn Soviet interference. On the other hand, the Soviets later claimed that Dubcek at Cierna was speaking for a "right-wing minority" (with the conservatives hesitant to speak because of the vast popular pressure that had been built up). Subsequent events showed that the Russians did in fact have at least half a dozen reliable supporters among the sixteen Czechoslovak delegates and that the opinions of Western Communist parties counted relatively little. It therefore seems likely that the perceptible lightening of the atmosphere which followed the Brezhnev-Dubcek talk resulted from a shift in the majority of the Politburo, an offer of secret concessions by Dubcek, or both. However, it should be noted that, nearly two years after the event, the Soviets have yet to specify the "promises" which they allege that Dubcek made at Cierna. The likelihood is that they were vague.

for the banquet; the pigs were delivered to the Junction Club an hour later.

However, there was no agreement among the group of eight, even on a communiqué. At 7:35, the Soviet leaders again walked out of the Junction Club alone. When the Czechoslovak leaders finally emerged, Smrkovsky was asked what had gone wrong. All he could say was that the talks would continue a fourth day.

On the last day, August 1, after further haggling, Brezhnev made a new proposal: a joint meeting with the other signatories of the Warsaw Letter. Dubcek accepted the proposal, on condition that the meeting be held in Czechoslovakia and that neither the Warsaw Letter nor Prague's reply be discussed. The meeting with Ulbricht, Gomulka, and the others was set for Bratislava on August 3. The Cierna conference, after three and a half days of tense discussions involving twenty-nine senior Communist leaders, ended with a cryptic, anti-climactic communiqué. It declared that "a broad comradely exchange of views" had been "held in an atmosphere of complete frankness," with the aim of "strengthening traditional friendly relations" on the basis of "Marxism-Leninism and proletarian internationalism."

Dubcek, exhausted, did not speak publicly that evening. Surrounded by anxious workmen at the Kosice airport, he merely remarked, "We have not take a single step back. Everything today is as it was four days ago."

It was Svoboda who reported to the nation on television. His speech was filled with traditional Communist jargon, and it dismayed the Prague revolutionaries even more than had the Cierna communiqué. The feeling spread that there had been a sellout.

Once again, the students rallied. They hastily posted hand-drawn notices on trees, walls, and auto windshields, announcing a protest demonstration in the Old Town Square. The students converged on the monument to Hus and the Reformation Martyrs, with banners reading *"We Want the truth!"* and *"Freedom and Independence!"* As night fell, more than 10,000 people had filled the square. They chanted, "What happened at Cierna?" and "We want Dubcek!" Student leaders demanded to know why Ulbricht and Gomulka were being invited to Bratislava, but not Tito and Ceausescu, Czechoslovakia's friends.

The crowd was at fever pitch when Smrkovsky arrived at the square in a black limousine. Radio men set up a microphone for him on a baroque balcony overlooking the monument. "Tell us the truth!" the crowd shouted. His voice hoarse, Smrkovsky began slowly: "We met our Soviet friends and I will tell you what we said. . . ."

"They are not our friends!" somebody shouted, and there was a roar of approval. Smrkovsky tried to begin again, but a student cried: "For how much did you sell us to the Russians?"

Smrkovsky warned that he would leave if the crowd did not hear him out. "If I told you that I am not ashamed to look our citizens in the eye after Cierna," he asked, "would you believe me?" He calmed the anxious crowd only gradually. He told them that the Bratislava meeting would only last a day, and that Tito ("our very close friend") and Ceausescu would visit Prague the following week.

Smrkovsky said that at Cierna it had been "agreed that polemics, mutual criticism, mutual accusations lead to nothing and will be ended. . . . We will forget that there ever was any Warsaw meeting." He insisted that Czechoslovakia's freedom of the press "was not even discussed" at Cierna. The final departure of the 8,000 Soviet troops still in the country was a "detail." The main thing was that Czechoslovakia had won the right to its own way in domestic affairs.

Smrkovsky pleaded with the students, in grave, measured tones, for patience. He pointed to a church tower across the square: "Most of you are too young to remember that before 1945 there were two towers" on the church; the other tower had been destroyed in the brief Prague anti-Nazi uprising. Such destruction should not happen again. "In the next few days," Smrkovsky concluded, "you will learn more, and then you can judge whether we dealt honorably."

The demonstrators finally dispersed, in a mood of relief tinged with faint skepticism. But the day's events had shown once more —as had been shown repeatedly since the Dresden meeting four months earlier—how precarious was the position of the Communist reformers between their own people and their Stalinist antagonists.

Dubcek was cheerful on arriving in Bratislava railroad station the next day. "If I was optimistic yesterday," he told a cheering throng, "I am even more optimistic today. The greatest hurdle is behind us."

Attacks on Czechoslovakia had ceased in the Soviet press and everywhere else except East Germany. Prague officials told journalists that the Russians had agreed to withdraw their troops, to regard the Warsaw Letter as "null and void," and to permit the Czechoslovak Communists to retain full responsibility for their internal affairs. On the other side, the Czechoslovak press would voluntarily refrain from criticism of Soviet policies, somewhat in the manner of Finland. This seemed to most Czechs a small price to pay for freedom. Cisar asserted in Prague that at the end of the Cierna meeting "the Soviets assured us that they would succeed in persuading the other four party leaderships to accept the agreement."

The Russians—Brezhnev, Podgorny, Kosygin, Suslov, and Shelest—also seemed relaxed on arriving at Bratislava. This time, Brezhnev had kisses and bear hugs for all the Czechoslovak leaders. But the arrival of Ulbricht's group was frosty—formal handshakes, and nary a smile. Gomulka, too, was cool to his hosts. His first question to the Russians, moreover, was, "What are we doing here? I thought everything was settled in Warsaw."

Czechoslovak spokesmen assured everyone that the Brastilava conference would be a mere formality. They pointed to the schedule: a ceremonial wreathlaying at a Soviet war memorial at noon, signature of a joint declaration at the old Archepiscopal Palace at 3 P.M., and a great open-air friendship rally, with speeches by Dubcek and Brezhnev, immediately afterward.

There seemed ample grounds for Czechoslovak optimism. *Pravda* on the morning of August 3 had hailed the Cierna conference "as an example of how socialist countries solve their problems by means of a comradely exchange of opinion in an atmosphere of sincerity and mutual understanding." Even the East German press that day had ceased to criticize Prague. And, as the Bratislava conference began, the Czechoslovak Defense Ministry announced that the last Soviet troops had left the country.

There was glorious sunlight and a cloudless sky at noon on August 3, when the assembled Communist leaders, on schedule, climbed the Slavin Hill overlooking the Danube to lay their wreaths at the massive monument for 8,000 Soviet soldiers who had perished in the battles for Slovakia during World War II. The crowd gathered along the mall leading to the monument was quick to raise the cry of "Dubcek! Dubcek!" Three or four members of the Workers Militia then began calling, "Long Live the Soviet Union!" but there were no echoes. As a local brass band played Czechoslovak and Soviet national anthems before the monument, observers could see that Ulbricht, Gomulka, and Shelest were grim, Kadar and Suslov tense, Kosygin mournful. Brezhnev looked ill, with a curious twitch under his right eye. Only Dubcek seemed serene.

The small Archepiscopal Square, a graceful mingling of Renaissance and baroque styles, was jammed long before the scheduled arrival at 3 P.M. of the leaders to sign the declaration. Thousands of other Slovaks began filling up Bratislava's broadest crossroads, where platforms, public-address systems, banners, and national flags were already in place for the friendship rally.

But time passed, the skies darkened, and both crowds were suddenly drenched by a thunderstorm. By 6 P.M. the friendship rally had been canceled; instead, it was said, Dubcek and Brezhnev would speak from the balcony of the Archepiscopal Palace. Yet it was not until 7:30 that Communist leaders began arriving in the Palace Square. Immediately, the cry went up, "Dubcek! Dubcek!" ("The savior of our nation," one Slovak youth cried.) Brezhnev and Kosygin were also warmly greeted, but there were boos and hisses for Ulbricht, and the old German Stalinist was visibly disturbed.

The Bratislava Declaration was signed in the Palace Hall of Mirrors, where the Hapsburg Emperor Francis II in 1805 had signed the Peace of Pressburg dictated by Talleyrand ("because," a plaque in the Hall made clear, "of the superior force of France"). There were no speeches afterward.

The Bratislava Declaration proved to be a ragbag of platitudes, literally culled verbatim from the Moscow Declarations of 1957 and 1960, various Warsaw Pact communiqués, and other bloc statements which Czechoslovakia had signed previously. From the sea of jargon, Czechoslovak officials proudly fished out the phrase "equality, sovereignty and national independence." (Others later fished out the words "mutual aid and support.")

Moreover, as the Czechs had predicted, there was no mention of the Warsaw Letter or any of the accusations that had been made against their reformation.

Jiri Hajek, the Czechoslovak foreign minister, told a news conference that the Warsaw Letter now belonged to history. Asked to what it owed its rapid passage into history, Hajek replied: "To its contents." He assured journalists that Prague would not restore censorship. The question of stationing Soviet troops in Czechoslovakia "had not been raised."

At Bratislava station that evening, both the Russians and the Czechoslovak leaders seemed completely relaxed. There were hugs and kisses all around, and Brezhnev raised the arms of both Svoboda and Dubcek in a gesture of triumph. Smrkovsky embraced Suslov with surprising affection—because, Smrkovsky explained, Suslov had contributed so much to the agreements achieved at Cierna and Bratislava.

Brezhnev, who on arriving at Cierna six days earlier had raged at the sight of photographers, now leaned from the steps of the dark green Soviet train to give an impromptu interview to Bratislava television. He said that the conference had been a complete success and wished the people of Czechoslovakia good health and happiness. He recalled that he had first seen Bratislava at the end of the war, had been back several times since, was impressed by the city's progress, and hoped to return again.

Brezhnev and his colleagues returned to Moscow, where the Politburo formally approved the results of the Cierna and Bratislava conferences. A *Pravda* editorial of August 5 praised the meetings because they had shown that differences between Communist parties could be solved by "calm and reasonable, reflective and patient study." Brezhnev and Podgorny went off on vacation August 7 to Pitsunda on the Black Sea coast. Kosygin, too, retired to his summer villa in the woods thirty miles from Moscow.

In Prague, Marshal Tito finally arrived and was given tumultuous popular ovations. Ceausescu came later that week, signed a new friendship treaty, and also received enthusiastic popular acclaim. Between their two visits, Ulbricht came to Karlovy Vary to meet with Dubcek. The public did not cheer him; nor were his talks with Dubcek very successful. But the two men held a joint press conference on August 12, at which Ulbricht declared:

> The workers of Czechoslovakia have embarked on an historically important road toward the construction of socialism. . . . It is entirely normal that difficulties arise during such a transformation, and we do not consider this as too tragic in your case. . . . The difficulties can easily be surmounted.

In Budapest meanwhile, the senior Hungarian ideologist, Zoltan Komocsin, who had attended the Bratislava conference, now disclosed that "from the beginning the Hungarian Communists have sympathized with the aims of the Czechoslovak Communists" to create "a better and more attractive socialism."

"What is good for them," the Hungarian leader said, "is also good for us and for all the socialist countries."

The trial seemed over. The President of the United States left for his ranch in Texas. The American ambassador in Moscow left for vacation in Italy. The West German foreign minister went fishing in Norway. The commander of the NATO armies in Europe decided to visit Greece.

From Czechoslovakia, too, scores of thousands of vacationers departed for Mediterranean and Adriatic beaches. One of Dubcek's sons went to Egypt; his wife and the other two boys were planning to go to Yugoslavia. The vacationers included Ota Sik, Jiri Hajek, and many other Czechoslovak leaders. They had been under great strain for months and would need their energy for the splendid days ahead: for the party congress in September, and for the joyous birthday celebration planned for October 28, the fiftieth anniversary of the Czechoslovak Republic created by Thomas Mazaryk.

Somebody must have been telling lies about Alexander D. for without having done anything wrong he was arrested one fine morning. It was the morning of August 21. Overnight, Stalin's heirs had invaded and occupied Czechoslovakia.

CHAPTER 17

The Empire's
New Clothes

The secret Soviet decision to invade Czechoslovakia appears to have been taken sometime between August 12 and 15, probably on August 13. Where and precisely by whom the decision was made remains a mystery. The Soviet party Central Committee was not convened until late October. The initial announcement of the invasion was made by Tass, the Soviet news agency, rather than the Soviet government as such; and the ideological justification for the invasion was provided in an unsigned article in *Pravda*. None of the Soviet leaders spoke, to justify the occupation in his own name, until a month later.

On August 12, the day of Ulbricht's visit to Dubcek at Karlovy Vary, the Soviet defense minister, Marshal Grechko, completed a review of the maneuvers which had ended three days earlier in the area of Minsk, Byelorussia. Another set of maneuvers had just begun in the Western Ukraine and the "southern regions" of Poland and East Germany.

The whereabouts and activities of both the Soviet political and military leaders on August 13 and 14 remain obscure. However, on August 14, criticism of Czechoslovakia was resumed by two

Soviet newspapers: the Writers' Union organ, *Literaturnaya Gazeta*, and the Red Army paper, *Krasnaya Zvezda*. That afternoon, the leader of the Italian Communist party, Luigi Longo, suddenly arrived in Moscow, presumably in an effort to prevent an invasion. Janos Kadar appears to have visited Brezhnev and Podgorny in Pitsunda on the same day.

On August 15, several of the vacationing Soviet political leaders were seen back in Moscow. The same day, Marshal Grechko and his chief political commissar, General Alexei Yepishev, arrived in East Germany to inspect the Soviet armies massed there. Marshal Ivan Yakubovsky, the Warsaw Pact commander in chief, was waiting to meet them at the airport.

The next day, Grechko, Yakubovsky, and Yepishev went off to inspect the Soviet forces in southern Poland. They were greeted there by General Sergei Shtemenko, the new Warsaw Pact chief of staff.* That morning, *Pravda*'s ranking propagandist, Yuri Zhukov, had launched the psychological buildup for the invasion with a 2,500-word article. By the end of the day, Dubcek in Prague had delivered an anxious speech warning his people against "excesses" and proclaiming unity with Moscow to be "the alpha and omega" of his policy.

The Soviet marshals appear to have had few illusions as to what the invasion would entail. According to letters by Soviet soldiers later found in Czechoslovakia, Grechko told the troops in Poland: "You are going to Czechoslovakia. You will not be welcomed with flowers."

From a purely military standpoint, the invasion on the night of August 20 was a triumph of Soviet arms, with some token assistance from East German, Polish, Hungarian, and Bulgarian units. The invading armies, estimated to number more than 250,-000 men, profited from the dress rehearsal conducted under the

---

* Shtemenko, Stalin's wartime chief of staff, was very much a "political" officer rather than a military professional; under Stalin, he was a marshal and a deputy defense minister. Immediately after Stalin's death, he was demoted to colonel-general and banished to the provinces. He did not appear in Moscow until 1962, and only became prominent again in 1965, when he helped launch the campaign to prettify Stalin's war record.

Strangely, Shtemenko's appointment as Warsaw Pact chief of staff was announced in East Berlin, rather than in Moscow, on August 4, 1968, the day after the Bratislava conference.

guise of "maneuvers" in June and July; they were also assisted by the Soviet advisers who had remained in the Czechoslovak Army and security police throughout the Prague spring. At 1 A.M. on August 21, the Czechoslovak party Presidium ordered the Czechoslovak Army of 175,000 men to offer no military resistance. Thus, there were fewer frontier incidents or casualties than when Hitler's Wehrmacht had occupied Bohemia and Moravia on March 15, 1939.

Politically, however, the invasion provided yet another demonstration of the Soviet leaders' ineptitude. Czechoslovak Communist conservatives, led by Indra and Bilak, had been assigned to depose Dubcek on the night of August 20 and then to "invite" the occupation of their country; but they bungled the assignment and before long, in the face of Czechoslovak popular outrage, were compelled to deny any part in the Kremlin plot. The Soviet armies thus arrived in Czechoslovakia in response to an anonymous "invitation" which never was signed.

Although the KGB kidnapped Dubcek, Smrkovsky, Cernik, Kriegel, and other reformers, President Svoboda refused to lend his name to the formation of a quisling government in Prague. He insisted on going to Moscow on August 23 and, once in the Kremlin, refused to negotiate with the Soviet leaders until his kidnapped colleagues were released.

From August 21 to 27, the invading armies encountered an amazing and unprecedented passive resistance from the 14 million people of Czechoslovakia. The resistance was led, in the streets, by the students. It was directed by the journalists of Czechoslovak radio and television, using emergency military transmitters. Through their efforts, the occupation and resistance were transmitted "live" to the outside world through the European television network.*

Neither the Politburo nor the Soviet conscripts occupying Czechoslovakia were psychologically prepared for this stunning passive resistance, which grew stronger with each passing hour. The resistance compelled the Soviet leaders to release Dubcek and his colleagues, and to recognize them anew—in the Moscow

---

* The hour-by-hour drama of invasion week is best described in *The Black Book*, prepared by the Czechoslovak Academy of Sciences, and the individual accounts by Ladislav Mnacko and Joseph Wechsberg (see bibliography).

agreement of August 27—as the legitimate heads of the Czechoslovak party and state. For their part, the Czechoslovak Communist leaders (with the exception of Kriegel) agreed to accept the "temporary" Soviet occupation, to curb the press and radio, and to take various other steps toward what the Kremlin chose to call "normalization" of Czechoslovakia.

Although Czechoslovak citizens at all levels—from Dubcek down to factory workers—sought for many months afterward to maintain the unity and spirit of the Prague spring, the Moscow Agreement proved to be decisive. Thereafter, employing their various pressures in more deliberate fashion, the Soviet rulers gradually succeeded in dividing the Czechoslovak Communist leadership, imposing concession after concession, and ultimately demoralizing the great mass of Czechs and Slovaks.

Nevertheless, the week of August 21–27 constituted the empire's gravest shock since 1956, in some respects an even greater shock than the intervention which crushed the Hungarian Revolution. In Prague in 1968, unlike Budapest in 1956, there could be no pretense that the situation had gotten out of control, that "bourgeois" politicians and clerics were returning to power, that "fascist" elements were hanging the "honest Communists" of the security police, that the government was preparing to leave the Warsaw Pact and declare the country a neutral state. The Soviet pretense that Dubcek and his fellow reformers represented only a "right-wing opportunist minority" (*Pravda*, August 22) in the Czechoslovak Communist leadership failed to last the week.

Despite fifteen years of Novotny's gray rule, despite all their efforts in the spring and summer of 1968 to locate or create a substantial pro-Kremlin Communist faction in Czechoslovakia, the Soviet leaders found themselves intervening against the virtually total resistance of 14 million Czechs and Slovaks, including 1.3 million Communist party members and their highest leaders. By intervening in this manner, Brezhnev and his colleagues destroyed within a week the pro-Russian sentiments which had existed among the Czechs and Slovaks for centuries. Many were the Czechoslovak mothers who took their small children to view their Soviet tanks in their streets, telling them: "I want you to remember this sight for the rest of your life."

The invasion was condemned, in the strongest terms, by virtually everyone who was not directly dependent on the Kremlin's favors: by the Italian Communist party as well as Pope Paul, by Herbert Marcuse as well as Richard Nixon, by Enver Hoxha as well as Bertrand Russell. Although Fidel Castro and Ho Chi Minh, whose militant activities required Soviet support, approved the Russian intervention, Chou En-lai called the Soviet leaders "fascists," Lin Piao called them "the new tsars."

In Rumania, Ceausescu mobilized the army and formed new para-military units, while Maurer and Manescu prodded President Johnson into warning the Kremlin against "unleashing the dogs of war" in the Balkans. Tito told the Soviet ambassador that there was a Yugoslav bullet waiting for every Warsaw Pact soldier who dared cross his frontier. The Czechoslovak Embassy in East Berlin received 2,500 letters of support from East Germans during invasion week, while in Poland, despite the pressure of Moczar's police, Jerzy Andrzejewski (the author of *Ashes and Diamonds*) and other intellectuals declared their solidarity with Czechoslovakia in open letters.

Historians may long dispute the motives which led Stalin's heirs deliberately to incur such universal odium, to evoke a suspicion of Soviet policy deeper than at any time since Khrushchev had begun his "opening" to the world in 1955.

From afar, it appeared to many that the principal Soviet motive was strategic: to maintain Czechoslovak territory as the empire's westernmost advanced military base. The influence exerted by Grechko, Yakubovsky, and other Soviet marshals during 1968 and 1969 was doubtless formidable. The first Soviet public figure to praise the invasion, long before either Brezhnev or Kosygin was ready to do so, was Marshal Konev on August 23. *Pravda* during the crisis of invasion week did not hesitate to cite Bismarck's alleged remark that "Whoever rules Bohemia holds the key to Europe.* And, early in 1969, one of the highest leaders of the

* The Legislative Reference Service of the U.S. Library of Congress attempted to discover when, if ever, Bismarck made such a remark. It was unable to find any such statement either in Bismarck's works or in the memoirs of his contemporaries. The "quotation" first appeared at the start of the twentieth century in works by Czech historians and statesmen, including Dr. Beneš, who used it as part of his argumentation at Versailles. The "quotation" thus appears to be an ironic example of nationalist propaganda boomeranging against its originators.

Yugoslav Communist party warned Western visitors not to over-estimate the influence of such Soviet civilian politicians as Suslov, Kirilenko, or Kosygin. "The political summit in the Soviet Union today," the Yugoslav leader said, "consists of Brezhnev, Grechko and Yakubovsky. Nobody else matters."

Only the opening of the Soviet archives may disclose whether, indeed, as many Western analysts believed, the occupation of Czechoslovakia was chiefly motivated by sheer militarism. On the ground—in Prague and Bratislava, and in Moscow as well—the Kremlin's primary motive appeared to be less strategic than political. Czechoslovakia had existed without a Soviet garrison since 1945, and military possession of its territory was considerably less essential in the age of supersonic rockets. Militarily, Russia might have tolerated even a neutral Czechoslovakia on its borders as easily as it had long tolerated a neutral Finland and an anti-Communist Turkey.

For the peoples of the empire, and doubtless their rulers as well, the issue in Czechoslovakia was liberty, not real estate. From the Dresden meeting onward, the Soviet leaders made it plain, in their repeated demands for the reimposition of censorship, that the cardinal "danger" in Czechoslovakia was freedom of the press —a freedom which not merely permitted independent criticism of the bases of orthodox Communist rule, but which gathered together in a new community millions of individuals who had been atomized in fearful isolation. To paraphrase Marx's words on a similar occasion, in Czechoslovakia in 1968 the revolution-aries suddenly counted themselves and discovered that they were the nation. As in 1848, the discovery leaped beyond the bounds of a single state, for Czechoslovakia was part of a repressive im-perial system no less vulnerable than that of Metternich.

In 1968 and afterward, Soviet propagandists often indicated the Kremlin's particular resentment of Dubcek's claim to be intro-ducing "socialism with a human face." Indeed, the very existence of such an alternative model immediately posed the question of what sort of "socialism" was represented by the faces of Brezh-nev, Shelest, and Marshal Yakubovsky.

Back in 1966, in his Budapest apartment overlooking the Dan-ube, the old Hungarian Marxist philosopher Georg Lukacs was asked whether, sooner or later, one of the ruling Communist leaders would have to face the problem of freedom. "Certainly," Lukacs replied, "and the first leader who does so will remain in power for 25 years." The tragedy which Lukacs did not foresee was that the first Communist leader to face the problem of freedom—and in doing so to gain the enduring affection of millions—proved to be a Slovak, Alexander Dubcek, rather than a Russian. Stalin's Soviet heirs, who in overthrowing Khrushchev had refused to confront their own past, were even less prepared to face a future in which their personal powers and imperial prerogatives might be called into question.

Viewed from Prague or Moscow, the invasion of Czechoslovakia was directed primarily at crushing the hopes that the Prague spring had aroused throughout the empire—the hope that Communism might yet be reformed from above without violence, the hope that Soviet leaders themselves might preside (as Khrushchev had occasionally seemed prepared to preside) over the liquidation of Stalin's empire of fear. Such hopes were highest in Czechoslovakia and the countries nearest to it—East Germany, Hungary, and Poland, the rebel nations of the mid-fifties—but the hopes were far from nonexistent in Russia itself, as the conduct both of the Soviet regime and of individual Soviet citizens was soon to show.

Confronted with the challenge of the Prague spring, the Soviet leadership could find no more adequate response than military force—and no justification less threadbare than the so-called Brezhnev Doctrine of "limited sovereignty." As explained by *Pravda* on September 25 and others later, neither state sovereignty nor international law nor the principle of self-determination mattered if any Communist-ruled country attempted to depart from what the "camp" regarded as "socialism." Then (as in fact Brezhnev and Kadar had already hinted in their Kremlin speeches on July 3, 1968), the imperial armies had both "the right and the duty" to impose their will even on states governed entirely by Communists.

To be sure, as the Russian worker Anatoly Marchenko had pointed out in July, the Soviet rulers did not dare (yet?) exercise their self-proclaimed "right" of intervention against 700 million Chinese, whose armies were trained in guerrilla war and whose scientists had produced nuclear weapons. However, Brezhnev's doctrine was a clear threat not merely to Rumania, Yugoslavia, and Albania (which denounced it furiously), but to all those young Communists in Poland, East Germany, and elsewhere who, as unknown in 1968 as Dubcek had been in 1958, might at some future time aspire to shape their own destiny.

It had been a popular belief, in the late fifties and until August 20, 1968, that "liberalization" in Eastern Europe might precede and compel change in the Soviet Union itself. The belief was based partly on the indisputable influence of Tito's Yugoslavia, partly on the resilience of older tradition in Poland and Hungary. In fact, this belief (shared in West and East alike) ran counter to the facts of 1955 and 1956. For then it had been Khrushchev—by his reconciliation with Tito, his meeting with Western leaders at Geneva, and his denunciation of Stalin at the 20th Party Congress—who had set off the "Polish October" and the Hungarian Revolution.

The Czechoslovak experience, and the Brezhnev Doctrine, made it plain that the benificent influence of the East European Communists on the Kremlin was limited, and that no great improvement was possible in Eastern Europe without corresponding change in Russia.

The London *Economist* argued in the aftermath of the invasion that "in stifling freedom in Prague, the men in the Kremlin may have sown the seeds of revolution in their own country." This remained to be seen. The *Economist's* conclusion, however, seemed indisputable: namely, that the future of freedom throughout the empire now lay "with the Russian people and their readiness to take their destiny in their own hands."

Such readiness would not come easily of itself, as the "inevitable" result of what were presumed to be irreversible, impersonal historic processes. In invading Czechoslovakia, Brezhnev and his colleagues destroyed what had become a traditional faith (in East and West alike) in the inevitability of progressive evolution of Soviet Russia after Stalin's death.

Under the impact of Soviet de-Stalinization and of Khrushchev's peculiar charm, it had been increasingly imagined that Soviet power would soon "mellow" and "erode" of itself (perhaps under the impact of the arms race, or else of what was loosely called *détente*)—that Russia was progressing irreversibly toward rationality, restraint, and traditional norms in its foreign policies, as well as toward more humane and responsive government of its own subjects. The Soviet Union, it was argued, had advanced from famine and scarcity to relative abundance; the old Stalinist ideology had lost credibility and relevance; and the new generation of scientists, managers, and technocrats was gradually compelling changes in the Soviet economic system which in turn would force modification of the political dictatorship.

Such assumptions—tenaciously maintained even in the face of the trial of Sinyavsky, the harassment of Solzhenitsyn, and the Middle East War—were clearly untenable after the invasion of Czechoslovakia. It became evident, to rulers and ruled alike, that whatever the Soviet people were to achieve, they would have to achieve by their own hard and lonely struggle. For the post-Khrushchev regime in the Kremlin, although unwilling to sanction a full-fledged return to the mass terror and paranoia of the Stalin years, was as plainly a deliberate "restoration" of the "old days" as the reign of Alexander III (1881–1895) embodied a conscious effort to reimpose the autocratic order of Nicholas I (1825–1852).

There were all too many reasons for the regression. The Soviet Union was a great power stubbornly embattled on two fronts, Western and Chinese; its rulers feared that any domestic disarray would be exploited by their rivals abroad. The Soviet state was a multinational empire, in which harsh centralism appeared the simplest response to nationalist stirrings on the periphery. The ruling generation of Soviet politicians was one of particular mediocrity, for it consisted of precisely those members of the party, state, army, and police apparatus capable of surviving or rising during Stalin's blood purges. The older generations of the intelligentsia were even more thoroughly decimated, terrorized, or corrupted, so that the young seemed to lack leaders. In fact, two world wars, the Civil War, two emigrations, successive purges, and leveling economic policies had "decapitated" Russian society as no other in modern history, destroying or atomizing the very groups and classes which elsewhere (including nineteenth-century Russia) set moral and cultural standards and were the bearers of liberal ideas.

In Soviet society at large, there had been a paralysis or atrophy of what might be called the political sense—the ability of an individual to relate the grim, inchoate details of social life to a larger, coherent political framework and to draw independent conclusions in theory and practice. This political sense, as well as the capacity for civil courage, had been deadened by decades of demeaning propaganda, censorship, police control, exaltation of brutality, and thorough isolation from the living world outside. It was the kind of atrophy familiar to students of postwar Germany, where the "middle generation" was (with very few exceptions) hopelessly disoriented by only twelve years of Hitler, Goebbels, and Himmler.

The disorientation in Russia was even more grave after half a century; and it was a kind of miracle that young men like Vladimir Bukovsky and Yuri Galanskov had nevertheless arisen to reenact the protests of the first radical "circles" in tsarist Russia a century earlier. Yet such young men seemed relatively rare, and those who sympathized with them were inhibited not merely by the sanctions of the party and the KGB but by the indifference of large Soviet masses to purely political issues so long as the regime could continue the slow but steady raising of living standards. For many ordinary Russians in August 1968, the Soviet regime's decisive argument was that "the Czechs live far better than we do."

In the months which followed, it became obvious that—contrary to previous theory—the very existence of profound contradictions and rising libertarian aspirations in Russia might well (as they did a century ago) lead its rulers to repression rather than reform. Some form of military rule, a reassertion of police power, or a new "strong man" had to be considered as being at least as possible in the decade ahead as the "erosion from despotism" or the "violent upthrust of liberty" which George F. Kennan had, in 1951, regarded as among the likelier consequences of Stalin's death.

Nevertheless, as Brezhnev proclaimed his imperial doctrine,

and as the legions of Grechko and Yakubovsky carried out almost continuous maneuvers in Eastern Europe for nearly a year, the passivity of the great Russian masses was less surprising than the insecurity of the regime in the face of increasingly determined resistance, passive and active, by individual Soviet citizens. Such resistance seemed to corroborate the initial judgment of Dr. Ivan Svitak, the Czech philosopher, who declared, barely a week after the Soviet invasion of his country, that

> The intervention was not against a nation of 14 million, but *against the Russian intellectuals.* Our hope for change is within the Soviet Union; that will be the end of Soviet imperialism. . . . The invasion of Czechoslovakia was an act of fear by the Soviet bureaucratic and military elite against their own intelligentsia, against their own people. . . .

Even some of the conscripted Russian youths who had carried out the invasion appear to have been swayed by the Czechoslovak resistance. The initial occupation units, it seems, had to be replaced after a few days. On August 22, Ladislav Mnacko watched the Russian soldiers in his native Bratislava:

> They sat there on their tanks and armored cars, afraid to look people in the face, patiently suffering the names they were being called and allowing the youngsters to paint anti-occupation slogans on their tanks. They sat behind their machine guns and gazed into the middle distance, each of them looking in a different direction. Were they ashamed? Or afraid?

The German novelist Heinrich Böll watched the Russian soldiers on their tanks that week in Prague. "I will be thinking about their faces for a long time," he said afterward. "They were in complete despair."

Böll, a personal friend of many Russian writers, also believed that "the genuine motive" for the intervention was fear of "opposition within the Soviet Union, the opposition of the intellectuals,"—fear especially of freedom of the press. "Take the Solzhenitsyn case," Böll said. "If he were suddenly allowed to publish, an entire avalanche would start to move."

In Moscow, Yevgeny Yevtushenko sent a telegram to Brezhnev and Kosygin on the night of August 21. "I can't sleep. I can't go on living. . . . I have many personal friends in Czechoslovakia and I don't know how I will be able to look into their eyes if I should ever meet them again." The Soviet cellist, Mstislav Rostropovitch, at a concert in London, played the Dvořák Cello Concerto and finished with tears in his eyes.

Soviet party organizers attempted vainly to obtain letters or resolutions of support for the invasion from the Russian elite. Even in the Governing Board of the Writers Union, despite two months of pressure, Tvardovsky, Konstantin Simonov, and Leonid Leonov refused to sign. Communist party cells in some of Russia's most prestigious atomic and space institutes were reportedly among the 800 party organizations which sent formal letters of protest to the Central Committee. At the Academic Village in Novosibirsk on August 25, slogans denouncing the invasion were painted on the walls. In Leningrad, they were painted on the statues.

However, the party had sent thousands of professional agitators to factories and villages, to "explain" that West Germany had been on the verge of invading Czechoslovakia—but that this "Nazi plot" had been nipped in the bud by Soviet intervention. As a result, the Soviet press during the week after the invasion was filled not only with shrill official calls for "liquidating 40,000 counterrevolutionaries" in Czechoslovakia, but with stereotyped statements of support signed by carpenters, lathe-operators, tractor-drivers, milkmaids.

Seven Moscow democrats decided (as one of them put it later) "to break through the sludge of unbridled lies and cowardly silence, and thereby demonstrate that not all the citizens of our country are in agreement with the violence carried out in the name of the Soviet people."

One of the seven was Larissa Daniel, who quit work on August 21, telling her superiors she was on strike. In deciding to demonstrate in Red Square four days afterward, she said, "I did not act on impulse. . . . I knew fully what the consequences might be. . . . I was faced with the choice of acting or keeping silent. To me, to have kept silent . . . would have been tantamount to lying."

Pavel Litvinov also understood what the consequences would be. "I knew it beforehand, when I made up my mind to go to Red Square. . . . I was positive that the employees of the KGB would stage a provocation against me. . . . I knew it from the person who followed me. I read my verdict in his eyes when he followed me into the metro. . . ." Nevertheless, "there was never any question" in Litvinov's mind that he had to demonstrate against the invasion.

There were five other demonstrators: Konstantin Babitsky, a linguistic scholar; Vadim Delone, the young poet (who had been among the group in Pushkin Square which had protested the arrest of Galanskov and Ginsburg at the start of the Jubilee Year); Vladimir Dremlyuga, a twenty-eight-year old factory worker; Victor Feinberg, an art critic from Leningrad; and Natalia Gorbanevskaya, a tiny poetess and the mother of two infants.

They came at noon on Sunday August 25 to Red Square, to the parapet called Lobnoe Mesto ("the Place of Skulls") in front of the Cathedral of St. Basil the Blessed. On this parapet, before Peter the Great opened his "window to the West," Ivan the Terrible and other Muscovite tsars had performed their executions.

They sat down on the parapet and unfurled their homemade banners. One of the banners, in Czech, read *"Long live a free and independent Czechoslovakia!"* The other banners were in Russian: *"Shame on the Occupiers!" "Free Dubcek!" "Hands off Czechoslovakia!"* and *"For your freedom and ours!"* The last slogan was that of the Polish insurrection of 1830 against Tsar Nicholas I.

Natalia Gorbanevskaya has described what happened when the banners were unfurled:

Almost immediately, whistles were heard from all corners of the square, and plainclothes agents of the KGB came running towards us. . . . They shouted: "These are all dirty kikes (*Zhidy*)" and "Beat the anti-Soviets!" We sat quietly and offered no resistance. They tore the banners from our hands and beat Victor Feinberg on the face until the blood flowed, breaking some of his teeth. Pavel Litvinov was beaten on the face with a heavy bag. A small Czechoslovak flag was ripped from my hands and destroyed. They shouted: "Get out of here, you scum!" We remained seated.

After a few minutes, automobiles arrived, and every one except me was pushed into them. I had my three-month-old son with me, and for this reason they did not seize me immediately. I remained on the parapet of Lobnoe Mesto for about ten minutes. Then I was beaten up in a car. . . .

All who had been detained were searched that night under charges of "group activities in flagrant violation of public order". . . . After the search I was released, apparently because I must care for my children.*

The critic Victor Feinberg, who had been badly disfigured, was dispatched to a mental hospital in Leningrad. The other five were brought to trial on October 9 in a small, ochre, three-story courthouse on the Moscow River.

Only twelve close relatives of the five defendants were admitted to the forty-seat courtroom, which was barred to the public and foreign press. However, some 150 of the defendants' friends and supporters were outside on the street before the trial began. They included not only the hardy nucleus of the informal "democratic movement" led by Pyotr Yakir, General Grigorenko, and Yesenin-Volpin, but scores of new faces, most of whom seemed to be young engineers and intellectuals.

Among the familiar faces on the street, however, were many of the same dark-suited KGB agents who had patrolled the Ginsburg-Galanskov trial ten months earlier. Their supervisor, in fact, was the same black-bearded young man who had then told the press that the "mystery witness" Brocks-Sokolov was carrying pictures of Andrei Sinyavsky and Yuli Daniel.

General Grigorenko, Yakir, and their friends had prepared a petition protesting the closed trial. But the black-bearded KGB man began tearing up the petition after fifty-six Russians had signed it. Grigorenko insisted that the agent accompany him to the nearest police station so that he could file a formal complaint. The general, swinging his cane to military measure, marched the agent (and a troop of curious followers) along the river and across a bridge to the station. Once there, however, the agent

* The charges were based on the September 1966 decree against which Shostakovich, Academician Sakharov, and others had unsuccessfully protested. Once Natalia Gorbanevskaya's infant boy had passed the age of a year and a half, she was seized and forcibly confined in a mental hospital. She is perfectly sane.

immediately passed through into a backroom, while police outside refused to permit Grigorenko to enter or to file a complaint. The general had nonetheless made his point about the hypocrisies of Soviet "legality."

On the second day of the trial, the KGB agents on the street were reinforced by organized workers' groups sent from nearby factories, who had been told by their Communist party chiefs that the democrats outside the courtroom were in the pay of foreign "imperialists." Despite intermittent rain, more than fifty democrats maintained a thirteen-hour vigil outside the court on the second day. But they were now outnumbered by KGB men, relays of workers' groups, and individuals who had come to vent their hostility. The divided crowd engaged all day in passionate arguments which ranged the full emotional and political scale. A bleached blonde in her mid-fifties screamed, "If it were up to me, you would all be shot, like in the old days!" A burly worker denounced the unkempt beards of some of the democrats, and was quietly reminded that Marx had worn a similar beard.

Continuous political discussion milled around General Grigorenko. The tall, erect soldier obviously fascinated both the workers and the young plainclothesmen, who found it difficult to understand how a Communist party member, Civil War fighter, and disabled veteran of World War II could now oppose Kremlin policy.

Grigorenko patiently explained that the essence of the matter, both at the trial and in Czechoslovakia, was free speech. "But we are speaking freely here," a worker said, "nobody is stopping us." Grigorenko answered that free speech also meant the right to publish freely, to hold discussions and meetings expressing views different from those of the nation's rulers. "That would be anarchy!" an old woman cried.

A younger man, ignoring her cry, said quietly that freedom was relative and subjective, and that total freedom existed nowhere. Grigorenko suggested that he read Alexander Herzen. The young man said he had. "Read him again," Grigorenko replied, recalling that Herzen had condemned the tsarist armies' suppression of both the Hungarian Revolution of 1848–49 and the Polish uprising of 1863. On and on the discussion raged. At nightfall, one young democrat, the historian Andrei Amalric, quietly observed: "It is hard to say what the effect of the trial may be throughout Russia. But here today at least, a few frozen minds may have been moved to think."

Inside the courtroom, Pavel Litvinov, Larissa Daniel, and their friends had firmly denied any "conspiracy" and reiterated their disapproval of the invasion of Czechoslovakia. At the end of the second day, Prosecutor Valentin Drel demanded three years at forced labor for Delone and Dremlyuga, who had figured in previous trials. However, returning to tsarist penal traditions, the prosecutor urged compulsory exile for the three principal defendants, who were first offenders. He recommended three years for Babitsky, four years for Mrs. Daniel, and five years for Litvinov. The next morning, they were sentenced accordingly.

In his final words after sentence had been pronounced, Pavel Litvinov discussed Article 125 of the Soviet Constitution, which guarantees the rights of free speech, press, and assembly "in the interests of socialism." The prosecutor interrupted to complain that this was irrelevant.

"This is relevant," Litvinov insisted. "Who is to judge what is in the interest of socialism and what is not? . . . Perhaps the prosecutor, who spoke with admiration, almost tenderness, of those who beat us and insulted us. . . . Evidently, such people are supposed to know what socialism is and what is counterrevolution. That is what I find terrible, and that is why I went to Red Square. That is what I have fought against, and what I shall continue to fight against for the rest of my life. . . ."

Pavel Litvinov was exiled to Siberia, as his grandfather Maxim had been under Tsar Nicholas II in 1901. But when his Aunt Tatyana and other relatives emerged from the courtroom, many with tear-stained faces, more than a hundred supporters greeted them with flowers, embraces, and kisses.

"True, it was a very small demonstration," the Soviet writer Anatoly Kuznetsov * later commented, "but in Russian terms they were acting in the same way as the Christian martyrs of

---

* For Kuznetsov, "the wailing of all the sirens in occupied Prague" on August 21 was the end. That day, he began making preparations to leave Russia. A year later, he managed to reach Britain and obtain political asylum.

ancient times. . . . All Russia heard about them and respects their bravery."

In Russia's vast silence, the hardy little band who had deliberately sacrificed themselves by demonstrating in Red Square appeared to be virtually alone in their courage. Yet, barely a hundred days after the conviction of Pavel Litvinov and Larissa Daniel, another young Russian attempted to commit an act of even greater daring—once again, in direct response to tragedy in Czechoslovakia.

By the end of 1968, such Prague liberals as Kriegel, Foreign Minister Hajek, and Interior Minister Pavel had been dismissed; Ota Sik, Goldstuecker, Liehm, and others were already in emigration. Husak had emerged as leader of the "realists" who sought, by conscious collaboration with the Kremlin, to preserve a "Hungarian" status for Czechoslovakia and avoid a Stalinist terror.

However, the "big four" of the Prague spring—Dubcek, Cernik, Svoboda, and Smrkovsky—had held together. In December, Husak launched a campaign to remove Smrkovsky as president of the National Assembly. Once again, as if the country had not been occupied, Prague students took to the streets for massive demonstrations of protest. But the Kremlin made clear its approval of Husak's initiative, and on January 8, 1969, Smrkovsky was removed.

Eight days later, on January 16, a twenty-one-year-old Prague student named Jan Palach set himself afire with gasoline in the center of Wenceslas Square. He made clear before his death on January 19 that he had deliberately sacrificed himself in protest against the Soviet occupation. Palach's funeral, a solemn ceremony held in the oldest courtyard of Charles University, was yet another massive, although tragic demonstration of the Czechoslovak national unity in support of the ideals of the Prague spring.

On the day after Palach's death, in distant Leningrad a twenty-two-year-old Soviet Army Engineers lieutenant named Ilyin left his post without reporting back to his unit to return his pistols. He went to Moscow, where a festive welcome was being prepared by the Kremlin leaders for four astronauts who had just completed a linkup of two spaceships. Lieutenant Ilyin borrowed a police

captain's uniform from a relative, in order to watch the astronauts' welcome to the Kremlin on January 22 more closely.
When the motorcade started from Vnukovo Airport, the four
triumphant astronauts were leading it in an open car. Directly
behind them, in a closed ZIL-112 limousine, were Brezhnev and
Podgorny. Lieutenant Ilyin, in his borrowed blue police uniform
with red piping, posted himself to wait for them just inside the
Kremlin's Borovitsky Gate. There, the motorcade would have to
slow down in order to climb a narrow 30-foot ramp, go through
the medieval archway, and make two successive sharp turns.

The motorcade reached the Borovitsky Gate shortly after 2
P.M. The returning astronauts' open car entered first, followed
by escort motorcyclists. A closed ZIL-112 limousine followed.
Through its frosted windowpanes, Lieutenant Ilyin could see a
burly face with thick black hair and bushy black eyebrows. From
his police holsters, he whipped two pistols and fired six shots,
wounding the chauffeur and an escort motorcyclist, before he was
clubbed into unconsciousness by KGB Kremlin guards.

Only a handful of Russians, and a Mongolian Communist from
a great distance, witnessed the scene, but rumors spread fast. By
the next day, Tass was compelled to state (without giving further
details) that a "provocation" had taken place, supposedly aimed
at four other astronauts riding in a closed ZIL-112 limousine. One
of them, General Gregory Beregovoy, bore a facial resemblance
to Brezhnev.*

Soviet officials made strong efforts to suppress all details of the
assassination attempt inside the Kremlin Gate. At the customary
scientific press conference for the returning astronauts on January
24, foreign journalists submitted numerous written questions about
the episode. Alexei Leonov, one of the astronauts in Beregovoy's
car, was chosen to answer all the questions at once. All he did
was to loosely paraphrase Tass. Even Leonov's vague remarks
were not printed in the Soviet press.

---

* It was unthinkable that anyone in Russia would have risked his life to kill
any of the astronauts, who were immensely popular. Furthermore, the wounding
of the motorcyclist suggested that the shots had ricocheted off bulletproof glass,
the kind of glass used in Politburo cars. (The chauffeur of the heated limousine
would have had his side vent open, in the sub-zero weather, to prevent fogging
of his windshield.)

After the Tass bulletin of January 23, 1969, and despite a *Washington Post* dispatch one week later reporting the essential facts, there was total official silence on the case for fourteen months. Only on March 20, 1970, was Ilyin's name mentioned for the first time in the Soviet press, in a brief statement announcing that he had been declared a "schizophrenic" and confined to a "strict" asylum. Even then, no other details were given—neither his first name, nor the fact that he was an army officer.

The Kremlin leaders had good reason to suppress all news of the young lieutenant who had attempted to assassinate Brezhnev. For Ilyin's act had a terrible precedent in Russian history: the attempt on April 4, 1866, by the student Dmitri Karakozov to assassinate Tsar Alexander II. That was the first of the terrorist acts by desperate revolutionaries who ultimately did kill Alexander II in 1881 and a long list of grand dukes, tsarist ministers, army generals, and police chiefs over the next three decades.

The student Karakozov's motivations in 1866 were known to every Soviet schoolboy a century later. Karakozov's act marked and symbolized the turn of Russian democrats, radicals, and socialists away from hope in liberal reform from above and toward terror as a means of awakening the Russian people to a struggle against autocracy.

The political circumstances of Karakozov's act were remarkably similar to those of Lieutenant Ilyin. In 1861, Alexander II had aroused enthusiastic hopes by abolishing serfdom in Russia, hopes as enthusiastic as those aroused by Khrushchev's de-Stalinization a century later. But the terms of peasant emancipation were disappointing, and within a year the Tsar's police were arresting leading Moscow and St. Petersburg intellectuals. In 1863, Alexander II had bloodily suppressed the Polish uprising— and Polish patriots had directly inspired the Russian revolutionary circles from which Karakozov sprung.

Now, in February 1969, there were rumors in Moscow underground circles that Lieutenant Ilyin, before serving in the Leningrad garrison, had been among the Soviet troops in Czechoslovakia. He had, clearly, decided on his act immediately after the suicide of Jan Palach in Prague. And there were reports that, when Ilyin was interrogated by KGB chief Andropov and asked why he had tried to shoot Brezhnev, the young lieutenant had replied, *"Chtob razbudit Rossiyu"*—"To wake up Russia."

Jan Palach's self-immolation, followed by the suicides of other Czech and Slovak students, produced profound shock and shame at all political levels in Moscow. Even hard-bitten Communists who had approved the invasion were stunned and bewildered.

In an open letter to their fellow Soviet citizens, General Grigorenko and his friend Ivan Yakhimovich * declared that Palach's protest

> . . . which has taken so horrible a form, is addressed primarily to us, the Soviet people. . . . We all bear some part of the guilt for his death, and for the deaths of other Czechoslovak brothers who have committed suicide. . . . The greatness of a country lies not in the might of its armed forces, brought down upon a numerically small, freedom-loving nation, but in its moral strength. Shall we then continue to look on in silence while our brothers perish?

The appeals of the small group of Russian democrats went unanswered. The Soviet masses struggled through the bitter winter to cope with food and other shortages. Most intellectuals remained silent and fearful. The Kremlin leaders, after the shooting at the Borovitsky Gate, became more fearful still. They did not dare go to Leningrad, even for long-scheduled ceremonies to mark the twenty-fifth anniversary of the lifting of the wartime blockade. Leningrad was closed to foreigners through February and March, as the KGB interrogated the officers of Lieutenant Ilyin's army garrison.

Then, suddenly, on March 2, there came a new shock. Thousands of miles across Russia and Siberia, on the frozen ice of the Ussuri River, a tiny island—barely a sandspit—overnight entered world history. The Russians called the island Damansky, the Chinese called it Chenpao. The Ussuri formed part of the disputed 5,000 mile boundary between Russia and China.

For three years, as China had struggled with the chaos of the

* Five years earlier, in the Khrushchev days, Yakhimovich had been praised as a model collective-farm chairman in Latvia. The Soviet press had even printed extracts from his diaries. But in February 1968, Yakhimovich protested the Galanskov-Ginsburg trial in an open letter to Suslov. He was dismissed from his post after further protests against the "vigilance" campaign.

"cultural revolution," Soviet Army units and KGB frontier troops had been having their way in hundreds of unpublicized skirmishes on the long frontier—from the deserts of Kazakhstan and Sinkiang to the islands of the Ussuri and the Amur near the Pacific. On March 2, 1969, his cultural revolution completed, Mao Tsetung struck back. Soviet soldiers wandering across the ice onto Chenpao/Damansky Island were ambushed by machine gunners of the Chinese Red Army. Thirty-four Russian soldiers were reported killed, many more wounded.

The shock produced in Moscow that night was incredible. The Tass news agency (accustomed to delay even the most innocuous Kremlin communiqués for five or six hours) rushed to report the Ussuri incident barely a few hours after the battle had ended. Ordinary Russians scoured the newspapers next morning as they had not in years. All over Moscow, one could see small groups gathered around newspaper bulletin boards, discussing the news. For this was the first time, after a decade of Soviet-Chinese tensions, that the Kremlin had announced that guns had been fired and Russian blood had been spilled.

On March 15, there was a second, even fiercer battle on the Ussuri, with tanks and artillery. Television and newsreel films of the two incidents heightened the tension in Moscow. One could feel among the Russians the rise of archetypal ancestral fears: the collective memory, transmitted from generation to generation by sagas, ballads, icons, monuments, and history books, of the Golden Horde of Genghis and Batu Khan—which had subjugated all Russia to the "Tatar yoke" for two centuries.

The retorts of the second Ussuri battle were still echoing when Brezhnev, Kosygin, Marshal Grechko, and Marshal Yakubovsky arrived in Budapest for a Warsaw Pact summit meeting on March 16. The meeting had been called earlier to discuss reorganization of the Warsaw Pact military command structure, and Soviet diplomats had been struggling for three days to overcome Rumanian resistance to "integration." Before the formal session, Brezhnev and Kosygin conferred separately on Margaret Island in the Danube with each of the other delegations, including General Svoboda, Cernik, and other Czechoslovak officials. Brezhnev did not say a word to them about the still-uneasy situation in Czechoslovakia. According to an eye-witness, "His face was red and he did not look well. He was nervous and impatient. His temper flared and he pounded on the table. He had only one thing on his mind—and that was China."

Brezhnev described how conflict with China would strain Russia's armed forces and overtaxed economy. He urged the East Europeans to raise their own military budgets, to help defend Russia against the Chinese threat.

The Kremlin leader encountered resistance, both open and silent. Ceausescu declared that Russia's conflict with China in no way concerned the Warsaw Pact, which was (as the treaty stated) a purely European alliance. The leaders of Hungary and Czechoslovakia were (according to a participant) "curiously detached, distant, quiet and enigmatic."

Both Magyars and Czechoslovaks understood (from the experiences of 1956 and 1968) that the Soviet occupation armies represented the principal obstacle to their nations' independent development. They were likewise painfully aware that their economic progress had been thwarted not only by Soviet commercial exploitation, but by the harsh policy toward West Germany demanded by Brezhnev, Ulbricht, and Gomulka.

Ironically, in March 1969, Brezhnev had arrived—in a weaker position—at the same crossroads which had faced Khrushchev five years earlier. From 1959 onward, Khrushchev had slowly come to realize that Russia could not simultaneously raise living standards while waging cold war on two fronts—against the Chinese to the East, against the Germans and Americans to the West. By the spring of 1964, when he visited Budapest for the last time, Khrushchev had made his choice—a truce with the West, struggle against China—and soon afterward had sent Adzhubei to Bonn to prepare the ground.

Brezhnev and the others who had overthrown Khrushchev had lost Russia five years. For nearly two of those years, they had pursued the will-o'-the-wisp of reconciliation with Peking. When the Social Democrats entered the Bonn Government in December 1966, Brezhnev, Ulbricht, and the marshals had prohibitively raised the price for an accommodation. They had also chosen to support new "fronts" in Southeast Asia and the Middle East.

The shock of the Ussuri incidents led the Budapest conference to issue a declaration on European security (March 17, 1969) which was the mildest Communist statement in years on the German problem. It might have been, and perhaps was, drafted by the Rumanians.

For more than a month thereafter, it seemed that the Kremlin might give the political green light to the professional Soviet and West German diplomats who had, in eight months of confidential talks, reached tentative agreement on a series of measures aimed at gradually easing Russo-German tensions. But Ulbricht successfully lobbied his old friends among the Stalinist ideologists and the marshals to prevent any Soviet accord with Bonn.

Even six months later, when the Social Democrat Willy Brandt became West German chancellor and negotiations recommenced, the Soviet leaders remained reluctant to ease the regime at the Wall. They were quick to be frightened, and to stiffen their terms, when the West German chancellor, visiting the East German town of Erfurt (March 22, 1970), was greeted by enthusiastic crowds crying *"Willy, Willy, Willy Brandt!"*

Even before Brandt's selection as chancellor, Kosygin had again visited Chou En-lai in Peking—with the result that formal negotiations were opened to settle the frontier dispute as well as other issues between the two parties and states. Few expected the new Soviet-Chinese negotiations to lead soon to any substantial agreement. But they permitted the Kremlin once more to defer, at least for the time being, any serious reconsideration of imperial policies in Central and Eastern Europe.

In 1961, Khrushchev had aroused the hope that the conflict with China would compel the Soviet leaders to permit a greater measure of independence to the nations of Eastern Europe. The Ussuri incidents of March 1969 produced precisely the opposite effect—dramatically, within a matter of weeks.

Four days after the Budapest conference, in a world championship hockey tournament at Stockholm, Czechoslovakia defeated the Soviet Union in the first of two games. The tournament, televised throughout Eastern Europe by the Intervision network, was watched avidly in both Moscow and Prague. The Swedish fans in the Stockholm arena cheered every Czech advance and rally.

Moscow sound engineers eliminated the crowd noise from the Soviet telecast of the game. Seconds after the final buzzer, Moscow cut off the Intervision picture as well, to avoid showing the jubilant pro-Czechoslovak demonstration at the Stockholm rink. In Prague, tens of thousands of proud Czechs poured out into Wenceslas Square to celebrate the hockey victory. As in all the spontaneous demonstrations since the spring of 1968, there was no violence.

A week later, on Friday night March 28, the Soviet and Czechoslovak teams clashed in Stockholm for the second time. In a hard-fought game, the Czechoslovak team, despite injuries to key players, rallied to win by a score of 4 to 3. Again, Moscow cut off the telecast immediately after the final buzzer. Hundreds of thousands throughout Czechoslovakia took to the streets in joyous demonstrations.

In Prague, they thronged around the equestrian statue of St. Wenceslas at the head of the square. Young workers, students, and Czech Army soldiers cheered and chanted "4–3! 4–3! 4–3!" Suddenly, five hundred yards down the square, an unidentified gang smashed the windows of Aeroflot, the Soviet airline, and sacked its office.

The next day, the new Czech regional interior minister, Josef Grosser, announced on his own that demonstrators had also pelted Soviet Army barracks at Mlada Boleslav and elsewhere in the provinces.* The national government, still headed by Svoboda and Cernik, swiftly reprimanded Grosser for having made such a statement before there had even been an official investigation.

New Soviet "routine" maneuvers began around the Czechoslovak borders, and on Monday afternoon, March 31, Marshal Grechko arrived at the main occupation headquarters at Milovice, two hours north of Prague. A Soviet deputy foreign minister, Vladimir Semyonov, joined him in Hradcany Castle next day to confront President Svoboda.

In the days that followed, Marshal Grechko fulfilled the political purposes for which the Warsaw Pact armies commanded by

---

* Weeks later, foreign journalists in Prague said that they were unable to find anyone who had actually seen any damage to Soviet barracks. European newspapers charged that the sacking of the Prague Aeroflot office was organized by the KGB.

his deputy, Marshal Yakubovsky, had invaded Czechoslovakia less than eight months earlier. Censorship was reimposed on liberal newspapers, the party organ *Rude Pravo* was itself officially condemned, and Smrkovsky was publicly reproved.

On April 17, 1969, the Dubcek era ended officially. The Central Committee replaced him with Husak as party leader and expelled Smrkovsky, Spacek, and other liberals from the Presidium. A long series of purges, transfers, expulsions, and demotions followed. Soon there were arrests, too. On the anniversary of the invasion, between August 19 and 21, there were violent demonstrations against the occupation in Prague, Brno, Bratislava, and other towns. This time, they were put down by the "normalized" Czechoslovak Army and security police. Tanks were used in Prague. There were 474 wounded and 2,174 arrested in Bohemia and Moravia alone.

Ironically, the deposition of Dubcek on April 17, accomplished by Marshal Grechko, came on the seventy-fifth birthday of Nikita Khrushchev, who had first called in the Soviet Army to act as the final arbiter of intraparty conflict in the Kremlin. In 1953, Marshal Moskalenko had helped Khrushchev oust Beria. In 1957, the support of Marshal Zhukov and other Army leaders had enabled Khrushchev to overcome a 7–4 Politburo majority against him and to defeat Malenkov, Molotov, and other rivals.

In 1960, military influence had committed Khrushchev to the doctrine of support for "wars of liberation," which had dimmed prospects for the Paris Big Four summit conference even before the U-2 incident. A glowering Marshal Malinovsky had accompanied Khrushchev to Paris to be sure that the agile party leader did not strike a bargain with President Eisenhower, whom Khrushchev had publicly proclaimed to be "a man of peace." In 1962, the marshals had helped plunge Khrushchev into the desperate gamble of installing offensive missiles in Cuba. At the end of 1963, the "military-industrial" leaders had blocked his plans for diverting arms spending to agriculture and the civilian economy.

In October 1964, the marshals had remained neutral—at the very least—when Khrushchev was overthrown. Soon afterward, under Brezhnev's nominal leadership, the Soviet Union concentrated on achieving strategic parity with the United States in nuclear weapons and the missiles to deliver them. The new regime had moved swiftly to supply military aid to North Vietnam, and the role of the Soviet Army in the Middle East expanded rapidly. Between 1967 and 1969, the Soviet military budget, even according to the official figures, had been increased by 25 percent. Soviet civilians paid the price.

At the end of April 1969, there were shortages of meat even in the Moscow hard-currency shops for privileged foreigners. By the end of the year, Brezhnev himself was denouncing the collapse of the Soviet civilian economy, and a French correspondent reported from Moscow: *

> For the population, at least in the big cities, it is a very somber winter. One can tell it even in Moscow, the privileged capital, not to speak of provincial towns plunged in their wintral night. Even recalling the soggy cornbread in the winter of 1963, there has been nothing like this for ten years. . . .
> No meat or chicken, or very little, for months. As for the true meat of Soviet citizens, sausages, even they are rare and of dubious taste. Butter, potatoes, even vodka are of very bad quality. The cunning travel to Leningrad—where "there is some"—to buy the staple of Moscow winters, pickled herring. Housewives have the reflexes of occupied Paris. They run along the sidewalks to learn in one place of a queue for fifty frozen Bulgarian chickens, then go miles to another queue for sour pickles. The same situation at pharmacies, electrical appliance stores, paper shops, hat shops. . . . Slump, too, in the field of clothing and shoes, despite Western imports. . . .
> [But] the industrial production statistics for 1969 present phenomenal figures. Where do the 110 million tons of steel go? For whose use are the 328 million tons of petroleum, the 183 billion cubic meters of gas extracted in 1969? . . . The Soviet Union is carrying Cuba, North Vietnam, and several Arab countries practically on its shoulders. Armaments weigh heavily on its development. . . .

Those who hoped that the Ussuri incidents and the new conflict with China might lead the Soviet rulers to reconciliation with their own people, in the interest of national unity, were rapidly disappointed. On May 7, 1969, former Major General

* *L'Express*, February 23, 1970.

Pyotr Grigorenko was arrested in Tashkent, where he had gone to attend a trial of Crimean Tatar leaders who had been trying vainly to regain the homes from which Stalin had deported them in 1944. The chief Tatar defendant, Roland Kadiyev, was a physicist who had been officially praised as late as November 1968 for his brilliant researches confirming Einstein's theory of relativity.

Grigorenko was interrogated and tortured, but refused to "confess." Like young Lieutenant Ilyin, the old general was declared a lunatic and forcibly confined in an asylum.

Just before the arrest of General Grigorenko, his friend Ivan Yakhimovich, the former model collective-farm chairman, was arrested in Riga. On the same day as Grigorenko's seizure in Tashkent, the KGB searched the Moscow apartment of the young historian Andrei Amalric, but the unexpected arrival of several Americans during the search and the subsequent publicity given to his case delayed his arrest for a year. Amalric used the time to compose an essay called "Will the Soviet Union Survive Until 1984?", in which he prophesied the dissolution of the Soviet empire in the course of a prolonged war with China.

Later in May 1969, Ilya Gabai (who had been one of the Pushkin Square demonstrators with Khaustov and Bukovsky back in 1967), was arrested in Moscow. But the arrests soon went beyond the well-known Moscow adherents of the informal "democratic movement," beyond the ranks of intellectual dissidents. According to reports by what seemed to be taking on the proportions of a genuine underground movement, three officers of the Baltic Fleet (Gavrilov, Kosyrev, Paramonov) were arrested in Tallin and Kaliningrad for having formed a "union of fighters for political freedom." The KGB established that the rebel officers had contacts in Moscow, Riga, Baku, Perm, and Khabarovsk. Their arrest had followed the seizure of another Baltic Fleet coast guard officer named Alexeyev.

The purge in the Baltic Fleet resulted in the arrest of a group of thirty-one civilians (only a few of them Estonians) in Tallin. One of the group's leaders was the engineer Sergei Soldatov, who in more than two months of interrogations declined to discuss his contacts either with the Baltic Fleet officers or with such Moscow democrats as General Grigorenko and Pyotr Yakir. Soldatov declined as well to discuss alleged plans to publish an underground newspaper, to be called *The Democrat*. But he firmly made clear his condemnation of the Soviet invasion of Czechoslovakia. As a result of the KGB investigations in Tallin, underground sources reported, two unnamed Soviet Army officers in Poland were later arrested.

The arrests of Grigorenko, Yakhimovich, Gabai, and other of their comrades failed to deter the members of the "democratic movement." At the end of May 1969, they sent an appeal to the United Nations Commission on Human Rights, protesting "the unending stream of political persecutions in the Soviet Union, which we see as a return to the Stalin era." Fifteen of the 52 signatories of this appeal formally constituted themselves "The Initiative Group for Defense of Civil Rights in the U.S.S.R." One of the signatories was a grandson of Gregory Gershuni, one of the leaders of the Socialist Revolutionary party which had won Russia's only genuinely free election in 1917 and which Lenin and Trotsky thought they had banished forever to the "rubbish heap of history."

The first name on the appeal, however, furnished an even more striking illustration of the dragons' teeth sown by Khrushchev's successors. He was listed on the appeal merely as "G. O. Altunian, engineer, Kharkov." Until 1968, however, he had been a major in the Soviet Army engineers. Born in 1933, a Communist party member since 1957, he had spent thirteen years as a lecturer in the Kharkov Higher Military School—receiving some fourteen official expressions of gratitude for loyal service from the Supreme Soviet and other institutions. Altunian became a rebel after Khrushchev's fall. At closed party meetings, he asked, "Where are all those who surrounded Khrushchev when he made all his mistakes?" Later, he criticized the rehabilitation of Stalin; still later, Brezhnev's policy in the Middle East (Altunian considered Nasser a Nazi). The invasion of Czechoslovakia proved the last straw. The KGB forced his dismissal from the Army and party in 1968, and his arrest on July 11, 1969. (Ten Kharkov citizens immediately signed a petition protesting the arrest.) Former Major Altunian was sentenced to three years at hard labor for having condemned Soviet "state anti-Semitism" and the invasion of Czechoslovakia.

Despite the arrests of Altunian and many others, the democratic movement managed to elaborate a political program later in 1969 —civil liberty and the rule of law were its principal demands— and to continue publishing, well into 1970, the remarkable underground *Chronicle of Human Rights in the Soviet Union*. The twelve issues of this onionskin *samizdat* publication, which had been launched in the Human Rights Year 1968, provided a fascinating portrayal of the struggle between the new Soviet generation and a regime which was living (in Amalric's phrase) off "the interest on the capital of fear amassed in Stalin's time."

Because the Soviet rulers did not wish, or did not dare to return to the murderous terror of Stalin, new repressions evoked new protests; and, after each arrest of a prominent democrat, a new voice was raised in his place. Thus, for example, after the arrest of Amalric on May 21, 1970, young Vladimir Bukovsky, who had returned to Moscow after serving three years for his part in the Pushkin Square demonstration of January 22, 1967, took the lead in new protests against the repressions and new exposures of the horrors of Soviet concentration camps, prisons, and political "mental asylums."

By the middle of 1969, the official repression had moved beyond the circles of active Soviet dissidents and had begun to touch members of the "loyal opposition" within the Establishment. In June 1969, a campaign began against Tvardovsky who had so long maintained the integrity of *Novy Mir* even in the last difficult years. The old Communist poet resisted for eight months, but finally resigned when four of his deputy editors were purged. One of them was Vladimir Lakshin, who had so ably championed Solzhenitsyn in 1963 and who in the summer of 1964 had recounted to young Mihajlo Mihajlov the Moscow saying, "Tell me what you think of *Ivan Denisovich* and I will tell you what you are."

On November 4, 1969, Solzhenitsyn was expelled from the Writers Union. The deed was done in Ryazan. Only six members of the local Writers Union branch, including Solzhenitsyn, were present. An emissary from Moscow brought the orders; the discussion lasted an hour and a half; Solzhenitsyn was condemned by a vote of five to one.

Two days later, the expulsion at Ryazan was confirmed at a conference of Writers Union officials in Moscow, to which Solzhenitsyn was not invited. In a letter of protest, the heir of Tolstoy wrote:

"Your clocks are behind our time. Lift those heavy curtains so dear to you. You do not even suspect that outside, day has broken. The time of the deaf is past, the somber epoch of no exit when with light heart you expelled Akhmatova. The timid, frigid time is past, too, when, shouting insults, you expelled Pasternak. Was that not shameful enough for you? . . .

"Blind leading the blind, you do not even notice that you are going in a direction opposite to the one which you yourselves proclaimed. In our time of crisis, you are incapable of proposing anything constructive, anything good, for our dangerously sick society—only your hatred, your vigilance, your 'hold-on-and-don't-let-go.' . . .

"'The enemies will find out'—that is your excuse. The eternal and permanent 'enemies' provide an easy justification for your functions and even for the fact that you exist. As if we had no enemies in the time we were promised that the truth would be told always and immediately.

"What would you do without 'enemies'? Without 'enemies,' you could not even exist! Hatred, a hatred no less evil than race hate, has become your sterile atmosphere. But just so is being lost the genuine, integral feeling of mankind; and that loss is near. If tomorrow the ice of the Antarctic melted and all humanity drowned, into whose head would you stuff the idea of 'class struggle'? Not to speak of the day when a few surviving bipeds will roam the radioactive earth and die.

"It is time to remember that, above all, we belong to humanity; that man is distinguished from beasts by thought and speech; and that men by nature must be free. And if they are fettered, we return to a bestial state. . . ."

On December 21, 1969, for the first time since 1955, *Pravda* celebrated the anniversary of the birth of Josef Stalin. So, sadly, ended a decade which had begun with optimistic hopes, even though in 1960 few outside the small town of Trencin, Slovakia, had ever heard of Alexander Dubcek, and not a word had ever been published by the cancer patient and former political prisoner Alexander Solzhenitsyn.

Before the new decade was six months old, Dubcek had been expelled from the Communist movement into which he had been born—and a new bust of Stalin was unveiled above his grave along the Kremlin wall. Yet only time would tell whether Stalin's ghost would have history's last word, or whether the power of his heirs would prove—as had the power of the Romanov tsars before them —as illusory as the Empire's new clothes.

BIBLIOGRAPHY

As indicated in the Foreword, the primary source of most of this book is eye-witness. As a Fellow of the Institute of Current World Affairs and *Washington Post* correspondent, I observed:

—Communist party congresses in Hungary (1962 and 1966), Yugoslavia (1964 and 1969), Rumania (1965), and Poland (1968).

—Meetings of the Warsaw Pact Political-Consultative Committee in Bucharest (1966), Sofia (1968), and Budapest (1969).

—State visits by Brezhnev to Yugoslavia (1962), Khrushchev to Yugoslavia (1963) and Hungary (1964), and Chou En-lai to Rumania (1966).

—The Soviet-Czechoslovak crisis meetings at Cierna-nad-Tisou and Bratislava (1968).

—Trials of Georgiev in Sofia (1963), Mihajlov in Zadar (1965), Ginsburg-Galanskov and Litvinov-Daniel in Moscow (1968).

—The consultative preparatory meeting of Communist parties in Budapest (1968).

—Countless memorial and anniversary occasions, including the 50th anniversary of the Bolshevik Revolution in Moscow and Leningrad (1967), and the 25th anniversary of the Yugoslav Anti-Fascist Liberation Front at Jajce (1969).

—Factories, farms, trade fairs, and cultural institutions too numerous to list. They include the Galati metallurgical complex, the Soviet factories, farms, institutes, and museums mentioned in Chapter 13, and all other sites mentioned elsewhere, as well as some not worth mentioning anywhere.

The original sources of most of the political quotations and economic figures given in the text are the respective Communist newspapers, press agency dispatches, statistical handbooks, and official collections of speeches—with the exception of cases (see Chapter 9) where the author and other witnesses heard speakers say things later censored by the official press.

In addition to Communist documentary sources, specialized Western journals were frequently consulted. They include *Survey* (London), *Problems of Communism* (Washington), *East Europe* (New York), the *Current Digest of the Soviet Press* (New York), and the regular background and situation reports issued by the Research Department of Radio Free Europe.

Acknowledgment is gratefully made for permission to quote in Chapter 7 from Max Hayward's translation of Boris Slutsky's "Andrei Rublyov" and Harry Willetts' translation of Solzhenitsyn's sketch, "Along the Oka"—both from *Encounter* magazine.

I have drawn directly for facts, dates, figures, or quotations on—or checked my own experience against—the books listed below. (English-language editions are listed, wherever possible, of works written in other languages; and the most recent editions of books which have been revised by their authors.)

Russia and the U.S.S.R., History and Politics, to 1956

Abramovitch, Raphael R. *The Soviet Revolution, 1917–1939*. New York, 1962.

> A valuable combination of personal experience and retrospective scholarship by a prominent antiwar Russian Social Democrat, participant in the events of 1917–22, and long-time editor of the newspaper *Sotsialisticheski Viestnik* (Socialist Courier) in Berlin, Paris, and New York. Rich in official early Soviet documentation.

Avtorkhanov, Abdurakhman. *Stalin and the Soviet Communist Party*. New York, 1959.

Avtorkhanov, Abdurakhman. *The Communist Party Apparatus*. Cleveland, 1968.

> The Soviet party *"apparat"* described and studied by a former insider, a contemporary of Suslov's at the Moscow Institute of Red Professors (1928–37). The first book describes the power struggle of that period; the second analyzes the party machine from Lenin to Brezhnev.

Conquest, Robert. *The Great Terror*. London, 1968.

> Until the Soviet party and KGB their files, the definitive work on the subject.

Dallin, Alexander. *German Rule in Russia, 1941–45*. New York, 1957.

> Similarly definitive.

Djilas, Milovan. *Conversations With Stalin*. New York, 1962.

> The most perceptive non-Russian close-up view of Stalin, with the possible exception of relatively brief passages in General de Gaulle's war memoirs.

Fainsod, Merle. *How Russia Is Ruled*. Cambridge, Mass., 1963.

> Authoritative description and analysis of the major Soviet institutions.

Kennan, George. *Siberia and the Exile System*. Chicago, 1958.
Originally published in 1891, this description of tsarist prison camps and exile settlements can be usefully compared with later descriptions of Soviet camps. The 1958 reissue contains a preface by the author's nephew, the contemporary historian and statesman George F. Kennan.

Kohn, Hans. *Pan-Slavism—Its History and Ideology*. New York, 1960.
The greatest twentieth-century historian of nationalism, Professor Kohn is as thorough and understanding in discussing Russia as in his more detailed studies of his native Central Europe.

Laqueur, Walter. *The Fate of the Revolution: Interpretations of Soviet History*. London, 1967.
A splendid guide to the existing literature on the Bolshevik Revolution and its consequences.

Luxemburg, Rosa. *The Russian Revolution* and *Leninism or Marxism?* Ann Arbor, 1961.
Reissue of the classic Marxist critique of Leninism from the left, the first work written in 1918, the second in 1904.

Nicolaevsky, Boris. *Power and the Soviet Elite*. New York, 1966.
Collected articles by the late Russian Social Democrat and grand master of Kremlinology. Includes the famous "Letter of An Old Bolshevik," based on Bukharin's conversations with the author and other Social Democrats in Paris in 1936.

Rigby, T. H. (ed.). *Stalin*. Englewood Cliffs, New Jersey, 1966.
An excellent documentary collection, superior to any biography extant, presenting Stalin in his own words, in the views of his contemporaries, and in the judgment of foreign historians.

Saikowski, Charlotte, and Gruliow, Leo (ed.). *The Documentary Record of the 22nd Congress of the Communist Party of the Soviet Union*. New York, 1962.
The basic source for the quotations from the Congress record cited in the Prologue.

Schapiro, Leonard. *The Communist Party of the Soviet Union*. London, 1960.
Authoritative and scholarly. (Specialists will find the author's *Origins of the Communist Autocracy* even more rewarding for the 1917–21 period.)

Shub, David. *Lenin: A Biography*. Revised edition, London, 1966.
Others beside myself consider my father's biography the standard work on the man and the origins of his movement.

Sukhanov, N. N. *The Russian Revolution 1917* (edited and translated by Joel Carmichael). Oxford, 1955.
The most vivid of contemporary accounts, originally published in Moscow in 1922 in seven volumes, here deftly abridged. Contains the famous offhand description of Stalin as "a gray blur."

Troyat, Henri. *Daily Life in Russia Under The Last Tsar*. London, 1961.

An excellent reconstruction from memories, reminiscences, and documents of the Russia of 1903, by the Russian-born French biographer, novelist, and historian.

Ulam, Adam B. *The Bolsheviks*. London, 1965.

Thoughtful critical biography of Lenin, written with a mature sense of historical ironies, contradictions, and paradoxes.

Wallace, Sir Donald Mackenzie. *Russia On the Eve of War and Revolution*. New York, 1961.

Reissue of what in 1912 was regarded as the standard work on Russia, by a correspondent and editor of *The Times* who had known the country since 1871. Rich in detail and written broadly from the viewpoint of moderate officialdom, a healthy corrective to later works influenced by revolutionaries, and still later essays pretending that nothing in Russia changed between Nicholas I and Stalin.

U.S.S.R., History and Politics, since 1956

Abel, Elie. *The Missile Crisis*. New York, 1966.

The best (and least self-serving) account of the Cuban crisis of October 1962, by the experienced correspondent of the National Broadcasting Company.

Alliluyeva, Svetlana. *Only One Year*. New York, 1969.

Fascinating not only because of Svetlana's insight into her father Stalin and his various heirs, but also because of her sensitive descriptions of the Moscow intellectual milieu (notably, her portrait of Andrei Sinyavsky).

Amalrik, Andrei. *Will the Soviet Union Survive Until 1984?* New York, 1970.

A brilliant meditation on the Russian future by a young dissident Soviet historian, including a valuable discussion of ideological trends within the "democratic movement" of 1968–69.

Brumberg, Abraham (ed.). *In Quest of Justice: Protest and Dissent in the Soviet Union Today*. New York, 1970.

A basic documentary collection, assembled by the editor of *Problems of Communism*, including fuller texts of many of the Solzhenitsyn and other protest documents mentioned in Chapters 13–17.

Conquest, Robert. *Power and Policy in the U.S.S.R.* London, 1962.

A valuable "study of Soviet dynastics"—i.e., Kremlinology—from 1945 to 1960, and thus a good bridge from Nicolaevsky (see above) to Tatu (below).

Hindus, Maurice. *The Kremlin's Human Dilemma*. New York, 1967.

Contains useful personal descriptions of the Soviet agricultural crisis of 1962–64, by a Russian-born reporter who had been revisiting many of the same farm areas since the 1930s.

Hyland, William, and Shryock, Richard, W. *The Fall of Khrushchev*. New York, 1968.

This "outside" view, by two analysts of the U.S. Central Intelligence Agency, can be usefully compared with the "Moscow" view provided by Tatu (below).

Labedz, Leopold, and Hayward, Max (ed.). *On Trial*. London, 1967.
The eloquent documentary record of the trial of Andrei Sinyavsky and Yuli Daniel in February 1966, partly based on the "White Book" compiled by Alex Ginsburg.

Laqueur, Walter. *The Road to War 1967: The Origins of the Arab-Israel Conflict*. London, 1968.
The definitive study.

Leonhard, Wolfgang. *Nikita Sergeyevich Khrushchev*. Luzern, 1965.
A fine German biography, in text and pictures, by the author of *Child of the Revolution* and other excellent works. Balanced, understanding treatment of Khrushchev's rise, power, and fall.

Levine, Isaac Don. *I Rediscover Russia 1924–1964*. New York, 1964.
Interesting personal travelogue by a journalist who knew Lenin, Trotsky, Gorky, and others in revolutionary days and then returned to Khrushchev's Russia.

Linden, Carl A. *Khrushchev and the Soviet Leadership 1957–1964*. Baltimore, 1966.
Useful Kremlinological study.

Litvinov, Pavel. *The Demonstration in Pushkin Square*. London, 1969.
The record of the trials of Khaustov, Bukovsky, and other Moscow demonstrators of January 22, 1967, with a good biographical description of Litvinov by Karel van Het Reve.

de Mauny, Erik. *Russian Prospect*. London, 1969.
The Moscow atmosphere of 1964–66, seen by the resident correspondent of the British Broadcasting Corporation.

Mehnert, Klaus. *Peking and Moscow*. London, 1963.
Penetrating study of the relations between Russia and China, as states and as nations, by a German scholar who has known both countries intimately.

Sakharov, Andrei. *Progress, Coexistence and Intellectual Freedom*. New York, 1968.
Fundamental to an understanding of the liberal viewpoint within the Soviet Establishment.

Salisbury, Harrison E. *War Between Russia and China*. New York, 1969.
Carries Mehnert's study (above) up to date, and supplements it with valuable eyewitness accounts of Soviet Asia and Mongolia. The veteran *New York Times* correspondent knows the U.S.S.R. since 1944, and Mongolia since 1959.

Tatu, Michel. *Power in the Kremlin*. London, 1969.
By far the best study of Soviet politics from 1959 to 1966, by the former Moscow correspondent (1957–64) of *Le Monde*, now that paper's deputy foreign editor.

Van der Post, Laurens. *Journey Into Russia*. London, 1964.
Uniquely perceptive travelogue which best catches the atmosphere and aspirations of the late Khrushchev period.

Russia and the U.S.S.R., Culture

Billington, James H. *The Icon and the Axe: An Interpretive History of Russian Culture.* New York, 1967.

Challenging scholarly exploration of Russian thought, especially strong on the religious heritage. Can be usefully compared with Masaryk and Weidle (below).

Blake, Patricia, and Hayward, Max (ed). *Dissonant Voices in Soviet Literature.* New York, 1964.

Contains, among other important works, Tendraykov's "Three, Seven, Ace," extracts from Ehrenburg's memoirs, Yevtushenko's "Babi Yar," and "This Is Moscow Speaking" by "Nikolai Arzhak" (Yuli Daniel). Max Hayward's introduction expertly reviews Soviet letters between 1917 and 1964.

Blake, Patricia, and Hayward, Max (ed.). *Halfway to the Moon: New Writing from Russia.* London, 1963.

Contains Solzhenitsyn's masterpiece "Matryona's Home," the title story by Aksyonov, and some of the best poems of Voznesensky, Yevtushenko, Slutsky, and others. Patricia Blake's introduction provides both vivid personal descriptions of leading Moscow writers in the fall of 1962, and a knowing account of the cultural-political crisis in the winter of 1962–63.

Masaryk, Thomas G. *The Spirit of Russia.* London, New York, 1955.

Reissue of Professor Masaryk's definitive cultural-political study first completed in 1911. Immensely valuable, not only as a corrective to post–1917 studies of Russian thought, but as itself an illustration of the reaction of an erudite, democratic Western Slav to various patterns of Russian thinking.

Mihajlov, Mihajlo. *Moscow Summer.* New York, 1965.

The full text of the literary travelogue, including the third part which never saw print in Yugoslavia.

Mihajlov, Mihajlo. *Russian Themes.* London, 1968.

Collected essays, including a preliminary assessment of "Abram Tertz" (see below), the *Forum* essay on "Dostoyevsky's and Solzhenitsyn's *House of the Dead,*" and "The Mission of *Novy Mir.*"

Okudzhava, Bulat. *Bulat Okoudjava, poète-compositeur Sovietique.* Paris, 1969.

A long-playing phonograph record, taped during the Soviet poet's visit to Paris in 1968, with his own renditions of many of his most famous ballads, including "François Villon," "Smolensk Highway," and "A Toy Soldier."

"Tertz, Abram" (Andrei Sinyavsky). *On Socialist Realism* and *The Trial Begins.* London, New York, 1960.

A brilliant essay and masterful short story, in which the young Soviet literary critic (in works first published abroad in the late 1950s) not only described the impact of "de-Stalinization" but already discerned his own fate. For an example of the mature Sinyavsky at the top of his critical form, see his essay on Yevtushenko for *Phoenix 66* ("In Defense of Pyramids," included in the Brumberg collection listed above).

Voznesensky, Andrei. *Anti-worlds* and *The Fifth Ace.* London, 1968.

The definitive, bilingual edition of the Soviet poet's best work to date.

Weidle, Wladimir. *Russia Absent and Present*. London, 1952.
The most impressive single meditation on the meaning of recent Russian history I have read, even more impressive on rereading.

Eastern Europe, General

Blumenfeld, Yorick. *Seesaw: Cultural Life in Eastern Europe*. New York, 1968.
Good reporting here on Czechoslovak theater and films, Hungarian poetry, Polish painting, and other aspects of East European culture between 1964 and 1967.

Burks, R. V. *The Dynamics of Communism in Eastern Europe*. Princeton, 1961.
Excellent analysis, including statistical studies, of the ethnic bases of Communist support before and after World War II.

Byrnes, Robert F. (ed.). *The United States and Eastern Europe*. Englewood Cliffs, New Jersey, 1967.
Valuable symposium of ranking specialists and a good general introduction to the area.

Fischer-Galati, Stephen (ed.). *Eastern Europe in the Sixties*. New York, 1963.
Useful symposium gathering expert analyses of the situation at the start of the decade.

Griffith, William E. (ed.). *Communism in Europe*. Cambridge, Massachusetts, 1964.
Contains Victor Meier's knowing essay on the Yugoslav party, and useful studies by Hansjakob Stehle and Francois Fetjo of the Polish and Hungarian parties respectively.

Hanak, Harry. *Great Britain and Austria-Hungary During the First World War*. London, 1962.
Excellent research study showing how Slavic exiles and British publicists helped turn the dissolution of the Hapsburg monarchy into an Allied war aim. Further documents many points made by Zeman (below).

Jaszi, Oscar. *The Dissolution of the Hapsburg Monarchy*. Chicago, 1929.
The most detailed and intimate study, by a Hungarian democrat and political associate of the late Count Michael Karolyi.

Lendvai, Paul. *Eagles and Cobwebs: Nationalism and Communism in the Balkans*. London, 1970.
Excellent studies, combining research and firsthand observation, by the Hugarian-born Eastern European correspondent of the *Financial Times* and *Die Presse* (Vienna).

London, Kurt (ed.). *Eastern Europe in Transition*. Baltimore, 1966.
Useful symposium of specialist opinion at mid-decade.

Macartney, C. A., and Palmer, A. W. *Independent Eastern Europe.* London, 1962.
> The most balanced, solid recent study of Eastern Europe between the two World Wars.

Pounds, Norman J. G. *Eastern Europe.* London, 1969.
> A definitive economic geography, indispensable to the specialist.

Pritchett, V. S. *Foreign Faces.* London, 1964.
> Superior travelogue by the British literary critic, especially perceptive in Poland and Hungary; I liked the Czechs better than he did.

Seton-Watson, Hugh. *Eastern Europe Between the Wars.* Cambridge, 1945.
> Still highly useful, although the author's views have evolved considerably since this early work. Remains valuable because of the author's combination of scholarly background and personal experience; as the son of the late Robert Seton-Watson, Britain's most distinguished scholar on Southeastern Europe (see below), the author practically grew up in the region and returned to it as a British officer during and after World War II.

Seton-Watson, Hugh. *The East European Revolution.* New York, 1951.
> The best single work on the Communist seizures of power between 1944 and 1950, containing such currently relevant nuggets as Gustav Husak's violent Slovak nationalism in personal conversation with the author.

Taylor, A. J. P. *The Hapsburg Monarchy.* London, 1948.
> Authoritative history by the wittiest of English-language historians. Professor Taylor's concluding vision of Tito as the heir of Franz Josef was uncommonly astute.

Wolff, Robert Lee. *The Balkans in Our Time.* Cambridge, Massachusetts, 1956.
> The definitive history to 1955.

Zauberman, Alfred. *Industrial Progress in Poland, Czechoslovakia and East Germany 1937–1962.* New York, London, 1964.
> Sophisticated economic analysis of official growth statistics, placing them in more sober perspective.

Zeman, Z. A. B. *The Breakup of the Hapsburg Monarchy 1914–1918.* London, 1961.
> A ground-breaking "revisionist" study of original sources, and thus a useful corrective to traditional liberal-nationalist accounts stressing the "inevitability" of November 1918.

Czechoslovakia

Kennan, George F. *From Prague After Munich.* Princeton, 1968.
> Dispatches of a young diplomat in Czechoslovakia between November 1938 and 1940. Useful in understanding a similar situation between September 1968 and 1970.

Liehm, Antonin. *Trois Generations: Entretiens Sur le Phenomene Culturel Tchecoslovaque.* Paris, 1970.
> Valuable collection of interviews with leading Czech and Slovak writers between 1966 and the spring of 1968, by a leading Czech publicist and film critic.

Littell, Robert (ed.). *The Czech Black Book.* London, 1969.
The basic source book, compiled by the Czechoslovak Academy of Sciences, on the week of the Soviet invasion.

Loebl, Eugen. *Sentenced and Tried: The Stalinist Purges in Czechoslovakia.* London, 1969.
A survivor of the Slansky trial of November 1952 describes how the trial was "prepared." The book includes a transcript of the trial proceedings.

Mnacko, Ladislav. *The Seventh Night.* London, 1969.
Eyewitness account of the Soviet invasion, seen from Bratislava, by the most popular of Czechoslovak Communist journalists.

Schwartz, Harry. *Prague's 200 Days.* London, 1969.
Solid, reliable account, based partly on personal experience, of the "spring" of 1968 by the Soviet-affairs specialist of the *New York Times.*

Seton-Watson, R. W. *A History of the Czechs and Slovaks.* London, 1943.
Authoritative, sympathetic, irreplaceable.

Sik, Ota. *La Verité sur L'Economie Tchecoslovague.* Paris, 1968.
Based on Professor Sik's Prague Television series in July 1968, which finally told the Czechs and Slovaks some of the truth about their economic plight. Helpful in understanding other Communist economies, then, now, and in the future.

Taborsky, Edward. *Communism in Czechoslovakia 1948–1960.* Princeton, 1961.
The standard reference work.

Tigrid, Pavel. *La Chute Irresistible d'Alexander Dubcek.* Paris, 1969.
Based largely on information and documents supplied by Czechoslovak liberal Communist leaders, and valuable for their versions of the Cierna meeting, the Moscow "agreement," and various subsequent phases of Soviet intervention.

Wechsberg, Joseph. *The Voices—Prague 1968.* New York, 1969.
A sensitive "ear-witness" account of the invasion, based on radio monitoring and refugee interviews, by the Czech-born East European correspondent of *The New Yorker.*

Whelan, Joseph. *Aspects of Intellectual Ferment and Dissent in Czechoslovakia.* A study prepared for the U.S. Senate Judiciary Committee, Washington, 1969.
An excellent resume by a Library of Congress specialist of the intellectuals' role in the Czechoslovak "liberalization" of 1963–67 and the revolution of 1968. Includes the texts of important speeches, resolutions, and manifestoes of 1967–68.

Windsor, Philip, and Roberts, Adam. *Czechoslovakia 1968.* London, 1969.
Attempts to examine the Czechoslovak drama in its geopolitical and strategic context.

Zeman, Z. A. B. *Prague Spring.* Harmondsworth, Middlesex, England, 1969.
A Czech-born, Oxford-trained historian returns to Prague in the spring of 1968. An unbeatable combination; even the translations of Czech speeches and documents are superior to all others.

East Germany

Doenhoff, Marion Gräfin; Leonhardt, Rudolf Walter; Sommer, Theo. *Reise in ein Fernes Land.* Hamburg, 1964.
Three editors of the liberal Hamburg weekly *Die Zeit* describe their visit to the DDR. Authentic, sensitive, brief, and best.

Dornberg, John. *The Other Germany.* New York, 1968.
A sympathetic attempt to understand and explain the DDR in its own terms, packed with useful information.

Elon, Amos. *Journey Through a Haunted Land—The New Germany.* New York, 1967.
A perceptive Israeli journalist compares West and East Germany with the historic Germany of the past.

Hangen, Welles. *The Muted Revolution.* New York, 1966.
Shrewd observation of East Germany at mid-decade.

Stern, Carola. *Ulbricht, a Political Biography.* London, 1965.
Definitive thus far.

Hungary

Lasky, Melvin J. (ed.). *The Hungarian Revolution.* London, 1957.
Invaluable, day-by-day documentary account of the 1956 revolution which remains the basic English-language source book.

Lengyel, Emil. *1,000 Years of Hungary.* New York, 1958.
A popular history with the authentic flavor.

Macartney, C. A. *Hungary—A Short History.* Edinburgh, 1962.
The standard scholarly reference.

Nagy, Imre. *On Communism—In Defense of the New Course.* New York, 1958.
Useful for its insights not only into internal Hungarian Communist politics, but into the satellite-Soviet relationship after Stalin's death.

Poland

Halecki, Oscar. *A History of Poland.* London, 1942.
The standard reference, despite Gomulka's frequent attacks on it.

Korbel, Josef, *Poland Between East and West.* Princeton, 1965.
Solid study of Soviet and German diplomacy toward Poland between 1919 and 1933, and therefore useful in considering the classic Polish geopolitical dilemma.

Kuncewicz, Maria (ed.). *The Modern Polish Mind*. New York, 1963.
A fine anthology including, *inter alia*, stories, memoirs, and essays by Slonimski, Maria Dobrowska, Kolakowski, Andrzejewski, and Mrozek.

Stehle, Hansjakob. *The Independent Satellite: Society and Politics in Poland since 1945*. London, 1965.
A sympathetic study by the *Frankfurter Allgemeine Zeitung* correspondent in Warsaw from 1957 to 1962, and best on that period.

Rumania

Churchill, Winston S. *The World Crisis 1911–1918*. London, 1923.
From which we filched the amusing description of Rumanian policy in World War I.

Floyd, David. *Rumania: Russia's Dissident Ally*. New York, 1965.
Solid account by the Communist-affairs specialist of the *Daily Telegraph*.

Ionescu, Ghita. *Communism in Rumania 1944–1962*. London, 1964.
The definitive work thus far.

Seton-Watson, R. W. *A History of the Rumanians: From Roman Times to the Completion of Unity*. Cambridge, 1934.
The classic reference.

Yugoslavia

Clissold, Stephen. *Whirlwind—Tito's Rise to Power*. New York, 1949.
Best account in any language of the Yugoslav Civil War. The author lived in Yugoslavia before the war and was there during the Axis invasion, returned as a British liaison officer to Tito's Partisans, and was Press Attaché of the British Embassy after the Liberation. A classic.

Dedijer, Vladimir. *Tito*. New York, 1953.
The authorized biography and a basic reference.

Djilas, Milovan. *Land Without Justice*. New York, 1958.
To my mind, the best of Djilas's works—a personal memoir describing the Montenegro of his childhood and youth, and thus the making of a Communist, writer, and fighter.

Djilas, Milovan. *The Unperfect Society*. New York, 1969.
Djilas's most recent book contains fascinating material on his own break with Tito in 1953–54, his experience in prison, and his impressions of Yugoslav Communism after his release.

Halperin, Ernest. *The Triumphant Heretic*. London, 1958.
The best book on Yugoslavia in the fifties, and particularly on the Djilas controversy, by the then East European correspondent of the *Neue Zuricher Zeitung*.

Hoffman, George W., and Neal, Fred W. *Yugoslavia and the New Communism*. New York, 1962.
A valuable standard reference.

Kardelj, Edvard. *Socialism and War*. London, 1961.

A "survey of the Chinese criticism of the policy of coexistence." Can be read on various levels: straight; as Tito's way of helping Khrushchev in the struggle with Mao; and as Kardelj's way of making it difficult for Tito to compromise with Khrushchev's colleagues and heirs. (The lofty principles expressed in the book did not prevent a rapprochement between Yugoslavia and China after the Soviet invasion of Czechoslovakia.)

Macek, Vladko. *In the Struggle for Freedom*. New York, 1957.

Memoirs of the prewar leader of the Croatian Peasant party. Interesting, honest, and needed as a corrective to the Serbian enthusiasm of Rebecca West (below).

Maclean, Fitzroy. *Disputed Barricade*. London, 1957.

The best biography of Tito, by the Commander of the wartime British Military Mission to the Partisans and later Conservative MP. Written with intimate knowledge and balanced judgment.

West, Rebecca. *Black Lamb and Grey Falcon—A Journey Through Yugoslavia*. New York, 1940.

The greatest of all Balkan historical-political travelogues, which still captures more authentic Yugoslav atmosphere and tradition than any work ever written by a foreigner. The book's chief political weakness, Miss West's absorption in the Serbian national myth, is also the source of its greatest literary strength.

INDEX